Instant Perl Modules

Douglas Sparling
Frank Wiles

Osborne/McGraw-Hill
New York   Chicago   San Francisco
Lisbon   London   Madrid   Mexico City
Milan   New Delhi   San Juan
Seoul   Singapore   Sydney   Toronto

Osborne/McGraw-Hill
2600 Tenth Street
Berkeley, California 94710
U.S.A.

To arrange bulk purchase discounts for sales promotions, premiums, or fund-raisers, please contact
Osborne/McGraw-Hill at the above address. For information on translations or book distributors
outside the U.S.A., please see the International Contact Information page immediately following the
index of this book.

Instant Perl Modules

1 2 3 4 5 6 7 8 9 0   DOC DOC   0 1 9 8 7 6 5 4 3 2 1

Book p/n 0-07-212961-1 and CD p/n 0-07-212960-3
parts of
ISBN 0-07-212962-X

Publisher Brandon A. Nordin	**Technical Editor** David Adler
Vice President & Associate Publisher Scott Rogers	**Page Layout** Patricia Wallenburg
Acquisitions Editor Rebekah Young	**Copy Editor** Anna Halasz
Acquisitions Coordinator Paulina Pobocha	**Proofreader, Indexer** Joann Woy
Project Manager Dave Nash	**Cover Design** William Chan

To our friends and families.

Contents

Contents

INTRODUCTION

About This Book

Instant Perl Modules is a collection of examples and applications that use modules the authors have found useful in their professional careers. The examples in this book explain the features of these modules that should be of use to most Perl programmers.

The book begins by showing detailed examples of modules that can be used in a variety of programming applications. The later chapters focus on specific application development, including CGI, Win32, Web, and XML applications.

This book was not written to be a tutorial of the Perl language, nor a complete reference to the modules discussed within. Only those options that we felt were of significant value to most Perl programmers were included.

Who Is the Book For?

This book is for programmers, system administrators, and webmasters who already have a basic understanding of the Perl language, but wish to harness the immense power the Comprehensive Perl Archive Network (CPAN) provides. A basic knowledge of HTML and SQL would be helpful, but is not required.

How to Use This Book

This book provides examples that explain the basic functionality of many Perl modules. There are also many practical applications, while fully functional, are tailored to be easily modified to fit your own needs.

Chapter Breakdown

This book consists of the following 17 chapters and 6 appendices.

Chapter 1: *Introduction to Perl Modules*, provides a gentle introduction to Perl modules and the Comprehensive Perl Archive Network (CPAN). This chapter covers installing, using, and finding Perl modules as well as module documentation.

Chapter 2: *The Standard Modules*, contains a list of all the standard Perl modules that are included with version 5.6 of Perl. Usage of several of the standard Perl modules is covered.

Chapter 3: *Dates and Times*, shows modules that are useful for manipulating date and time values. Converting, parsing, and determining values of different types are covered. How to determine work and holiday dates are also shown.

Chapter 4: *Databases*, provides examples on working with all manners of databases. From simple hash style DBM files to full relational databases using Perl's DBI are explained.

Chapter 5: *Graphics*, gives a brief introduction on how to build and modify images using available Perl modules. In these examples determining size, scaling, watermarking, and the building of graphs are explained.

Chapter 6: *Perl/Tk*, presents an overview of building GUI interfaces using the Perl/Tk module. Widgets and geometry managers are covered in detail.

Chapter 7: *E-mail*, focuses on the most used portion of the Internet. This chapter provides you with all the tools necessary to build robust applications that send and receive E-mail messages.

Chapter 8: *Internet Protocols*, discusses the most common networking protocols used on the Internet. This chapter shows you how easy it is to connect to remote computers, transfer files, resolve DNS domains, and build TCP clients and servers using Perl modules.

Chapter 9: *CGI.pm*, introduces the CGI module that is used extensively in the next few chapters. Learn the basics of CGI programming with CGI.pm including form processing, HTML shortcuts, cookies, file uploads and debugging.

Chapter 10: *Fun CGI Applications*, contains a few fun CGI applications using the CGI.pm module introduced in chapter 9. Build a voting booth, a guestbook, a postcard script, and a web-based chat.

Chapter 11: *CGI and Databases*, shows how to use a relational database with your CGI scripts. Includes a feedback form, a resume submit form, a job board, and a CD database application.

Chapter 12: *CGI: Commerce and Community*, shows how to apply Perl CGI programming to business and interactive websites. This chapter discusses how to build an online store and a fully threaded discussion forum.

Chapter 13: *Site Administration*, covers many administration utilities and functions that are useful in the day-to-day upkeep of a website. The examples provided show how to build an online HTML editor, handle user authentication, parse log files, and most importantly notify you when your server is not functioning.

Chapter 14: *Site Utilities*, outlines some Perl CGI scripts that can be used on a website to provide common functionality. Concepts such as banner ad rotation, recommending a site, and searching are outlined.

Chapter 15: *Web Programming*, discusses many common web programming tasks including web automation, getting web pages, specifying and converting URLs, parsing HTML, extracting links from a web page, checking for dead links, and converting HTML character entities.

Chapter 16: *Win32*, covers the Win32 library that comes with the ActiveState distribution of Perl for Microsoft Windows. This chapter explains how to retrieve and format Win32 error messages, create and manage processes, use OLE automation and connect to a Microsoft Access database using ODBC.

Chapter 17: *XML*, covers the basics of parsing XML documents with Perl. Creating an RDF channel and converting an RSS news feed to HTML are also covered.

Appendix A: *Pragmas*, looks at some of the common pragmatic modules that come with Perl, such as 'use diagnostics', 'use strict', and 'use vars'.

Appendix B: *Creating Perl Modules*, shows how building your own modules can save time by facilitating code reuse. Coding guidelines and style are also discussed.

Appendix C: *Perl Security*, gives a few examples of common programming mistakes that often lead to dangerous security problems.

Appendix D: *Perl Resources*, provides many online and offline resources which help in finding answers to programming questions. Many books, websites, articles are detailed.

Appendix E: *Installing the PostgreSQL Database*, is a brief introduction to building, configuring, and installing a PostgreSQL database.

Appendix F: *Installing Apache*, is a brief overview of how to compile and install the popular Apache web server.

Contacting the Authors

While the authors, editors, and everyone involved strived to make this book as close to perfect as possible, the occasional error does seem to be inevitable. Because we want you to get the most out of this book we are making ourselves available for questions, comments, and suggestions. We are available individually via email at ipm@dougsparling.com and ipm@wiles.org. We maintain a compilation of answers to common questions and errata regarding this work at the following URLs. http://www.dougsparling.com/ipm/ and http://www.wiles.org/ipm/.

A complete copy of the CD-ROM will be available at ftp://ftp.wiles.org/pub/ipm/.

ACKNOWLEDGMENTS

We would like to give special thanks to Rebekah Young for providing us the opportunity to write this book. Her patience has been a virtue and her guidance has been a blessing. We would like to extend our gratitude to David H. Adler, whose keen eye (and keen wit) has been invaluable in the writing of this book. A special thanks goes to Patty Wallenburg, who went the extra mile and never hesitated in providing last minute changes to the manuscript. And certainly a big thank you to the McGraw-Hill staff and anyone we've neglected to mention who were involved in the production of this book.

We would like to thank Larry Wall for inventing Perl and all those who have contributed to making it the wonderful language that it is today. Also deserving of thanks are the numerous CPAN developers and module maintainers who have shared their code and made the life of every Perl programmer easier. Without them we would all be reinventing the wheel on a daily basis.

First and foremost I would like to thank my wife Kim whose love and support I rely and depend on. I would also like to thank my children Dylan and Shea. I hope they didn't mind too much that I spent so much time hunkered over the keyboard instead of playing basketball or peek-a-boo. I won't thank Harry the cat, as I don't think he noticed a thing.

I'd like to thank my parents, Dr. Robert and Marilyn Boyd, for being the best parents a son could ever ask for. Their encouragement and love has been an inspiration. I would also like to thank my late father, Dr. William E. Sparling, who unwittingly gave me a passion for 1s and 0s. I hope he would have been proud.

I can't go with out thanking those with whom I work. A big thanks to Chris Pizey for giving me the opportunity to do what I love to do most: programming Perl on a UNIX box. Thanks to Mike Admire for constantly increasing my knowledge and respect for the UNIX operating system. I'd also like to thank Mark Smith for helping me sort out the intricacies of that other operating system. I'd also like to acknowledge Scott Kahler, Jason Garcia, Scott Shorter, Derek Nolen and all the others at the office.

Here's a nod to Greg Melvin who has always made sure that my grammar was proper. Thanks to David 'Yow' Albrecht, Terry Adams, Todd Greene and all my other friends for putting up with the wacky way I deal with life. And thanks to all the other members of my family, friends, and people I forgot to mention.

I'd like to thank all those in the Perl community who have inspired me to be the best Perl coder I can be. A special tip of the hat to Randal L. Schwartz, whose code I've read with much pleasure and which has never failed to teach me something new.

And finally, I'd like to thank my co-author Frank Wiles. I couldn't have done this book without him.

—*Doug Sparling*

I must first thank my parents, Stanley and Janet Wiles, for generously providing me with not only a loving environment, but also computers and books without which I would not be the geek I am today. I would also like to thank my grandparents, aunt, and cousin for their support and for being so understanding when my job and this book have pulled me away from family functions and events.

A special thanks to The World Company and all my friends and co-workers for their support and their (somewhat failing) attempt at not overloading me with work during the writing of this book.

A very special acknowledgement to my mentors Chris Bell, Stephen Spencer, and Ben Singer, without whose constant tutoring, encouragement, and nearly boundless knowledge I would not know half of what I do about Unix and Perl.

To my favorite English teachers Mrs. Bushman and Mrs. Gladman without who I would not be fit to write this sentence let alone an entire book.

To Joe Larcher, Nicholas Studt, and David Hageman and all of the other members of the Kansas UNIX & Linux Users Association (KULUA) the best user group and group of friends a guy could ask for.

Also I would like to thank Cody, Julie, Kathy, John, Liz, Lori, Juli, Kim, Joe, Nathan, Devin, Liz, and my many other friends who were supportive and kept me sane through this whole processes. I would also like to specially thank Erin Daily who has taught me much about life, and who daily inspires me to become a better person.

And finally my co-author Doug Sparling for giving me the opportunity to work on this book with him and for helping keep my disorganized brain organized throughout the process.

—Frank Wiles

Introduction to Perl Modules

Introduction

The standard Perl library is a collection of code that comes with the standard Perl distribution and consists of modules, pragmas (see Appendix A), and scripts whose actual contents and location will differ depending on the port of Perl used and the whims of your system administrator.

The standard modules tend to be written to perform common and useful tasks. By using existing code, the programmer can save valuable time by not having to reinvent the wheel. Because standard modules are distributed with Perl, there is no need to be concerned about the portability of scripts written using standard modules. Some modules are system dependent, however, and will not be portable across operating systems.

Getting Perl Modules from the CPAN

If you cannot find a module that suits your needs in the standard library or if you are missing a module from the standard library, you should try the Comprehensive Perl Archive Network (CPAN). The CPAN is a huge Perl repository containing Perl ports, scripts, documentation, and all available Perl modules.

Installing Perl Modules

Once you have downloaded a module from CPAN, you will need to install it on your system. Modules can be installed manually, which is normally a four-step process:

1. Decompress the file.
2. Unpack the file.
3. Build the module (not always necessary).
4. Install the module.

You should always read the instructions in the README file for the specific module before performing the installation.

Modules may also be installed in an automated process using the CPAN (UNIX) or PPM (ActiveState Perl for Windows) module.

Manual Installation on UNIX

Decompress the File

```
% gzip -d module.tar.gz
```

Unpack the File

```
% tar -xvf module.tar
```

Note that steps 1 and 2 can be combined with the following command:

```
% gzip -dc module.tar.gz | tar -xvf -
```

Build the Module

Go into the directory created in step 2 and run the following commands. Be sure to read the instructions in the README file first.

```
% perl Makefile.PL
% make
% make test
```

Install the Module

You must be logged in as root to install the module into the Perl library.

```
% make install
```

It is also possible to install modules into your own private directory, which is handy if you don't have root access. This is covered later in this chapter in the section "Installing Modules to a Private Directory."

Manual Installation on Windows

Decompress and Unpack

Use a Windows utility such as WinZip to decompress and unpack the module. If your browser changed the name of your file to something like `module_tar.tar`, be sure to rename it `module.tar.gz` before running WinZip.

You will need nmake installed on your system (and possibly a C compiler for some modules) before running the following commands. If you don't have nmake, you can download it from Microsoft at:

```
ftp.microsoft.com/Softlib/MSLFILES/nmake15.exe
```

Build

```
% perl Makefile.PL
% nmake
% nmake test
```

Install

```
% nmake install
```

Automated Installation on UNIX using the CPAN Module

The CPAN module, CPAN.pm, can be used to query, download, and install Perl modules. The CPAN module is included with version 5.004 or greater of Perl and can be installed manually if you are using an older version of Perl on your system (in that case, it might be wise to upgrade your version of Perl). Once the module is installed you can enter the interactive mode by typing the following command:

```
% perl -MCPAN -e shell
```

The first time you use the CPAN module, you will be asked a series of configuration questions. The default answers should work fine for most of the questions, although you may wish to change the default CPAN site.

Once you are in the interactive mode, you can install a module by typing the following command:

```
cpan> install Module::Name
```

It's also possible to do this in one step by typing the following text at the command line:

```
% perl -MCPAN -e "install 'Module::Name'"
```

Before actually installing the module, CPAN.pm checks if the module is already installed. If the module isn't found on your system, then the module is loaded. The module is also installed if you have an older version of the module already installed. If you already have the latest version of the module, then CPAN.pm prints the message "module up to date" and won't reinstall the module (unless you force it to).

Be sure to read the CPAN.pm module documentation for more detailed information.

Automated Installation on Windows using PPM

If you are using ActiveState Perl for Windows, the Perl Package Manager (PPM) will be installed on your system. PPM allows you to use a command line interface to query, install, and remove Perl modules. PPM connects to package repositories instead of using the CPAN.

To run PPM, type ppm at the command prompt:

```
C:\> ppm
PPM interactive shell (2.0) - type 'help' for available commands.
```

Typing help at the PPM> prompt will produce an output similar to:

```
PPM> help
Commands:
 exit            - leave the program.
 help [commands] - prints this screen, or help on 'command'.
 install PACKAGES- installs specified PACKAGES.
 quit            - leave the program.
 query [options] - query information about installed packages.
 remove PACKAGES - removes the specified PACKAGES from the system.
 search [options]- search information about available packages.
 set [options]   - set/display current options.
 verify [options]- verifies current install is up to date.
 version         - displays PPM version number.
```

By default, PPM will connect to the ActiveState Web site (http://www.activestate.com/PPMPackages/) to download modules, behaving much like the CPAN module. For example, to install the Tk module, type the following command at the PPM> prompt:

```
PPM> install Tk
```

It is also possible to download a package and install it from a local directory. For example, ActiveState has packages available for download at http://www.activestate.com/PPMPackages/zips/. Once you download a package to a local directory on your machine, you need to unzip the file. Unzipping a file named `module.zip` should provide you with a file named `module.ppd`. You can then run the following command from the directory where `module.ppd` is located:

```
D:\path\to\file>ppm install module.ppd
```

Installation on Other Operating Systems

For information on installing Perl modules on other operating systems, including Macintosh, DOS, and VMS, take a look at the `perlmodinstall` manpage or the "Installing CPAN Modules" page on the CPAN site.

Installing Modules to a Private Directory

If you don't have root permission or you can't install modules to the standard installation directories, you may still install a module to a nonstandard or private directory. You may use any directory that you have write permissions to.

There is more than one way to install a module to a private directory. The easiest way is to use the LIB variable to specify the install directory when running `Makefile.PL`.

```
% perl Makefile.PL LIB=/path/to/private/directory
```

For example, if I have a private library directory under my home directory, I would type the command:

```
% perl Makefile.PL LIB=/home/doug/modules
```

Now complete the remaining steps to install the module into your private directory:

```
% make
% make test
% make install
```

A program that uses a module installed in a private directory must know how to find that module. It is necessary to modify the `@INC` variable so that it includes the path to your private directory. This can easily be done with the `lib` pragma.

```
use lib '/path/to/private/directory';
```

For example, if I have installed the `DBI.pm` module in my private directory /home/doug/modules, then I could use this module with the following code:

```
use lib '/home/doug/modules';
use DBI;
```

NOTE

If a module is installed in the same directory as the program using it, then the module will be found without modifying the `@INC` variable. The current directory `.` is included in `@INC` by default.

To see how a private directory is added to `@INC`, run a short script similar to the following (using the path to your private directory):

```
use lib '/home/doug/modules';
for ( @INC ) {
    print "$_\n";
}
```

You should see your private directory added to the list of standard directories.

You can also set the `PERL5LIB` environment variable with a colon-separated list of directories. These directories will be searched first, before the standard library and current directory.

UNIX

```
% export PERL5LIB='/home/doug/modules'
```

Windows

```
D:\> PERL5LIB=D:\doug\modules
```

Using Perl Modules

You can include a Perl module in your program by using the following line near the top of your program:

```
use Module;
```

This is the same as:

```
BEGIN { require Module; import Module; }
```

The use statement will load the module at compile time and import the functions listed in the module's @EXPORT array.

It is also possible to supply a list of functions to be imported by using:

```
use Module LIST;
```

This is the same as:

```
BEGIN { require Module; import Module LIST; }
```

The functions in the LIST must be included in the @EXPORT or @EXPORT_OK arrays of the module or an error will be generated.

To import a module without importing any functions, use the following:

```
use Module ();
```

Which is the same as:

```
BEGIN { require Module; }
```

Once a module has been loaded and its functions have been imported, you may use the module's functions without providing a package qualifier. For example, the Date::Calc module includes the Today() method, so once we load the Date::Calc module, we can use the Today() method without using the package qualifier.

```
use Date::Calc qw/Today/;
Today();
```

Most modules contain functions that are imported into the program, as we have seen in the previous examples. However, some modules use an object-oriented interface and do not import functions into the program. When using an object-oriented module, you first need to create a new object and then access the object's methods. Let's use the CGI.pm module as an example:

```
use CGI;
$query = new CGI;
print $query->header;
```

Some modules provide both a function-oriented and an object-oriented interface, thus providing two ways to use the module. We can use a function-oriented interface to the CGI.pm module as follows:

```
use CGI qw/:standard/;
print header;
```

You can include a module at run time by using a the require statement:

```
require MODULE;
```

However, in almost all cases, it is preferable to use use rather than require.

Finding Installed Modules

You may want to find out what modules are already installed on your system. We'll also take a look at how to determine what nonstandard modules have been added to your installation.

Where Are Modules Located?

The location of the modules on your system will differ according to the port and version of Perl being used. @INC is a list of standard locations where Perl modules are installed and this is where your program will look for modules. The directories in the @INC array are set when Perl is compiled (although it can be modified with the lib pragma and the PERL5LIB environment variable).

To find the locations of all the modules installed on your system, run one of the following simple scripts from the command line:

For UNIX, type:

```
% perl -e 'print "@INC\n"'
```

For Windows; type:

```
C:\>perl -e "print join(' ',@INC),\n"
```

or

```
C:\>perl -e "print qq(@INC)"
```

As an alternative (UNIX and Windows), you can also use:

```
% perl -V
```

This will also print the configuration information used when Perl was compiled.

Which Modules Are Installed?

If you want to determine whether a specific module is already installed on your system, run one of the following script at the command line:
For UNIX, type:

```
% perl -e 'use ModuleName'
```

or

```
% perl -MModuleName -e 'print'
```

For Windows; type:

```
C:\>perl -e "use ModuleName"
```

or

```
C:\>perl -MModuleName -e "print"
```

If this command is successful, then you know that this module is installed on your system.
To find modules that have been installed but are not part of the standard distribution, run the following command:

```
% perldoc perllocal
```

For a sorted list (UNIX only), try:

```
% perldoc perllocal | col -b | grep Module | cut -c 45-100 | cut
-d '' -f 1 | sort | uniq
```

To find all modules installed on a UNIX system, run the following command:

```
% find `perl -e 'print "@INC"'` -name '*.pm' -print
```

This will find all modules, including modules that aren't part of the standard distribution or that don't have documentation.

Module Documentation

To find documentation for a Perl module, take a look at the module's manpage or use the `perldoc` command.

```
% man CGI
% perldoc CGI
```

Modules are also normally documented as pod. You may also have HTML documentation on your system (HTML documentation is installed automatically with ActiveState Perl). Documentation will usually include a description of the module, detailed descriptions of the methods that the module provides, and examples on how to use the module. A list of the standard modules and their descriptions can be found in the `perlmod` manpage.

Summary

In this chapter, we have introduced you to Perl modules and the advantages of their use. We've also taken a detailed look at how to install and use Perl modules, and how to determine which modules are loaded on your system.

CHAPTER **2**

The Standard Modules

Overview of the Standard Perl Modules

The standard Perl modules are the modules that are included with the standard Perl distribution. These modules perform many common and useful tasks, including text processing, file handling, error handling, networking, interfacing with databases, object-oriented programming, advanced mathematics, manipulating times and dates, graphics, language extensions, and more. It is imperative that you become familiar with the standard modules, as knowledge of them will save you time and prevent you from reinventing the wheel. You are also guaranteed that your programs will be portable, because these modules come with all distributions of Perl and all Perl developers should have access to them.

A list of the standard modules can be found in the `perlmodlib` man page, which lists descriptions of the standard modules that should be included with all distributions of Perl. Some of these modules will be system dependent and thus not be portable across operating systems. Note that the standard modules actually found on your system will differ depending on the port of Perl used and whether or not the system administrator (or whoever installed Perl on your system) chose to leave any out during the installation. Windows comes with several standard Win32 modules and these will be covered in a later chapter.

Typing:

`% `**`man perlmodlib`**

or

`% `**`perldoc perlmodlib`**

will display the Perl module library man page. Included in the output is the list of standard modules presented in Table 2.1.

TABLE 2.1

Standard Modules

Module	Function
AnyDBM_File	Provide framework for multiple DBM libraries
AutoLoader	Load subroutines only on demand
AutoSplit	Split a package for autoloading

(continued on next page)

TABLE 2.1

Standard Modules
(continued)

Module	Function
B	Guts of the Perl code generator (aka compiler)
B::Asmdata	Autogenerated data about Perl ops, used to generate bytecode
B::Assembler	Assemble Perl bytecode
B::Bblock	Walk basic blocks
B::Bytecode	Perl compiler's bytecode back end
B::C	Perl compiler's C backend
B::CC	Perl compiler's optimized C translation back end
B::Debug	Walk Perl syntax tree, printing debug info about ops
B::Deparse	Perl compiler back end to produce Perl code
B::Disassembler	Disassemble Perl bytecode
B::Lint	Module to catch dubious constructs
B::Showlex	Show lexical variables used in functions or files
B::Stackobj	Helper module for CC backend
B::Stash	XXX NFI XXX
B::Terse	Walk Perl syntax tree, printing terse info about ops
B::Xref	Generates cross reference reports for Perl programs
Benchmark	Benchmark running times of code
ByteLoader	Load byte-compiled Perl code
CGI	Simple Common Gateway Interface class
CGI::Apache	Make things work with CGI.pm against Perl-Apache API
CGI::Carp	CGI routines for writing to the HTTPD (or other) error log
CGI::Cookie	Interface to Netscape cookies
CGI::Fast	Interface for Fast CGI
CGI::Pretty	Module to produce nicely formatted HTML code
CGI::Push	Simple interface to server Push
CGI::Switch	Try more than one constructor and return the first object available

(continued on next page)

TABLE 2.1

Standard Modules
(continued)

Module	Function
CPAN	Query, download, and build Perl modules from CPAN sites
CPAN::FirstTime	Utility for CPAN::Config file initialization
CPAN::Nox	Wrapper around CPAN.pm without using any XS module
Carp	Act like warn/die from perspective of caller
Carp::Heavy	Carp guts
Class::Struct	Declare struct-like datatypes as Perl classes
Config	Access Perl configuration information
Cwd	Get pathname of current working directory
DB	Programmatic interface to the Perl debugging API (experimental)
DB_File	Perl5 access to Berkeley DB version 1.x
Data::Dumper	Serialize Perl data structures
Devel::Dprof	A Perl execution profiler
Devel::Peek	A data debugging tool for the XS programmer
Devel::SelfStubber	Generate stubs for a SelfLoading module
DirHandle	Supply object methods for directory handles
Dumpvalue	Provide screen dump of Perl data
DynaLoader	Dynamically load C libraries into Perl code
English	Use English (or awk) names for ugly punctuation variables
Env	Access environment variables as regular ones
Errno	Load the libc errno.h defines
Exporter	Implement default import method for modules
Exporter::Heavy	Exporter guts
ExtUtils::Command	Utilities to replace common UNIX commands in Makefiles etc.
ExtUtils::Embed	Utilities for embedding Perl in C/C++ programs
ExtUtils::Install	Install files from here to there
ExtUtils::Installed	Inventory management of installed modules

(continued on next page)

TABLE 2.1

*Standard Modules
(continued)*

Module	Function
ExtUtils::Liblist	Determine libraries to use and how to use them
ExtUtils::MM_Cygwin	Methods to override UNIX behavior in ExtUtils::MakeMaker
ExtUtils::MM_OS2	Methods to override UNIX behavior in ExtUtils::MakeMaker
ExtUtils::MM_Unix	Methods used by ExtUtils::MakeMaker
ExtUtils::MM_VMS	Methods to override UNIX behavior in ExtUtils::MakeMaker
ExtUtils::MM_Win32	Methods to override UNIX behavior in ExtUtils::MakeMaker
ExtUtils::MakeMaker	Create an extension Makefile
ExtUtils::Manifest	Utilites to write and check a MANIFEST file
ExtUtils::Miniperl, writemain	Write the C code for perlmain.c
ExtUtils::Mkbootstrap	Make a bootstrap file for use by DynaLoader
ExtUtils::Mksymlists	Write linker options files for dynamic extension
ExtUtils::Packlist	Manage .packlist files
ExtUtils::testlib	Add blib/* directories to @INC
Fatal	Replace functions with equivalents which succeed or die
Fcntl	Load the libc fcntl.h defines
File::Basename	Split a pathname into pieces
File::CheckTree	Run many filetest checks on a tree
File::Compare	Compare files or filehandles
File::Copy	Copy files or filehandles
File::DosGlob	DOS-like globbing and then some
File::Find	Traverse a file tree
File::Glob	Perl extension for BSD filename globbing
File::Path	Create or remove a series of directories
File::Spec	Portably perform operations on file names
File::Spec::Funtions	Portably perform operations on file names
File::Spec::Mac	File::Spec for MacOS

(continued on next page)

TABLE 2.1

Standard Modules
(continued)

Module	Function
`File::Spec::OS2`	Methods for OS/2 file specs
`File::Spec::Unix`	Methods used by `File::Spec`
`File::Spec::VMS`	Methods for VMS file specs
`File::Spec::Win32`	Methods for Win32 file specs
`File::stat`	By-name interface to Perl's built-in `stat()` functions
`FileCache`	Keep more files open than the system permits
`FileHandle`	Supply object methods for filehandles
`FindBin`	Locate installation directory of running Perl program
`GDBM_File`	Access to the gdbm library
`Getopt::Long`	Extended processing of command line options
`Getopt::Std`	Process single-character switches with switch clustering
`I18N::Collate`	Compare 8-bit scalar data according to current locale
`IO`	Front-end to load various IO modules
`IO::Dir`	Supply object methods for directory handles
`IO::File`	Supply object methods for filehandles
`IO::Handle`	Supply object methods for I/O handles
`IO::Pipe`	Supply object methods for pipes
`IO::Poll`	Object interface to system poll call
`IO::Seekable`	Supply seek based methods for I/O objects
`IO::Select`	OO interface to the select system call
`IO::Socket`	Object interface to socket communications
`IO::Socket::INET`	Object interface for `AF_INET` domain sockets
`IO::Socket::UNIX`	Object interface for `AF_UNIX` domain sockets
`IPC::Msg`	SysV Msg IPC object class
`IPC::Open2`	Open a process for both reading and writing
`IPC::Open3`	Open a process for reading, writing, and error handling
`IPC::Semaphore`	SysV Semaphore IPC object class

(continued on next page)

TABLE 2.1

Standard Modules
(continued)

Module	Function
IPC::SysV	SysV IPC constants
Math::BigFloat	Arbitrary length float math package
Math::BigInt	Arbitrary size integer math package
Math::Complex	Complex numbers and associated mathematical functions
Math::Trig	Trigonometric functions
Net::Ping	Check a remote host for reachability
Net::hostent	By-name interface to Perl's built-in gethost*() functions
Net::netent	By-name interface to Perl's built-in getnet*() functions
Net::protonet	By-name interface to Perl's built-in getproto*() functions
Net::servent	By-name interface to Perl's built-in getserv*() functions
O	Generic interface to Perl compiler backends
Opcode	Disable named opcodes when compiling Perl code
POSIX	Perl interface to IEEE Std 1003.1
Pod::Checker	Check POD documents for syntax errors
Pod::Html	Module to convert POD files to HTML
Pod::InputObjects	Manage POD objects
Pod::Man	Convert POD data to formatted *roff input
Pod::Parser	Base class for creating POD filters and translators
Pod::Select	Extract selected sections of POD from input
Pod::Text	Convert POD data to formatted ASCII text
Pod::Text::Color	Convert POD data to formatted color ASCII text
Pod::Usage	Print a usage message from embedded POD documentation
SDBM_File	Tied access to SDBM files
Safe	Compile and execute code in restricted compartments
Search::Dict	Search for key in dictionary file
SelectSaver	Save and restore selected file handle
SelfLoader	Load functions only on demand

(continued on next page)

TABLE 2.1

Standard Modules
(continued)

Module	Function
Shell	Run shell commands transparently within Perl
Socket	Load the libc socket.h defines and structure manipulators
Symbol	Manipulate Perl symbols and their names
Sys::Hostame	Try every conceivable way to get hostname
Sys::Syslog	Interface to the libc syslog(3) calls
Term::cap	Termcap interface
Term::Complete	Word completion module
Term::ReadLine	Interface to various 'readline' packages
Test	Provides a simple framework for writing test scripts
Test::Harness	Run Perl standard test scripts with statistics
Text::Abbrev	Create an abbreviation from a list
Text::ParseWords	Parse text into a list of tokens or array of tokens
Text::Soundex	Implementation of the Soundex Algorithm as described by Knuth
Text::Tabs	Expand and unexpand tabs per expand(1) and unexpand(1)
Text::Wrap	Line wrapping to form simple paragraphs
Tie::Array	Base class for tied arrays
Tie::Handle	Base class definitions for tied handles
Tie::Hash	Base class definitions for tied hashes
Tie::RefHash	Use references as hash keys
Tie::Scalar	Base class definitions for tied scalars
Tie::SubstrHash	Fixed-table-size, fixed-key-length hashing
Time::Local	Efficiently compute time from local and GMT time
Time::gmtime	By-name interface to Perl's built-in gmtime() function
Time::localtime	By-name interface to Perl's built-in localtime() function
Time::tm	Internal object used by Time::gmtime and Time::localtime
UNIVERSAL	Base class for ALL classes (blessed references)
User::grent	By-name interface to Perl's built-in getgr*() functions
User::pwent	By-name interface to Perl's built-in getpw*() functions

There are scores of Perl modules included in the standard Perl library, and each comes with its own documentation. However, to give you an idea of how useful these modules are, we'll take a closer look at a few of the available standard modules.

Benchmark

The Benchmark module is used to determine and compare the execution times of code. Elapsed time is measured to an accuracy of 1 second, and an accuracy of 1 millisecond is used for user, system, and CPU time. For an accurate benchmark, it is necessary to have an elapsed time of 5 seconds or more. For this reason, short snippets of code will need to be run within a loop. The Benchmark module exports the following functions, most of which we will now discuss: timeit(), timethis(), timethese(), timediff(), timesum(), and timestr().

The timethis() function is used to measure the running time of a piece of code. The timethis() function takes two arguments: the number of loop iterations and the code to be benchmarked. The code can be either a string or a reference to a subroutine.

For example, running the following short script:

```
use Benchmark;
my $count = 1000000;
timethis($count, "sqrt($count)");
```

produces an output something like this:

```
timethis 1000000: 2 wallclock secs ( 2.15 user + 0.00 sys = 2.15
CPU)
```

Of course, the actual time will depend on your system. You may increase the value of $count depending on the speed of your CPU.

The timethese() function benchmarks multiple snippets of code and reports each snippet separately. This is useful for comparing snippets of code that perform a similar function.

The following short bit of code compares the running times of the different methods of division by two.

```
use Benchmark;

my $test = 1000000;
```

```
my $count = 1000000;

timethese($count, {division  => '$test = $test/2',
                   assign_op => '$test /= 2',
                   shift     => '$test >>= 1'
});
```

Running this script should give you a comparison of the speed of each algorithm. This is the output I got on my old Pentium desktop:

```
Benchmark: timing 1000000 iterations of assign_op, division,
shift...
 assign_op:  9 wallclock secs ( 9.06 usr +  0.00 sys =  9.06 CPU)
  division: 11 wallclock secs ( 9.67 usr +  0.00 sys =  9.67 CPU)
     shift:  1 wallclock secs ( 0.47 usr +  0.00 sys =  0.47 CPU)
```

As before, the running times will depend on your system.

It is also possible to benchmark a section of code contained in an actual program. The Benchmark constructor creates an object that contains the current time. You can benchmark a section of code by placing a constructor at the beginning and the end of a section of code and then computing the difference in the time values of the two Benchmark objects.

```
use Benchmark;

my $MAX_COUNT = 1000000;

my $time_start = new Benchmark;   # Begin benchmark
for (1..$MAX_COUNT) {
    my $sqrt = sqrt $_;
}
my $time_end = new Benchmark;   # End benchmark

my $td = timediff($time_end, $time_start);
print "$MAX_COUNT iterations of code took: ", timestr($td), "\n";
```

Running the previous script will produce an output similar to the following script. Once again, your mileage will vary.

```
1000000 iterations of code took: 7 wallclock secs (7.03 usr +
0.00 sys =  7.03 CPU)
```

The timediff() function returns a Benchmark object that contains the difference between two Benchmark times. This Benchmark object can then be passed to the timestr() function, which will return a formatted string.

The `timeit()` function is similar to the `timethis()` function, except that it returns a `Benchmark` object instead of printing a string. To see the results, you must use the `timestr()` function.

```
use Benchmark;

my $count = 1000000;
my $t = timeit($count, "sqrt($count)");
print "$count iterations of code took: ", timestr($t), "\n";
```

Running this script will give you an output similar to following:

```
1000000 iterations of code took: 2 wallclock secs ( 2.15 usr +
0.00 sys =  2.15 CPU)
```

Carp

The `Carp` module exports three functions: `carp()`, `croak()`, and `confess()`. These functions create error messages similar to those generated by Perl's `warn()` and `die()` functions. However, unlike `warn()` and `die()`, which identify the exact line number where the error occurred, these functions report the line number of the call to the subroutine in which the error is generated. This is useful when using modules because the error message will contain the line number from where a module's subroutine is called, not the line number in the subroutine where the error occurred.

To see the difference between `warn()` versus `carp()` and `die()` versus `croak()`, we'll run the same script twice, first using `warn()` and `die()` and then a second time using `carp()` and `croak()`.

First, try the following script using `warn()` and `die()`.

```
package MyPackage;

sub my_routine {
    # warn will issue a warning and report the line number of the
    # error
    # die will cause the program to die and report the line
    # number of the error
    warn("warn");
    die("die");
}

package main;
MyPackage::my_routine();
```

Running the following script:

```
% perl die.pl
```

will generate the following output:

```
warn at die.pl line 6
die at die.pl line 7
```

Compare this output with the following script that uses carp() and croak().

```
package MyPackage;
use Carp;

sub my_routine {
    # carp warns of an error and reports the line number of the
    # calling routine
    # croak dies and reports the line number of the calling
    # routine
    carp("carp");
    croak("croak");
}

package main;
MyPackage::my_routine();
```

Running this script

```
% perl carp.pl
```

will produce this output:

```
carp at carp.pl line 12
croak at carp.pl line 12
```

Notice that now the error is generated by line 12, MyPackage::my_routine();.

The confess() function is like croak(), but it also prints a stack trace. This is demonstrated in the following short program.

```
use Carp;

sub one {
    two();
}
```

```
sub two {
    three();
}

sub three {
    confess("confess");
}

one();
```

Running the following script,

% **perl confess.pl**

will produce the following output:

```
confess at confess.pl line 12
        main::three() called at confess.pl line 8
        main::two() called at confess.pl line 4
        main::one() called at confess.pl line 15
```

Class::Struct

The Class::Struct module allows the creation of C-style, struct-like data types such as Perl classes. Class::Struct provides a single function, struct(), which takes as an argument a list of scalars, arrays, hashes, and classes.

The struct function has three forms:

```
struct( CLASS_NAME => [ ELEMENT_LIST ]);
struct( CLASS_NAME => { ELEMENT_LIST });
struct( ELEMENT_LIST );
```

The first two forms explicitly define the name of the new class being created, and the third form uses the current package name as the name for the new class. The first and third forms are based on an array, which tend to be smaller and faster, and the second form is hash based, which can be more flexible.

The ELEMENT_LIST argument uses the following form:

```
NAME => TYPE
```

Each element of the struct is represented by a name-type pair. The NAME is the name of the element in the new class, and the TYPE is either the string '$', '@', '%' (corresponding to a scalar, array, or hash) or a class name.

The following code creates a struct-like employee record. This struct consists of several scalar elements, one hash element, and one array element. Note that the constructor method new must be used to create a new object.

```perl
use Class::Struct;

# Declare employee struct
struct( employee => {
                first_name => '$',
                 last_name => '$',
                   address => '$',
                      city => '$',
                     state => '$',
                       zip => '$',
                     phone => '%',
                      dept => '@'
});

# Create new employee object
my $emp = new employee;

# Assign values
$emp->first_name('Jake');
$emp->last_name('Barnes');
$emp->address('123 Maple St.');
$emp->city('Warrensburg');
$emp->state('MO');
$emp->zip('64093');
$emp->phone('home', '555-5555');
$emp->phone('cell', '555-6666');
$emp->dept(0, '101');
$emp->dept(1, '103');
$emp->dept(2, '104');

# Print values
print $emp->first_name, " ", $emp->last_name, "\n";
print $emp->address, "\n";
print $emp->city, ", ", $emp->state, " ", $emp->zip, "\n";
print "Home: ", $emp->phone('home'), "\n";
print "Cell: ", $emp->phone('cell'), "\n";
print "Dept: ", join(',', sort @{$emp->dept}), "\n";
```

This code will produce the following output:

```
Jake Barnes
123 Maple St.
```

```
Warrensburg, MO 64093
Home: 555-5555
Cell: 555-6666
Dept: 101,103,104
```

In the following code, the struct consists of two class elements, one hash element and one array element. The output is identical to that of the previous code.

```perl
use Class::Struct;

# Declare employee struct
struct( employee => {
            name     => 'name',
            address  => 'address',
              phone => '%',
               dept => '@'

});

# Class element
struct( name => {
            first_name => '$',
            last_name  => '$'
});

# Class element
struct( address => {
            street  => '$',
            city    => '$',
            state   => '$',
            zip     => '$'
});

# Create new employee object
my $emp = new employee;

# Assign values
$emp->name->first_name('Jake');
$emp->name->last_name('Barnes');
$emp->address->street('123 Maple St.');
$emp->address->city('Warrensburg');
$emp->address->state('MO');
$emp->address->zip('64093');
$emp->phone('home', '555-5555');
$emp->phone('cell', '555-6666');
$emp->dept(0, '101');
$emp->dept(1, '103');
$emp->dept(2, '104');

# Print values
```

```
print $emp->name->first_name, " ", $emp->name->last_name, "\n";
print $emp->address->street, "\n";
print $emp->address->city, ", ", $emp->address->state, " ",
    $emp->address->zip, "\n";
print "Home: ", $emp->phone('home'), "\n";
print "Cell: ", $emp->phone('cell'), "\n";
print "Dept: ", join(',', sort @{$emp->dept}), "\n";
```

Config

The `Config` module is used to access all the configuration information that was saved at Perl build time. The configuration information is stored in the hash `%Config`, which is part of `Config.pm`. `%Config` is always exported. Individual configuration parameters may be found by name.

For example, the following code finds the name of the operating system on which your Perl script is running:

```
use Config;
print "Operating System: $Config{'osname'}\n";
```

When I run this short script, I get the following output:

```
Operating System: linux
```

There are three functions that may be exported on demand: `config_sh()`, `config_vars()`, and `myconfig()`.

config_sh()

This function returns all the configuration information:

```
use Config qw(config_sh);
print config_sh();
```

The output is quite long, so it won't be reproduced here.

config_vars(@name)

This function prints the values of the specified configuration variable names to STDOUT.

```
use Config qw(config_vars);
print config_vars(qw(osname cc));
```

When I run this on my machine, I get the following output:

```
osname='linux';
cc='cc';
```

myconfig()

This function returns a text summary of the major Perl configuration values.

```
use Config qw(myconfig);
print myconfig();
```

The output should look familiar because it is the same as when you type:

% **perl -V**

The following script is one example of using the configure information. This script will print out the individual paths from the $PATH environment variable, using the osname configuration parameter to determine the separator character.

```
use Config;

my $path = $ENV{PATH};

if ($Config{osname} eq 'MSWin32') {
    $path =~ tr/;/\n/;
} else {
    $path =~ tr/:/\n/;
}

print $path, "\n";
```

On a Linux machine, it produces the following output:

```
/usr/bin
/usr/local/bin
/bin
/usr/bin
/usr/X11R86/bin
```

```
/home/doug/bin
```

On Windows 98, the following output is produced:

```
C:\PERL\BIN
C:\WINDOWS
C:\WINDOWS\COMMAND
```

Cwd

The Cwd module retrieves the current working directory. Cwd exports three methods: cwd(), getcwd(), and fastcwd().

The safest way to get the current working directory is with the cwd() function. This function is guaranteed to work on all operating systems and should be used in most cases.

```
use Cwd;
my $dir = cwd();
```

The getcwd() function is same as the cwd() method except that it reimplements the C getcwd(3) or getwd(3) functions in Perl.

```
use Cwd;
my $dir = getcwd();
```

The fastcwd() function is a faster but more dangerous way to get the current working directory. The danger comes from the remote possibility that fastcwd() could chdir() out of a directory and then find it impossible to chdir() back.

```
use Cwd;
my $dir = fastcwd();
```

You can also override Perl's built-in chdir() function. This will ensure that the PWD environment variable is updated.

```
use Cwd;

my $dir = cwd();
print "\$DIR = $dir\n\n";

use Cwd 'chdir';
chdir '..';
```

```
print "\$DIR = $dir\n";
print "\$PWD = $ENV{PWD}\n";
```

Assuming that we start in /home/doug, we'll get the following output:

```
$DIR = /home/doug

$DIR = /home/doug
$PWD = /home
```

Notice that $dir does not reflect the change made by chdir(). However, the PWD environment variable is updated and contains the current working directory.

Env

The Env module imports environment variables from the %ENV hash as simple scalars. The imported environment variables (keys %ENV) are tied to similarly named global scalars. For example, $PATH will be equivalent to $ENV{PATH}.

To import all the environment variables, use

```
use Env;
```

You can import specific environment variables by using the following form:

```
use Env qw(var1, var2 …);
```

Thus, if you only need to import the PATH and HOME environment variables, you would use this line:

```
use Env qw(PATH HOME);
```

Once the environment variable has been tied, it may be used like any other scalar variable.

1. You may find the value of an environment variable:

   ```
   use Env;
   print "$PATH\n";
   ```

   and produce the following output:

```
/usr/bin:/usr/local/bin:/bin:/usr/bin:/usr/X11R6/bin:/home/
doug/bin
```

2. You may modify the value of an environment variable:

```
use Env;
$PATH .= ':/this/is/a/newpath';
print "$PATH\n";
```

to produce the following output:

```
/usr/bin:/usr/local/bin:/bin:/usr/bin:/usr/X11R6/bin:/home/
doug/bin:/this/is/a/newpath
```

3. You can remove the tied environment variable by assigning it a value of `undef`. This will also cause `$ENV{PATH}` to become `undef`.

```
undef $PATH
```

Otherwise, the variable will be removed when the program exits.

File::Basename

The `File::Basename` module makes it easy to parse the filename, file extension, and the directory containing that file from a string containing a full path. `File::Basename` provides three functions: `basename()`, `dirname()`, and `fileparse()`.

The `basename()` function is used to parse the filename from a full path.

```
use File::Basename;
my $fullpath = '/home/doug/myfile.pl';
print 'Basename: ', basename($fullpath), "\n";
```

This code will produce the following output:

```
Basename: myfile.pl
```

The `dirname()` function is used to parse the name of the directory that contains the basename.

```
use File::Basename;
my $fullpath = '/home/doug/myfile.pl';
print 'Directory Name: ', dirname($fullpath), "\n";
```

This function will generate the following output:

```
Directory Name: /home/doug
```

The `fileparse()` function is used to parse the filename, directory, and file suffix.

```
use File::Basename;

my $fullpath = '/home/doug/myfile.pl';
my ($name, $dir, $extension) = fileparse($fullpath, '\..*');

print "Name: $name\n";
print "Dir: $dir\n";
print "Extension: $extension\n";
```

This code produces the following output:

```
Name: myfile
Path: /home/doug
Extension: .pl
```

The `fileparse()` function takes two arguments: the full path and a regular expression used to match the file suffix. If you have a file name such as `file.tar.gz`, you can use the regular expression to extract only the extension you need. The `regex '\..*'` expression will extract `.tar.gz` as the extension and `file` as the file name. Using the regular expression `'\.[^.]*'` will extract `.gz` as the extension and `file.tar` as the file name.

File::Compare

The `File::Compare` module is used to compare the contents of two files. The `compare()` function takes two arguments, each being either a file or file handle. The `compare()` function returns a 0 if the files are equal, 1 if they're not equal, and −1 if there is an error.

The following short script takes two file names as command-line arguments and then the files are compared for equality.

```
use File::Compare;

if (@ARGV < 2) {
    print "Insufficient number of arguments\n";
```

```
        print "Usage: filecompare.pl file1 file2\n";
        exit;
}

my ($file1, $file2) = @ARGV;

if (compare($file1, $file2) == 0) {
    print "Files are equal\n";
} elsif (compare($file1, $file2) == 1) {
    print "Files are not equal\n";
} else {
    print "Error comparing files: $!\n";
}
```

Therefore, if `file1.txt` and `file2.txt` are the same, the command

```
% perl filecompare.pl file1.txt file2.txt
```

would create the following output:

```
Files are equal
```

File::Copy

The `File::Copy` module is used for copying and moving files. It exports two functions: `copy()` and `move()`. The `copy()` function takes two arguments: the source file and the destination file. Either argument may be a file name or a file handle, although the file handle may not be portable across operating systems. The `move()` function also takes two arguments: the current name and the new name.

In the following code, the `copy()` function will create a copy of the file `test.txt` and name it `test.bak`. Then the `move()` function will rename the file `test2.bak`.

```
use File::Copy;

# Make copy of test.txt named test.bak
copy('test.txt', 'test.bak');

# Then rename the file test2.bak
move('test.bak', 'test2.bak');
```

`File::copy` can be used with STDIN and STDOUT. STDIN may be copied into a file:

```
copy(\*STDIN, 'test.txt');
```

A file's contents may be copied to STDOUT:

```
copy('test.txt', \*STDOUT);
```

File::Find

The `File::Find` module is used to recursively search a directory structure for files that match a given criterion. The `find()` function takes two arguments: a reference to a subroutine and a list of directories. The subroutine is called for each file found in the list of specified directories (and the respective subdirectories).

Within the subroutine, you will find the following scalars:

- `$_` will contain the name of the current file.
- `$File::Find::Dir` will contain the name of the current directory.
- `$File::Find::Name` will contain the full path and file name (that is, `$File::Find::Dir/$_`).
- `$File::Find::prune` is used to stop the `find()` function from moving into a directory.

The following code will seek all `.txt` files under the `/home/doug` directory and its subdirectories. Note that `$Find::File::prune` is set to block the find function from looking through any directory named `images` (for example, the directory `/home/doug/images` will not be entered, even if it contains any `.txt` files).

```perl
use File::Find;

find(\&wanted, '/home/doug');

sub wanted {
    # Don't search the images dir
    $File::Find::prune = 1 if /images/;

    if ($_ =~ /\.txt$/i) {

        print "FILE: $_\n";
        print "DIR: $File::Find::dir\n";
        print "PATH: $File::Find::name\n";
    }
}
```

Getopt::Long

The `Getopt::Long` module allows you to process multicharacter command-line options. Multicharacter options normally begin with two dashes (although a multicharacter option may start with a single dash or a plus sign) and may take an argument after a space or an equals sign (=). Using the default configuration, the long options are case insensitive and may be abbreviated if the abbreviation is unambiguous.

The `Getopt::Long` module contains the `GetOptions()` function, which takes one argument: a list of option descriptions. Each option description consists of two parts: an *option specification*, which is the name of the multicharacter switch (and an optional argument specifier), and an *option destination*, which is normally a reference to a variable that is associated with the option if it is present.

Argument Specifiers

The argument specifier describes the type of value an argument can take for a multicharacter option. If an option doesn't take an argument, then there will be no argument specifier and the option variable will be set to 1 if the option is used.

The following is a list of values that the argument specifiers may take:

- `!` The option does not take an argument and may be negated by appending a "no" to the beginning of the option name.

  ```
  GetOptions("option!" => \$option);
  ```

  `-option` will set its option variable (`$option`) to 1, whereas `-nooption` will set the `$option` to 0.

- `+` The option does not take an argument. The option variable will be incremented by 1 for each occurrence of the option on the command line.

  ```
  GetOptions("option+" => \$option);
  ```

  `--option -option -option` will set `$option` to 3, assuming that it was set to 0 or was undefined.

- =s   The option takes a mandatory string argument. The string is assigned to the option variable.

```
GetOptions("option=s" => \$option);
```

  --option=name will set $option to name.
- :s   The option takes an optional string argument. The string is assigned to the option variable. If the string argument is absent, the option variable is set to an empty string.

```
GetOptions("option:s" => \$option);
```

  --option=name will set $option to name, and -option will set $option to "".
- =i   The option takes a mandatory integer argument. The integer is assigned to the option variable.

```
GetOptions("option=i" => \$option);
```

  --option=3 will set $option to 3.
- :i   The option takes an optional integer argument. The integer is assigned to the option variable. If the integer argument is absent, the option variable is set to 0.

```
GetOptions("option:i" => \$option);
```

  --option=3 will set $option to 3, and -option will set $option to 0.
- =f   The option takes a mandatory floating-point argument. The floating-point number is assigned to the option variable.

```
GetOptions("option=f" => \$option);
```

  --option=3.14 will set $option to 3.14.
- :f   The option takes an optional floating-point argument The floating-point number is assigned to the option variable. It the floating-point argument is absent, the option variable is set to 0.

```
GetOptions("option:f" => \$option);
```

  --option=3.14 will set $option to 3.14, and -option will set $option to 0.

Option Destination

The option destination is normally a reference to a variable (scalar or array) or a subroutine.

```
GetOptions("option", \$option);
```

The option destination is optional. If the destination of the option isn't explicitly specified and a hash reference is passed, then the option values are placed in that hash.

```
%opts = ();
GetOptions(\%opts, "option=s");
```

`--option=name` will set `$opts{option}` to name.

If the destination of the option isn't explicitly specified and no hash reference is passed, then the option values are placed in a global variable with the same name as the option with a prefix of `opt_`.

```
GetOptions("option=s");
```

`--option=name` will set `$opt_option` to name.

The following script uses a few different argument specifiers.

```perl
use Getopt::Long;
my($name, $nickname, $age, @hobby, $geek);

GetOptions("name=s"      => \$name,
           "nickname:s"  => \$nickname,
           "age=i"       => \$age,
           "hobby:s"     => \@hobby,
           "geek!"       => \$geek);

print "Name: $name\n" if $name;
print "Nickname: $nickname\n" if $nickname;
print "Age: $age\n" if $age;
foreach my $hobby (@hobby) {
    print "I like $hobby\n";
}
if(defined $geek) {
    if($geek) {
        print "Certified geek\n";
    } else {
        print "Not a geek\n";
    }
}
```

The following command line:

```
% perl getoptslong.pl --name=Jake --nickname=X123 --age=23
--hobby=Perl --hobby=Linux --geek
```

will produce the following output:

```
Name: Jake
Nickname: X123
Age: 23
I like Perl
I like Linux
Certified geek
```

In contrast, the following command line:

```
% perl getoptslong.pl --name=Howy  --hobby=football
--hobby=basketball --nogeek
```

will produce this output:

```
Name: Howy
I like football
I like basketball
Not a geek
```

This is an extremely useful module so be sure and read all the documentation.

Getopt::Std

The Getopt::Std module allows you to process single-character command-line options. These command-line options, also known as *switches*, are single letters than begin with a dash (-a, -b, -c). If there is more than one switch on the command line, the switches may be clustered (-abc). In some cases, a switch may also have a value associated with it (-f file.dat). As the command line is processed, each switch is assigned to a variable, and then the switch is removed from @ARGV.

Getopt::Std provides two functions: getopt() and getopts(). The getopt() function takes one argument, a string that contains all the switches that must take an argument. Each switch found will have its argument placed in a corresponding variable, where $opt_x corresponds to the switch –x. If no argument is set, an error will occur. Switches other than those passed to `getopt()` can be used. Their corresponding variables will be set to 1.

For example, let's say we have a program named `getopt.pl`, and we include the following line in this program:

```
getopt('df');
```

Calling our program from the command line as follows:

```
% perl getoptstd1.pl –d 20000423 –f file.dat –o
```

will set `$opt_d` to 20000423, `$opt_f` to file.dat, and `$opt_o` to 1.

Note that warnings will be thrown if you subsequently use the option variables once (that is, as a one-time flag). The use of a hash reference, shown below, avoids this difficulty.

If you pass a hash reference as the second argument to `getopt()`, a hash with the options as keys will be used instead of the individual scalar variables.

Using our previous example, we would change the line in our program to:

```
getopt('df', \%opts);
```

Now when we run our program as before:

```
% perl getoptstd1.pl –d 20000423 –f file.dat –o
```

This will set `$opts{d}` to 20000423, `$opts{f}` to file.dat, and `$opts{o}` to 1.

Here's the code for our `getoptstd1.pl` program:

```perl
use Getopt::Std;

getopt('df');

print "\$opt_d => $opt_d\n" if $opt_d;
print "\$opt_f => $opt_f\n" if $opt_f;

# I've included a check for $opt_o so that you can see that it
# gets set to 1.
# If you really need a Boolean switch, use getopts()
print "\$opt_o => $opt_o\n" if $opt_o;
```

And here's the output:

```
$opt_d => 20000423
$opt_f => file.dat
$opt_o => 1
```

If you use the `strict` pragma, you must pre-declare your variables. For example:

```
use strict;
use vars qw($opt_d $opt_f $opt_o);
```

The same script using the hash reference:

```
use Getopt::Std;

my %opts;

getopt('df', \%opts);

print "\$opts{d} => $opts{d}\n" if $opts{d};
print "\$opts{f} => $opts{f}\n" if $opts{f};
print "\$opts{o} => $opts{o}\n" if $opts{o};
```

produces the following output:

```
$opts{d} => 20000423
$opts{f} => file.dat
$opts{o} => 1
```

The `getopts()` function gives you a little more flexibility processing command-line options. The argument to `getopts()` is a string that contains all of the *allowed* switches. In this case, the arguments to the switches are optional. The switches are considered Boolean by default and do not take any arguments unless they are followed by a colon.

The following program will parse only the three variables listed in the `getopts('d:f:o')` statement. The –d and –f switches both take arguments because each is followed by a colon.

```
use Getopt::Std;
use vars qw ($opt_d $opt_f $opt_o);

getopts('d:f:o');

print "\$opt_d => $opt_d\n" if $opt_d;
print "\$opt_f => $opt_f\n" if $opt_f;
```

```
print "\$opt_o => $opt_o\n" if $opt_o;
```

When this script is run at the command line:

```
% perl getoptstd3.pl -d 20000423 -f file.dat -o
```

the output produced would be:

```
$opt_d => 20000423
$opt_f => file.dat
$opt_o => 1
```

The hash reference can also be used with getopts():

```
use Getopt::Std;

my %opts;

getopts('d:f:o', \%opts);

print "\$opts{d} => $opts{d}\n" if $opts{d};
print "\$opts{f} => $opts{f}\n" if $opts{f};
print "\$opts{o} => $opts{o}\n" if $opts{o};
```

When this script is run at the command line:

```
% perl getoptstd4.pl -d 20000423 -f file.dat -o
```

the following output is received:

```
$opts{d} => 20000423
$opts{f} => file.dat
$opts{o} => 1
```

IO::File

The IO::File module supplies an object-oriented interface to file handles. This module is part of a group of I/O modules written by Graham Barr and is meant to replace the FileHandle module. By creating a reference to a file-handle object, the limitations of using a traditional file handle can be avoided. Some advantages include the ability to pass a file handle to a subroutine without resorting to "typeglobbing" and limiting the scope of a filehandle with my.

The open() method takes one required argument: the name of the file to open. There are also two optional arguments: open mode and file permission value. The open-mode argument may take the form of either a Perl mode string ("<", ">", ">>", etc), a POSIX fopen mode string ("w", "wb", "r+", etc.), or a POSIX constant (O_CREAT, O_RDONLY, O_WRONLY, etc.).

For example, a file could be opened for reading in several ways:

```
$IO::File->new("<file.dat");
$IO::File->new("file.dat", "r");
$IO::File->new("file.dat", O_RDONLY);
```

The constructor will return an object reference if the file is open successfully; otherwise, undef is returned if there is an error opening the file.

The close() method explicitly closes a file handle. A file handle will close implicitly when a program terminates or when the file handle is no longer valid.

The following script will open and write to a file and then reopen the file and read from it.

```
use IO::File;

my $file = 'iofile.txt';

# Write to the file
my $out = IO::File->new(">$file")
    or die "Cannot open $file for writing: $!\n";

print $out "Test data - line 1\n";
print $out "Test data - line 2\n";
$out->close();

# Read from file
my $in = IO::File->new("<$file")
    or die "Cannot open $file for reading: $!\n";

print while(<$in>);
```

The next script is similar to the previous one but shows how file handles can be passed to a subroutine.

```
use IO::File;

sub write_file {
    my $fh = shift;
    print $fh "Test data - line 1\n";
```

```perl
        print $fh "Test data - line 2\n";
}

sub read_file {
    my $fh = shift;
    print while(<$fh>);
}

my $file = 'iofile.txt';

# Write to file
my $out = IO::File->new(">$file")
    or die "Cannot open $file for writing $!\n";

# Pass the file handle
write_file($out);
$out->close();

# Read from file
my $in = IO::File->new("<$file")
    or die "Cannot open $file for reading: $!\n";

# Pass the file handle
read_file($in);
```

Text::Abbrev

The Text::Abbrev module is used to create a hash containing unique and unambiguous abbreviations from a given list of words. The keys are the abbreviations, and the values are equal to the corresponding words.

The following example uses Text::Abbrev to create a hash of unique, abbreviated commands that correspond to actual full, unabbreviated commands. This example could be used in your programs to allow the user to type fewer keystrokes when entering program commands.

```perl
use Text::Abbrev;

my %commands = abbrev qw(query start stop);

print "Enter a command: ";
chomp(my $key = <>);

if (exists $commands{$key}) {
    print "$key corresponds to the actual command."
        "\"$commands{$key}\"\n";
} else {
    print "There is no corresponding command for \"$key\"\n\n";
    foreach my $key (sort keys %commands) {
```

```
        print "$key => $commands{$key}\n";
    }
}
```

When running this example, you could enter the abbreviation "q" to run the query command:

```
Enter a command: q
q corresponds to the actual command "query"
```

If you enter an ambiguous abbreviation (or an abbreviation that doesn't exist as a key in the hash), you will see something like the following:

```
Enter a command: st
There is no corresponding command for "st"

q => query
qu => query
que => query
quer => query
query => query
sta => start
star => start
start => start
sto => stop
stop => stop
```

Text::Wrap

The `Text::Wrap` module wraps a simple text string into a multiline paragraph. The default column width is 76 but may be specified in the `Text::Wrap::column` scalar. The wrap function takes three arguments: a string to indent the first line of the paragraph, a string to indent all remaining lines of the paragraph, and the string to be wrapped.

This simple example will take a long string and wrap it into a paragraph with a width of 20 columns per line.

```
use Text::Wrap;

my $string = 'This is a long line of text that will be wrapped
with 20 columns per line. The first line will be indented with
">>>>>" and the remaining lines will be indented with ">".';

$Text::Wrap::columns = 20;
my $indent1 = ">>>>>";
```

```
my $indent2 = ">";
print wrap($indent1, $indent2, $string), "\n";
```

When the following script is run, it produces the following output:

```
>>>>>This is a
>long line of text
>that will be
>wrapped with 20
>columns per line.
>The first line
>will be indented
>with ">>>>>" and
>the remaining
>lines will be
>indented with ">".
```

Time::Local

The `Time::Local` module is used to convert local time and Greenwich mean time to UNIX time (epoch seconds) using the functions `timelocal()` and `timegm()`, respectively. These two functions have the opposite functionality of the Perl core functions `localtime()` and `gmtime()`. The arguments to the `Time::Local` functions are the corresponding time and date fields that are returned from Perl's `localtime()` and `gmtime()` functions. Once the upper integer limit is exceeded, both `timelocal()` and `timegm()` will return –1. This will occur in the year 2038 on most 32-bit systems.

The following short example will convert the date January 1, 2000 to epoch seconds using the `timelocal()` function contained in the `Time::Local`. The epoch seconds are then used as an argument to Perl's `localtime()` function and converted back to the date and time with which we began. The same function is then performed with `timegm()` and `gmtime()`.

```
use Time::Local;

# Set the date/time fields to January 1, 2000
my $sec   = 0;
my $min   = 0;
my $hours = 0;
my $mday  = 1;
my $mon   = 0;      # months 0..11
```

```
my $year  = 100;   # year = year - 1900

# Get local UNIX time (epoch seconds)
my $timelocal = timelocal($sec, $min, $hours, $mday, $mon,
$year);

print "timelocal($sec, $min, $hours, $mday, $mon, $year) =>
$timelocal\n";

# Convert UNIX time back to local time.
my $localtime = localtime($timelocal);

print "localtime($timelocal) => $localtime\n\n";

# Get GMT UNIX time (epoch seconds)
my $timegm = timegm($sec, $min, $hours, $mday, $mon, $year);

print "timegm($sec, $min, $hours, $mday, $mon, $year) =>
$timegm\n";

# Get GMT time from the epoch seconds
my $gmtime = gmtime($timegm);

print "gmtime($timegm) => $gmtime\n";
```

This function produces the following output:

```
timelocal(0, 0, 0, 1, 0, 100) => 946713600
localtime(946713600) => Sat Jan  1 00:00:00 2000

timegm(0, 0, 0, 1, 0, 100) => 946684800
gmtime(946684800) => Sat Jan  1 00:00:00 2000
```

The output will differ slightly with the time zone in which you run the code.

Time::gmtime

The Time::gmtime module provides two functions, gmtime() and gmctime(), which override the Perl core gmtime() function. The gmtime() function returns a Time::tm object. The methods associated with the returned object have the same names as the tm structure fields in the C time.h file. The gmctime() function overrides the core gmtime() function in a scalar context, returning a string containing the date and time.

```
use Time::gmtime;

my $time = gmtime;

# Print the individual fields
print '$time->sec   => ', $time->sec, "\n";
print '$time->min   => ', $time->min, "\n";
print '$time->hour  => ', $time->hour, "\n";
print '$time->mday  => ', $time->mday, "\n";
print '$time->mon   => ', $time->mon, "\n";
print '$time->year  => ', $time->year, "\n";
print '$time->wday  => ', $time->wday, "\n";
print '$time->yday  => ', $time->yday, "\n";
print '$time->isdst => ', $time->isdst, "\n";

# Use Perl core gmtime function in scalar context
print gmctime(time), "\n";
```

The output will look something like this:

```
$time->sec   => 57
$time->min   => 37
$time->hour  => 5
$time->mday  => 24
$time->mon   => 4
$time->year  => 100
$time->wday  => 3
$time->yday  => 144
$time->isdst => 0
Wed May 24 05:37:57 2000
```

Obviously the output will differ depending on when you run the script.

Time::localtime

The `Time::localtime` module provides two functions, `localtime()` and `ctime()`, which override the Perl core `localtime()` function. The `localtime()` function returns a `Time::tm` object. The methods associated with the returned object have the same names as the `tm` structure fields in the C `time.h` file. The `ctime()` function overrides the core `localtime()` function in a scalar context, returning a string containing the date and time.

```
use Time::localtime;
```

```
my $time = localtime;

# Print the individual fields
print '$time->sec   => ', $time->sec, "\n";
print '$time->min   => ', $time->min, "\n";
print '$time->hour  => ', $time->hour, "\n";
print '$time->mday  => ', $time->mday, "\n";
print '$time->mon   => ', $time->mon, "\n";
print '$time->year  => ', $time->year, "\n";
print '$time->wday  => ', $time->wday, "\n";
print '$time->yday  => ', $time->yday, "\n";
print '$time->isdst => ', $time->isdst, "\n";

# Use Perl core localtime function in scalar context
print ctime(time), "\n";
```

The output will look something like this:

```
$time->sec    => 6
$time->min    => 43
$time->hour   => 22
$time->mday   => 23
$time->mon    => 4
$time->year   => 100
$time->wday   => 2
$time->yday   => 143
$time->isdst  => 1
Tue May 23 22:43:06 2000
```

Obviously, the output will differ depending on when you run the script.

Summary

The standard Perl distribution comes with a collection of standard Perl modules. These modules can be used to perform many common and useful tasks that will in turn save you time and simplify your coding. Don't reinvent the wheel: if you familiarize yourself with the standard modules, you may avoid writing code that is already freely available with your distribution of Perl.

Dates
and Times

Overview of Dates and Times

Working with dates and times in any programming language is not typically considered difficult. However, it is time consuming to write your own routines to handle this common task. In this chapter, we look at five modules that will definitely make your life easier and cut your development time.

Date::Calc

Date::Calc, written by Steffen Beyer, is a self-described low-level toolkit approach to working with dates. Its purpose is not only to use these date routines directly but also in building larger more robust routines.

Date::Calc: /CPAN/Date-Calc-4.3.tar.gz

Date::Calc provides many easy-to-use functions for calculating items such as the number of days in a particular month, the number of days between two dates, and whether or not a given year is a leap year, to name a few. Holding true to the toolkit approach to building your own date-handling routines, Date::Calc is built off a small C library, which makes it much faster than other Perl-only implementations.

The following is a simple example:

```
use Date::Calc qw(Days_in_Month Month_to_Text Today);

my ($year, $month, $day) = Today();
my $days_in_month = Days_in_Month($year, $month);
my $month_text = Month_to_Text($month);

print "There are $days_in_month days in the month of
$month_text\n";
```

This example will print out the number of days of the current month, provided that your computer's date is accurate. Your results may vary; however, when I run this program, I get the following output:

```
There are 31 days in the month of May
```

To dissect this example, you will notice the use Date::Calc line, which includes the three functions from Date::Calc used in the example. To be able to use all of the functions without having to list them by name, you must replace that line with:

```
use Date::Calc qw(:all);
```

The Today() function used in the first line of the example returns an array containing the numeric values for the current year, month, and day. These values will be used later for the inputs to our other functions.

```
my $days_in_month = Days_in_Month($year, $month);
my $month_text = Month_to_Text($month);
```

These lines provide the number of days in the current month with Days_in_Month() and the textual name for the current month with Month_to_Text().

NOTE

Unlike Perl's built in localtime() *function, these values start at 1, not at 0. Instead of January being month 0, it will be month 1 when using* Date::Calc. *Also, the year is represented by a 4-digit year instead of Perl's standard number of years since 1900. This method makes working with dates much easier and makes more sense than the typical computer-science method of starting indices at 0.*

When dealing with years in Date::Calc make sure you pass the function with 4-digit years. In other words, pass "1999" rather than "99" because the program may attempt to decode "99" as "99 A.D." and not as the expected "1999."

One common problem in working with dates is generating a calendar representation of a month. Date::Calc solves this problem beautifully with one simple function call:

```
use Date::Calc qw(Calendar);

my $calendar = Calendar(2000, 5);
print "$calendar\n\n";
```

This function will output the following:

```
        May 2000
Mon Tue Wed Thu Fri Sat Sun
  1   2   3   4   5   6   7
  8   9  10  11  12  13  14
 15  16  17  18  19  20  21
 22  23  24  25  26  27  28
 29  30  31
```

Now that you understand the basics of how Date::Calc works, let's use a more complex example.

```perl
use Date::Calc qw(:all);

my ($year, $month, $day);

print "Enter a date using numeric representation: ".
      "( i.e. 1999, 5, 14 )\n";

print "Year: ";
chomp($year = <STDIN>);

print "Month: ";
chomp($month = <STDIN>);

print "Day: ";
chomp($day = <STDIN>);

if( check_date($year, $month, $day) ) {
    print Date_to_Text_Long($year, $month, $day) .
          " is a valid date\n";
}else {
    print "You have entered an invalid date.\n";
    exit(1);
}

if( leap_year($year) ) {
    print "$year is a leap year\n";
}else {
    print "$year is not a leap year\n";
}
exit(0);
```

This example first prompts the user to enter numerical values equivalent to the year, month, and day he or she wishes to use as input. These values are chomp()ed so that they do not contain any extra characters such as a return or newline character.

These user-supplied values are then passed to the check_date() function, which states whether or not the date is valid. A date such as that in the example, May 14, 1999, is a valid date, whereas a date such as May 40, 1999 is not. If the user enters an invalid date, the function immediately stops rather than pass erroneous data onto `leap_year()`.

If the date the user entered is valid, a nicely formatted textual representation of the date is made by using `Date_to_Text_Long()`. We finish by checking whether the year the user entered is a leap year.

The output for this program, using the inputs 1999, 5, 14 for the year, month, and day, is:

```
Friday, May 14th 1999 is a valid date
1999 is not a leap year
```

 # Date::Format

 Date::Format: /CPAN/TimeDate-1.09.tar.gz

`Date::Format` provides functions that correspond to the standard C-library functions `strftime()` and `ctime()`. `Date::Format` includes four functions:

- `time2str()`—Converts a time into an ASCII string by using a given conversion format.
- `strftime()`—Similar to the `time2str` except that it takes an array like the one returned by `localtime()`.
- `ctime()`—Calls `time2str`, with some preset arguments; an example output is "Mon May 15 20:42:22 2000."
- `asctime()`—Almost identical to `ctime()` except that it takes the array returned by `localtime()` as its argument.

NOTE *Each of these functions takes an optional third argument of a time zone; however, these functions default to using your current time zone.*

`time2str()` and `strftime()` both take templates as their first arguments. These templates determine how the ASCII output of these functions will appear. Let's build a simple example using first `time2str()` and then `strftime()`:

```
use Date::Format;
print time2str("%A the %o of %B", time);
print "\n";

use Date::Format;
my @lt = localtime(time);
print strftime("%A the %o of %B", @lt);
print "\n";
```

The output of each of these functions on my system was the following:

```
Monday the 15th of May
```

As you can plainly see, for quick operations time2str() seems to save you the step of having to fill an array with the results of localtime(); however, each function has its purpose. Having two functions with different inputs gives you the choice of which to use, based on what format your input is in. The output of time(), which we pass to time2str(), is the number of seconds since the epoch (midnight of January 1, 1970), whereas the output of localtime(time) consists of the date and time broken up into more usable chunks. localtime(time) returns an array with the seconds, minutes, hours, day of the month, month, year, weekday, day of the year, and time zone.

The following is a list of the possible values you can use in your templates:

%%	A literal '%'
%a	A day-of-the-week abbr
%A	A day of the week
%b	Month abbr
%B	Month
%c	MM/DD/YY HH:MM:SS
%C	ctime format: Sat Nov 19 21:05:57 1994
%d	Numeric day of the month, with leading zeros
%e	Numeric day of the month, without leading zeros
%D	MM/DD/YY
%h	Month abbr
%H	Hour, 24-hour clock, leading 0's
%I	Hour, 12-hour clock, leading 0's
%j	Day of the year
%k	Hour
%l	Hour, 12-hour clock
%m	Month number, starting with 1

%M	Minute, leading 0s
%n	NEWLINE
%o	Ornate day of month: "1st," "2nd," "25th," etc.
%p	AM or PM
%r	Time format: 09:05:57 PM
%R	Time format: 21:05
%s	Seconds since the epoch, UCT (aka GMT)
%S	Seconds, leading 0s
%t	TAB
%T	Time format: 21:05:57
%U	Week number, with Sunday as the first day of the week
%w	Day of the week, numerically, Sunday == 0
%W	Week number, with Monday as the first day of the week
%x	Date format: 11/19/94
%X	Time format: 21:05:57
%y	Year (2 digits)
%Y	Year (4 digits)
%Z	Time zone in ASCII, for example, PST
%z	Time zone in format -/+0000

Now let's build a slightly more complex example. In this example, we're going to attach the last access and modification times to a text file.

```
use Date::Format;

# Check to make sure we get a filename as a command line argument
if( scalar(@ARGV) != 1) {
    die "ERROR: Invalid filename(s) given\n";
}

# Get info about our file
# This will error here if the file does not exist.
# Error handling removed for clarity.
my @stats = stat($ARGV[0]);

# Open our file and read it into @lines
open(INPUT, "$ARGV[0]") or die "Can't open $ARGV[0]: $!\n";
my @lines = <INPUT>;
close(INPUT);

# Format our time info. stats() returns us an array of
# information
# about our file, of which we only need the last access time and
# last modify times
my $access_time = ctime($stats[8]);
my $mod_time = ctime($stats[9]);
```

```
open(OUTPUT,">$ARGV[0]")
    or die "Can't open $ARGV[0] for writing: $!\n";
print OUTPUT "Last Access: $access_time\n";
print OUTPUT "Last Modification: $mod_time\n";
print OUTPUT join(",@lines);
close(OUTPUT);

exit(0);
```

Date::Manip

Date::Manip is probably the most powerful module for working with dates and times available in CPAN. It makes all operations such as comparing dates, determining time intervals, and parsing dates much easier than with Perl's built-in routines. However, ease of use can come at the cost of speed. Date::Manip is written entirely in Perl without the benefit of a speedy C back end. Unfortunately, Date::Manip is also one of the more complicated CPAN modules, and a complete account of its uses is beyond the scope of this book.

Date::Manip: /CPAN/DateManip-5.39.tar.gz

This module, like many others, uses a specific representation of dates and times internally. Therefore, it is necessary to "convert" your date into this module before working with any of the other functions. Date::Manip's ParseDate() function handles this by converting from almost every common date format. ParseDate() returns a scalar that contains the specific date/time representation, which is passed into the other member functions.

```
use Date::Manip;

$date = ParseDate("today");
$date = ParseDate("05/28/00");
$date = ParseDate("Sun May 28 17:17:19 CDT 2000");
$date = ParseDate("3rd sunday in May 2000");
```

All of these formats, as well as many others, are supported. Below is a list of the internal representations:

- ParseDate("today"); 2000052817:18:34
- ParseDate("05/28/00"); 2000052800:00:00
- ParseDate("Sun May 28 17:17:19 CDT 2000"); 2000052817:17:19
- ParseDate("3rd sunday in May 2000"); 2000052100:00:00

To output a date from `Date::Manip`, the function `UnixDate()` is used. It is very similar to `strftime()` and other date-formatting functions, except that it takes the internal representation returned from `Parse-Date()` as its date and time arguments.

`DateCalc()` is `Date::Manip`'s function for determining the difference between two dates and for performing simple mathematical operations on a date (adding one day, adding one business day, finding the first Monday after the date, etc.).

In addition to using `Date::Manip`'s almost entirely readable formatting such as "3rd Sunday of May 2000," `Date:Manip`'s most powerful feature to the average programmer is the "business" mode. This mode makes the calculation of typical business days a snap. It should be noted that `Date:Manip` will reference a configuration file where all of these values can be assigned by default, for example, which days are holidays, the beginning and ending times of the work day, what default time zone to use, etc.

The following example calculates three business days from the current day to determine by what date a product must ship:

```
use Date::Manip;

my $date = ParseDate("today");
my $future_date = DateCalc($date, "+3 days", 2);
print UnixDate($future_date, "Product must be shipped by %D\n");
```

Let's dissect this example in detail. The first line containing the `ParseDate()` function determines the current day and time and formats it in `Date::Manip`'s internal representation. This is then passed, on the second line, to `DateCalc()` along with two other arguments. The second argument to `DateCalc()` tells it we want the date three days into the future from the date we passed in as `$date`. The third argument of "2" tells `DateCalc()` to use "business mode," skipping holidays and weekends in its calculations.

The output of this script from the command line is:

```
% perl 3biz_days.pl
Product must be shipped by 06/01/00
```

I ran this on 05/28/00, which is a Sunday. However, Monday is Memorial Day, which `DateCalc()` properly skipped because it was told to run in business mode. It should be noted that `DateCalc()` also calculates based on the time of day given. The output of the example will very based upon the time of day that you run it. For testing purposes, you can change the "today" argument of `ParseDate()` to be more specific about the time.

Another useful function of `Date::Manip` is the `Date_IsHoliday()` function. This function returns `undef` if the date passed is not a holiday or a string containing the name of the holiday. If the holiday is unnamed, it returns an empty string.

Finding the time between two different dates is a common requirement in many programs. More importantly, `Date::Manip` can format the output of these delta dates in very convenient ways, such as the number of hours between the two dates, the number of days, and so on. Let's build a very small payroll example.

```
use Date::Manip;

my ($start, $stop);

print "Start Date/Time: ";
chomp( $start = <STDIN> );
print "Stop Date/Time: ";
chomp( $stop = <STDIN> );

# Determine number of hours worked

my $delta = DateCalc($start, $stop);
# Arguments are the time offset, the number of decimal places to
# round to, and the format of the output.
print Delta_Format( $delta, 3,
      "That employee worked %hd hours\n");
```

When run from the command line, I got the following output:

```
% perl payroll.pl
Start Date/Time: Sun May 28 18:26:34 CDT 2000
Stop Date/Time: Sun May 28 21:14:09 CDT 2000
That employee worked 2.793 hours
```

The first few lines of this script prompt the user for the beginning and ending times of this employee's shift. Then it uses `DateCalc()` to determine the delta time between the two inputs and `Delta_Format()` to determine the number of hours worked rounded to three decimal places.

Date::Parse

`Date::Parse` is a very low-level function that should be used when creating your own date-handling routines. It has only two uses: it converts a string representation of a date into UNIX seconds, or it converts the string into an array similar to what is returned by the standard `localtime()` function.

Date::Parse: /CPAN/TimeDate-1.09.tar.gz

```
use Date::Parse;

my $date = "Sun May 28 18:37:46 CDT 2000";

my $seconds = str2time($date);
my ($seconds, $minutes, $hours, $day,
$month, $year, $zone) = strptime($date);
```

The function `str2time()` returns the number of epoch seconds at which the date occurred or `undef` upon failure. `strptime()`, as shown in the example above, returns an array of values that it parsed from the string representation. Only those values that could be calculated are included; the others will be undefined.

An example of where `Date::Parse` would be useful is a database-loading program. If you have a large amount of input to load into a database and you are going to be storing a date value from that input as epoch seconds, `Date::Parse` would be the perfect choice to determine the number of seconds. As opposed to using something like `Date::Manip`, which would be more appropriate for the outputting of the user interface, because `Date::Parse` is much faster than `Date::Manip`.

Time::HiRes

`Time::HiRes` is a very useful Perl module for dealing with time values shorter than 1 second. Common uses are to determine the amount of time a task took, having the program sleep for less than 1 second, or having it issue an alarm in less than 1 second. This module simply provides a Perl interface to the system calls `gettimeofday()`, `ualarm()`, and `usleep()`.

```
Time::HiRes: /CPAN/Time-HiRes-01.20.tar.gz
```

The following is an example of calculating execution time:

```
use Time::HiRes qw( gettimeofday tv_interval );
# gettimeofday is in brackets to make sure it returns
# its information in list context.
my $start_time = [gettimeofday];
my $counter = 0;

foreach (1..1000) {
    $counter++;
}

my $interval = tv_interval($start_time, [gettimeofday]);

print "Counting to 1000 on this computer took ".
      "$interval seconds.\n";
```

The output when run on my Pentium-II class machine was:

```
% perl interval.pl
Counting to 1000 on this computer took 0.000978 seconds.
```

Let's also make this example sleep for a few microseconds between each iteration of the loop:

```
use Time::HiRes qw( gettimeofday tv_interval usleep );

my $start_time = [gettimeofday];
my $counter = 0;
my $sleep = 0.001;

foreach my item (1..10) {
    $counter++;
    usleep($sleep);
}

my $interval = tv_interval($start_time, [gettimeofday]);
print "Counting to 10 took $interval seconds, sleeping $sleep " .
      "seconds after each count.\n";
```

The output on my computer is:

```
% perl interval.sleep.pl
Counting to 10 took 0.09789 seconds, sleeping 0.001 seconds after
each count
```

Do those numbers look funny to you? What is going on is the overhead of calling the `usleep()` function itself. There will always be some overhead associated with these sorts of system calls, but they are usually minor and shouldn't affect the overall results very much.

Summary

Working with dates is always bothersome. It is never the most exciting or intriguing aspect of any project, but it is almost always necessary. In this chapter we have tried to show you quick, useful, and, most importantly, open-source modules that can be used in a variety of applications. Hopefully, their usefulness and their ability to reduce development time has been made apparent.

Databases

Introduction

One of Perl's most useful abilities is working with databases. Databases allow you to store large amounts of data efficiently, in a logical manner, and quickly. They also allow for the fast retrieval of specific information from the database.

With databases you do not have to be concerned with how the data is stored or how to most effectively retrieve it. All of these details are handled by your database system.

DB_File

Perl's DB interface allows you to store data in a file but access it as if it were a normal in-memory hash. This is very useful when working with a large amount of data that would be impractical to actually store in memory.

Let's build a small database of user names and passwords. We are going to tie a hash called %users to our DB file, called users.dat in the current directory. This example wouldn't be practical with the small amount of data with which we're working, but if you were working with 10,000 user names and passwords it should be self-evident why using a database would be better than trying to store this amount of information in memory.

```perl
use Fcntl;
use SDBM_File;
my %users;

tie(%users, 'SDBM_File', 'users.dat', O_RDWR|O_CREAT, 0666)
    or die "Can't create or open users.dat: $!\n";

# Add our users to the hash, with really bad passwords
$users{'root'} = 'secret';
$users{'admin'} = 'password';
$users{'webmaster'} = 'www';

print "Login: ";
my $current_user = <STDIN>;
chomp($current_user);

print "Password: ";
my $pass = <STDIN>;
chomp($pass);
```

```
if($users{$current_user} eq $pass ) {
    print "Authorization accepted\n";
} else {
    print "Authorization failed!\n";
}

untie(%users);
```

Most of the code in the example above should be self-explanatory, with the exceptions of the included modules and the `tie` function. We include the `Fcntl` module to give us the ability to use the `tie` function, and we also include the `SDBM_File` module for our database.

We pass the tie function five arguments:

1. We pass it in the hash `%users` as the variable we want tied
2. The type of DB we want (`SDBM_File`)
3. The filename we want to use
4. The file options
5. The file's permissions

The file's options may seem cryptic but they signify that we want to open the database in read/write mode (`O_RDWR`) and that we want to create it, if it does not exist (`O_CREAT`). These are equivalent to file flags in the C programming language's `open` function or Perl's own `sysopen` function.

As you might have guessed, `SDBM_File` is not the only type of database available, but it is typically the only one that comes as a default with your installation of Perl. Some of the other types are NDBM, GDBM, MLDBM, and Berkeley DB. Each of these has its pros and cons, and for your individual application something besides `SDBM_File` may be appropriate.

For instance, MLDBM allows you to store references (similar to pointers in C/C++) in your database, which lets you store complex data structures in your database files. However, Berkeley DB is the fastest of all the DB modules, so if you are looking for speed, it is definitely the right choice.

In agreement with the Perl motto, "there's more than one way to do it," there is more than one effective way to "tie" a hash to a DB file. This is accomplished with the `dbmopen` and `dbmclose` commands built into Perl, but these functions only work with DBM, NDBM, SDBM, GDBM, and Berkeley DB; they do not work with MLDBM. The following are the pertinent lines of code from our previous example using this alternate method:

```
use DB_File;
my %users = ();
dbmopen(%users, 'users.dat', 0666)
    or die "Can't open or create users.dat: $!";

# Previous code to set and retrieve users and passwords removed

dbmclose(%users);
```

MLDBM: /CPAN/MLDBM-2.00.tar.gz

The most significant problem with using DB files is storing and retrieving data more complicated than simple key or value pairs. This is accomplished with Gurusamy Sarathy's MLDBM module. The following stores phone numbers and e-mail addresses keyed by the individual's name. It is stored as a hash of hashes (It's really easier than it sounds).

```
use MLDBM;
use Fcntl;
my %addresses;

tie(%addresses, 'MLDBM', 'addresses.dat', O_RDWR|O_CREAT, 0666)
    or die "Can't open or create addresses.dat: $!\n";

# Insert our data into addresses.dat
$addresses{'Bob'} = { phone => '555-5555',
                      email => 'bob@bob.com' };
$addresses{'Steve'} = { phone => '555-5050',
                        email => 'steve@nowhere.com' };

untie(%addresses);
```

To retrieve that data you would use the following script:

```
use MLDBM;
use Fcntl;
my %adds;

tie(%adds, 'MLDBM', 'addresses.dat', O_RDWR, 0666)
    or die "Can't open or create addresses.dat: $!\n";

foreach my $name ( keys(%adds) ) {
```

```
    print "Name   : $name\n";
    print "Phone : $adds{$name}->{phone}\n";
    print "E-mail: $adds{$name}->{email}\n\n";
}

untie(%adds);
```

The output should appear as follows:

```
% perl mldbm-retrieve.pl
Name   : Bob
Phone : 555-5555
E-mail: bob@bob.com

Name   : Steve
Phone : 555-5050
E-mail: steve@nowhere.com
```

One thing to note about using DB files is that the data resides in one or more files on your disk, so having to load the data as we did in our previous examples would be necessary only once. This is very useful if you need to load a large amount of data, process it slightly, and then need to retrieve the processed data at a later date. By using a DB file or any persistent data storage method, you would have to process the data one time.

Now let's build an example using Berkeley DB. One interesting feature of Berkeley DB is that it gives you the ability to tie an array as well as a hash. This feature is useful if you need to store only one value and not a key/value pair or complex data structure. Another interesting feature of Berkeley DB is that it takes the normal five arguments to tie, along with a special sixth argument that defines how you want it to store the data. The options are:

- $DB_HASH—This allows for storing key/value hashes, equivalent to all our previous examples.
- $DB_BTREE—This allows for storing key/value pairs in a sorted binary tree. You can also supply a user-defined sorting routine if you wish.
- $DB_RECNO—This allows for using fixed-length and variable-length flat text files just like $DB_HASH or $DB_TREE. The "key" of the key/value pair will be the line number on which the data resides.

Because using $DB_HASH is equivalent to our previous examples, let's build a small database of names and take advantage of Berkeley DB's ability to store information in sorted order. We'll also write our own sort routine to perform case-insensitive sorting.

```perl
use DB_File;
my %people = ();

sub case_insensitive_sort {
    my ($key_one, $key_two) = @_;

    # Make them lowercase
    $key_one = lc($key_one);
    $key_two = lc($key_two);

    return( $key_one cmp $key_two );
}

# Setup DB_File to use our sort
$DB_BTREE->{'compare'} = \&case_insensitive_sort;

tie(%people, "DB_File", 'sorted_people.dat',
    O_RDWR|O_CREAT, 0666, $DB_BTREE) or
  die "Can't open or create sorted_people.dat: $!\n";

# Add and remove some people
$people{'Frank Wiles'} = '1';
$people{'doug sparling'} = '2';
$people{'frank sinatra'} = '3';
$people{'John Doe'} = '4';
$people{'jane doe'} = '5';
$people{'Linus Torvalds'} = '6';
$people{'Wayne Newton'} = '7';

# Remove Linus
delete( $people{'Linus Torvalds'} );

# Now display our people in sorted order
foreach my $person ( keys(%people) ) {
    print "$people{$person}: $person\n";
}

untie(%people);
```

The output should appear as follows:

```
% perl sorted_db.pl
2: doug sparling
3: frank sinatra
1: Frank Wiles
5: jane doe
4: John Doe
7: Wayne Newton
```

If we run the same example without our case-insensitive sort, it would sort based on lexical order, or as follows:

```
% perl unsorted_db.pl
1: Frank Wiles
4: John Doe
7: Wayne Newton
2: doug sparling
3: frank sinatra
5: jane doe
```

DBI

DBI: /CPAN/DBI-1.14.tar.gz

Perl's database interface module, DBI, connects your Perl programs with SQL databases, not just one SQL database, but almost every SQL database ever written. It will access Oracle, Sybase, Informix, MySQL, PostgreSQL, mSQL, and ODBC databases.

DBI is basically a wrapper to DBD (DataBase Driver) modules that hold the specific code for whichever database you happen to be using. However, each database has different features, so certain DBI methods may not work as expected or not function at all.

DBI's API approach to using DBD modules allows for much easier migration from one database to another. For instance, if you originally wrote an application using MySQL on a Linux box and later realized that you needed more horsepower. Provided you had used all ANSI standard SQL in your program, it would be trivial to move to using Oracle on a Solaris machine.

You may be asking, "What is this SQL thing he keeps referring to?" SQL stands for Structured Query Language, and a complete introduction to it is beyond the scope of this book. However, I will give a brief introduction so that the rest of this chapter makes sense. SQL is a language that is used to insert data into, change data within, and retrieve data from an SQL database. SQL databases are laid out using tables; you can think of a table as a spreadsheet with rows and columns. Each column is a field in the database, with each row being a specific item in it.

```
DBD::Pg:  /CPAN/DBD-Pg-0.95.tar.gz
```

NOTE

All examples in this chapter use the PostgreSQL database which is the most robust open-source database available. See http://www.postgresql. org for more information or to download your own copy.

First we need to make a connection to our database so that we can create a table:

```
use DBI;

my $dbh = DBI->connect('dbi:Pg:dbname=chapter4', 'reader', 'ipm')
    or die "Cannot connect to database: $!";
```

`DBI->connect` creates an instance of a DBI object that we store in `$dbh`. This will be our gateway into the database for the rest of the program. We pass it three arguments.

`'dbi:Pg:dbname=chapter4'` uses database type PostgreSQL (Pg) and the database named `'chapter4'`. You can you can have multiple "databases" on a single database server. For example, a small business might have one computer running PostgreSQL and have a database for employee information, sales, inventory, etc.

We also pass the user name and the password; we used `'reader'` and `'ipm'` for this example. You would replace these with whatever user name and password you have created for your program in your database system. A user name with this system is typically different from a user's UNIX or NT user name. Consult the documentation that came with your specific database.

New let's create a table so we have something with which to work:

```
use DBI;
my $dbh = DBI->connect('dbi:Pg:dbname=chapter4', 'reader', 'ipm')
    or die "Cannot open database connection: $!";

$dbh->do("CREATE TABLE people (
            first_name      text,
            last_name       text
        ) "
);

$dbh->disconnect;
```

In the previous example, we first make our usual connection to the database and then use DBI's do() method to run an SQL statement. The do() method is the appropriate method to use when you expect no output other than errors from the database. SQL insertions, deletions, and updates are typically run with the do() method. Select statements, which return data are accomplished with other methods.

The SQL statement we passed to our database simply creates a table named 'people' with two text fields, first_name and last_name. To add information to our table, we need to construct and pass another type of SQL statement, aptly named INSERT. Afterward, we call DBI's disconnect method to close the connection to the database.

```
use DBI;
my $dbh = DBI->connect('dbi:Pg:dbname=chapter4', 'reader', 'ipm')
    or die "Cannot make a database connection: $!\n";

$dbh->do("INSERT INTO people VALUES( 'Frank',  'Wiles')");
$dbh->do("INSERT INTO people VALUES( 'Doug',   'Sparling')");
$dbh->do("INSERT INTO people VALUES( 'John',   'Reader')");
$dbh->do("INSERT INTO people VALUES( 'John',   'smith')");
$dbh->do("INSERT INTO people VALUES( 'Jane',   'smith')");

$dbh->disconnect;
```

This will insert the people above into our table 'people', so that we have some values to work with in the next few examples. The structure of a SQL insert statement is:

```
INSERT INTO tablename VALUES( field1, field2, ... fieldN )
```

As you might have noticed from the names above, we forgot to capitalize the two "smith" surnames. We can fix this with another type of SQL statement, the UPDATE statement. Updates are used to modify data that already resides in the database. The format of an update statement is:

```
UPDATE tablename SET field1=value1, field2=value2 WHERE
field1=identifier

use DBI;
my $dbh = DBI->connect('dbi:Pg:dbname=chapter4', 'reader', 'ipm')
    or die "Cannot make a database connection: $!\n";

$dbh->do("UPDATE people SET last_name='Smith' WHERE
last_name='smith'");

$dbh->disconnect;
```

Now let's retrieve all the names in alphabetical order from the database and display them. This is accomplished with an SQL select statement and some DBI methods that will be new to you. Following is the code:

```
use DBI;
my $dbh = DBI->connect('dbi:Pg:dbname=chapter4', 'reader', 'ipm')
    or die "Cannot make a database connection: $!";

my $sth = $dbh->prepare("SELECT * FROM people ORDER BY last_name,
first_name");
$sth->execute;

while( my($first_name, $last_name) = $sth->fetchrow ) {
    print "$last_name, $first_name\n";
}
$sth->finish;

$dbh->disconnect;
```

We call $dbh->prepare, which tells the database that we want to run this query and to please "prepare" itself for it to be run. This gives the database forewarning and optimizes its internal processes to produce the results as fast as possible. We assign a variable to this query because with certain databases you can have multiple queries running in tandem. Afterward, we tell the database to actually execute the query with $sth->execute. Because we did a SELECT *, which means to pull back all of the fields from the table 'people' that fit our conditions, we should be getting back our two name fields.

The while loop assigns two variables, $first_name and $last_name each time we call $sth->fetchrow. $sth->fetchrow instructs the database to assign the next row from our query to $sth. We then output each name to the screen. With $sth->finish we tell the database that we are done with this query, so that it can stop working on it and free up internal resources. We then disconnect from the database. Provided you ran each of the three examples above before running this one, the output should be:

```
% perl outputdb.pl
Reader, John
Smith, Jane
Smith, John
Sparling, Doug
Wiles, Frank
```

Now that you understand the basics, we can build a slightly more complex example and show some of the features that really make SQL databases shine. We are going to build a script that will take a text file as input and contains tab-separated values; one value will be a person's name and the other value will be that person's phone numbers. In today's world of cellular phone, pagers, fax machines, etc., an individual may have many phone numbers. Here is our data file.

```
Frank Wiles      (555) 555-5555   (555) 555-5000   (555) 555-5001
Doug Sparling    (555) 555-4000   (555) 555-4001
John Doe         (555) 555-3000
Jane Doe         (555) 555-3001
Larry Wall       (555) 555-2000   (555) 555-2050   (555) 555-2051
```

As you can see, some people have only one phone number, some have two numbers, and others have three numbers. With this problem we cannot use only one table because we have no idea how many numbers could be in our data file. So we will use two tables and two sequences. Sequences are SQL's answer to unique ID numbers. Think of a sequence as a variable in the database that is the largest ID currently being used. We then use PostgreSQL's NEXTVAL SQL function to give us the next number and increment the sequence. Note that NEXTVAL is a PostgreSQL function. Sequences typically work slightly differently from database to database. Here are our tables:

```
CREATE TABLE people (
    person_id   int,
    name        text
);

CREATE SEQUENCE people_seq;

CREATE TABLE phone_numbers (
        phone_id    int,
        person_id   int,
        number      text
);

CREATE SEQUENCE phone_numbers_seq;
```

You can load these SQL statements the same way as in our first example by using the DBIs; however, most database systems come with an interactive SQL monitor that behaves much like a command-line shell, where you can simply type these statements in and have them executed. Loading SQL statements is much easier than writing a script each time. From here on, we will assume that you have built these two tables and two sequences using whichever method you choose in a database named `'numbers'`, and that you have a data file in the same format named `'numbers.dat'`. Now for the Perl code:

```perl
use DBI;
my $dbh = DBI->connect('dbi:Pg:dbname=numbers', 'reader', 'ipm')
    or die "Cannot make a database connection: $!";

# Load our data into the database
open(DATAFILE, "numbers.dat")
    or die "Cannot open numbers.dat: $!\n";

while( my $line = <DATAFILE> ) {
    chomp($line);

    # Break our line up by tabs
    my @info = split(/\t/, $line);

    # Get our next sequence number.
    my $sth = $dbh->prepare("SELECT NEXTVAL('people_seq')");
    $sth->execute;
    my $next_seq = $sth->fetchrow;
    $sth->finish;

    # Insert our name into the people table
    $dbh->do("INSERT INTO people VALUES($next_seq, '$info[0]')");

    # Remove the first element of our line
    # which should be the person's name, which we have
    # already inserted into the database above
    shift(@info);

    # Insert each phone number into the database, with this
    # person's ID number.
    foreach my $number ( @info ) {
        $dbh->do("INSERT INTO phone_numbers VALUES(
            NEXTVAL('phone_numbers_seq'),
            $next_seq,
            '$number')");
    }

}
close(DATAFILE);

# Retrieve each person, and their phone number
my $sth = $dbh->prepare("SELECT * FROM people");
$sth->execute;

while( my($id, $name) = $sth->fetchrow ) {
    print "$name:\n";

    # Get phone numbers for this person
    my $sth2 = $dbh->prepare("SELECT * FROM phone_numbers
                WHERE person_id=$id");
```

```
    $sth2->execute;

    while( my($phone_id, $person_id, $number ) = $sth2->fetchrow
) {
        print "\t$number\n";
    }
    $sth2->finish;
    print "\n";
}
$sth->finish;

$dbh->disconnect;
```

After making our database connection in the usual way, we open our data file `'numbers.dat'` for processing. We loop through the file one line at a time in our while loop. We process each line by splitting on tab characters, inserting the first element into the `'person'` table. It is necessary to remember the person's unique ID number so that we can insert it with each of their phone numbers to maintain their relationship. Then we insert each of their phone numbers by looping over the array with a `foreach` statement returned by the `split` function.

Displaying the information again is then very trivial. We start by running a SELECT query to retrieve each and every person in the database. As we are looping through these names, we use the current person's ID number to start another query where we retrieve all the phone numbers and where the `'person_id'` field in the phone_numbers table is equal to the ID number of the person we are currently processing. We then print out their name and numbers to the screen, finish our queries, and properly disconnect from the database to not waste any system resources.

Provided everything went according to plan, the output should appear as follows:

```
Frank Wiles:
        (555) 555-5555
        (555) 555-5000
        (555) 555-5001

Doug Sparling:
        (555) 555-4000
        (555) 555-4001

John Doe:
        (555) 555-3000

Jane Doe:
        (555) 555-3001
```

```
Larry Wall:
        (555) 555-2000
        (555) 555-2050
        (555) 555-2051
```

Summary

Hopefully, through the examples given here, you have a better understanding of how to work with databases in Perl programs. Simply having this knowledge will greatly increase your flexibility as a programmer. The examples in this chapter were simplistic in nature and definitely don't show all the power that is inherent in these modules and in databases themselves. However, they should provide a solid foundation for learning more on these topics.

The most difficult part of building database-backed systems is all the variables are outside of your program. Items such as table structure, the data, the user interface of the program, the choice of database system, and the implementation of that system determine the quality of the finished product. I cannot stress enough the need to fully understand all of these variables in making your programs the best they can be.

Graphics

Graphics

One of the most difficult areas for many programmers is working with graphics. It is so difficult that the user interface often suffers due to the programmer's fear of it. However, with the help of the Perl modules detailed in this chapter, you should be able to incorporate the creation of dynamically built graphics into your programs.

This chapter shows how to gather information such as image size, build entire images from scratch, modify existing images, and, most importantly, how to build graphs.

Finding the Size of an Image

Something especially useful to Web programmers is finding the visual size of an image. There are two very useful modules that help with this process: `Image::Magick` and `Image::Size`. These modules allow you to gather the size of an image dynamically from a variety of different image formats, most notably GIF, JPEG, PNG, and TIFF.

By being able to determine an image's size with a Perl script or CGI, a programmer can include width and height attributes in HTML or use the attributes in other graphics manipulations, such as resizing an image.

Finding the Size of an Image with Image::Magick

```
ImageMagick: /misc/ImageMagick-5.2.2.tar.gz
PerlMagick: /misc/PerlMagick-5.22.tar.gz
```

`Image::Magick` allows you to retrieve an image's size from its `Get()` method. This method of size retrieval should probably only be used when using `Image::Magick` for some of its other image manipulation features, because it requires more lines of code than the `Image::Size` method and more overhead.

Let's build a simple example:

```
use Image::Magick;

# Create a new Image::Magick object
my $img = new Image::Magick;

# Read in our image
$img->Read("test.gif");

($width, $height) = $img->Get("width", "height");

print "The size of test.gif is $width x $height\n";
```

The output of this program using my test image is below; your results will differ:

```
% perl image_size.pl
The size of test.gif is 287 x 70
```

Finding the Size of an Image with Image::Size

Image::Size: /CPAN/Image-Size-2.903.tar.gz

With Image::Size, you can generate the WIDTH and HEIGHT attributes for the HTML image tag dynamically. Image sizes are cached, so once the size of an image is found, it won't be recalculated if the same image is called again. The Image::Size module provides the following methods: imgsize(), html_imgsize(), and attr_imgsize(). Only imgsize() is exported by default.

imgsize()

The imgsize() method returns a list containing three elements: the width, the height and the image type. If there is an error, both width and height return undef and the image type returns an error string.

```
use Image::Size;

my ($image_width, $image_height, $image_type) =
imgsize('ipm.gif');

print "Width: $image_width, Height: $image_height, ".
    "Type: $image_type\n";
```

Running this script will produce this output (when using the image on the CD):

```
Width: 90, Height: 30, Type: GIF
```

html_imgsize()

The `html_imgsize()` method will return the dimensions of an image in a formatted string that can be placed in an HTML IMG tag. If there is an error, `undef` is returned.

```
use Image::Size 'html_imgsize';

my $html_size = html_imgsize('ipm.gif');

print $html_size, "\n";
```

Running this script will produce this output:

```
width="90" height="30"
```

The following script will create a valid HTML image tag:

```
use Image::Size 'html_imgsize';

my $html_size = html_imgsize('ipm.gif');
my $html_string = qq!<img src="/images/ipm.gif" $html_size>!;

print $html_string, "\n";
```

This script will produce the following output:

```
<img src="/images/ipm.gif" width="90" height="30">
```

attr_imgsize()

The `attr_imgsize()` method will return the dimensions of an image as a four-element list. If there is an error, `undef` is returned.

```
use Image::Size 'attr_imgsize';

my @attrs = attr_imgsize('ipm.gif');

print join (',', @attrs), "\n";
```

Running this script will produce this output:

```
-width,90,-height,30
```

This list can be used with the `CGI.pm img()` method, which uses a hash for its parameters.

```
use CGI ':standard';
use Image::Size 'attr_imgsize';

my $image = '/home/httpd/html/images/ipm.gif';
my $image_vir = '/images/ipm.gif';

my @attrs = attr_imgsize($image);

print header,
    start_html('Image::Size Example'),
    img({-src=>$image_vir, $attrs[0]=>$attrs[1],
                           $attrs[2]=>$attrs[3]}),
    end_html;
```

To view the output of this script, you can either run it in the "offline" mode (you'll need to terminate your input using **Ctrl-D** or **Ctrl-Z** for Windows) or place the script in your cgi-bin and call it with your browser and use the view source function of your browser:

```
<!DOCTYPE HTML PUBLIC "-//IETF//DTD HTML//EN">
<HTML><HEAD><TITLE>Image::Size Example</TITLE>
</HEAD><BODY><IMG WIDTH="90" SRC="/images/logos/ipm.gif"
HEIGHT="30">
</BODY></HTML>
```

Manipulating Images with Image::Magick

The `Image::Magick` library also provides many ways to manipulate images. With this module you can add noise or borders and blur, crop, or animate your images. This module allows you to do almost everything that you can do with image-editing programs such as GIMP or Photoshop. This allows for simple tasks such as adding borders to several images with a script instead of manually with an editing program.

This example blurs the image slightly and adds a border:

```
use Image::Magick;

my $img = new Image::Magick;
```

```
$img->Read("test.gif");
my ($width, $height) = $img->Get("width", "height");

$img->Blur( order => 7 );

$img->Border(geometry => "${width}x{$height}+0+0",
             width    => 5,
             height   => 5,
             color    => "black"
);

$img->Write(filename => 'output.png');
```

This example will create a PNG file named output.png that will be very slightly blurred when compared with the original and have a 5-pixel-wide black border around the image. First, we have to read our original with the Read() method, after which we get the width and height of the image so we can have the proper information for the Border command.

We then blur the image, giving it an order of 7, which sets how blurred the result will be. The call to Image::Magick's Border() method is the most complex in this example. We have to pass to it the geometry of the image, which will look very familiar to UNIX users. The format is WIDTHxHEIGHT+X-OFFSET+Y-OFFSET. We then specify the width and height of the border and its color. We then output our transformed image into the file output.png.

Creating Dynamic Images with GD.pm

GD is a graphics library originally used for drawing GIF files. However, with the recent patent disputes over the compression algorithm in GIF images, GD has been converted to using only PNG and JPEG image files. The GD CPAN module allows you to interface with the GD library from your Perl programs.

GD: /CPAN/GD-1.30.tar.gz

Let's build an example script that will generate a PNG file that has a black border and a red circle in the center:

```perl
use GD;

# Create our GD object
my $img = new GD::Image(100,100);

# Make some colors
my $black = $img->colorAllocate(0,0,0);
my $red = $img->colorAllocate(255,0,0);

# Draw the outline of our circle
$img->arc(50,50,75,75,0,360, $red);

# Fill the circle with red
$img->fill(50,50, $red);

# Fill the rest of the image with black
$img->fill(0,0, $black);

# Convert into PNG format
my $image_data = $img->png;

# Write our image to a file for viewing.
open(OUTPUT, ">output2.png") or
  die "Can't write output2.png: $!";
print OUTPUT $image_data;
close(OUTPUT);
```

As you can see from this example, working with GD is similar in some ways to working with Image::Magick. We start by creating an image object we named $img and setting its size to 100 × 100 pixels. We then build our two colors, red and black, using RBG triplet values. We then draw the border to our circle using the arc() method. arc() takes arguments of the center of the arc, the width and height of the arc, and the beginning and ending degrees. To build a circle one merely picks a point. In this example, we used the center point, the radius of the circle, and 0 through 360 degrees. After drawing the border, we fill the circle with red using the fill method. We give the image its black background by filling the rest of the image with black.

GD has its own internal format for storing all of the image information, so we must use the png() method to convert it into a portable image format that can be viewed on an image viewer. Using standard Perl functions, we can output the image data to a file.

If all went well, you should have an image that resembles the one shown in Figure 5.1.

Another useful function of GD is the ability to manipulate text and place it into an image file. This has many applications, from building dynamically created image buttons on Web pages to watermarking

Figure 5.1
Red circle on black
background.

images with a website URL or company name. Let's build a simple example where we create an image with a single phrase, "Perl makes this easy!".

ON THE CD

GDTextUtil: /CPAN/GDTextUtil-0.75.tar.gz

```perl
use GD;
use GD::Text::Align;

# Create our image object
$img = new GD::Image(150,50);

# Create our text alignment object
my $align = GD::Text::Align->new($img,
                                 valign => 'top',
                                 halign => 'left',
);

# Build our colors
my $black = $img->colorAllocate(0,0,0);
my $white = $img->colorAllocate(255,255,255);

# Fill the image to have a white background
$img->fill(0,0,$white);

# Set our font to be GD's built in internal "small" font
# Also set the color
$align->set_font(gdSmallFont);
$align->set( color => $black);

# Set our text string
$align->set_text("Perl makes this easy!");

# Actually draw the text
$align->draw(5,5,0);

# Output the image data in the usual way
my $image_data = $img->png;

open(OUTPUT, ">output3.png");
```

```
print OUTPUT $image_data;
close(OUTPUT);
```

Figure 5.2 shows the output of this example.

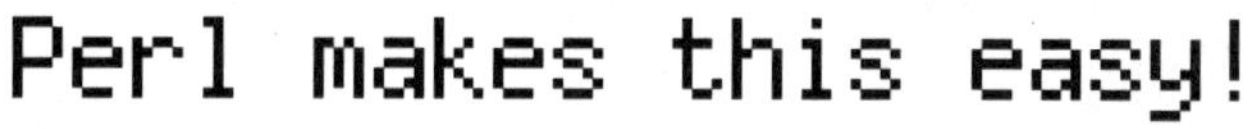

Figure 5.2
Text output example.

Perl makes this easy!

This example creates an image that is 150 pixels wide by 50 pixels tall, with a white background and black text, with the text reading "Perl makes this easy!". To use fonts other than those built into GD, you must use *true type fonts* (TTFs). Using TTF with GD isn't difficult, but it is more difficult than using the built-in fonts. It also makes the code less portable because you have to specify a font path for GD::Text::Align to look for fonts. You accomplish this with a colon-separated list:

```
$align->font_path('/usr/fonts:/usr/local/fonts');
```

This list sets GD to look in the two following directories for fonts you specify for the rest of the program:

```
/usr/fonts
/usr/local/fonts
```

We can also use GD::Text::Align to write text at a particular angle when calling the draw method. If we create our image slightly larger, we can write our string vertically instead of horizontally.

```
use GD;
use GD::Text::Align;

# Create our image object
$img = new GD::Image(150,150);

# Create our text alignment object
my $align = GD::Text::Align->new($img,
                                 valign => 'top',
                                 halign => 'left',
);

# Build our colors
my $black = $img->colorAllocate(0,0,0);
my $white = $img->colorAllocate(255,255,255);

# Fill the image to have a white background
$img->fill(0,0,$white);
```

```
# Set our font to be GD's built in internal "small" font
$align->set_font(gdSmallFont);

# Set our text string and our color
$align->set_text("Perl makes this easy!");
$align->set( color => $black);

# Actually draw the text
$align->draw(75,145,90);

# Output the image data in the usual way
my $image_data = $img->png;

open(OUTPUT, ">output4.png");
print OUTPUT $image_data;
close(OUTPUT);
```

Figure 5.3 shows the vertical output.

Figure 5.3
Vertical text example.

Perl makes this easy!

A very common use for GD is "watermarking" images. If you publish many copyrighted images online, it is nice to be able to place some text on the image, such as a company name, URL, and copyright information. If you are developing only a few images, it is probably easier to edit the images by hand with your favorite image editor. But what if you're converting hundreds or thousands of images? It would much simpler to be able to do something like:

```
% copyright_images.pl *.png
```

GD supports only an 8-bit color depth, so this routine probably won't be acceptable for use on photographs.

NOTE

Let's build this script:

```perl
use GD;
use GD::Text::Wrap;

my $output_string = "Acme Image Company http://www.acme.com
Copyright 2000";

foreach $file ( @ARGV ) {

  print "Processing $file...";

  # Make a backup copy of our file
  `cp $file $file.bak`;

  # Get our image
  my $img = GD::Image->new($file) or
    die "Can't open image: $!\n";

  # Setup our colors
  my $black = $img->colorAllocate(0,0,0);

  # Setup our text object
  my $text = GD::Text::Wrap->new($img,
                                 line_space => 4,
                                 color      => $black,
                                 text       => $output_string,
  );

  # Get this image's width and height
  my( $width, $height ) = $img->getBounds();

  # Setup our font, text string, etc.
  $text->set_font(gdTinyFont);
  $text->set(align => 'left', width => 120);

  # Actually draw the text
  $text->draw( $width - 125, $height - 65 );
  # Output our converted image
  my $image_data = $img->png;
```

```perl
# Remove file extension
$file =~ s/\..*?$//;

open(OUTPUT, ">$file.png") or
   die "Can't write $file.png: $!\n";
print OUTPUT $image_data;
close(OUTPUT);

print "done\n";

}

print "Converstion complete.\n\n";
```

Creating Graphs with GD::Graph

One task that is often demanded of programmers is the creation of graphs based on dynamic data. Graphs are a very useful tool in showing trends in data as well as overall pictures, but they are generally difficult for the programmer to implement. GD::Graphs attempts to solve this by giving a fairly easy-to-use interface for building different styles of graphs.

GDGraph: /CPAN/GDGraph-1.32.tar.gz

Let's use a simple bar graph of system load versus time as an introduction to building graphs:

```perl
use GD::Graph::bars;
use GD::Graph::colour;
use GD::Graph::Data;

# Build our dataset as an array of two arrays
my $datavalues = GD::Graph::Data->new(
    [[ "12am", "2am", "4am", "6am", "8am", "10am", "12pm", "2pm",
      "4pm", "6pm", "8pm", "10pm" ],
     [ .98, .63, .08, .07, .12, .54, .32, .89, .81, .43, .21, .05]]);

# Create our graph object
my $graph = GD::Graph::bars->new();

# Set useful variables such as our axis labels, title,
# coloring, etc
$graph->set(
```

```
        x_label => 'Time',
        y_label => 'System Load',
        title => 'System Load vs. Time',
        y_max_value => 1.1,
        bar_spacing => 6,
        shadow_depth => 4,
        shadowclr => 'dred',
);

# Actually plot the data
$graph->plot($datavalues) or die $graph->error;

# Output the image as a PNG
open(OUTPUT, ">output5.png") or
  die "Can't open output5.png: $!\n";
print OUTPUT $graph->gd->png();
close(OUTPUT);
```

Figure 5.4 shows the bar graph.

Figure 5.4
Sample bar graph.

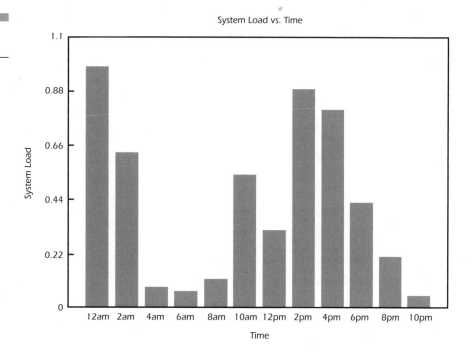

This example looks complex at first glance, but the only difficult part is the data generation and the graph options. The rest should be very familiar by now.

Our data generation is accomplished by passing an anonymous array, which contains an array of x-axis labels and an array of y-axis values. We then set up some options to the graph itself, such as the spacing between the bars in the graph, how deep to make the shadow, and the color of the bars.

Some examples of defined colors are white, gray, black, blue, yellow, green, red, and purple. Some of these colors can be modified by prefixing them with an 'l' or a 'd' indicating light or dark. Play around for awhile to get the color you want or consult the GD::Graph::colour documentation for more information.

Now that we've built our first bar graph, let's convert it to a continuous line graph:

```
use GD::Graph::lines;

my @data = (
  [ "12am", "2am", "4am", "6am", "8am", "10am", "12pm", "2pm",
    "4pm", "6pm", "8pm", "10pm" ],
  [ .98, .63, .08, .07, .12, .54, .32, .89, .81, .43, .21, .05],
);

my $graph = new GD::Graph::lines();

$graph->set(
    x_label => 'Time',
    y_label => 'System Load',
    title   => 'System Load vs. Time',
    y_min_value => 1.1,
    y_min_value => 0,
    y_tick_number => 11,
    box_axis => 1,
    line_width => 2,
    show_values => 1,

);

$graph->plot(\@data);

open(OUTPUT, ">output6.png") or
  die "Can't open output6.png: $!\n";
print OUTPUT $graph->gd->png();
close(OUTPUT);
```

Did you notice that the data are represented differently? This is an alternative method for building a dataset. Also notice, that, when building line graphs, there are more options, such as line_width. I also turned on show_values, which displays the value of each data point at its location on the image. Figure 5.5 shows the output of this example.

Figure 5.5
Line chart example.

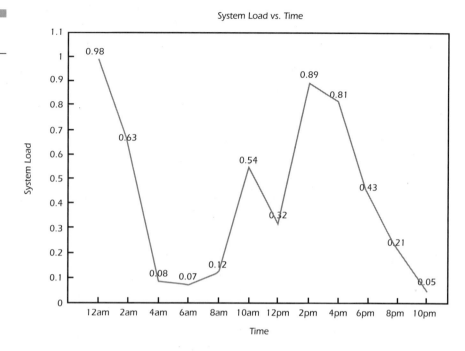

Another often-requested graph type is the pie chart. So let's build one of those:

```perl
use GD::Graph::pie;

# Build our dataset
my @data = (
  [ "1st quarter", "2nd quarter", "3rd quarter", "4th quarter" ],
  [ 33.7, 14.8, 7, 44.5 ]
);

# Generate our Graph object, forcing it to produce images
# of 200 pixels by 200 pixels.
my $graph = new GD::Graph::pie(200,200);

# Setup our graph options
# start_angle is the angle where GD begins
# drawing our data values
$graph->set(
  start_angle => 90,
  '3d' => 0,
  label => 'Company Productivity',
);

# Actually plot our data
$graph->plot(\@data);
```

```
# Output normally.
open(OUTPUT, ">output7.png") or
    die "Can't open output7.png: $!\n";
print OUTPUT $graph->gd->png();
close(OUTPUT);
```

Figure 5.6 shows our pie chart.

Figure 5.6
Pie chart.

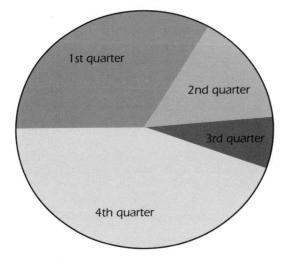

We can also build a pseudo–three-dimensional pie chart by changing the line of code from `'3d' => 0` to `'3d' => 1`. Figure 5.7 shows this pie chart.

Figure 5.7
Three-dimensional pie chart.

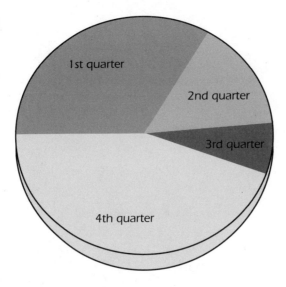

Summary

Working with graphics is not nearly as difficult as most people believe. Unfortunately, most programmers aren't familiar with factors such as color depth and image quality. GD provides a very simple programming interface for building images and graphs. It does, however, have the slightly annoying restriction of an 8-bit color depth. If more complicated images are necessary, such as high-quality photographs, then other technologies must be used.

Perl/Tk: Creating Graphical User Interfaces

Introduction to Perl/Tk

 Perl/Tk: /CPAN/Tk800.022.tar.gz

The Perl/Tk extension to Perl is a toolkit used to create graphical user interfaces (GUIs). Tk was originally developed by John Ousterhout as a graphical toolkit for Tcl (a scripting language that he also developed) and was later ported to Perl by Nick Ing-Simmons. Perl/Tk makes it easy to create a visual interface to Perl and possible to build windows-based, event-driven applications for both UNIX and Windows.

Brief Overview of Perl/Tk

A Perl/Tk interface consists of a hierarchy of *widgets*. A widget is a graphical component or control such as a button, label, or menu. The topmost, or parent, widget of this hierarchy is normally a special top-level widget known as the main window. The main window is the primary container that will hold the children widgets that make up the interface. A geometry manager is used to arrange the widgets in the container. Once the main window is created and the widgets are added, the event loop is entered and the application will wait to handle user events. User events are handled by *callbacks*, which is code attached to widgets that will be called in response to the user event.

Simple Example: Hello World

I'm sure that you're eager to see how easy it is to create a Perl application with a graphical interface. Before digging into the details we'll take a look at a simple example consisting of a window and two buttons.

First, let's list the steps necessary to build a simple GUI application:

1. Create the main window.
2. Create and configure the widgets contained in the main window.
3. Add the widgets to the main window. This is usually done with the `pack()` function, which positions and sizes the widgets.
4. Start the event loop. From this point on, the application will respond to user events such as mouse movements and key presses.

Now for the code:

```
use Tk;

my $mw = MainWindow->new();

$mw->Button(-text => 'Hello, World',
            -command => sub { print STDOUT "Hello, World!\n" }
)->pack();

$mw->Button(-text => 'Goodbye, World',
            -command => sub { exit })->pack();

MainLoop;
```

Figure 6.1 shows the window created by our example program. Note that the title of the window is set to the name of the program by default. We'll show how to change the title a little later on. Figure 6.2 shows the output generated after clicking the "Hello, World" button.

Figure 6.1
Simple example window.

The first line:

```
use Tk;
```

loads the Tk module. Next, we need to create a MainWindow object:

```
my $mw = MainWindow->new();
```

Once the MainWindow object is created, we can add the other widgets. First, we'll add a button:

```
$mw->Button(-text => 'Hello, World',
            -command => sub {print STDOUT "Hello, World!\n";}
)->pack();
```

This code uses the widget creation method to create a new button. Note that two configuration options, -text and –command, are passed to the cre-

Figure 6.2
Output created by
clicking "Hello,
World" button.

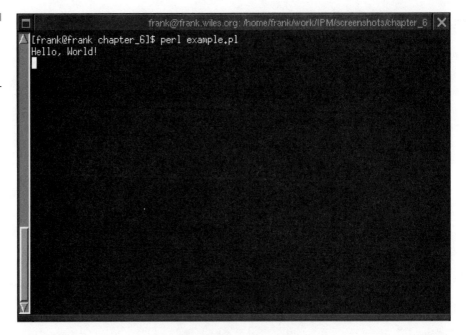

```
[frank@frank chapter_6]$ perl example.pl
Hello, World!
```

ation method. The -text option sets the text that will be displayed on the
button. The -command option binds an anonymous subroutine that will
run when the button is clicked. In this case, when the button is clicked,
"Hello, World!" is printed to STDOUT. Finally, the button is *packed*. Packing
the button will place it in the main window. A widget can be packed when
it is created or it can be packed separately. For example:

```
# pack when widget is created
$mw->Button(-text => 'Hello, World',
            -command => sub {print STDOUT "Hello, World!\n" }
)->pack();
```

or

```
# pack button separately
$button = $mw->Button(-text => 'Hello, World',
                      -command => sub { print STDOUT "Hello,
World!\n" });
$button->pack();
```

You must pack a widget for it to be displayed.

NOTE

Let's add another button:

```
$mw->Button (-text => 'Goodbye, World',
             -command => sub { exit })->pack();
```

This button will cause the application to exit when the button is clicked.

The last line

```
MainLoop;
```

activates the event loop. The application will now wait for user events and respond with the corresponding callbacks that were configured with the widgets.

NOTE

You must call the MainLoop for your widgets to be displayed.

Widgets

There are several widgets for creating graphical interfaces. The main widgets included in the Tk toolkit are:

- Button
- Canvas
- Checkbutton
- Entry
- Frame
- Label
- Listbox
- Menu
- Menubutton
- Message
- Radiobutton
- Scale
- Scrollbar
- Text
- Toplevel

Perl/Tk comes with a widget demo application that will demonstrate the various Tk widgets. Assuming that `/usr/bin` (`\perl\bin` on Windows) is in your path, type the following line to run the demo:

```
% widget
```

This will open a window containing links to several sample scripts that you can run. Each script comes with code that you can modify and rerun.

Creating the MainWindow

Before you start creating widgets, you must create a main window to place them in. The MainWindow widget is a container that is a parent to other widgets in the interface. The MainWindow is a Toplevel widget. The use of multiple top-level windows is allowed in Perl/Tk, but the MainWindow is the first window created. You can create a new window by using the new() method of the Tk::MainWindow module as follows.

```
use Tk;

my $mw = MainWindow->new();

MainLoop;
```

To display the window, you must enter the event loop by calling the MainLoop method. User events are handled in the event loop. You may have noticed that the caption in the titlebar of the window is set by default to the name of the Perl script that created it. You can add your own caption by calling the title() function. Figure 6.3 shows the window created with the following code.

```
use Tk;

my $mw = MainWindow->new();

$mw->title('My Title');

MainLoop
```

Creating Widgets

Widgets are created with the widget construction method. You may pass options to the widget's construction method using -option => value

Figure 6.3
Window created using title() function.

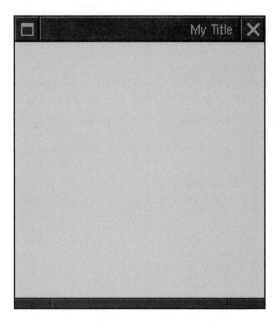

pairs. These options are configuration parameters that allow you to configure the widget when you create it. The following example creates a button with two options, -text and -command.

```
use Tk;

my $mw = MainWindow->new();

$mw->Button(-text => 'Exit',
            -command => sub { exit })->pack();

MainLoop;
```

The -text option sets the text displayed on the button. The -command option determines how the widget will interact with the application. Figure 6.4 shows the window created by this simple script.

Figure 6.4
Window with Exit button.

A reference to the created widget can be stored in a *scalar*, which is useful when you need to refer to a particular widget after it is created.

```
$button_exit = $mw->Button(-text => 'Exit',
                          -command => sub { exit })->pack();
```

Once a widget has been created, it is possible to change the value of an existing option or assign a value to a new option by using the `configure()` method. For example, to change the text of a button after it has been created, you could use the following code:

```
$button_exit->configure(-text => 'Goodbye');
```

To determine the value of an option, the widget may be queried with the `cget()` method as follows:

```
$text = $button_exit->cget(-text);
```

Common Widget Options

There are several configuration options that are common to many of the widgets.

-anchor => position
Description: Sets position of text in a widget
Possible values: 'n', 'ne', 'e', 'se', 's', 'sw', 'w', 'nw' and 'center'
Default value: 'center'
Example: `-anchor => 'nw'`
Widgets: Button, Checkbutton, Label, Menubutton, Radiobutton

-background => color
Description: Sets background color of widget
Possible values: String or hex RGB value
Default value: SystemButtonFace
Example: `-background => 'red'`
         `-background => '#ff0000'`
Widgets: Button, Canvas, Checkbutton, Entry, Frame, Label, Listbox, Menu, Menubutton, Radiobutton, Scale, Scrollbar, Text, Toplevel

-bitmap => bitmap
Description: Determines bitmap that is displayed in the widget
Possible values: Default Tk bitmap (error, gray12, gray25, gray50, gray75, hourglass, info, question, questhead or warning) or location of a bitmap file
Default value: undef

Example: `-bitmap => 'question'`
    `-bitmap => '@filename'`
Widgets: Button, Checkbutton, Label, Menubutton, Radiobutton

-borderwidth => amount
Description: Sets width of widget border
Possible values: Valid screen units [pixels, (c)cm, (i)inch, (m)mm, (p)points]
Default value: 2 pixels
Example: `-borderwidth => 4`
    `-borderwidth => 1c`
Widgets: Button, Canvas, Checkbutton, Entry, Frame, Label, Listbox, Menu, Menubutton, Radiobutton, Scale, Scrollbar, Text, Toplevel

-command => callback
Description: Action to be performed on default widget event
Possible values: Anonymous routine or reference to function to be called
Default value: undef
Example: `-command => \&function`
    `-command => sub { exit }`
Widgets: Button, Checkbutton, Radiobutton, Scale, Scrollbar

-font => font
Description: Sets font used for text in widget
Possible values: Valid font in X or Windows format
Default value: {MS Sans Serif} 8
Example: `-font => '-adobe-times-medium-r-12-120-75-75-p-64-`
        `iso8859-1'`
    `-font => '9x15'`
    `-font => '{Times New Roman} 12 {normal}'`
Widgets: Button, Checkbutton, Entry, Label, Listbox, Menu, Menubutton, Radiobutton, Scale, Text

-foreground => color
Description: Sets foreground color (color of text)
Possible values: String or hex RGB value
Default value: SystemButtonText
Example: `-background => 'red'`
    `-background => '#ff0000'`
Widgets: Button, Checkbutton, Entry, Label, Listbox, Menu, Menubtton, Radiobutton, Scale, Text

-height => height
Description: Sets the height of a widget
Possible values: Number of characters for text, screen units [pixels, (c)cm, (i)inch, (m)mm, (p)points] for images and bitmaps
Default value: 0 pixels
Example: -height => 2
       -height => 150
Widgets: Button, Canvas, Checkbutton, Frame, Label, Listbox, Menubutton, Radiobutton, Text, Toplevel

-image => image_ref
Description: Determines image that is displayed in the widget
Possible values: Reference to Image or Photo object
Default value: undef
Example: -image => $image
Widgets: Button, Checkbutton, Label, Menubutton, Radiobutton

-relief => relief_style
Description: Sets border style of widget
Possible values: 'flat', 'groove', 'raised', 'ridge', and 'sunken'
Default value: 'raised'
Example: -relief => 'groove'
Widgets: Button, Canvas, Checkbutton, Entry, Frame, Label, Listbox, Menu, Menubutton, Radiobutton, Scale, Scrollbar, Text, Toplevel

-state => state
Description: Current status or responsiveness of widget
Possible values: 'normal', 'disabled' and 'active'
Default value: 'normal'
Example: -state => 'disabled'
Widgets: Button, Checkbutton, Entry, Menubutton, Scale, Text

-text => text
Description: Sets text that is displayed in widget
Possible values: Text string
Default value: undef
Example: -text => 'Exit'
Widgets: Button, Checkbutton, Label, Radiobutton

-textvariable => variable_reference
Description: Reference to scalar variable that contains text to be displayed in widget
Possible values: Reference to scalar variable
Default value: undef

Example: `-textvariable => \$text`
Widgets: Button, Checkbutton, Entry, Label, Radiobutton

`-width => width`
Description: Sets the width of a widget
Possible values: Number of characters for text, screen units [pixels, (c)cm, (i)inch, (m)mm, (p)points] for images and bitmaps
Default value: 0 pixels
Example: `-width => 2`
`-width => 150`
Widgets: Button, Canvas, Checkbutton, Frame, Label, Listbox, Menubutton, Radiobutton, Scale, Scrollbar, Text, Toplevel

Callbacks and Binding

Perl/Tk is used to build event-driven applications. Once the interface is displayed, the program will wait quietly for events to be generated. An event is normally a user action such as a mouse click, mouse movement, or a key press. It is possible to bind events to a widget so that a certain action will take place in response to a specific event. Many widgets have a default event that can be handled with the `-command` option. The `-command` option will evoke a callback, normally a subroutine that will be called in response to an event. For example, the following code has a button that calls a subroutine that prints a simple text string to STDOUT when it is clicked. Figure 6.5 shows the interface. The output is printed to STDOUT, as shown in Figure 6.6.

```
use Tk;

my $mw = MainWindow->new();

$mw->Button(-text => 'Say Goodnight Irene',
            -command => \&display)->pack();

MainLoop;

sub display {
    print "Goodnight Irene\n";
}
```

You can bind other nondefault events to a widget by using the bind method. For example, the following code will create a label and bind a double-left mouse click event to a subroutine that will print the label

Figure 6.5
Window created by
callback example.

Figure 6.6
Output generated by
callback example.

text to STDOUT. Figure 6.7 shows the interface. The output produced is the same as the previous example.

```perl
use Tk;

my $mw = MainWindow->new();

my $label = $mw->Label(-text => 'Say Goodnight Irene')->pack();

$label->bind('<Double-Button-1>', \&display);

MainLoop;

sub display {
    print "Goodnight Irene\n";
}
```

Event Sequences

The event that we bind to a widget is defined with a string made up of three parts: an optional modifier, an event type, and an optional detail.

The modifier is a special key that is held down when the main event occurs, such as Control, Shift, Alt, Meta, or Lock. Other modifiers include mouse buttons, such as Button1, Button2, ... Button5 and Double and Triple for double and triple clicks, respectively. The event type is the event being processed such as a button press (e.g., Button1), button release (e.g., ButtonRelease-1), cursor entry (Enter), focus in (FocusIn), focus out (FocusOut), key press (KeyPress or Key), or key release (KeyRelease). The detail gives us specific information about the event. For example, a detail can be used with the KeyPress event to check for a particular key press (e.g., KeyPress-d). It should now be clear that the event sequence <Double-Button-1> in the previous example describes an event consisting of a double-click of button 1 (the left mouse button) where Double is the modifier, Button is the event type, and 1 the detail.

Label Widget

A label widget is used to display static noneditable text. A label widget is often used to describe another widget on the screen.

The following code demonstrates the various -relief options that give a 3-D effect to the label's border. The -text option is used to set the text string displayed in the label. The window created is shown in Figure 6.8.

```
use Tk;

my $mw = MainWindow->new();

$mw->Label(-text => 'Label with flat (default) relief')->pack();

$mw->Label(-text => 'Label with groove relief',
           -relief => 'groove')->pack();

$mw->Label(-text => 'Label with raised relief',
           -relief => 'raised')->pack();

$mw->Label(-text => 'Label with ridge relief',
           -relief => 'ridge')->pack();
```

```
$mw->Label(-text => 'Label with sunken relief',
           -relief => 'sunken')->pack();

MainLoop;
```

Figure 6.8
Label widgets using
the -relief option.

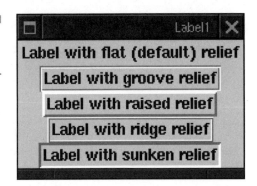

This next example will use the -textvariable option to update the label as various buttons are pressed. Each button has a callback that updates the variable pointed to by the -textvariable option. The label's text will change accordingly as this variable is updated. Figure 6.9 shows the window after the user clicks the Hello button. Note that this example uses the -fill and -side options of the pack geometry manager. These options are discussed later in the chapter.

```
use Tk;

my $mw = MainWindow->new();

$mw->Label(-textvariable => \$greeting,
           -relief => 'groove')->pack(-fill => 'x');

$mw->Button(-text => 'Hello',
            -command => [ \&say_hello, 'Hello' ]
)->pack(-side => 'left');

$mw->Button(-text => 'Bonjour',
            -command => [ \&say_hello, 'Bonjour' ]
)->pack(-side => 'left');

$mw->Button(-text => 'Guten Tag',
            -command => [ \&say_hello, 'Guten Tag' ]
)->pack(-side => 'left');

$mw->Button(-text => 'Exit',
            -command => sub { exit })->pack(-side => 'left');

MainLoop;
```

```
sub say_hello {
    my ($greet) = @_;
    $greeting = $greet;
}
```

Figure 6.9
Label widget using
the –textvariable
option.

Note that we pass an argument to the callback. There are three main ways to define a callback, all of which we have seen by now.

1. The -command option takes an anonymous subroutine, as shown in the first simple example in this chapter:

```
$mw->Button(-text => 'Hello, World',
            -command => sub { print STDOUT "Hello, World!\n" }
)->pack();
```

2. The -command option takes a reference to a subroutine, as shown previously in the callback example. This is useful for longer or more complex callbacks and has the benefit that several widgets can use the same subroutine.

```
$mw->Button(-text => 'Say Goodnight Irene',
            -command => \&display)->pack();
```

3. The -command option takes an anonymous list, with the first element being a reference to the subroutine and the remaining elements being arguments that are passed to the subroutine. This is what we just saw in the previous example.

```
$mw->Button(-text => 'Hello',
            -command => [ \&say_hello, 'Hello' ]
)->pack(-side => 'left');
```

Button

The button widget is one of the most commonly used widgets. When a button is clicked, the callback assigned to that button will perform some action.

The following example is similar to the label widget example. One button updates the text in a label and another button clears the text. An Exit button is also provided. Figure 6.10 shows the window after the user clicks the Hello button.

```perl
use Tk;

my $mw = MainWindow->new();

my $text = '';

$mw->Label(-textvariable => \$text,
           -relief => 'groove')->pack(-fill => 'x');

$mw->Button(-text => 'Hello',
            -command => \&update_label)->pack(-side =>'left');

$mw->Button(-text => 'Clear',
            -command => \&clear_label)->pack(-side => 'left');

$mw->Button(-text => 'Exit',
            -command => sub { exit })->pack(-side => 'left');

MainLoop;

sub update_label {
    $text = 'Hello';
}

sub clear_label {
    $text = '';
}
```

Figure 6.10
Button widget
example.

Checkbutton

Checkbuttons allow you to present a user with a list of nonexclusive options. Any number of items may be selected at a time. Figure 6.11 shows a window with three checkbuttons and a text box to display their values. The window is produced from the code below:

```perl
use Tk;

my $cb1 = 'Off';
my $cb2 = 'Off';
my $cb3 = 'Off';

my $mw = MainWindow->new();

$mw->Checkbutton(-text => 'Checkbutton 1',
                 -variable => \$cb1,
                 -onvalue => 'On',
                 -offvalue => 'Off')->pack();

$mw->Checkbutton(-text => 'Checkbutton 2',
                 -variable => \$cb2,
                 -onvalue => 'On',
                 -offvalue => 'Off')->pack();

$mw->Checkbutton(-text => 'Checkbutton 3',
                 -variable => \$cb3,
                 -onvalue => 'On',
                 -offvalue => 'Off')->pack();

my $text = $mw->Text(-width => 20,
                     -height => 3)->pack();

$mw->Button(-text => 'Show Me',
            -command => \&show_me
)->pack(-side => 'bottom', -anchor => 'center');

MainLoop;

sub show_me {
    my $show_buttons = "Checkbutton 1: $cb1\n";
    $show_buttons .= "Checkbutton 2: $cb2\n";
    $show_buttons .= "Checkbutton 3: $cb3\n";
    $text->delete('1.0', 'end');
    $text->insert('1.0', $show_buttons);
}
```

This example uses the -text, -variable, -onvalue, and -offvalue
checkbutton options. The -text option sets the text displayed next to
the checkbutton. The -variable option associates a variable with the
on/off values. Because multiple checkbuttons can be selected, each
checkbutton should have a unique scalar variable associated with it.
The -onvalue option specifies the value of the variable when the
checkbutton is selected. The -offvalue option specifies the value of
the variable when the checkbutton is deselected. The default values
for -onvalue and -offvalue are 1 and 0, respectively.

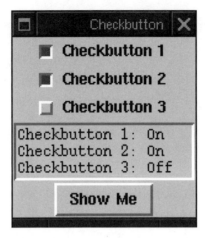

Figure 6.11
Window with three
checkbuttons.

This example also uses the insert() and delete() methods of the text widget, which are explained in the section on text widgets later in this chapter.

Radiobutton

Radiobuttons allow you to present a user with a list of exclusive options. Only one item may be selected at a time. Figure 6.12 shows a window with three radiobuttons and a text box to display their values. The window is produced from the code below:

```
use Tk;

my $rb = 0;

my $mw = MainWindow->new();

$mw->Radiobutton(-text => 'Radiobutton 1',
                 -value => 1,
                 -variable => \$rb)->pack();

$mw->Radiobutton(-text => 'Radiobutton 2',
                 -value => 2,
                 -variable => \$rb)->pack();

$mw->Radiobutton(-text => 'Radiobutton 3',
                 -value => 3,
                 -variable => \$rb)->pack();
```

```perl
my $text = $mw->Text(-width => 20,
                     -height => 3)->pack();

$mw->Button(-text => 'Show Me',
            -command => \&show_me
)->pack(-side => 'bottom', -anchor => 'center');

MainLoop;

sub show_me {
    my $show_buttons;

    if($rb) {
        $show_buttons = "Radiobutton $rb\n";
        $text->delete('1.0', 'end');
        $text->insert('1.0', $show_buttons);
    } else {
        $show_buttons = "None selected\n";
        $text->delete('1.0', 'end');
        $text->insert('1.0', $show_buttons);
    }
}
```

Figure 6.12
Window with three
radiobuttons.

This example uses the -text, -variable, and -value radiobutton options. The -text option sets the text displayed next to the radiobutton. The -variable option associates a variable with the on/off value. Because only one radiobutton can be selected at a time, each radiobutton should have the same scalar variable associated with it. The -value option is the value assigned to the variable when the radiobutton is selected.

Entry

An entry widget is a singe-line editable text field. The entry widget can be used to obtain information from the user, but the application will need to validate the input. The following example shows a typical use of an entry widget. The interface for this example is shown in Figure 6.13. For demonstration, the username and password are printed to STDOUT, as shown in Figure 6.14.

```perl
use Tk;

my $mw = MainWindow->new();

$mw->Label(-text => 'User Name: ')->grid
   (my $name_entry = $mw->Entry);

$mw->Label(-text => 'Password: ')->grid
   (my $password_entry = $mw->Entry(-show => '*'));

$mw->Button(-text => 'OK',
            -command => \&display)->grid(-column => 1);

MainLoop;

sub display {
    my $name = $name_entry->get();
    my $password = $password_entry->get();
    print "NAME: $name\n";
    print "PASSWORD: $password\n";
    exit;
}
```

Figure 6.13
Window with two entry widgets.

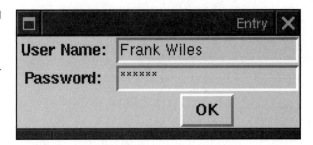

This example uses the -show option, which sets the character to be displayed in place of the actual text entered. This is often used for password fields. This example also uses the get() method, which returns the text string in the entry widget. The -textvariable option (not used in this example) could also be used to assign a variable to store the text

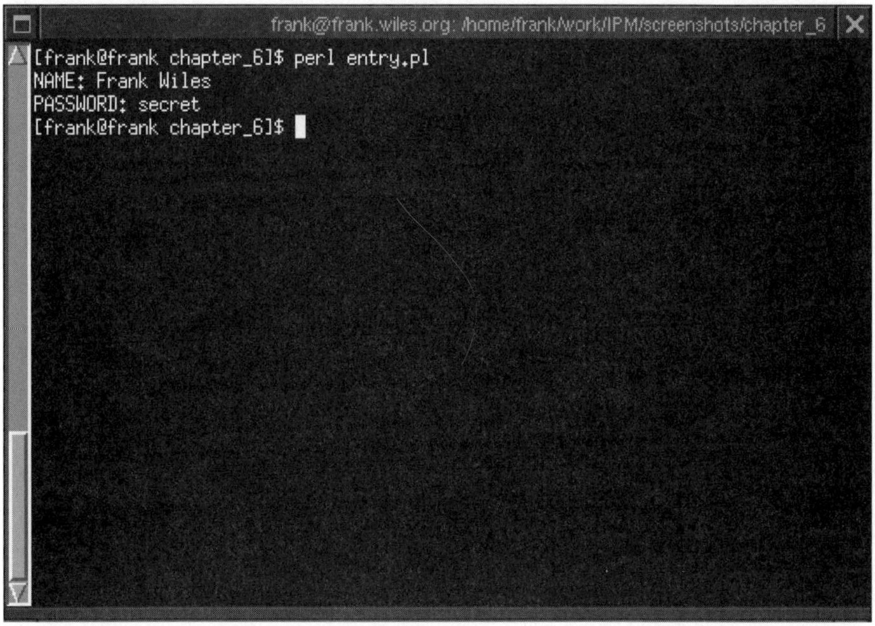
frank@frank.wiles.org: /home/frank/work/IPM/screenshots/chapter_6
[frank@frank chapter_6]$ perl entry.pl
NAME: Frank Wiles
PASSWORD: secret
[frank@frank chapter_6]$

Figure 6.14 Text from entry widgets printed to STDOUT.

string. You may have noticed that this example uses the grid geometry manager instead of pack. The pack and grid geometry managers will be discussed later in the chapter.

Text

The text widget is a multiline editable text field. In fact, the text widget is essentially a small text editor. It is possible to navigate through the text using the cursor, and the text widget also supports several editing, motion, and selection keyboard shortcuts. It is possible to display read-only text and disable the navigation. Text tags allow you to manipulate selected portions of the text. The following code is a fairly simple example that demonstrates some of the basic editing that is possible with a text widget. Text can be typed in the input text widget and displayed in the output text widget by clicking either the Display All or Display First Line button. The output text widget can be cleared by clicking the Clear Output button. Figure 6.15 shows the window after entering text and clicking the Display All button.

```
use Tk;

my $mw = MainWindow->new();
```

```
$mw->Label(-text => 'In:')->pack();

my $text_in = $mw->Text(-width => 30,
                        -height => 5)->pack();

$mw->Label(-text => 'Out:')->pack();

my $text_out = $mw->Text(-width => 30,
                         -height => 5)->pack();

my $bottom_frame = $mw->Frame()->pack(-side => 'bottom',
                                      -pady => 5);

$bottom_frame->Button(-text => 'Display All',
                      -command => \&display_all
)->pack(-side => 'left');

$bottom_frame->Button(-text => 'Display First Line',
                      -command => \&display_first
)->pack(-side => 'left');

$bottom_frame->Button(-text => 'Clear Output',
                      -command => \&clear_output
)->pack(-side => 'left');

MainLoop;

sub display_all {
    $text_out->configure(-state => 'normal');
    $text_out->delete('1.0', 'end');
    my $text_string = $text_in->get('1.0', 'end');
    $text_out->insert('end', $text_string);
    $text_out->configure(-state => 'disabled');
}

sub display_first {
    $text_out->configure(-state => 'normal');
    $text_out->delete('1.0', 'end');
    my $text_string = $text_in->get('1.0', '2.0');
    $text_out->insert('end', $text_string);
    $text_out->configure(-state => 'disabled');
}

sub clear_output {
    $text_out->configure(-state => 'normal');
    $text_out->delete('1.0', 'end');
    $text_out->configure(-state => 'disabled');
}
```

This example creates two text widgets, one for text entry and one for read-only display. We use three options, -width, -height, and -state.

Figure 6.15
Text widgets.

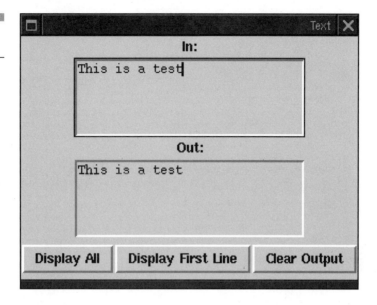

The -width option sets the number of characters wide the text widget will be, the default being 80. The -height option sets the height of the text widget, the default being 24. The -state option indicates whether text can be inserted by the user or the program, the default being 'normal' (text entry allowed). The -state option is used with the configure method to create a read-only text widget. After writing to the text widget, we use the configure method to set the value of the -state option to 'disabled'. The -state option must be set to 'normal' before writing to the text widget by either the user or the program.

The program also uses two text widget methods, get() and delete(), to manipulate the text. Both methods use index values to specify the line number to manipulate. This example uses the "n.m" format, where *n* is the line number and *m* is the character number. Line numbers start with 1, and character numbers start with 0. Therefore, the first character of the first line would be 1.0. The other index format used by this example is "end", which specifies the very last character in the text. For example, the line

```
$text_out->delete('1.0', 'end');
```

specifies that all the text in $text_out is to be deleted (that is, delete all text from the first character of the first line to the last character of the document).

The line

```
my $text_string = $text_in->get('1.0', 'end');
```

gets all the text from $text_string by similar reasoning.
    The line

```
my $text_string = $text_in->get('1.0', '2.0');
```

gets the text from the first line (all the text from the first character of the first line up to, but not including, the first character of the second line).

Listbox

The listbox widget provides a list of items from which the user may select one or multiple items depending on the listbox configuration. Listboxes can be used in place of large groups of checkbuttons or radiobuttons to save screen space. Figure 6.16 shows the interface produced by the following code.

```
use Tk;

my $mw = MainWindow->new();

$mw->Label(-text => 'Select a Saxophonist')->pack();

my $listbox = $mw->Listbox(-width => 25,
                           -height => 6,
                           -selectmode => 'extended')->pack();

# Fill the listbox
$listbox->insert('end', 'John Coltrane', 'Coleman Hawkins',
'Dexter Gordon', 'Charlie Parker', 'Lester Young',
'Ben Webster');

# Bind a left double-click to the listbox
$listbox->bind('<Double-1>', \&get_item);

my $text = $mw->Text(-width => 20,
                     -height => 6)->pack();

$mw->Button(-text => 'Display',
            -command => \&get_item)->pack(-side => 'bottom');

MainLoop;
```

```
sub get_item {
    # Clear textbox and display selected element
    $text->delete('1.0', 'end');
    # Get selected items
    my @sel = $listbox->Getselected;
    # Add selected items to textbox
    for (0..$#sel) {
        # add one to index since insert starts at 1.0
        my $index = $_ + 1;
        $index .= '.0';
        $text->insert($index, "$sel[$_]\n");
    }
}
```

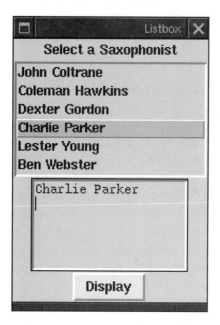

Figure 6.16
Listbox widget.

This example uses the −width, −height, −selectmode listbox options and the insert() method. The −width and −height options specify the width and height, respectively, of the listbox in characters. The value of the −height option corresponds to the number of lines visible in the list-box. By setting the value of the −width option to 0 or less, the width of the listbox is determined by the widest item in the list. The −selectmode option determines whether the user can select one or multiple items. Setting the value of −selectmode to 'single' or 'browse' allows the user to select only one item at a time (similar to a radiobutton), and setting the value to 'multiple' or 'extended' lets the user select multiple items (similar to a checkbutton). The default value of −selectmode is 'browse'.

Before discussing the listbox methods, it will be helpful to briefly mention the listbox indexes. The first item in a listbox has an index of 0, the second item has an index of 1, and so on down the list. The following list shows valid index values that may be used in listbox methods.

- n—An integer value.
- `'active'`—The index for the item that has the location cursor.
- `'anchor'`—The index that is set with the `selectionAnchor` method.
- `'end'`—The last item in the listbox.

Now let's take a look at some listbox methods.

- `insert(index, item, item, …)`—The `insert` method allows you to insert a list of items before the specified index.
- `delete(firstindex [, lastindex])`—The `delete` method allows you to delete one or more items from the listbox. One item will be deleted if only the `firstindex` is given. Multiple items from `firstindex` through `lastindex` will be deleted if a `lastindex` is provided.
- `get(index)`—The `get` method returns the string at `index`.
- `selectionSet(index)`—The `selectionSet` method selects an item in the listbox.
- `activate(index)`—The `activate` method sets an item as active, allowing you to refer to this item later as the `"active"` index.

Scrollbar

Scrollbars allow you to display more items than will fit in a widget. There are two ways to create scrollbars: the scrollbar method and the scrollbar widget. The scrollbar method allows you to add scrollbars to certain widgets, such as entry, text, and listbox. A separate scrollbar widget is more robust but is more difficult to code. We'll take a look at both types.

Scrollbar Method

This first example uses the `Scrolled` method and adds vertical and horizontal scrollbars. Example 6.17 shows the interface produced by the following code.

```
use Tk;

my $mw = MainWindow->new();
```

```perl
my $listbox = $mw->Scrolled('Listbox',
                            -width => 25,
                            -height => 5,
                            -scrollbars => 'se')->pack();

my @woods = ('European spruce', 'Sitka Spruce',
'Engelmann spruce', 'Western redcedar', 'Redwood',
'Brazilian rosewood', 'Indian rosewood', 'Cocobolo',
'Mahogany, Honduran', 'Mahogany, sapele', 'Mahogany, African',
'Cypress, Monterey', 'Canadian cypress (Alaskan yellow cedar)',
'Maple, European', 'Maple, bigleaf',
'Maple, rock (hard or black)', 'Buginga (African rosewood)',
'Spanish cedar', 'Ebony (Sri Lankan, Indian)',
'Ebony (African)');

$listbox->insert('end', @woods);

MainLoop;
```

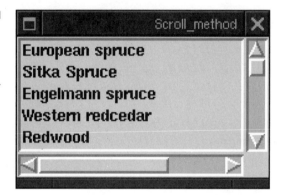

Figure 6.17
Listbox widget using
the Scrolled
method.

The following snippet shows the usage for the Scrolled method:

```perl
my $listbox = $mw->Scrolled('Listbox',
                            -width => 25,
                            -height => 5,
                            -scrollbars => 'se')->pack();
```

The first argument to the Scrolled method is the type of widget to create, in this case a listbox. The -scrollbars option specifies which scrollbars are created and where they will be placed. The valid values for the -scrollbars option are n, s, e, and w and on, os, oe, and ow for optional scrollbars. The values signify scrollbar placement on a widget: n for north, or the top of a widget; e, for east, or the right side of a widget; etc. A maximum of one horizontal and one vertical scrollbar per widget can be used.

Scrollbar Widget

The scrollbar widget is often used when controlling multiple listboxes with one scrollbar. The following code produces the simple scrollbar widget shown in Figure 6.18.

```
use Tk;

my $mw = MainWindow->new();

my $listbox = $mw->Listbox(-width => 25,
                           -height => 5);

my @woods = ('European spruce', 'Sitka Spruce',
'Engelmann spruce', 'Western redcedar', 'Redwood',
'Brazilian rosewood', 'Indian rosewood', 'Cocobolo',
'Mahogany, Honduran', 'Mahogany, sapele', 'Mahogany, African',
'Cypress, Monterey', 'Canadian cypress (Alaskan yellow cedar)',
'Maple, European', 'Maple, bigleaf',
'Maple, rock (hard or black)', 'Buginga (African rosewood)',
'Spanish cedar', 'Ebony (Sri Lankan, Indian)',
'Ebony (African)');

$listbox->insert('end', @woods);

my $scrollbar_x = $mw->Scrollbar(-command => ['xview', $listbox],
                                 -orient => 'horizontal');

$listbox->configure(-xscrollcommand => ['set', $scrollbar_x]);

my $scrollbar_y = $mw->Scrollbar(-command => ['yview',
                                              $listbox]);

$listbox->configure(-yscrollcommand => ['set', $scrollbar_y]);

$scrollbar_x->pack(-side => 'bottom', -fill => 'x');
$scrollbar_y->pack(-side => 'right', -fill => 'y');
$listbox->pack();

MainLoop;
```

Figure 6.18
Scrollbar widget.

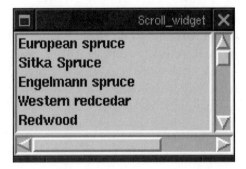

In this example, we create a listbox and scrollbar widgets separately and then connect the scrollbars to the listbox. For example, the following line uses the `Scrollbar` method of the parent widget to create a horizontal scrollbar:

```
my $scrollbar_x = $mw->Scrollbar(-command => ['xview', $listbox],
                                 -orient => 'horizontal');
```

The `-command` option then sets the function to be invoked when the scrollbar is clicked on. In this case, we are using the `xview()` method of the listbox. The `xview()` method is used with horizontal scrollbars and the `yview()` method is used with vertical scrollbars. These methods are used to move (scroll) the widget contents. We're using a listbox widget, but these methods can be used with other widgets that have a scrollbar attached. The `-orient` option sets the orientation of the scrollbar. Valid values are `vertical` (default) and `horizontal`.

Next we configure the listbox to use the scrollbar we just created:

```
$listbox->configure(-xscrollcommand => ['set', $scrollbar_x]);
```

Then we pack the scrollbar and the listbox.

```
$scrollbar_x->pack(-side => 'bottom', -fill => 'x');
$listbox->pack();
```

Scale

The scale widget is used to display a continuous range of sliding values, very much like a thermometer. The scale widget may be placed either horizontally or vertically in an interface. As the slider button is moved, a variable associated with the scale is updated. Figure 6.19 shows a simple horizontal scale with a range from 1 to 100. This example is built from the following code:

```
use Tk;

my $value = 0;
my $label_text = '';

my $mw = MainWindow->new();

$mw->Scale(-orient => 'horizontal',
           -from => 0,
```

```
        -to => 100,
        -tickinterval => 10,
        -label => 'Select Value:',
        -length => 400,
        -variable => \$value,
        -command => \&display)->pack();

$mw->Label(-textvariable => \$label_text)->pack();

MainLoop;

sub display {
    $label_text = "Scale Value: $value\n";
}
```

Figure 6.19
Horizontal scale
widget.

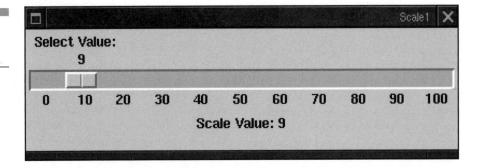

This example uses the -orient, -from, -to, -tickinterval, -label, -length, -variable, and -command scale options. The -orient option sets the direction of the scale, either horizontal or vertical, with a default setting of vertical. The -from and -to options set the minimum and maximum values of the scale, with default settings of 0 and 100, respectively. The -tickinterval option sets the spacing between the ticks on the scale. The -length option sets the length of the slider. The -variable option specifies the variable that stores the slider value. The -command option specifies the callback invoked when the value of the scale is updated.

The next example, as shown in Figure 6.20, is a simple color viewer application using three scale widgets. The graphics in the book aren't in color, so you'll have to run this program to see the actual colors. This example uses the get() method to return the value of the scale's variable.

```
use Tk;

my $mw = MainWindow->new();
$mw->title('Colors');
```

```perl
    my $scale_red = $mw->Scale(-orient => 'horizontal',
                               -from => 0,
                               -to => 255,
                               -label => 'Red:',
                               -command => \&display)->pack();

    my $scale_green = $mw->Scale(-orient => 'horizontal',
                                 -from => 0,
                                 -to => 255,
                                 -label => 'Green:',
                                 -command => \&display)->pack();

    my $scale_blue = $mw->Scale(-orient => 'horizontal',
                                -from => 0,
                                -to => 255,
                                -label => 'Blue:',
                                -command => \&display)->pack();

my $text1 = $mw->Text(-width => 25,
                      -height => 4)->pack();

my $text2 = $mw->Text(-width => 25,
                      -height =>4)->pack();

MainLoop;

sub display {
    # Get scale values
    my $red_value = $scale_red->get();
    my $green_value = $scale_green->get();
    my $blue_value = $scale_blue->get();

    # Create hex value
    my $hex_value = sprintf("#%2.2x%2.2x%2.2x",
                            $red_value,
                            $green_value,
                            $blue_value);

    # Build text string for display
    my $color_values = "Red: $red_value\n";
    $color_values .= "Green: $green_value\n";
    $color_values .= "Blue: $blue_value\n";
    $color_values .= "Hex: $hex_value";

    # Clear text widget and display color values
    $text1->delete('1.0', 'end');
    $text1->insert('end', $color_values);

    # Set background color to current color
    $text2->configure(-background => $hex_value);
}
```

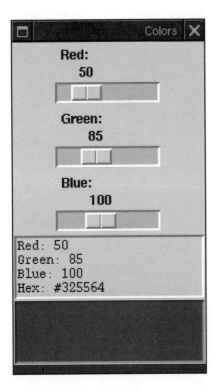

Figure 6.20
Color picker using
three scale widgets.

Frame

The frame widget is a container that is used to organize other widgets into groups. The frame can be quite useful when creating complex widget layouts, giving you more control over individual widget placement than is normally possible with a geometry manager alone. The next example demonstrates how to use three frames to create three vertical columns of widgets. The window shown in Figure 6.21 is produced by the following code.

```
use Tk;

my $mw = MainWindow->new();

my $left_frame = $mw->Frame()->pack(-side => 'left', -padx => 5);
my $middle_frame = $mw->Frame()->pack(-side => 'left', -padx => 5);
my $right_frame = $mw->Frame()->pack(-side => 'left', -padx => 5);

$left_frame->Label(-text => 'Left Frame')->pack();
$left_frame->Button(-text => 'Button1')->pack();
$left_frame->Button(-text => 'Button2')->pack();
```

```
$left_frame->Button(-text => 'Button3')->pack();

$middle_frame->Label(-text => 'Middle Frame')->pack();
$middle_frame->Button(-text => 'Button4')->pack();
$middle_frame->Button(-text => 'Button5')->pack();
$middle_frame->Button(-text => 'Button6')->pack();

$right_frame->Label(-text => 'Right Frame')->pack();
$right_frame->Button(-text => 'Button7')->pack();
$right_frame->Button(-text => 'Button8')->pack();
$right_frame->Button(-text => 'Button9')->pack();

MainLoop;
```

Figure 6.21
Window using three
frame widgets.

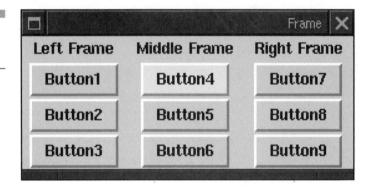

Menu

A pull-down menu is a common feature of almost all GUIs. The menu is used to keep less frequently used options off the main screen of an application.

To create a menu, the following steps are performed:

1. Create a menu bar that will hold individual menu buttons. The menu bar is normally a frame widget.
2. Create the individual menu buttons and pack them into the menu bar.
3. Create the individual menu items using the `MenuButton` widget methods.

The following code creates the menu shown in Figure 6.22.

```
use Tk;

my $cb1 = 0;
```

```perl
my $cb2 = 0;
my $rb = 0;

my $mw = MainWindow->new();

# Create the menubar
my $menubar = $mw->Frame(-relief => 'raised',
                          -borderwidth => 2
)->pack(-side => 'top', -fill => 'x');

# Create the menubuttons
my $menu_file = $menubar->Menubutton(-text => 'File',
                                      -underline => 0,
                                      -tearoff => 0
)->pack(-side => 'left');

my $menu_edit = $menubar->Menubutton(-text => 'Edit',
                                      -underline => 0,
                                      -tearoff => 0
)->pack(-side => 'left');

my $menu_options = $menubar->Menubutton(-text => 'Options',
                                         -underline => 0,
                                         -tearoff => 0
)->pack(-side => 'left');

my $menu_help = $menubar->Menubutton(-text => 'Help',
                                      -underline => 0,
                                      -tearoff => 0
)->pack(-side => 'right');

# Create menu items

# File menu items
$menu_file->command(-label => 'Open',
                    -command => [\&display, 'Open selected'],
                    -underline => 1);

$menu_file->separator();

$menu_file->command(-label => 'Exit',
                    -command => sub { exit },
                    -underline => 1);

# Edit menu items
$menu_edit->command(-label => 'Cut',
                    -command => [\&display, 'Cut selected'],
                    -underline => 2);

$menu_edit->command(-label => 'Copy',
                    -command => [\&display, 'Copy selected'],
                    -underline => 0);

$menu_edit->command(-label => 'Paste',
```

```
                                -command => [\&display, 'Paste selected'],
                                -underline => 0);

    # Options menu items

    # Checkbutton
    $menu_options->checkbutton(-label => 'Checkbutton1',
                               -command => \&display_checkbutton,
                               -variable => \$cb1);

    $menu_options->checkbutton(-label => 'Checkbutton2',
                               -command => \&display_checkbutton,
                               -variable => \$cb2);

    $menu_options->separator();

    # Radiobutton
    $menu_options->radiobutton(-label => 'Radiobutton1',
                               -command => \&display_radiobutton,
                               -variable => \$rb,
                               -value => 'Radiobutton1');

    $menu_options->radiobutton(-label => 'Radiobutton2',
                               -command => \&display_radiobutton,
                               -variable => \$rb,
                               -value => 'Radiobutton2');

    $menu_options->separator();

    # Cascade
    my $menu_cascade = $menu_options->menu->Menu();

    $menu_cascade->add('command', -label => 'Cascade',
                       -command => [\&display,
                                    'Cascade item selected']);

    $menu_options->cascade(-label => 'Cascade');

    $menu_options->entryconfigure('Cascade', -menu => $menu_cascade);

    # Help menu items
    $menu_help->command(-label => 'Help',
                        -command => [\&display, 'Help selected']);

    $menu_help->separator();

    $menu_help->command(-label => 'About',
                        -command => [\&display, 'About selected']);

    my $text = $mw->Text(-width => 50,
                         -height => 15)->pack(-side => 'bottom');

    MainLoop;
```

```
sub display {
    my ($item) = @_;
    $text->delete('1.0', 'end');
    $text->insert('end', $item);
}

sub display_checkbutton {
    my $item = "Checkbutton1: $cb1\n";
    $item .= "Checkbutton2: $cb2\n";
    $text->delete('1.0', 'end');
    $text->insert('end', $item);
}

sub display_radiobutton {
    my $item = "$rb selected";
    $text->delete('1.0', 'end');
    $text->insert('end', $item);
}
```

Figure 6.22
Menu widget.

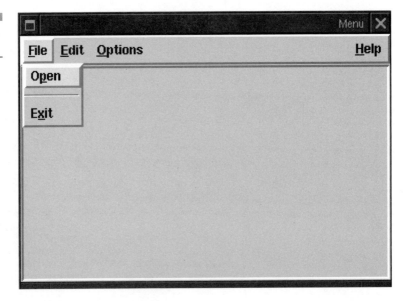

Let's take a closer look at what's going on here. First, we create a menu bar using a frame widget:

```
# Create the menubar
my $menubar = $mw->Frame(-relief => 'raised',
                         -borderwidth => 2)->pack(-side => 'top',
                                                  -fill => 'x');
```

Next we create a menu button:

```
# Create the menubuttons
my $menu_file = $menubar->Menubutton(-text => 'File',
                                     -underline => 0,
                                     -tearoff => 0
)->pack(-side => 'left');
```

This example uses the -text, -underline, and -tearoff options when creating the menu button. The -text option sets the text displayed on the button. The -underline option specifies the index of the character in the text that will be underlined. The underlined character indicates a shortcut key that can be used if the menu button has keyboard focus. The -tearoff option determines whether the tear-off dashed line will be displayed. A default value of 1 displays the line and 0 does not. If the tear-off line is visible, then the menu can be "torn off" of its window and moved around the screen. The other menu buttons are added in a similar fashion. Note that we use the pack option -side => 'left' when packing the menu buttons. Menu buttons will be added to the menu bar from left to right in the order that they are packed.

Once the menu button is created we can create the individual menu items. Menu items are added to the menu button in the same order as they are listed in the code. In the following code, we create the 'Open' command menu item.

```
$menu_file->command(-label => 'Open',
                    -command => [\&display, 'Open selected'],
                    -underline => 1);
```

Other types of menu items include radiobutton, checkbutton, cascade, and separator.

The separator is simply a visual separator between menu items with no other functionality. The separator can be created as follows:

```
$menu_file->separator();
```

Geometry Managers

A geometry manager is used to display and arrange widgets on the screen. The size and position of a widget are controlled by the geometry manager. There are three types of geometry managers: pack, grid, and place. pack is the most commonly used geometry manager and that's where we'll begin.

Pack

Using the `pack` geometry manager is a lot like packing a suitcase or box. Each item is packed one at time in the space that remains after packing the previous items. When using the `pack` geometry manager, widgets are added to the frame or window one at a time in the order that they are packed. The order is important and will affect the appearance of your window. As each widget is packed, it is placed into the space that remains in the frame or window. By default, the `pack` method places a widget at the top center of the available space in a window or frame and then arranges widgets vertically from top to bottom. There are several options that can be used with `pack` to give you more control when arranging the widgets. Widgets cannot overlap or touch each other.

The following code uses the `-side`, `-fill`, and `-expand` options explained in the next section to produce the window shown in Figure 6.23.

```perl
use Tk;

my $mw = MainWindow->new();

$mw->Button(-text => '(1) Top')->pack(-side => 'top',
                                      -fill => 'both',
                                      -expand => 1);

$mw->Button(-text => '(2) Bottom')->pack(-side => 'bottom',
                                         -fill => 'both',
                                         -expand => 1);

$mw->Button(-text => '(3) Left')->pack(-side => 'left',
                                       -fill => 'both',
                                       -expand => 1);

$mw->Button(-text => '(4) Right')->pack(-side => 'right',
                                        -fill => 'both',
                                        -expand => 1);

MainLoop;
```

To see how the ordering of the pack statements affects the layout, we'll use the code from the previous example but alter the order in which the widgets are packed. Compare our new window, as shown in Figure 6.24, with that of the previous window.

```perl
use Tk;
```

Figure 6.23
Buttons packed with
–side, –fill, and
–expand options,
ordered from top,
bottom, left, to right.

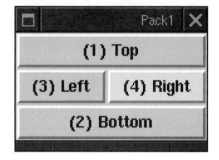

```
my $mw = MainWindow->new();

$mw->Button(-text => '(1) Top')->pack(-side => 'top',
                                      -fill => 'both',
                                      -expand => 1);

$mw->Button(-text => '(2) Left')->pack(-side => 'left',
                                       -fill => 'both',
                                       -expand => 1);

$mw->Button(-text => '(3) Bottom')->pack(-side => 'bottom',
                                         -fill => 'both',
                                         -expand => 1);

$mw->Button(-text => '(4) Right')->pack(-side => 'right',
                                        -fill => 'both',
                                        -expand => 1);

MainLoop;
```

Figure 6.24
Buttons packed with
–side, –fill, and
–expand options,
ordered from top,
left, bottom, to right.

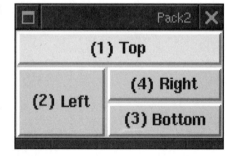

Options for Pack

The following options can be used with the `pack` method to give you
more control over the layout of your application.

```
-anchor => position
```

This option anchors a widget within its allotted space. The values are n, ne, e, s, s, sw, w, nw, and center. The default value is center.

-expand => boolean
The -expand option determines whether a widget's allotted area will expand to fill any remaining space in the window after all the individual widgets have been inserted. The values are 1 or 0. The default is 0 (no expansion).

-fill => direction
The -fill option determines in which direction the widget will fill its allotted area. The values are none, x, y, and both. The default value is none.

-padx => amount
This option adds padding to the left and right of a widget. The amount must be a valid screen distance [pixels, (c)cm, (i)inch, (m)mm, (p)points]. The default value is 0 pixels.

-pady => amount
This option adds padding to the top and bottom of a widget. The amount must be a valid screen distance [pixels, (c)cm, (i)inch, (m)mm, (p)points]. The default value is 0 pixels.

-side => side
This option sets the side of the window or frame where the widget is placed. The values are left, right, top, and bottom. The default value is top.

Grid

The grid geometry manager divides the window into a grid consisting of columns and rows. Column and row numberings begin with 0, so the top left-hand corner of a grid is at location 0,0. Widgets may be placed in a specific location using the grid method. Figure 6.25 shows the grid created by the following code.

```
use Tk;

my $mw = MainWindow->new();
```

```
for my $r(0..2) {
    for my $c(0..2) {
        $mw->Button(-text => "Button $r, $c")->grid
            (-row => $r, -column => $c);
    }
}

MainLoop;
```

Figure 6.25
Window using grid
geometry manager.

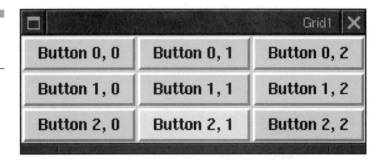

It is also possible to use one `grid` method call for each row. The following code produces the same grid as the previous example.

```
use Tk;

my $mw = MainWindow->new();

$mw->Button(-text => 'Button 0,0')->grid
  ($mw->Button(-text => 'Button 0,1'),
   $mw->Button(-text => 'Button 0,2'));

$mw->Button(-text => 'Button 1,0')->grid
  ($mw->Button(-text => 'Button 1,1'),
   $mw->Button(-text => 'Button 1,2'));

$mw->Button(-text => 'Button 2,0')->grid
  ($mw->Button(-text => 'Button 1,1'),
   $mw->Button(-text => 'Button 1,2'));

MainLoop;
```

Place

The `place` geometry manager allows us to position widgets at specific *x,y* coordinates. The values for *x* and *y* can be in any valid screen unit [pixels, (c)cm, (i)inch, (m)mm, (p)points]. The top left-hand corner is coordinate 0,0. The –x and –y options correspond to the *x,y* location on the screen. Figure 6.26 shows a window with several buttons using the `place` geometry manager.

```
use Tk;

my $mw = MainWindow->new();

$mw->Button(-text => 'Button 0,0')->place(-x => 0, -y => 0);
$mw->Button(-text => 'Button 50,50')->place(-x => 50, -y => 50);
$mw->Button(-text => 'Button 75,100')->place(-x => 75,
                                             -y => 100);
$mw->Button(-text => 'Button 25,150')->place(-x => 25,
                                             -y => 150);

MainLoop;
```

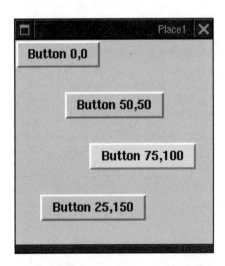

Figure 6.26
Window using place geometry manager.

It is also possible to overlap widgets using the `place` geometry manager. Figure 6.27 shows a window with overlapping buttons.

```
use Tk;

my $mw = MainWindow->new();

$mw->Button(-text => 'Button 0,0')->place(-x => 0, -y => 0);
$mw->Button(-text => 'Button 20,20')->place(-x => 20, -y => 20);

MainLoop;
```

Figure 6.27
Overlapping buttons
using place geometry
manager.

Summary

Perl/Tk makes it easy to create a GUI to your Perl scripts. You can create windows-based programs that use widgets such as labels, buttons, text and entry fields, listboxes, scrollbars, and menus. Although certainly not necessary, using a GUI can make some tasks easier, such as getting information from a user or interacting with a database.

E-mail

There is a joke among programmers that every program written that is worth its weight in code ends up sending or receiving e-mail. Assuming that you write worthwhile programs, at some point you are going to be asked to modify it to send and/or receive e-mail.

Sending E-mail

Net::SMTP: /CPAN/libnet-1.0703.tar.gz

The ability of applications that may be running in the background, with no visual representation to the user, to communicate with the user in a convenient manner is important. The incorporation of e-mail into programs occurs most in server applications such as log file analysis, intrusion detection, and other system-monitoring applications. You will also find programs that generate e-mails, for example, automated mailing lists, web postcard applications, and e-mail authoring programs themselves. CPAN's Net::SMTP module handles all your e-mail needs except for attaching files to your e-mails.

It is usually a surprise to most programmers that sending and receiving e-mail is so easy to do, so they start sending e-mails about everything. This should be avoided, because the main benefit of e-mail notification is that it is actually read by the user. If users receive so much e-mail that they begin to ignore and delete their messages, they may miss the most important information.

To better understand this module, it is helpful to understand how e-mail clients and mail servers themselves talk to each other. They communicate by a protocol known as the simple mail transfer protocol, or SMTP. If you connect to port 25 of a mail server (the standard SMTP port), you can interact with the mail server on the lowest possible level. Table 7.1 shows a basic session.

As in all polite conversation, we start off by saying HELO to each other, which establishes the connection and lets the remote server know who is talking to it. We then give the MAIL FROM command, which represents from whom this mail is supposedly sent. Then we tell the server the receiver's address with the RCPT TO command. After all this is finished, we give the DATA command, which tells the server we are going to transmit the actual body of the message. Now you can see why it is known as the simple mail transfer protocol!

TABLE 7.1

Simple Mail
Transfer Protocol

Client Command	Server Response
HELO myhost.mydomain.com	Hello myhost, pleased to meet you
MAIL FROM: me@mydomain.com	me@mydomain.com... Sender OK
RCPT TO: you@yourdomain.com	you@yourdomain.com... Recipient OK
DATA	Enter mail, ending with a .
Hello World!	
.	Message accepted for delivery
QUIT	

Now let's build a simple Perl script that sends the well-known "Hello World!" message to a specific e-mail address. For this example to work, you must supply your e-mail address, the e-mail address of the person receiving this message, and the hostname of the mail server for your Internet connection.

```perl
use Net::SMTP;

my ($to_user, $from_user, $mailserver);

# Gather our input from the user
print "Your E-mail Server's hostname: ";
$mailserver = <STDIN>;
print "To: ";
$to_user = <STDIN>;
print "From: ";
$from_user = <STDIN>;

# Make sure to remove any trailing \n characters
chomp($mailserver);
chomp($to_user);
chomp($from_user);

# Create our SMTP connection
my $smtp = Net::SMTP->new("$mailserver") or
  die "Can't create smtp: $!\n";

# Tell our mail server what user we are sending as
$smtp->mail($from_user);

# Tell it who we are trying to send to
```

```
$smtp->to($to_user);

# Start actually sending the body of our message
$smtp->data();
$smtp->datasend("\nHello World!\n");
$smtp->dataend();
$smtp->quit;
```

As you can see, sending an e-mail message is not as complicated as most people first assume. After we have gathered our command-line input from the user we remove any stray characters such as newlines. We then simply create a new SMTP object with the new command by passing it on to the local relay mail server.

By using our mail server rather than the mail server of the e-mail address to which we are sending, we eliminate having to deal with DNS and the complexity of finding the correct MX (Mail eXchange) IP address to send to. We will learn more about working with DNS in Chapter 8.

The rest of the code should look very similar to the example from Table 7.1 above, only in Perl. We then tell our SMTP object our e-mail address and the e-mail address to which we are attempting to send our message. The smtp->data call lets our mail server know that we are going to start sending the actual body of the message. We then send our message with the smtp->datasend function and end it with the smtp->dataend call. After we're done with all of that, we tell our SMTP object to close its connection to our mail server with the smtp->quit command.

Now let's add a small variation to the previous example adding a subject to our message and sending the message to multiple recipients. This script will e-mail some simple system statistics from a computer running UNIX or Linux to each e-mail address in a file we'll call sysadmins.txt.

```
use Net::SMTP;

# Change this to your mail server
my $mailserver = 'yourmailserver.yourcompany.com';

# Set up our senders E-mail address and text
# file full of system administrators
my $sender_address = 'sysstats@unixbox.yourcompany.com';
my $email_list = 'sysadmins.txt';

# Get current time
my $time = localtime;

# Get our uptime from the system
# NOTE: The actual location of the uptime binary may vary
# depending on your Unix system.
my $stats = `/usr/bin/uptime`;
```

```
# Subroutine to actually send the mail
sub send_mail {
  my $address = shift;
  # Connect to our mail server
  my $smtp = Net::SMTP->new($mailserver) or
      die "Can't connect to $mailserver: $!\n";

  $smtp->mail($sender_address);
  $smtp->to($address);

  $smtp->data();
  $smtp->datasend("Subject: Server Stats at $time\n\n");
  $smtp->datasend("$stats\n");
  $smtp->dataend();

  $smtp->quit;

} # END send_mail

# Get our list of addresses and
# pass them off to send_mail() to process
open(LIST, "$email_list") or die "Can't open $email_list: $!\n";

while( my $current_address = <LIST> ) {
  chomp($current_address);
  send_mail($current_address);
}

close(LIST);
```

Example sysadmins.txt:

```
info@wiles.org
frank@wiles.org
ides@inetdb.com
```

As you can see, this example is very similar to the previous one. There are only two major differences: we pass off handling of the actual e-mail to a subroutine, and we have added a Subject: line as the first line of smtp->datasend().

Receiving E-mail

Mail::POP3Client: /CPAN/POP3Client-2.6.tar.gz

Now that we have learned how to send e-mail, we should learn how to receive it. There are two common ways Perl is used to receive e-mail. One is as a POP3 client for getting normal mail, and another is by having Sendmail (the standard Internet mail server) pipe incoming e-mail to a Perl script for filtering, auto response, or mailing list purposes.

POP3 is one of the standard ways for e-mail clients to remotely receive e-mail from a mail server. CPAN has a nice module called `Mail::POP3Client` that helps reduce the standard POP3 protocol into an object-oriented Perl interface. Let's build a simple example, which will query our mail server and show us all the messages waiting for us and from whom they are.

```
use Mail::POP3Client;

# Make our connection to the pop server
my $pop_connection = new Mail::POP3Client( USER => 'username',
                       PASSWORD => 'password',
                       HOST => 'mail.mydomain.com'
) or die "Error in making connection to pop server: $!\n";

my $total_messages = $pop_connection->Count();

# Loop through each message
for( my $i = 1; $i <= $total_messages; $i++ ) {

  # Read each message's headers looking from the From: line
  foreach my $line ( $pop_connection->Head($i) ) {
    if($line =~ /^From:\s/) { print "$i: $line\n"; }
  }
}

print "Total Messages: $total_messages\n";

# Disconnect from the pop server
$pop_connection->Close();
```

After including the necessary `Mail::POP3Client` library, we attempt to make our connection to the POP3 server at `mail.mydomain.com` as user `username` with a password of `password`. Obviously, you will have to change these values to test this script and modify it to fit your settings.

We then count the total number of messages currently waiting on the POP3 server with the `Count()` function. We loop through each message, looking at its headers with the `Head()` function. The `Head()` function returns a list of lines that consists of that message's headers. We search for a line that starts with `From:` which denotes from whom this message is sent, and display it with the number of the message. After printing a total count for the user, we disconnect from the POP3 server.

The other typical way of using Perl to receive mail is by having the UNIX mail server, Sendmail, deliver e-mails directly to a Perl script's standard input. This is how mailing-list mangers such as Majordomo (http://www.greatcircle.com/majordomo/) work. To have e-mail sent directly to a Perl script, you have to make an entry like this in your Sendmail aliases file (typically /etc/aliases or /etc/mail/aliases):

```
mylist: "|/usr/bin/mylist.pl"
```

The account you wish to send mail to is in mylist and the program you wish to have parse this e-mail is /usr/bin/mylist.pl. Implementation of this sort of mail filtering may require additional Sendmail configuration, depending on which version of Sendmail you are using. Please consult the Sendmail documentation for more information.

This method works basically like any other Perl script you would write, except for the fact that your standard input (STDIN) consists of the actual headers and body of an e-mail message and you are expected to deal with it.

One of the more annoying things about e-mail is spam, or unsolicited commercial e-mail. The junk mail of the Internet clogs almost everyone's mailbox. One possible way to avoid spam is to set up a spam@yourdomain.com account, which is really an alias to a Perl script. With this account you could log all incoming messages to a log file that would show who the mail is from, to whom it's addressed, and the subject of the message without actually having to store the message itself. This will save you disk space and allow you to ask a sender to resend a message if you would really like to receive it.

```
my $logfile = '/home/frank/spam.log';

open(SPAMLOG, ">>$logfile") or die "Can't open $logfile: $!\n";

while( my $line = <STDIN> ) {
  if($line =~ /^(To|From|Subject):/) {
    print SPAMLOG $line;
  }
}

close(SPAMLOG);
```

As you can see this is a *very* simple example, but it illustrates all the important aspects of reading an e-mail message from Sendmail.

The previous example showed the basic elements of receiving e-mail using Sendmail aliases. Let's build one more slightly larger example to show how most mailing-list mangers work. This example will receive an e-mail, modify its headers slightly, and send a copy to each e-mail address in a file we will call list.txt.

```perl
use Net::SMTP;

# Our list of addresses
my $listfile = 'list.txt';

# Our list's E-mail address
my $address = 'mylist@mydomain.com';

# Our mail server
my $mailserver = 'mail.mydomain.com';

# The contents of our message
my @in_message = <STDIN>;

# Variable to store our modified message
my @out_message;

foreach my $line ( @in_message ) {

  # Skip the To: header
  if( $line =~ /^To:/i ) { next; }

  # Skip the From header and setup a Reply-To: header
  # so that the original sender of this message will
  # receive all replies.
  if( $line =~ /^From:(.*)/i ) {
    push(@out_message, "Reply-To: $1\n");
  } else {
    push(@out_message, $line);
  }
}

# Free up the resources associated with the original message
undef(@in_message);

open(USERS, "$listfile") or die "Cannot open $listfile: $!\n";

# Loop over $listfile, sending a copy to each user
while( my $user = <USERS> ) {
  chomp($user);

  my $smtp = Net::SMTP->new($mailserver) or
      die "Cannot connect to $mailserver: $!\n";

  # Setup From: and To: headers
  $smtp->mail($address);
  $smtp->to($user);
```

```
    # Start sending the body of the message
    $smtp->data();

    # Send the entire body
    $smtp->datasend( join('', @out_message) );

    $smtp->dataend();

    $smtp->quit;
}

close(USERS);
```

Sending Attachments

MIME::Lite: /CPAN/MIME-Lite-2.102.tar.gz

Sometimes it is necessary to send information that is not text or to attach a file that is not text in your e-mails. This is accomplished through *multi-purpose Internet mail extensions* (MIME), which encodes messages. You may want to do something as simple as send your message as HTML, or maybe you have a mailing list in which you send an interesting weather photograph daily to everyone on the list. All of these require some sort of MIME magic to work correctly. This magic is simplified with CPAN's MIME::Lite module.

There are two different approaches to using MIME::Lite. You can have MIME::Lite build only the encoded body of your message and use Net::SMTP or even Sendmail directly to actually send your message, or you can have MIME::Lite do it for you automatically. It should be noted that using MIME::Lite when *not* sending attachments is not considered good form. It creates useless MIME headers in your e-mails and may cause problem with certain mail readers, not to mention tarnish a good programmer's reputation.

Let's build an example using the first method:

```
use Net::SMTP;
use MIME::Lite;

my $from_address    = 'frank@wiles.org';
my $to_address      = 'spam@wiles.org';
my $mail_server     = 'mail.wiles.org';
```

```perl
my $image_file = '/home/frank/test.gif';

my $message_body = "Here is my test using MIME::Lite ".
   "and Net::SMTP\n".
   "to send a multipart message with some text and\n".
   "an image. You should find an image attached to\n".
   "this message. -- Frank\n";

# Create our initial text of our message
my $mime_msg = MIME::Lite->new(
   From      => $from_address,
   To        => $to_address,
   Subject   => 'My MIME Test Using Net::SMTP',
   Type      => 'TEXT',
   Data      => $message_body
) or die "Error creating MIME body: $!\n";

# Attach our image file
$mime_msg->attach(
   Type       => 'image/gif',
   Path       => $image_file,
   Filename   => 'test.gif'
) or die "Error attaching image: $!\n";

# This retrieves the encoded version of our message's body
# with the attached image
$message_body = $mime_msg->body_as_string;

my $smtp = Net::SMTP->new($mail_server) or die
"Can't connect to mail server ($mail_server): $!\n";

$smtp->mail($from_address);
$smtp->to($to_address);

$smtp->data();
$smtp->datasend($message_body);
$smtp->dataend();

$smtp->quit;
```

In the example above, we first set up some variables to store our information, such as to whom we are sending, who we are, our mail server, our actual message, etc. We then create a new instance of a MIME::Lite object by passing it relevant information about what type of MIME-encoded message we wish to send. This encodes the body and the headers of the message, but we still need to attach our image. The attachment is done with MIME::Lite's attach() function, which requires the MIME type, path to the file we are attaching, and what we wish the filename to be when it is received. We then have MIME::Lite return us the encoded body of our message with its body_as_string()

function. We only want the body of the message because we are going to be using Net::SMTP for the headers and the actual transmission of the message. From there, the code should be very familiar from our previous dealings with Net::SMTP.

Sending messages using MIME requires that you know the MIME type of the data being sent. Table 7.2 shows a list of common MIME types.

TABLE 7.2

Common MIME
Types

PDF file	application/pdf
Postscript file	application/postscript
MS Word document	application/msword
Excel spreadsheet	application/vnd.ms-excel
Powerpoint	application/vnd.ms-powerpoint
Mac BinHex	application/mac-binhex40
Gziped file	application/x-gzip
Zipped file	application/zip
GIF image	image/gif
JPEG image	image/jpeg
PNG image	image/png
TIFF image	image/tiff
HTML	text/html
SGML	text/sgml
XML data	application/xml
Plain text	text/plain
RTF format	text/rtf
Quicktime video	video/quicktime
Tab-delimited data	text/tab-separated-values

We can also have MIME::Lite handle all of the messy Net::SMTP details by using some more of its functions. Let's build an example of this:

```
use MIME::Lite;

my $from_address = 'frank@wiles.org';
my $to_address   = 'spam@wiles.org';
```

```
my $mail_server = 'mail.wiles.org';
my $image_file  = '/home/frank/test.gif';
my $word_doc    = '/home/frank/test.doc';

my $message_body = "Here is my test using MIME::Lite ".
    "without Net::SMTP\n".
    "to send a multipart message with some text and\n".
    "an image. You should find an image and Word doc\n".
    "attached to this message. -- Frank\n";

# Create our initial text of our message
my $mime_msg = MIME::Lite->new(
  From       => $from_address,
  To         => $to_address,
  Subject    => 'My MIME Test Without Using Net::SMTP',
  Type       => 'TEXT',
  Data       => $message_body
) or die "Error creating MIME body: $!\n";

# Attach our image file
$mime_msg->attach(
  Type       => 'image/gif',
  Path       => $image_file,
  Filename   => 'test.gif'
) or die "Error attaching image: $!\n";

# Attach our Word Document
$mime_msg->attach(
  Type       => 'application/msword',
  Path       => $word_doc,
  Filename   => 'test.doc'
) or die "Error attaching document: $!\n";

# Actually have MIME::Lite send the message.
$mime_msg->send('smtp', $mail_server, Timeout => 60) or
  die "Error sending message: $!\n";
```

The following example is similar to the one above, except that we have replaced all of the Net::SMTP codes with one call to MIME::Lite's send function. MIME::Lite's default is to attempt to use the local copy of Sendmail on your system, but that is only effective if you are running a UNIX variant. If you are using a UNIX system and wish to use Sendmail, you can replace

```
$mime_msg->send('smtp', $mail_server,Timeout => 60);
```

with

```
$mime_msg->send;
```

Summary

Hopefully this chapter has shown you how easy, with a little help from CPAN, it is to send and receive e-mail using Perl. This knowledge will become even more valuable over time, as more and more applications become Web based and as people desire more information through e-mail.

The ability to attach binary files to your generated e-mails opens up even greater possibilities, namely having a Perl script that gathers system statistics and, from those statistics, generates a PNG file using GD, which we have already discussed. With the modules we've covered in this chapter, that image could be waiting every morning for system administrators in their inbox.

Internet
Protocols

Introduction

It is often necessary for Perl scripts to send information back and forth across a network or simply to retrieve some data from another computer somewhere on the Internet. Unlike many programming languages, this is very easy with Perl, thanks to some CPAN modules that we will be discussing in this chapter.

Tasks such as DNS lookups, pinging a remote host, transferring files via FTP, gathering whois information, or interacting with a remote computer with Telnet have become almost trivial thanks to CPAN. And by using one of Perl's standard modules, IO::Socket, you can create your own network clients and servers.

DNS Lookups

The *domain name system* (DNS) is the way domain names (www.yahoo.com, www.mydomain.com, www.wiles.org, etc.) are transformed into the actual Internet addresses, known as IP addresses. Computers can only talk in IP addresses. At their lowest level, they understand nothing about domain names. When you type http://www.wiles.org into your browser, the computer performs what is called a DNS lookup; it translates the name www.wiles.org into an IP address (in this case 24.124.35.230). From that point on it only uses the IP address for its communications.

Let's build a simple example:

```perl
use Socket;
my $address;
my $hostname;

# Check to make sure we got a commandline argument
if( scalar(@ARGV) != 1 ) {
    print "Usage: dns1.pl <domain_name>\n";
    exit(1);
}

$hostname = $ARGV[0];

my $binary = inet_aton($hostname);

if( !defined($binary) ) {
    $address = 'Could not resolve';
```

```
    } else {
        $address = inet_ntoa($binary);
    }

    print "$hostname == $address\n";
```

We include the Socket library, which gives us the two functions: inet_ntoa() and inet_aton(). inet_aton() takes as its argument a hostname and returns that hostname's IP address in binary form. The function inet_ntoa() takes the binary form returned by inet_aton() and returns an IP address in the xxx.xxx.xxx.xxx format that we are accustomed to. In our example, if inet_aton() cannot find the hostname given at the command line, $binary will be undefined. We handle this error by checking for it with our if statement. Whether or not the hostname is found, we print out the hostname the user requested and the IP address or "could not resolve," if we could not find it.

The output of the previous example should resemble the following:

```
$ perl dns1.pl www.wiles.org
www.wiles.org == 24.124.35.230
```

The previous example will only work correctly if a hostname has only one IP address associated with it. For hosts such as www.yahoo.com that have many IP addresses using DNS's Round Robin feature, we must modify our code to the following:

```
use Socket;
my @addresses;
my $hostname;

# Check to make sure we got a commandline argument
if( scalar(@ARGV) != 1 ) {
    print "Usage: dns2.pl <domain_name>\n";
    exit(1);
}

$hostname = $ARGV[0];

# Use gethostbyname() to find all IP addresses
@addresses = gethostbyname($hostname) or
    die "Could not resolve $hostname: $!\n";

# Run inet_ntoa() on all members of @addresses to
# get textual IP addresses
@addresses = map {inet_ntoa($_)} @addresses[ 4 .. $#addresses ];

print "$hostname == ";
```

```
# Print out a list of the addresses we found
while( @addresses ) {
    my $tmp_addr = shift(@addresses);

    if(!@addresses) {
        print "$tmp_addr\n";
    } else {
        print "$tmp_addr, ";
    }
}
```

In the previous example, all we really did was use `gethostbyname()` instead of `inet_aton()`. We still ran `inet_ntoa()` on the IP address to get our textual representation in the dotted decimal notation. This example will also work with sites that have only one IP address.

The output of this example should resemble:

```
$ perl dns2.pl www.yahoo.com
www.yahoo.com == 216.32.74.55, 216.32.74.50, 216.32.74.51,
216.32.74.52, 216.32.74.53
```

A *reverse lookup* is when you have an IP address such as 24.124.35.230 and you want to know the hostname of the site that resides there. Using the `Socket` library makes this task very simple:

```
use Socket;
my $ipaddress;

# Check to make sure we got a commandline argument
if( scalar(@ARGV) != 1 ) {
    print "Usage: dns3.pl <domain_name>\n";
    exit(1);
}

$ipaddress = $ARGV[0];

my $hostname = gethostbyaddr( inet_aton($ipaddress), AF_INET) or
    die "Could not resolve $ipaddress: $!\n";

print "$ipaddress is $hostname\n";
```

In one of our previous examples, we used `gethostbyname()` when the input we had was a hostname. It is only fitting that we use `gethost-byaddr()` when all we have is a host's IP address. We use this in combination with `inet_aton()` to do a reverse lookup of that IP address. `gethostbyaddr()` takes two arguments: the first is the output of `inet_aton()` and the second is the type of network address it is supposed to be working with, in this case AF_INET. AF_INET is the notation for standard Internet addresses.

The output of our reverse example should be:

```
$ perl dns3.pl 24.124.35.230
24.124.35.230 is frank.wiles.org
```

Pinging a Host

Pinging a host is very much like asking someone if they are alive. If they are, most likely they will respond. Because of the physical space between computers on networks, especially the Internet, ping is a very useful tool. Ping will only tell you if a computer is active, but not whether it is performing its normal functions.

To test whether or not a host is simply alive, we use the Net::Ping module from the Perl standard distribution:

```perl
use Net::Ping;
my $hostname;

if( scalar(@ARGV) != 1 ) {
    print "Usage: ping1.pl <hostname>\n";
    exit(1);
}

# Store our hostname in a variable
$hostname = $ARGV[0];

# Create our Ping object
my $ping = Net::Ping->new('tcp', 10, 56)
    or die "Cannot create new Ping object: $!\n";

# Print a message telling our user whether or not
# $hostname is alive
if( $ping->ping($hostname) ) {
    print "$hostname is alive\n";
} else {
    print "$hostname is not responding\n";
}

# Destroy our ping object
$ping->close;
```

After we check to make sure we have received a commandline argument, we create our Net::Ping object. To create our object, we must define three parameters: the protocol we wish to use, the number of seconds to ping the host, and the size of each ping packet we wish to send.

The default timeout and the size are somewhat arbitrary; they only modify the performance of the script. As for the protocol, there are three choices: `tcp`, `udp`, and `icmp`. When using `tcp` and `udp`, ping actually connects to the echo port (port 7) of the host and waits to see whether the data it has sent is returned. If the protocol is `icmp`, Net::Ping actually uses the Internet control message protocol and executes a true ping request. On UNIX systems, the script must be run as root when using the `icmp` protocol.

Getting Whois Information

Net::Whois: /CPAN/Net-Whois-1.9.tar.gz

Domain names are registered through one of many domain registrars. (Until recently, all domains were registered through InterNIC, which is still the unofficial standard.) Domain registrars keep what is known as a *whois database* that will provide Internet users some limited information about the owner of that domain. This information includes contact e-mail address, physical address, name, which name servers service the domain, etc. This information is useful to contact the owner of the domain when they have not adequately provided contact information on their website, for instance.

Let's grab some whois information:

```perl
use Net::Whois;
my $domain;

# Check to make sure we have gotten our commandline
# arguments
if( scalar(@ARGV) != 1 ) {
    print "Usage: whois1.pl <domain_name>\n";
    exit(1);
}

$domain = $ARGV[0];

# Create our Net::Whois object
my $whois = Net::Whois::Domain->new($domain)
```

```
   or die "Could not connect to a Whois server: $!\n";

# Error out if we do not find a domain
if( !$whois->ok ) {
    print "No match for $domain\n";
    exit();
}

# Print out what information we received
print "Domain:  " . $whois->domain  . "\n";
print "Name:    " . $whois->name    . "\n";
print "Country: " . $whois->country . "\n\n";
print "Name Servers:\n";
print map { "\t$$_[0] ($$_[1])\n" } @{$whois->servers};
```

After we create our `Net::Whois::Domain` object by passing it the name of the domain we wish to query, all we do to get our information is call a few member functions of the CPAN module. `Net::Whois::Domain` handles all the decoding of the information, which makes getting whois information simple.

Some other possible member functions for `Net::Whois::Domain` are shown in Table 8.1.

TABLE 8.1

Net::Whois::
Domain Member
Functions

$whois->record_created	Creation date for the domain
$whois->record_updated	Last modification of the domain
$whois->address	Address of the domain
$whois->contacts	Administrative, technical, and billing contacts for the domain

Using FTP in Perl

Net::FTP: /CPAN/libnet-1.0703.tar.gz

Transferring files across a network is a common task. Whether it be interactively from the commandline or completely automated running in the background, it is a simple task with CPAN's `Net::FTP`.

FTP stands for file transfer protocol, and it does just that, transfers files. There are two different modes of an FTP server: anonymous access and nonanonymous access. As you probably guessed, anonymous access typically allows you to download files but not modify or delete them. With nonanonymous access, you have the same access to the files as the user you logged in as.

Let's build a simple example that will retrieve a file we'll call /pub/test.txt from a fictitious anonymous FTP server we'll call ftp.anonftp.net:

```
use Net::FTP;

# Make our FTP object
my $ftp = Net::FTP->new('ftp.anonftp.net')
    or die "Cannot connect to ftp server: $!\n";

# Login to the remote server anonymously,
# sending our E-mail address as our password
$ftp->login("anonymous", "me\@somewherefake.com");

# Move to the public directory
$ftp->cwd("/pub");

# Actually retrieve test.txt
$ftp->get("test.txt");

# Close our connection
$ftp->quit;
```

We create a new instance of Net::FTP object by passing the new host-name of the FTP server to which we wish to connect. After we create our object, we set the user name and password we are going to use to login via the login() member function. Note that we had to escape the @ symbol so that Perl does not think it is an array. After we have logged in, we change our current working directory to /pub with the cwd() function. /pub is the unofficial standard directory for files available for download by anonymous users. Because we are now in the correct directory we simply use the get() function to retrieve our file and then we quit. As you can see, using Net::FTP is simple and mimics the interface of most command driven FTP clients. Some other member functions for Net::FTP are shown in Table 8.2.

TABLE 8.2	`ascii()`	Retrieve ASCII data (this is the default)
Net::FTP member functions	`binary()`	Retrieve binary data
	`rename(oldname, newname)`	Renames a file from oldname to newname
	`cdup()`	Moves the current directory up one level
	`pwd()`	Returns the full path of the current directory
	`rmdir(DIR)`	Removes a directory
	`mkdir(DIR)`	Makes a new directory
	`ls([DIR])`	Get a directory listing of DIR
	`dir([DIR])`	Get a directory listing of DIR in long format
	`put(FILE)`	Sends a file to the FTP server
	`size(FILE)`	Returns the file in bytes

Using Telnet in Perl

`Net::Telnet: /CPAN/Net-Telnet-3.02.tar.gz`

Telnet is the protocol for remotely accessing a UNIX machine as if you were logged in locally. It allows for shell commands to be executed remotely with the same permissions as the user you authenticate as.

Telnet should not be used in environments where security is a concern; ssh (Secure SHell) should be used instead because it encrypts all data that passes between the two machines.

NOTE

CPAN has a nice module for handling and executing remote commands on a system known as `Net::Telnet`. `Net::Telnet` provides all the basic functionality of a person sitting at a Telnet session, including user authentication and handling of prompts. (Prompts in this case mean what `Net::Telnet` waits to see before executing any commands.) Let's build a simple example that will show us the uptime and load of a remote machine:

```
use Net::Telnet;

# Create our Telnet object
my $telnet = new Net::Telnet (Timeout => 20,
                              Prompt  => '/bash\$ /');

# Have our object connect to our remote server
$telnet->open("remotehost.somewhere.com");

# Login as myusername with mypassword
$telnet->login('myusername', 'mypassword');
my @lines = $telnet->cmd('/usr/bin/uptime');

print join('', @lines) . "\n";

$telnet->close;
```

After we create our instance of the `Net::Telnet` object by setting our default timeout and prompt, we use the `open()` method to make our connection to our remote server. Then, with the `login()` method, we pass in our user name and password for the user we wish to connect as. After we have completely connected and authenticated with the remote server, `Net::Telnet` waits until it sees what you have set with the Prompt argument to the `new()` method. Upon seeing Prompt, it allows you to run a command via the `cmd()` method. When you are finished, you close the connection simply by calling the `Net::Telnet close()` method.

The following script provided this output when running on my system:

```
[frank@frank frank]$ perl telnet1.pl
8:36pm  up 29 days, 29 min,  5 users,  load average: 0.12, 0.03,
0.01
```

When using `Net::Telnet`, it is imperative that you correctly describe the shell prompt using regular expressions. Without a properly described Prompt, `Net::Telnet` will not function normally. For instance, if you are running a default Red Hat Linux system, your shell prompt will resemble the following when logging in:

```
[user@host user]$
```

If your prompt looks like the one above, then your module must be created like this:

```
my $telnet = new Net::Telnet
            (Timeout => 20,
             Prompt  => '/\[user\@host user\]\$ $/');
```

Creating a TCP Client

When you need to have code that doesn't necessarily fall into the categories of connections such as Telnet, FTP, whois, ping, etc., you must craft your own routines to send this data. This can be accomplished in many ways with the standard Perl library IO::Socket, which provides a clear and open pipe between two processes on two different machines (or the same machine, as in our example). Whatever is passed down the local end of the pipe reaches the remote end in the same order, much like a queue.

Networking with sockets is a very low-level and complicated task and should only be explored when all other options have proven ineffective.

Our examples below and in the upcoming TCP server section use TCP protocol. TCP stands for transmission control protocol; its alternative UDP does not guarantee that the information passed will reach its target in the same order as it was sent, or the information may not reach the target at all. TCP sockets should be used in most cases to simplify your programs.

Telnet is a good example of a TCP protocol; the user types a command at a prompt that is in turn received on the remote side of the connection. It would cause the user many problems if his or her commands reached the remote server in a jumbled order or never reached the remote server. UDP sockets should be used when the order or transmission integrity does not matter quite so much. A remote logging program, for instance, would be a good example. A client sending logs to a remote server wishes for the information to be logged, but it is not terribly crucial to its task. By using UDP sockets, the client program can "fire and forget" the log information and continue its business. The server portion of the logging program would try its best to actually receive and store this information, but, if the server were down or network connectivity were lost, the client would not stop processing its other tasks.

The following example assumes that both the TCP client and the TCP server, described in the next section, are running, which is necessary for it to work.

Now let's build the client portion:

```
use IO::Socket;

my $server_address = '24.124.35.230';     # Modify this to be your
                                          # IP address

my $server_port = 5555;                   # This must match your
```

```
                                        # TCP server's port
                                        # number for this to
                                        # work.

# Set up our socket with the remote server address,
# remote server port, tcp protocol and that we want streamed data
my $connection = IO::Socket::INET->new(
                    PeerAddr => $server_address,
                    PeerPort => $server_port,
                    Proto    => 'tcp',
                    Type     => SOCK_STREAM)
       or die "Couldn't connect to $server_address on port ".
             "$server_port: $!\n";

# Send some output to our server by
# looping 25 times and transmitting the time
for my $count(0..25) {

    # Get the current time
    my $time = localtime;

    print $connection "$count: $time\n";

    # Sleep for one second
    sleep(1);
}

# Now close it like any normal file
close($connection);
```

After we have initialized our TCP socket, we simply print to it as if it were a standard file handle. Working with sockets is just like working with a regular file or special file handle such as STDIN, except that the initial opening of the file handle differs greatly.

Creating a TCP Server

Holding true to client and server architecture, we now need a TCP server for our client to talk with. Below is the code for creating a simple TCP server. If all goes well when you run the server in one window and then the client in another window, you should get lines of output in the server's window.

```
use IO::Socket;

my $server_port = 5555;
```

```
# Make our socket connection and begin
# listening on our port
my $connection = IO::Socket::INET->new(
                    LocalPort   => $server_port,
                    Type        => SOCK_STREAM,
                    Reuse       => 1,
                    Listen      => 5)
    or die "Could not initialize on port ".
            "$server_port: $!\n";

# Wait for a client to connect and after it has,
# output all data it sends to STDOUT
while( my $new_client = $connection->accept() ) {
    while( my $line = <$new_client> ) {
        print $line;
    }
}

close($server_port);
```

The main difference between the client and server is in the construction of the socket itself. We still tell IO::Socket which port we want to open up, but this time we're the listening party, so we have to define how many "ears" we want to have listen. The Listen command sets up the maximum number of sockets we are willing to use at any given time.

The previous code will allow up to five different clients to send information to this server at any given time. If more than five connections are made, they will be queued until they can be handled. After our connection is established and we are listening on our port, we simply spin through a while loop looking for incoming connections with the accept() method. Inside of this loop, we process the information being sent by the client by outputting it to the screen.

The output of the server when run on my computer is:

```
[frank@frank src]$ perl tcp_server1.pl
0: Wed Sep  6 13:30:42 2000
1: Wed Sep  6 13:30:43 2000
2: Wed Sep  6 13:30:44 2000
3: Wed Sep  6 13:30:45 2000
4: Wed Sep  6 13:30:46 2000
5: Wed Sep  6 13:30:47 2000
6: Wed Sep  6 13:30:48 2000
7: Wed Sep  6 13:30:49 2000
...
18: Wed Sep  6 13:31:00 2000
19: Wed Sep  6 13:31:01 2000
20: Wed Sep  6 13:31:02 2000
21: Wed Sep  6 13:31:03 2000
22: Wed Sep  6 13:31:04 2000
```

```
23: Wed Sep  6 13:31:05 2000
24: Wed Sep  6 13:31:06 2000
```

Summary

As you can see, the black magic of network programming isn't quite as hard as most people believe. Network programming is not, however, simple. Debugging problems found within networking code can be difficult even for the most experienced programmer. Following Perl's motto, these modules make the easy things easy and the hard things possible.

CGI.pm

Overview of CGI.pm

The CGI.pm module, written by Lincoln Stein, is a package that makes it easy to write CGI scripts using Perl. CGI.pm is included with the standard Perl distribution as of version 5.004 and will work with most operating systems, including UNIX, Linux, Windows, Macintosh, and VMS. CGI.pm simplifies the process of creating, parsing, and processing web forms and providing shortcuts for dynamically generating HTML. CGI.pm can also be used to manage cookies, handle file uploads, and maintain the state of your CGI scripts.

Interface

CGI.pm provides two separate interfaces: a function-oriented interface and an object-oriented interface. Unless you need to create multiple CGI objects, the function-oriented interface should work for most of your needs.

Function-Oriented Interface

In the function-oriented interface, there is only one implicit, default CGI object. When using this interface, you must first import the functions or sets of functions into your program's namespace. Once a function is imported, it may be called directly without first creating a CGI object. Normally, you would import a set of functions using one or more of the following import tags:

- `:cgi`—Imports all the CGI-handling methods such as `param()` and `redirect()`.
- `:form`—Imports all the methods used for generating forms.
- `:html2`—Imports all the methods used to generate HTML 2.0 elements.
- `:html3`—Imports all the methods used to generate HTML 3.0 elements.
- `:netscape`—Imports all the methods used to generate Netscape-specific HTML.
- `:html`—Imports all the methods from `:html2`, `:html3`, and `:netscape`.
- `:standard`—Imports all the methods from `:cgi`, `:html2`, `:html3`, and `:form`.

- :all—Imports all the methods available in CGI.pm as defined by variable %TAGS.

The following code is a simple example using the function-oriented interface:

```
use CGI qw/:standard/;

# Get parameter from query string
# If no parameter, assign 'World' to $name
my $name = param('name') || 'World';

# Get environment variable
my $host = remote_host;

# Generate HTML
print header,
      start_html("Hello, $name from $host"),
      h1("Hello, $name from $host"),
      end_html;
```

This script checks for a name parameter in the query string. If a name is passed, then $name is set to the name; otherwise, $name is set to 'World'. The $host variable is set to the value of the REMOTE_HOST environment variable. Figure 9.1 shows the output of this script.

Figure 9.1
Output from simple function-oriented script.

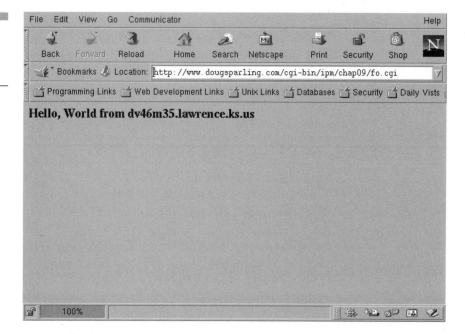

Object-Oriented Interface

In the object-oriented interface, you must explicitly create one or more CGI objects using CGI.pm's `new()` method. Note that the import tags are not needed. Each CGI object that is created contains the parameters passed to it (parameters passed from the query string or STDIN and from the environment variables) and provides methods to access those parameters. The following code is a simple example using the object-oriented interface.

```
use CGI;

# Create CGI object
my $query = new CGI;

# Get parameter from query string
# If no parameter, assign 'World' to $name
my $name = $query->param('name') || 'World';

# Get environment variable
my $host = $query->remote_host;

# Generate HTML
print $query->header,
      $query->start_html("Hello, $name from $host"),
      $query->h1("Hello, $name from $host"),
      $query->end_html;
```

This script performs the same function as the previous script, this time using the object-oriented interface. For variety, let's pass a name in the query string. Figure 9.2 shows the output of this script.

Processing the Form

Parameters are passed from a form to a CGI program either in the QUERY_STRING environment variable (GET request) or in the standard input (POST request). The input is encoded so that white space and other special characters are replaced with a percent sign and their corresponding hexadecimal codes. The request method used can be found in the REQUEST_METHOD environment variable. However, you really don't need to worry about these details, as CGI.pm will take care of them for you. CGI.pm will determine the request type and decode the URL. The input passed from a form is made up of key/value pairs, with the key corre-

Figure 9.2
Output from simple
object-oriented script
(with name
parameter).

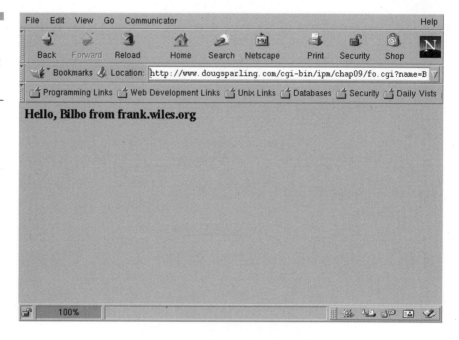

sponding to the name of a form element and the value to the user typed or selected. These keys and values are placed into a parameter array, where they can be accessed using CGI.pm's `param()` function.

Getting the Value(s) of a Single Named Parameter

The value of the key/value pair will be returned when the key is used as the argument to the `param()` function. The value returned is normally a scalar, but some form elements allow multiple selections, and you would want to use an array to take these values. The `param()` function will return `undef` if there is no value for the key used as an argument.

You can get the scalar value of a parameter:

```
$value = param('key');
```

You can get a list of values if the element allows multiple selections:

```
@values = param('key');
```

Getting the Values of All Parameters

If no arguments are given to the `param()` function, it will return a list of all the keys in the parameter array:

```
@keys = param();   # Gets keys (form element names)
```

This can be used to see whether the form has been filled out in scripts that generate both the form and the dynamic output.

```
if ( param() ) {
    # Form has been filled out - process form
} else {
    # No parameters - print initial form.
}
```

Calling `param()` without any arguments can also be used if you want to print out all the keys and their corresponding values.

```
foreach $key ( param() ) {
    print "$key => ", param($key), "\n";
}
```

Generating HTML Output

CGI.pm can be used to generate dynamic HTML documents, including fill-out forms and output produced in response to running a CGI script. CGI.pm provides methods for generating various HTTP headers and form elements and a set of HTML shortcuts for generating HTML tags. One advantage of using CGI.pm is that your program can generate its own fill-out form, thereby eliminating the need to have a form and CGI script being in different locations.

Generating Headers

An HTTP header must precede any output. This header will tell the browser what type of document is to follow. The HTTP header is required by the server and the server will return an error if it is omitted.

Generating HTTP Headers

An HTTP header is generated by the `header()` method. If no arguments are passed to the `header()` method, the default header type, `text/html`, is generated.

```
print header;
```

This will produce the following header:

```
"Content-type: text/html\n\n"
```

Other types of document headers can be produced by providing the MIME type:

```
print header('text/plain');
print header('image/gif');
```

You may also use the named argument form:

```
print header(-type=>'text/plain');
print header(-type=>'image/gif');
```

Generating a Redirection Header

It is possible to use the `redirect()` method to send the browser to a different URL:

```
print redirect('http://www.perl.com/');
```

Generating an HTML Header

The `start_html()` method is used to generate the top part of an HTML document. This method will generate the opening `<HTML>` and `<BODY>` tags as well as the `<HEAD>` and `<TITLE>` sections.

```
print start_html;
```

The title of the page will be set to 'Untitled Document' by default. If you want to set your own title, you can enter the title of the page with a simple string argument:

```
print start_html('Title of  Document');
```

It is possible to pass named arguments to the `start_html()` method to set optional attributes to the `<BODY>` tag.

```
print start_html(-title=>'Instant Perl Modules',
                 -author=>'name@email.org',
                 -meta=>{keywords=>'perl modules'},
                 -bgcolor=>'white');
```

The following arguments can be used with the named argument form of the `start_html()` method:

- `-author`—The author's email address.
- `-base`—Creates a `<BASE>` tag containing the URL of the script if set to a true value.
- `-dtd`—DTD is added before the `<HTML>` tag if set to a true value.
- `-meta`—Adds one or more `<META>` tags.
- `-onLoad`—Specifies JavaScript function to be executed when the page is loaded.
- `-onUnload`—Specifies JavaScript function to be executed when the page is unloaded.
- `-noScript`—Specifies HTML to display if the browser can't run JavaScript or scripting languages set by the `-script` attribute.
- `-script`—Adds scripting declarations to a page.
- `-title`—The title of the page.
- `-xbase`—Specifies a URL for the `<BASE>` tag.

Other arguments can be provided to create additional attributes to the `<BODY>` tag. Some of the more common attributes include the following:

- `-background`—Sets the background image for the page. Value is a URL pointing to GIF or JPEG.
- `-bgcolor`—Sets the background color of the page.
- `-link, -vlink, -alink`—Sets the color for hypertext links.
- `-text`—Sets the color of normal text on the page.

The `end_html()` method is used to end the HTML document. This method will generate the closing `</BODY>` and `</HTML>` tags.

```
print end_html;
```

Generating Standard HTML Elements

CGI.pm provides methods referred to as HTML shortcuts to create nearly every HTML tag. An HTML shortcut normally has the same name as the HTML tag that it creates. The tag's content may be passed as a string argument to the HTML shortcut. Attributes for HTML tags may also be specified by creating an anonymous hash containing the attribute's key/value pairs and passing it to the HTML shortcut. There are too many HTML shortcuts to list them all here. Take a look at the CGI.pm documentation for more details.

Here are a few examples:

```
print p;
print p('This is a paragraph');
print p({-align=>'right'});
print p({-align=>'right'}, 'This is a paragraph, aligned right');
print h1('This is an h1 heading');
print h1({-align=>'center'}, 'This is an h1 heading, centered');
print a({-href=>'http://www.perl.com', -alt=>'Perl homepage'},
        'Perl homepage');
```

If you are using the function-oriented interface, then only the shortcut methods that you imported will be available.

Generating Form Elements

A fill-out form is used to gather information from a user. A form can contain elements or widgets that include textfield, textarea, password field, a single checkbox, checkbox group, radio group, popup menu, scrolling list, hidden value, submit button, and reset button. One difference between form elements and HTML shortcuts is that the methods used to generate form elements have a different name than the element they create. There are many arguments that can be passed to the form-element methods, and these will be covered in the following sections.

Creating a Form

The `start_form()` method is used to generate the HTML `<FORM>` tag. This method can normally be called without any arguments.

```
print start_form;
```

The request method, form action, and encoding scheme may be passed as arguments:

```
print start_form('POST', '/cgi-bin/script.cgi',
                 'multipart/form-data');
```

or

```
print start_form(-method=>'POST',
                 -action=>'/cgi-bin/script.cgi',
                 -encoding=>'mulitpart/form-data');
```

- -method—The form request method, either POST or GET; the default is POST.
- -action—The URL of the CGI; the default is the current script.
- -encoding—Encoding scheme, either application/x-www-form-url-encoded (default) or multipart/form-data.

The end_form() method is used to close a form by generating the </FORM> tag. All form elements must be contained between the start_form() and end_form() tags.

```
print end_form;
```

Sticky Behavior of Form Elements

Each time a form is regenerated, it will remember and display its previous settings. There may be times when you want the form to display an element using its default settings. Fortunately, it is possible to override the sticky behavior of form elements by using the -override() method. The following code will force a text field to display the default text, even if there is a previous value provided by a CGI parameter with the same name as the text field. This is accomplished by setting the -override() method to a nonzero value:

```
print textfield(-name=>'first_name',
                -default=>'Doug',
                -override=>1);
```

The -override() method can be used with most of the form elements, including the textfield, textarea, single checkbox, checkbox group, radio group, popup menu, and scrolling list methods.

Textfield

The `textfield()` method generates a text entry field:

```
print textfield('first_name');

print textfield('first_name', 'Doug', 25, 40);
```

or

```
print textfield(-name=>'first_name',
                -default=>'Doug',
                -size=>25,
                -maxlength=>40);
```

- `-name`—Name of the text field (required).
- `-default`—Initial string in text field (optional).
- `-size`—Size of text field in characters (optional).
- `-maxlength`—Maximum number of characters that can be entered in text field (optional).

Textarea

The `textarea()` method generates a multiline text input box:

```
print textarea('comments');
```

or

```
print textarea(-name=>'comments',
               -default=>'This is a comment.',
               -rows=>10,
               -cols=>50);
```

- `-name`—Name of the text area (required).
- `-default`—Initial string in text area (optional).
- `-rows`—Number of rows to display (optional).
- `-cols`—Number of columns that to display (optional).

Password Field

The `password_field()` method will generate a password entry field. The `password_field()` and `textfield()` methods are almost identical, the only difference being that the content of the password field is displayed as asterisks:

```
print password_field('passwd');

print password_field('passwd', 'starting_value', 25, 40);
```

or

```
print password_field(-name=>'passwd',
                     -default=>'starting_value',
                     -size=>25,
                     -maxlength=>40);
```

- `-name`—Name of the password field (required).
- `-default`—Initial string in password field (optional).
- `-size`—Size of password field in characters (optional).
- `-maxlength`—Maximum number of characters that can be entered in password field (optional).

Standalone Checkbox

The `checkbox()` method will generate a single standalone checkbox.

```
print checkbox(-name=>'checkbox_name',
               -checked=>1,
               -value=>'ON',
               -label=>'Check box label');
```

- `-name`—Name of the checkbox (required).
- `-checked`—Specifies whether the checkbox is checked by default. A nonzero value will cause the checkbox to be initially checked (optional).
- `-value`—Value of the checkbox when it is checked. Default is 'ON' (optional).
- `-label`—The user-readable label for the checkbox (optional). If the `-label` argument is not supplied, the checkbox name will be used by default.

Checkbox Group

The `checkbox_group()` method will generate a group of related checkboxes.

```
%labels = (value1=>'one', value2=>'two', value3=>'three',
           value4=>'four');

print checkbox_group(-name=>'group_name',
```

```
                    -values=>['value1', 'value2', 'value3',
                              'value4'],
                    -default=>['value1', 'value2'],
                    -linebreak=>'true',
                    -labels=>\%labels);
```

- -name—Name of the checkbox group (required).
- -values—Array reference containing the values of the each checkbox (required).
- -default—List or single value to be checked by default (optional).
- -linebreak—Places line breaks between checkboxes, creating a vertical list, if set to true (optional).
- -labels—Pointer to a hash containing labels relating to the checkbox values (optional). If the -labels argument is not supplied, the checkbox values will be used by default.

Radio Button Group

The radio_group() method will generate a group of related radio buttons.

```
%labels = (value1=>'one', value2=>'two', value3=>'three',
           value4=>'four');

print radio_group(-name=>'group_name',
                    -values=>['value1', 'value2', 'value3',
                              'value4'],
                    -default=>'value2',
                    -linebreak=>'true',
                    -labels=>\%labels);
```

- -name—Name of the radio-button group (required).
- -values—Array reference containing the values of the each radio button (required).
- -default—Radio button to be selected by default (optional).
- -linebreak—Places line breaks between radio buttons, creating a vertical list, if set to true (optional).
- -labels—Pointer to a hash containing labels relating to the radio-button values (optional). If the -labels argument is not supplied, the radio-button values will be used by default.

Popup Menus

The popup_menu() method will generate a popup menu.

```
%labels = (value1=>'one', value2=>'two', value3=>'three',
           value4=>'four');
```

```
print popup_menu(-name=>'menu_name',
                 -values=>['value1', 'value2', 'value3',
                          'value4'],
                 -default=>'value2',
                 -labels=>\%labels);
```

- ▪ `-name`—Name of the popup menu (required).
- ▪ `-values`—Array reference containing a list of menu items (required).
- ▪ `-default`—Menu item to be selected by default (optional).
- ▪ `-labels`—Pointer to a hash containing labels relating to each menu item (optional). If the `-labels` argument is not supplied, the menu item text will be used by default.

Scrolling Lists

The `scrolling_list()` method will generate a scrolling-list form element.

```
%labels = (value1=>'one', value2=>'two', value3=>'three',
           value4=>'four');

print scrolling_list(-name=>'menu_name',
                     -values=>['value1', 'value2', 'value3',
                              'value4'],
                     -default=>'value2',
                     -size=>4,
                     -multiple=>'true',
                     -labels=>\%labels);
```

- ▪ `-name`—Name of the scrolling list (required).
- ▪ `-values`—Array reference containing a list of menu items (required).
- ▪ `-default`—Single value or list of values to be selected by default (optional).
- ▪ `-size`—Size of the list (optional). If the `-size` parameter is not supplied, the size of the list will be equal to the number of items it contains.
- ▪ `-multiple`—Multiple selections can be made if set to true (optional).
- ▪ `-labels`—Pointer to a hash containing labels relating to each menu item (optional). If the `-labels` argument is not supplied, the menu item text will be used by default.

Hidden Fields

The `hidden()` method will generate a hidden text field:

```
print hidden('name', 'value1', 'value2', 'value3');
```

or

```
print hidden(-name=>'name',
             -value=>['value1', 'value2', 'value3']);
```

- -name—Name of the hidden text field (required).
- -value—Single scalar value or array reference containing multiple values (required).

Submit Button

The submit() method will generate a submit button:

```
print submit('name', 'value');
```

or

```
print submit(-name=>'name',
             -value=>'value');
```

- -name—Name of the submit button; also the label if no -value argument is supplied (optional).
- -value—The value of the button; also used as the label (optional).

Reset Button

The reset() method will generate a reset button. The reset button will return a form to its initial state.

```
print reset;
```

An optional string argument may be passed to change the default label.

```
print reset('Do Over');
```

Default Button

The defaults() method will generate a default button. A default button will return a form to its default values. An optional string may be passed that will set the label of the button; otherwise, the label is defaults:

```
print defaults;
```

or

```
print defaults('Start Over');
```

Example

The following example uses most of the form elements covered in the previous section to create an online order form. The first time the program is called the parameter array is empty, so the fill-out form is displayed as shown in Figure 9.3. After the form is filled out and the user clicks the submit button, the CGI parameter names and values will be displayed. Figure 9.4 shows the output of this program.

```
use CGI qw/:standard/;

print header,
      start_html('Le Rendez-Vous');

if( param() ) {
    print_results();
} else {
    print_form();
}

print end_html;

######

sub print_form {
    print h1('Le Rendez-Vous'),
          'Online Lunch Special',

          start_form,

          hidden('type', 'lunch special'),

          "<STRONG>Order Type: </STRONG>",
          br,

          popup_menu(-name=>'order_type',
                     -values=>['Dine In', 'Carry Out',
                               'Delivery'],
                     -default=>'Dine In'),

          p,
          "<STRONG>Quiche: </STRONG>",
          br,

          radio_group(-name=>'quiche',
                      -values=>['Dijon (tomato, mustard)',
```

```
                              'Menton (tomato, black olives,
                               cheese)',
                              'Aix en Provence (zucchini, goat
                               cheese, basil)'],
                     -linebreak=>'yes'),

    p,
    "<STRONG>Tarte: </STRONG>",
    br,

    radio_group(-name=>'tarte',
               -values=>['Choco-poire (chocolate, pear)',
                         'Pomme-cannelle (apple,
                                          cinnamon)',
                         'Fraises Frangipane (strawberry
                                             almond
                                             custard)'],
               -linebreak=>'yes'),

    p,
    "<STRONG>Optional: </STRONG>",
    br,

    checkbox_group(-name=>'optional',
                  -values=>['Salade du Jour', 'Tea'],
                  -linebreak=>'yes'),

    p,
    "<STRONG>Name: </STRONG>",
    br,

    textfield(-name=>'name',
             -size=>25),

    p,
    "<STRONG>Email: </STRONG>",
    br,

    textfield(-name=>'email',
             -size=>25),

    p,

    checkbox(-name=>'mail_list',
            -label=>'Add me to your mailing list'),

    p,
    "<STRONG>How did you hear about us?: </STRONG>",
    br,

    scrolling_list(-name=>'hear_about',
                  -values=>['Newspaper', 'Radio',
                            'Friend', 'I\'m a regular'],
                  -size=>4,
                  -multiple=>'true'),
```

```
            p,
            "<STRONG>Comments</STRONG>",
            br,

            textarea(-name=>'comments',
                     -rows=>8,
                     -columns=>60),

            p,

            reset(-name=>'Reset'),
            submit,
            end_form;
}

sub print_results {
    print h1('Order Results');

    foreach my $key ( param() ) {
        print "<STRONG>$key</STRONG> = ";
        my @values = param($key);
        print join(", ",@values),"<BR>\n";
    }
}
```

Figure 9.3
Online order form
created by CGI.pm.

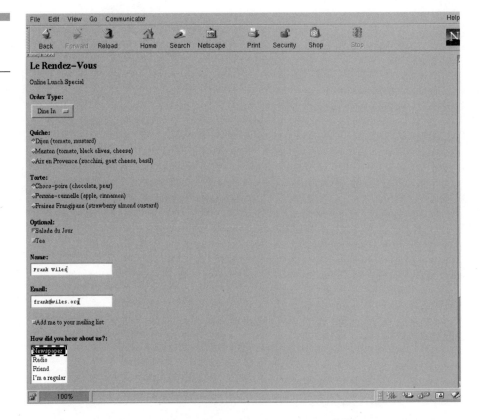

Figure 9.4
Output generated by
online order form.

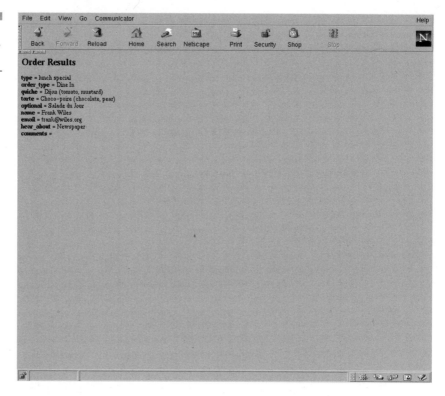

File Edit View Go Communicator   Help

Back Forward Reload Home Search Netscape Print Security Shop Stop

Order Results

type = lunch special
order_type = Dine In
quiche = Dijon (tomato, mustard)
tarte = Choco-poire (chocolate, pear)
optional = Salade du Jour
name = Frank Wiles
email = frank@wiles.org
hear_about = Newspaper
comments =

Cookies

CGI.pm provides several methods that make it easy to work with cookies. A *cookie* is a small piece of information that is stored on a client computer and can be used to maintain the state of a CGI script. A cookie consists of a name/value pair and optional information such as expiration date, cookie domain, cookie path, and whether the cookie must come from a secure server.

This example creates a simple cookie:

```
use CGI qw/:standard/;

my $cookie = cookie(-name=>'user_name',
                    -value=>'doug');

print header(-cookie=>$cookie);
```

Here's a cookie with some additional information:

```
use CGI qw/:standard/;
```

```
my $cookie = cookie(-name=>'user_name',
                    -value=>'doug',
                    -expires=>'+24h',
                    -path=>'cgi-bin/cookiejar',
                    -domain=>'mydomain.com',
                    -secure=>1);

print header(-cookie=>$cookie);
```

- `-name`—The name of the cookie (required).
- `-value`—The value of the cookie; can be a scalar, array reference, or anonymous array (optional).
- `-expires`—The expiration date of the cookie (optional). This value can be either an absolute or a relative value. Examples of relative expiration dates: '+30s' is 30 seconds from now, '+15m' is 15 minutes from now, '+2h' is 2 hours from now, '+2d' is 2 days from now, '-1d' is immediately, 'now' is immediately, '+2M' is 2 months from now, '+1y' is 1 year from now. An absolute date can also be used, for example: Wed, 05-Apr-2000 14:00:00 CDT.
- `-path`—Path for which the cookie is valid; default is '/' (optional).
- `-domain`—Partial or complete domain names for which cookie is valid; default is host name of the server that set the cookie (optional).
- `-secure`—If set to true, the cookie will only be valid when requested from a secure server.

Now let's read the cookie and retrieve it's value:

```
my $user = cookie('user_name');
```

or

```
my $user = cookie(-name=>'user_name');
```

The simple example that follows will take the name entered in the text field and save it to a cookie. Figure 9.5 shows the initial form. The number of times you visit the web page is also stored in the cookie and updated with each visit to the page. Figure 9.6 shows the output of the CGI after one visit. A check box is provided that can be selected to request that the cookie be deleted. This is done by sending a cookie with a '-1d' expiration date, which will immediately delete the cookie from the client's machine.

```perl
use CGI qw/:standard/;

my $cookie;

# Get cookie values
my %info = cookie('info');

# Set name and visits
my $name = $info{'name'} || param('name');
my $count = $info{'count'} || 0;

if( param('clear_cookie') ) {
    clear_cookie();
    print_form();
} elsif(!$name) {
    print_form();
} else {
    say_hello();
}

#####

sub clear_cookie {
    # Clear cookie if 'clear cookie' box is checked
    $cookie = cookie(-name=>'info',
                     -value=>\%info,
                     -expires=>'-1d');
}

sub print_form {
    # Send proper header
    if( param('clear_cookie') ) {
        print header(-cookie=>$cookie);
    } else {
        print header;
    }

    # Print form
    print start_html('Cookie Example'),
          h1('Welcome to the Cookie Example'),
          start_form,
          'Name: ',
          textfield(-name=>'name'),
          p,
          submit,
          reset,
          end_form,
          end_html;
}

sub say_hello {
    $info{'name'} = $name;

    $count++;
    $info{'count'} = $count;

    # Set cookie, expires in 60 days
    $cookie = cookie(-name=>'info',
```

```
                        -value=>\%info,
                        -expires=>'+60d');

    print header(-cookie=>$cookie),
          start_html("Hello, $name"),
          h1("Hello, $name"),
          "Visit number $count",
          start_form,
          checkbox(-name=>'clear_cookie',
          -label=>'Clear Cookie'),
          p,
          submit,
          end_form,
          end_html;
}
```

Figure 9.5
Form used to store a
name in a cookie.

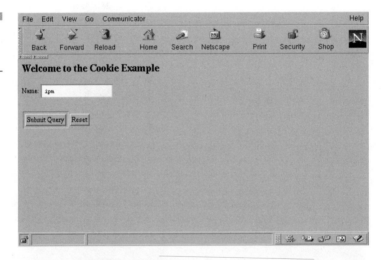

Figure 9.6
Output from CGI
script showing the
value of a cookie.

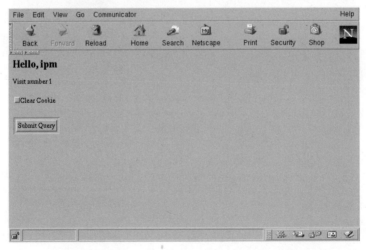

File Uploads

Files can be uploaded to a server from a web browser, and CGI.pm allows you to implement this easily. In the following example, we use CGI.pm to generate a multipart form that includes a `filefield()` method. The `filefield()` method creates both an editable text field, where the path of the file to be uploaded can be entered, and a browse button that allows the user to use a file browser to select a file.

```
use CGI qw/:standard/;
print header,
    start_html,
    start_multipart_form,
    filefield(-name=>'upload_file',
            -default=>'filename',
            -size=>50,
            -maxlength=>75),
    br,
    submit(-label=>'Upload File'),
    end_form,
    end_html;
```

- `-name`—Name of the file field (required).
- `-default`—Default value for file name; ignored by browsers for security reasons (optional).
- `-size`—Size of file field in characters (optional).
- `-maxlength`—Maximum number of characters that can be entered in a file field (optional).

After the file is uploaded, it can be accessed by using the `param()` method:

```
$filename = param('upload_file');
```

The returned value will contain the name of the file, which can be used as a file handle to read the contents of the file. You may print the file:

```
# Print text file
    while (<$filename>) {
        print $_;
    }
```

or

```
# Print binary file
```

```
while (read($filename,$data,1024)) {
      print $data;
}
```

You may also wish to save the file and store it on the server:

```
# Save text file
   open (OUTFILE,">>/home/doug/files/file.out");
   while (<$filename>) {
      print OUTFILE $_;
   }
```

or

```
# Save binary file
   open (OUTFILE,">>/home/doug/files/file.out");
   while (read($filename,$data,1024)) {
      print OUTFILE $data;
   }
```

The following example will upload a file to the server and then display the file's contents to the browser if it has a text or image MIME type. Any other type of file will cause the file's name and MIME type to be displayed. You could easily change the script so that it saves the file to the server instead of displaying it. Figure 9.7 shows the file upload form generated by this script. Figure 9.8 shows a file dialog box that is generated by clicking the Browse button.

```
use CGI qw/:standard/;

if( param() ) {
    print_output();
} else {
    print_form();
}

#####

sub print_form {
    print header,
    start_html('File Upload'),
    h1('File Upload'),

    start_multipart_form,
    filefield(-name=>'upload_file',
              -size=>50,
              -maxlength=>75),
```

```
        br,
        submit(-label=>'Upload File'),
        end_form,
        end_html;
}

sub print_output {
    my $file_name = param('upload_file');

    if(!$file_name) {
        print_error();
        return;
    }

    # Use uploadInfo() to determine MIME type of uploaded file
    my $file_type = uploadInfo($file_name)->{'Content-Type'};

    # Check MIME type of file
    if($file_type =~ /^text/) {
        # Print text (plain or html) file
        print header;
        while (<$file_name>) {
            print $_;
        }
    } elsif($file_type =~ /^image/) {
        # Print binary (image) file
        print header('image/gif');
        my $data;
        while (read($file_name,$data,1024)) {
            print $data;
        }
    } else {
        # Catch MIME types that aren't text or image
        print header,
        start_html('Not text or image'),
        h1('Not text or image'),
        "Filename: $file_name", br,
        "Filetype: $file_type", br,
        end_html;
    }
}

sub print_error {
    print header,
    start_html('No File'),
    h1('No File to Upload'),
    end_html;
}
```

You may want to limit the size of the files that can be uploaded. You could limit upload files to 50K by adding the following line to your script:

```
$POST_MAX = 1024 * 50;
```

Figure 9.7
Upload form.

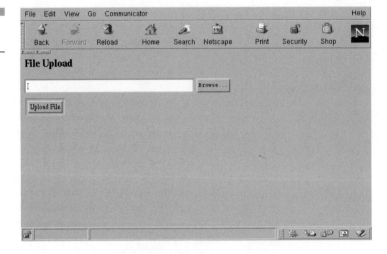

Figure 9.8
File-selection dialog
box.

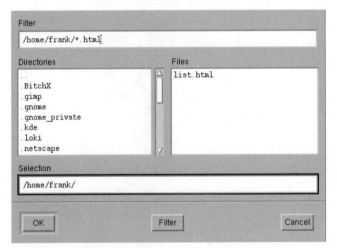

Debugging

A nice feature of CGI.pm is the ability to run CGI scripts at the command line. This is useful for debugging scripts without having to deal with the web server environment. You can enter an "offline" mode by running your CGI script at the command line without any arguments (in later versions of CGI.pm, you must pass the -debug flag on the "use CGI" line). Once in the offline mode, you may enter name/value pairs one at a time. After entering all of the name/value pairs, type **Ctrl-D** (**Ctrl-Z** on Windows) to end the input. You will then see the CGI output on the console.

We'll use this simple script for our examples:

```
# hello.cgi
use CGI qw/:standard/;

my $name = param('name');

print header,
      start_html,
      h1("Hello, $name"),
      end_html;
```

Now let's run this script at the command line:

```
% perl hello.cgi
(offline mode: enter name=value pairs on standard input)
name=Doug
^D
Content-Type: text/html

<!DOCTYPE HTML PUBLIC "-//IETF//DTD HTML//EN">
<HTML><HEAD><TITLE>Untitled Document</TITLE>
</HEAD><BODY><H1>Hello, Doug</H1></BODY></HTML>
```

It is also possible to enter the name/value pairs at the command line with your script.

```
% perl hello.cgi name=Doug
```

The CGI::Carp module can be used to debug your CGI script from the browser. By importing the fatalsToBrowser() method, CGI::Carp will output fatal errors (die, confess) as HTML to your browser.

```
use CGI qw/:standard/;
use CGI::Carp qw/fatalsToBrowser/;
die "die--Fatal Error";
```

Summary

CGI.pm isn't necessary for writing CGI scripts, but it does simplify the process. CGI.pm makes it easy to create and process forms and will save you from some typing by providing HTML shortcuts for dynamically generating HTML. CGI.pm can also handle more advanced CGI features such as cookies, file uploading, cascading style sheets, image maps, and frames. We've only scratched the surface in this chapter, so be sure to read the documentation that comes with the CGI.pm module. Another valuable resource is Lincoln Stein's book, *The Official Guide to Programming with CGI.pm*.

Fun CGI Applications

Introduction

In the previous chapter you learned how to use Lincoln Stein's CGI.pm module. In this and the following few chapters, we are going to build some practical web applications using CGI.pm. In this chapter, we'll put together some fun applications that many websites use: a voting booth, a guestbook, a postcard script, and a web-based chat.

Voting Booth

A very common application is a voting booth or poll. A voting booth script can be used to gather information from users or it can be a fun way to add dynamic content to your site.

Overview

The voting booth application will have a separate HTML form that calls the CGI script. The reason for creating a separate HTML form is so that it may be added directly to the main page of the site instead of having CGI.pm create the form.

You can have many polls when using this CGI script; just be sure to give each poll a different name, which is done with a hidden variable. Each poll will have two additional files: a data file and a log file. The data file will store the results of the poll and the log file will track IP addresses.

For our example, we'll build a voting booth where users can vote for their favorite stout. Slainte!

HTML Form

The following HTML will generate the web page shown in Figure 10.1.

```
<HTML>
<HEAD>
<TITLE>IPM Vote</TITLE>
</HEAD>

<BODY BGCOLOR="#FFFFFF">
```

```
<H1>Vote</H1>

<FORM ACTION="/cgi-bin/vote/vote.cgi">

<H3>What is your favorite stout?</H3>
<INPUT TYPE="HIDDEN" NAME="vote" VALUE="stout">
<INPUT TYPE="RADIO" NAME="choice" VALUE="Beamish" CHECKED>
Beamish<BR>
<INPUT TYPE="RADIO" NAME="choice" VALUE="Guinness">Guinness<BR>
<INPUT TYPE="RADIO" NAME="choice" VALUE="Murphys">Murphys<BR>

<P>
<INPUT TYPE="SUBMIT">
<INPUT TYPE="RESET">

</FORM>

<A HREF="/cgi-bin/vote/vote.cgi?view=stout">View Results</A>

</BODY>
</HTML>
```

Figure 10.1
Voting form.

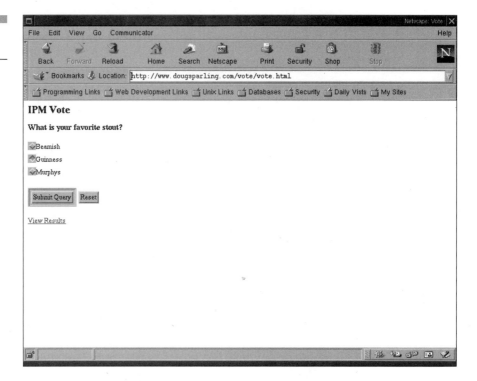

This is nothing more than a standard HTML form. You will have to configure the form slightly to match your poll (and your system).

You'll need to set the path to the CGI script that we'll put together a bit later in this section:

```
<FORM ACTION="/cgi-bin/vote/vote.cgi">
```

The name of the poll is set in a hidden variable. You can have as many polls as you want as long as each has a unique name:

```
<INPUT TYPE="HIDDEN" NAME="vote" VALUE="stout">
```

Next, you'll need to add the names of the items that are being voted on. The first item is checked to prevent a user from voting for nothing. If you remove the checked attribute, the script will catch it.

```
<INPUT TYPE="RADIO" NAME="choice" VALUE="Beamish" CHECKED>
Beamish<BR>
<INPUT TYPE="RADIO" NAME="choice" VALUE="Guinness">Guinness<BR>
<INPUT TYPE="RADIO" NAME="choice" VALUE="Murphys">Murphys<BR>
```

The last thing you'll need to set is a link to the poll results:

```
<A HREF="/cgi-bin/vote/vote.cgi?view=stout">View Results</A>
```

Data and Log Files

Data File

The data file stores the number of votes for each choice. Your data file should look something like this (after receiving a few votes):

```
Beamish:5
Guinness:12
Murphys:8
```

The CGI script will create this file as long as the web server has permission to write to the directory where the data file is located. If not, set the permission of the data file to 666. You might want to create the file manually by setting all the values to zero so that each choice will show up when viewing the results even if not all of the choices have votes.

The $DATA_PATH variable in the CGI script must be set to the full path to the directory containing the data file. It is best to store the data file somewhere outside of the document root path. Normally a directory under /home works fine.

Log File

The log file is used to store IP addresses. The CGI script will create this file automatically (assuming the IP option is set). Issues concerning permissions and location also apply to the log file. An entry in the log file will look similar to:

```
127.0.0.1
```

CGI Script

The CGI script will be located somewhere in the cgi-bin directory. Be sure to set the permissions to this file so that it is executable.

```perl
#!/usr/bin/perl -Tw
use strict;
use CGI qw/:standard/;
use Fcntl qw/:flock/;
$|++;

### config
my $DATA_PATH = '/home/doug/vote/';
my $LOG_PATH = '/home/doug/vote/';
my $CHECK_IP = 0; # 0 to turn off
my $CHECK_COOKIE = 0; # 0 to turn off
my $IMAGE = '/vote/vote_image.gif';
my $IMAGE_HEIGHT = 15; # height of image
my $IMAGE_MULT = 5; # img width = percent X $IMG_MULT
### end config

# Check what user wants to do
if ( param('vote') ) {
    # User wants to vote

    # Get name of poll
    my $poll = param('vote');

    # check for cookie
    if( cookie('vote') ne $poll or !$CHECK_COOKIE ) {
    # no cookie, let 'em vote
        print_header( $poll );
        vote( $poll );
    } else {
        # cookie found
        # allow user to view results but not vote
        print_header();
        print 'A vote has already been made ' .
                'from your machine.',
                br;
```

```
            view( $poll );
        }
    } elsif ( param('view') ) {
        # User wants to view

        # Get name of poll
        my $poll = param('view');
        print_header();
        view( $poll );
    } else {
        # Error (Not 'vote' or 'view' - what's the user up to?)
        print_header();
        print 'Not a valid option.',
                br;
    }

    print end_html;

    #############################################

    sub print_header {
        # Get name of our poll (if one is sent)
        my $poll = shift;

        # If poll is passed, then we need to set a cookie
        # We'll excuse user if no choice was selected
        if( $poll && param('choice') ) {
            my $cookie = cookie(-name=>'vote',
                                -value=>$poll);
            print header(-cookie=>$cookie);
        } else {
            print header;
        }

        print start_html(-title=>'Results',
                        -bgcolor=>'#FFFFFF');
    }

    sub vote {
        # Determine poll name and create full path to data file
        my $poll = shift;

        # Untaint data
        $poll =~ /^(\w*)$/ or die "Tainted data\n";
        $poll = $1;
        my $data_file = $DATA_PATH . $poll . '.dat';

        # Don't open symlinks for security
        if (-l $data_file) {
            die "File does not exist\n";
        }

        # Read the data file
        my %data = read_data($data_file);
```

```perl
    # Get total votes
    my $total = 0;
    foreach my $key (keys %data) {
        $total += $data{$key};
    }

    # Check IP
    my $ip = 0;
    $ip = check_ip($poll) if $CHECK_IP;

    if ($ip) {
        print "A vote from $ip has already been made",
            br;
    } else {
        # Add vote (only if choice is selected)
        if ( param('choice') ) {
            # Get user's vote
            my $choice = param('choice');

            # Up the count
            $data{$choice}++;
            $total++;

            # Save data
            save_data($data_file, \%data);

            # Log IP
            log_ip($poll) if $CHECK_IP;
        } else {
            print 'No choice selected - try again.',
                br;
        }
    }

    # Display results
    display(\%data, $total);

}

sub view {
    # Determine poll name and create full path to data file
    my $poll = shift;
    my $data_file = $DATA_PATH . $poll . '.dat';

    # Read data file
    my %data = read_data($data_file);

    # Get total votes
    my $total = 0;
    foreach my $key (keys %data) {
        $total += $data{$key};
    }
```

```perl
    # Display results
    display(\%data, $total);

}

sub read_data {
    # Get full path to data file
    my $data_file = shift;
    my %data = ();

    # Read file if it exists and is not empty
    if( -e $data_file and !-z $data_file ) {
        open(FILE, "$data_file") or
          die "Cannot open $data_file: $!\n";
        flock(FILE, LOCK_SH); # Shared lock for reading

        while(<FILE>) {
            # split name and count and put in hash
            chomp;
            my($name, $count) = split(/:/, $_);
            $data{$name} = $count;
        }

        flock(FILE, LOCK_UN); # Unlock the file
        close FILE;
    } else {
        # Data file doesn't exist or is empty
        print "You're the first voter for this poll!",
              br;
    }

    return %data;

}

sub save_data {
    # Get full path to data file and data
    my $data_file = shift;
    my $data_ref = shift;
    my %data = %$data_ref;

    open(FILE, ">$data_file") or
      die "Cannot open $data_file: $!\n";
    flock(FILE, LOCK_EX); # Exclusive lock for writing

    foreach my $key (sort keys %data) {
        print FILE $key . ':' . $data{$key} . "\n";
    }

    flock(FILE, LOCK_UN); # Unlock the file
    close FILE;

}
```

```perl
sub display {
    # Get data and total
    my $data_ref = shift;
    my %data = %$data_ref;
    my $total = shift;
    my $total_string = $total == 1 ? 'vote' : 'votes';

    print h1('Results');
    print "<TABLE BORDER=0 CELLPADDING=5 CELLSPACING=0>\n";

    # Calculate percentage
    foreach my $key (sort keys %data) {
        my $percent = 0;
        if ($total != 0) {
            $percent = ($data{$key} / $total) * 100;
        }

        # Percent display formatting
        $percent = sprintf("%3.2f", $percent);
        # Set width of image bar
        my $width = $percent * $IMAGE_MULT;
        # Round to integer for IMG SRC width tag
        $width = sprintf("%.0f", $width);
        my $vote_string = $data{$key} == 1 ? 'vote' : 'votes';

        print "<TR>\n";
        print "<TD ALIGN=\"LEFT\"><STRONG>$key</STRONG>" .
              "</TD>\n";
        if ($width == 0) {
            print "<TD>\n";
        } else {
            print "<TD><IMG SRC=\"$IMAGE\" " .
                  "HEIGHT=$IMAGE_HEIGHT WIDTH=$width>\n";
            print "   \n";
        }

        print "$data{$key} $vote_string ($percent %)</TD>\n";
        print "</TR>\n";
    }

    print "</TABLE>\n";
    print p,
          "$total total $total_string",
          br,
          p,
          a({-href=>referer()},'Back');

}

sub check_ip {
    # Get poll name and IP address of user
    my $poll = shift;
    my $ip = remote_addr();
    my $logfile = $LOG_PATH . $poll . '.log';
```

```perl
        # Read IP log file - see if this IP already exists
    if ( -e $logfile && !-z $logfile ) {
        open(FILE, "$logfile") or
          die "Cannot open $logfile: $!\n";
        flock(FILE, LOCK_SH); # Shared lock for reading

        while(<FILE>) {
            chomp;
            if ( $_ eq $ip ) {
                # This IP has already voted - return IP
                return $_;
            }
        }

        flock(FILE, LOCK_UN); # Unlock the file
        close FILE;
    }

    return 0;

}

sub log_ip {
    # Get poll name
    my $poll = shift;
    my $logfile = $LOG_PATH . $poll . '.log';

    # Save IP address to log file
    open(FILE, ">>$logfile") or
      die "Cannot open $logfile: $!\n";
    flock(FILE, LOCK_EX); # Exclusive lock for writing

    print FILE remote_addr(), "\n";

    flock(FILE, LOCK_UN); # Unlock the file
     close FILE;

}
```

We'll now cover some of the main features of this script.

We're using the `Fcntl` module that comes with the standard distribution. We use this module to load the C `fcntl.h` constants for the `flock` function.

```perl
use Fcntl qw/:flock/;
```

We want to lock our data and log files to prevent race conditions as more than one process could attempt to write to the same file simultaneously.

We disable buffering on the STOUT stream with the line:

```
$|++;
```

We set configuration variables for the script after setting the full path to the log and data files on the system. Make sure that this is the full path, not a relative path.

This script uses cookies or IP logging to prevent users from voting more than once (stuffing the ballot box). Set these options to a non-zero value to turn them on. Neither method is truly foolproof or accurate. A knowledgeable user can turn cookies off in the browser or delete the cookie, thus allowing the user to vote an unlimited number of times. Also, different users would not be allowed to vote from the same machine. With IP logging, many users go through a proxy server (for example, corporate users behind a firewall or users of some ISPs).

Once an IP is blocked, other users going through the same proxy server cannot vote. Dial-up and cable modem users can log back in with a different IP address because each session has a different IP assigned to it. Probably the best way to prevent multiple votes is to have a user login with an ID and password. This may be overkill for a "fun" or trivial poll, so the cookie or IP logging may be all you need.

Other configuration variables you may want to change are the $IMAGE_HEIGHT and $IMAGE_MULT. These are used to control the height and width of the bar graph image.

The two main functions used in this script are vote() and view(). Before entering vote(), the cookie is checked (unless $CHECK_COOKIE is set to zero). If no cookie is found or the check-cookie option is turned off, the name of the poll (a hidden variable passed from the form) is passed to the vote() function. The name of the poll is used to determine the name of the data file to write to. Because the name of the poll is passed from the form, it is considered tainted input. To use the poll name, we must first untaint the variable:

```
# Untaint data
$poll =~ /^(\w*)$/ or die "Tainted data\n";
$poll = $1;
my $data_file = $DATA_PATH . $poll . '.dat';
```

To untaint a variable, you must use a regular expression, as above. Note that we only accept word characters (a–z, A–Z, 0–9, _) in our poll name. If anything else is passed from the form, the script will die. As an extra bit of precaution, we make sure that the script won't open a symlink:

```
# Don't open symlinks for security
if (-l $data_file) {
    die "File does not exist\n";
}
```

Next we read the file and get the total number of votes accumulated so far. Then we check if a vote from the user's IP has already been made. If the IP address of the user has not been logged or if the IP logging has been shut off, we then get the user's choice, increment the count for the user's choice, and save the results to the data file. If the IP logging is turned on, the user's IP address is added to the log file. The results are displayed by calling the display() function.

The view() function just reads the data file and displays the results. Figure 10.2 shows the results page.

Figure 10.2
Viewing poll results.

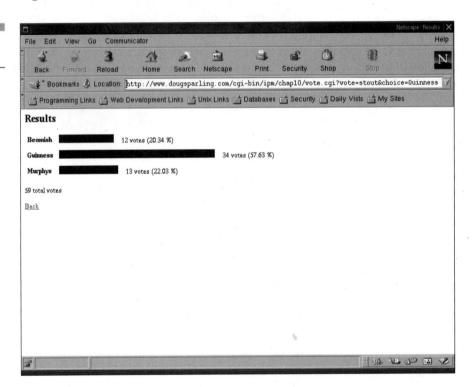

You might have noticed that, if there was an error opening a file, the screen is blank. In Chapter 9, we used the CGI::Carp module to print error messages back to the browser:

```
use CGI::Carp qw/fatalsToBrowser/;
```

This is a security risk to leave in production. If you want to give the user a friendly message when something goes wrong, you can add an error reporting function similar to:

```perl
sub print_error {
    my $error = shift;
    print h1('Error'),
          p($error),
          end_html;
    die $error;
}
```

Call this function by replacing the `die` statements with `print_error()`:

```perl
open(FILE, "$data_file") or
  print_error("Cannot open data file");
```

Be sure not to send too much information, such as filenames or path information, back to the user.

Guestbook

Another common script on many web sites is a guestbook. Guestbooks normally provide two functions: sign guestbook, which allows users to leave their name, email address, and comments; and view guestbook, which allows a user to view entries in the guestbook. Figure 10.3 shows the form used to sign the guestbook, and Figure 10.4 shows sample output when viewing the guestbook.

Here's the code for our guestbook application:

```perl
#!/usr/bin/perl -Tw
use strict;
use CGI qw/:standard escapeHTML/;
use Fcntl qw/:flock/;
$|++;

# Config
my $GUESTBOOK = '/home/doug/guestbook/guestbook.txt';
my $TITLE = 'IPM Guestbook'; # Title of guestbook
my $MAX_MSGS = 5;            # Maximum number of messages
my $MAX_NAME = 50;           # Maximum length of name field
my $MAX_EMAIL = 50;          # Maximum length of email field
my $MAX_COMMENTS = 300;      # Maximum length of comments field
# End Config

# Print header
```

Figure 10.3
Sign guestbook form.

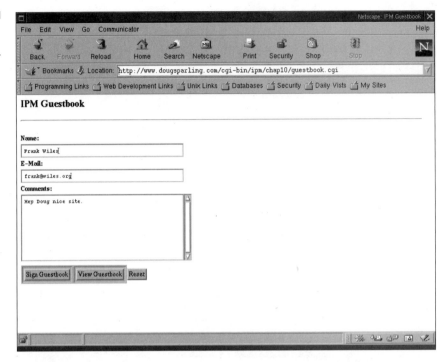

Figure 10.4
View guestbook.

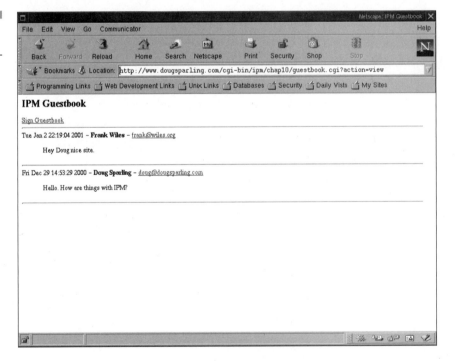

```perl
print header,
    start_html(-title=>$TITLE, -bgcolor=>'white'),
    h1($TITLE);

# Get action
my $action = param('action');

# Check action
if ($action =~ /^sign/i) {
    # Sign guestbook
    sign_guestbook();
} elsif ($action =~ /^view/i) {
    # View guestbook
    view_guestbook();
} else {
    print_form();
}

# End html
print end_html;

#######################################

sub print_form {
    print hr,
        start_form,
        '<STRONG>Name: </STRONG>',
        br,
        textfield(-name=>'name', -size=>50),
        br,
        '<STRONG>E-Mail: </STRONG>',
        br,
        textfield(-name=>'email', -size=>50),
        br,
        '<STRONG>Comments: </STRONG>',
        br,
        textarea(-name=>'comments', -rows=>10,
                -columns=>50, -wrap=>1),
        br,
        submit(-name=>'action', -value=>'Sign Guestbook'),
        submit(-name=>'action', -value=>'View Guestbook'),
        reset,
        end_form;

}

sub sign_guestbook {
    my $time = localtime;
    my $name = param('name');
    my $email = param('email');
    my $comments = param('comments');

    # Check that name was entered
    if ($name eq '' or $name =~ /^\s+$/) {
```

```perl
      print_error('You must enter a name');
  }

  # Check lengths of user input
  $name = substr($name, 0, $MAX_NAME);
  $email = substr($email, 0, $MAX_EMAIL);
  $comments = substr($comments, 0, $MAX_COMMENTS);

  # Remove leading/trailing white space
  $comments =~ s/^\s+//;
  $comments =~ s/\s+$//;

  # Escape HTML
  $name = escapeHTML($name);
  $email = escapeHTML($email);
  $comments = escapeHTML($comments);

  # Deal with line breaks
  $comments =~ s/(?:\015\012?|\012)/<BR>/g;

  open(FILE, ">>$GUESTBOOK") or
    die "Can't open $GUESTBOOK: $!\n";
  flock(FILE, LOCK_EX); # Exclusive lock for writing

  print FILE $time, ':::', $name, ':::',
             $email, ':::', $comments, "\n";

  flock(FILE, LOCK_UN); # Unlock the file
  close FILE;

  # Check number of messages
  max_msgs();

  my $script = url();
  print hr,
        'Thank you for signing my guestbook',
        p,
        a({-href=>"${script}?action=view"},'View Guestbook');

}

sub view_guestbook {
  my $script = url();

  print a({-href=>$script}, 'Sign Guestbook'),
        hr;

  # Check number of messages
  max_msgs();

  # Read message file
  open(FILE, "$GUESTBOOK") or
    die "Cannot open $GUESTBOOK: $!\n";
  flock(FILE, LOCK_SH); # Shared lock for reading
```

```perl
    my @messages = <FILE>;

    flock(FILE, LOCK_UN); # Unlock the file
    close FILE;

    @messages = reverse (@messages);
    foreach my $item (@messages) {
        my($time, $name, $email, $comments)
            = split(':::', $item);

        # Format fields
        my $f_name = "<STRONG>$name</STRONG>";
        my $f_email = "<A HREF=mailto:$email>$email</A>";

        # Output a record
        print "$time - $f_name - $f_email",
            p(blockquote($comments)),
            hr;
    }

}

sub max_msgs {
    # If more than MAX_MSGS messages, delete oldest

    # Read message file
    open(FILE, "$GUESTBOOK") or
        die "Cannot open $GUESTBOOK: $!\n";
    flock(FILE, LOCK_SH); # Shared lock for reading

    my @messages = <FILE>;

    flock(FILE, LOCK_UN); # Unlock the file
    close FILE;

    if(@messages > $MAX_MSGS) {
        open(FILE, ">$GUESTBOOK") or
            die "Cannot open $GUESTBOOK: $!\n";
        flock(FILE, LOCK_EX); # Exclusive lock for writing

        shift @messages while @messages > $MAX_MSGS;

        print FILE @messages;

        flock(FILE, LOCK_UN); # Unlock the file
        close FILE;
    }

}

sub print_error {
    my $error = shift;
    my $script = url();
```

```
print hr,
      h2('Error'),
      p($error),
      a({href=>$script}, 'Try Again'),
      end_html;
  die $error;

}
```

This script imports the escapeHTML() function from CGi.pm:

```
use CGI qw/:standard escapeHTML/;
```

The escapeHTML() function will replace special HTML characters with their HTML entities. We'll use this function later to prevent a user from entering HTML. For example, if a user types a line like this in the comments field:

```
<H1>Hello</H1>
```

the special characters < and > will be replaced with their HTML entities:

```
&lt;H1&gt;Hello&lt;/H1&gt;
```

If you want to allow the user to enter HTML in your guestbook, then comment out the lines containing the escapeHTML() function calls.

The configuration section allows you to set this script up for your system and gives you some options on running the guestbook. $GUESTBOOK should be set to the path to your data file; this must be the full path, including the name of the file. $TITLE sets the title to the page. $MAX_MSGS sets the number of messages saved in the data file and displayed when a user views the guestbook. $MAX_NAME, $MAX_EMAIL, and $MAX_COMMENTS set the maximum length of the name, email, and comments fields.

There are three possible actions for the guestbook CGI: print_form(), sign_guestbook(), and view_guestbook(). If no parameters are sent (the first time the script is called), then the print_form() function is called and the guestbook form is generated. From there, a user may choose to sign or view the guestbook.

sign_guestbook() makes some checks before saving the users' information to the data file.

First we check that a user has actually entered a name, making this a required field. If no name is entered, an error message is displayed, with a link back to the form. The following lines:

```
if ($name eq '' or $name =~ /^\s+$/) {
    print_error('You must enter a name');
}
```

call the error function:

```
sub print_error {
    my $error = shift;
    my $script = url();
    print hr,
          h2('Error'),
          p($error),
          a({href=>$script}, 'Try Again'),
          end_html;
    die $error;
}
```

This function could also be used in place of die, as with the voting script.

The lengths of the name, email, and comments fields are limited to the lengths set in the configuration file:

```
# Check inputs
$name = substr($name, 0, $MAX_NAME);
$email = substr($email, 0, $MAX_EMAIL);
$comments = substr($comments, 0, $MAX_COMMENTS);
```

All text after the limit will simply be truncated if the length of the field exceeds the limit. This will prevent a user from downloading the form locally and changing the size parameters of the fields.

Next we tidy up the comments field. First, we remove any leading or trailing white space:

```
# Remove leading/trailing white space
$comments =~ s/^\s+//;
$comments =~ s/\s+$//;
```

To prevent a user from using HTML (or preventing the HTML from being parsed by the browser), we use the escapeHTML() function that we imported with CGI.pm:

```
# Escape HTML
$name = escapeHTML($name);
$email = escapeHTML($email);
$comments = escapeHTML($comments);
```

Because the user is typing comments into a text area, we convert line breaks into <BR> tags to allow the HTML presentation to stay uncluttered:

```
# Deal with line breaks
$comments =~ s/(?:\015\012?|\012)/<BR>/g;
```

\015\012 is the Windows line break, \015 is the Mac line break, and \012 is the UNIX/Linux line break. All these line breaks are converted to <BR> tags.

The time, name, email, and comments are stored in a flat file separated by ':::'. The file is locked, written to (in the append mode), and then unlocked.

Next we call the max_msgs() function, which checks if the maximum number of messages has been exceeded; if so, it shifts off the oldest messages until the number is within the limit set by $MAX_MSGS.

```
sub max_msgs {
    # If more than MAX_MSGS messages, delete oldest

    # Read message file
    open(FILE, "$GUESTBOOK") or
      die "Cannot open $GUESTBOOK: $!\n";
    flock(FILE, LOCK_SH); # Shared lock for reading

    my @messages = <FILE>;

    flock(FILE, LOCK_UN); # Unlock the file
    close FILE;

    if(@messages > $MAX_MSGS) {
        open(FILE, ">$GUESTBOOK") or
          die "Cannot open $GUESTBOOK: $!\n";
        flock(FILE, LOCK_EX); # Exclusive lock for writing}

        shift @messages while @messages > $MAX_MSGS;

        print FILE @messages;

        flock(FILE, LOCK_UN); # Unlock the file
        close FILE;
    }

}
```

Last, we create a link to view the guestbook. We use the `url()` function from CGI.pm to get the URL of the script.

`view_guestbook()` reads the data file and checks whether the maximum number of messages has been exceeded (and deletes the oldest messages if it has). We then reverse the order of the messages so that the newest message is in the first element of the array. We process the array by using a `foreach` to loop through the array. We split each line and format the name and email fields. Finally, we display each guestbook entry.

Postcards

If your site has many images, allowing users to send postcards featuring these images might be a good way to promote your site. Our postcard script generates a form that allows a user to select an image for the postcard and up to five email addresses for sending the card. Figure 10.5 shows the main form.

Here's the code for the postcard CGI:

```perl
#!/usr/bin/perl -Tw
use strict;
use CGI qw/:standard escapeHTML/;
$|++;

# Config
# Title
my $TITLE = 'IPM Postcard';
# Directory containing postcard images
my $IMG_DIR = '/images';
# Directory containing postcard html files
my $PCARD_DIR = '/usr/local/apache/htdocs/postcard';
# URL to postcard directory
my $PCARD_URL = 'http://localhost/postcard';
# Main form text
my $TEXT = 'Send a postcard to a friend or family member!';
# End config

# Setup Environment for taint
$ENV{PATH} = '';

# Set hidden variables
my $hidden = '';
foreach my $name ( param() ) {
    next if $name eq 'action';
    my $value = param($name);
```

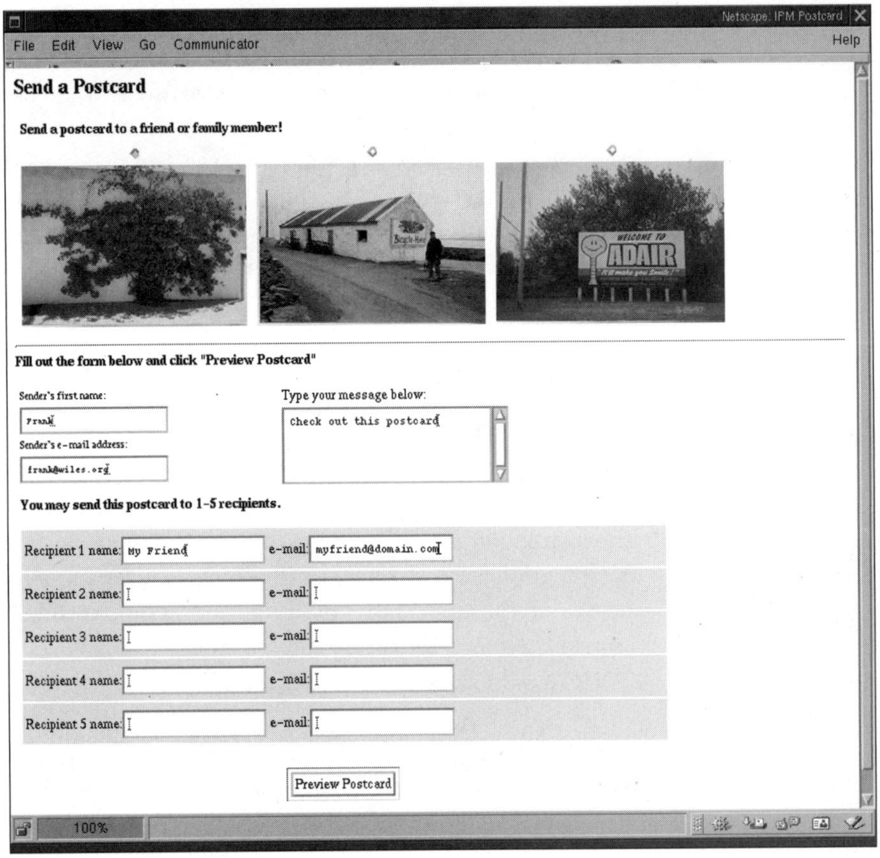

Figure 10.5
Postcard form.

Figure 10.5
Postcard form.

```
        # Escape HTML
        $value = escapeHTML($value);
        $hidden .= qq!<INPUT TYPE=HIDDEN NAME="$name" ! .
                   qq!VALUE="$value">\n!;
}

# Print header
print header,
      start_html(-bgcolor=>'white',
                 -title=>$TITLE);

my $action = param('action');

# Check action
if($action =~ /Preview/) {
    preview_card();
} elsif ($action =~ /Send/) {
    send_card();
} elsif ($action =~ /Redo/) {
```

```
        print_form();
} else {
        print_form();
}

# End html
print end_html;

#############################################

sub preview_card {
    # Print the Preview Postcard page

    # Get form vars
    my $graphic = param('graphic');
    my $display_message = param('message');

    # Full path to graphic
    $graphic = $IMG_DIR . '/' . $graphic;

    # Format message
    # Escape HTML
    $display_message = escapeHTML($display_message);
    # Deal with line breaks
    $display_message =~ s/(?:\015\012?|\012)/<BR>/g;

    print h1("Here's a preview of your postcard"),
          hr,
          img({-src=>$graphic}),
          p(b($display_message)),
          br,
          start_form,
          $hidden,
          submit(-name=>'action', -value=>'Send My Postcard'),
          submit(-name=>'action', -value=>'Redo My Postcard'),
          end_form;

}

sub send_card {
    # Get form vars
    my $graphic = param('graphic');
    my $display_message = param('message');
    my $from_name = param('sender_name');
    my $from_email = param('sender_email');

    # Full path to graphic
    $graphic = $IMG_DIR . '/' . $graphic;

    # Format message
    # Escape HTML
    $display_message = escapeHTML($display_message);
    # Deal with line breaks
    $display_message =~ s/(?:\015\012?|\012)/<BR>/g;
```

```perl
my $pcount = 0;      # Count number of recipients
my $people = '';     # Variable to hold recipients
my $filelist = '';   # URLs of postcards to print

# Save cards and send email to recipients
for (my $i=1;$i<=5;$i++) {
    my $recp_name = "name" . $i; # Name of textbox
    my $recp_email = "email" . $i;  # Name of textbox

    # Check that both recipient name
    # and email are filled out
    if ( param($recp_name) ne '' and
         param($recp_name) !~ /^\s+$/ and
         param($recp_email) ne '' and
         param($recp_email) !~ /^\s+$/) {

        # Get recipients name
        my $to_name = param($recp_name);

        # Get script URL
        my $script = url();

        my $greeting = "Hi <STRONG>$to_name</STRONG>, " .
                       "this postcard was sent to you " .
                       "by <STRONG>$from_name</STRONG>." .
                       "<P>";

        my $footer = 'Send a postcard: ' .
                     qq!<A HREF="$script">$script</A>!;

        # Save card
        my $time = time();
        my $file = $time . $i . '.html';
        my $filename = $PCARD_DIR . '/' . $file;
        my $pcard_url = $PCARD_URL . '/' . $file;

        open(FH, ">$filename") or
          die "Can't open $filename: $!\n";

        print FH start_html(-bgcolor=>'white',
                            -title=>$TITLE);
        print FH $greeting;
        print FH img({-src=>$graphic});
        print FH p(b($display_message));
        print FH hr;
        print FH $footer;
        print FH end_html;

        close FH;

        # Send Email to Recipient
        # Recipient email
        my $to_email = param($recp_email);
```

```perl
                # Remove any spaces
                $to_email =~ s/\s+//g;
                # Untaint data
                $to_email =~ /^([a-zA-Z0-9_\.\@\+\-]+)$/ or
                  die "Tainted data\n";
                $to_email = $1;

                # Message
                my $rcpt_message = "$from_name ($from_email) " .
                                   "has sent you an electronic " .
                                   "postcard.\n";
                $rcpt_message .= "The postcard may be found at: ";
                $rcpt_message .= "$pcard_url\n\n";
                $rcpt_message .= "This card will expire in " .
                                 "14 days\n";

                # Subject
                my $subject = 'Postcard';

                # Send mail
                mail_card($to_email, $from_email,
                          $subject, $rcpt_message);

                $pcount++;
                $people .= "$to_name ($to_email)<BR>\n";
                $filelist .= "<A HREF=\"$pcard_url\">" .
                             "$pcard_url</A><BR>";
        }
}

if( $pcount == 0 ) {
    print "No messages sent: Check recipients' names " .
          "and email addresses<BR>\n";
} elsif( $pcount == 1 ) {
    print "Thanks for sending your e-postcard to " .
          "<STRONG>$people</STRONG>";
    print "<BR><P>\n";
    print "The recipient of your e-postcard has been " .
          "e-mailed the information needed to view " .
          "the page online.<P>\n";
    print "You may view your e-postcard at the " .
          "following URL:<P>\n";
    print "$filelist<BR>\n";
} else {
    print "Thanks for sending your e-postcards to:" .
          "<P><STRONG>$people</STRONG>";
    print "<BR><P>\n";
    print "The recipient of your e-postcard has been " .
          "e-mailed the information needed to view " .
          "the page online.<P>\n";
    print "You may view your e-postcards at the " .
          "following URLs:<P>\n";
    print "$filelist<BR>\n";
}
```

```
}

sub mail_card {
    my $to_email = shift;
    my $from_email = shift;
    my $subject = shift;
    my $message = shift;

    open(SENDMAIL, "| /usr/lib/sendmail -oi -t $to_email");
    print SENDMAIL "From: $from_email\n";
    print SENDMAIL "To: $to_email\n";
    print SENDMAIL"Subject: $subject\n\n";
    print SENDMAIL $message;
    print SENDMAIL "\n\n.\n\n";
    close SENDMAIL;

}

sub print_form {
    print h1('Send a Postcard'),
        start_form;

    # Use here doc to print tables
print <<EOF;

<TABLE CELLPADDING=0 CELLSPACING=5>
<TR>
<TD COLSPAN=3>
<STRONG>$TEXT</STRONG>
</TD>
</TR>

<TR>
<TD ALIGN=CENTER>
<INPUT TYPE="RADIO" NAME="graphic" VALUE="image1.jpg"><BR>
<A HREF="$IMG_DIR/image1.jpg">
<IMG SRC="$IMG_DIR/s_image1.jpg" BORDER=0 ALT="image1"></A>
</TD>

<TD ALIGN=CENTER>
<INPUT TYPE="RADIO" NAME="graphic" VALUE="image2.jpg"><BR>
<A HREF="$IMG_DIR/image2.jpg">
<IMG SRC="$IMG_DIR/s_image2.jpg" BORDER=0 ALT="image2"></A>
</TD>

<TD ALIGN=CENTER>
<INPUT TYPE="RADIO" NAME="graphic" VALUE="image3.jpg"><BR>
<A HREF="$IMG_DIR/image3.jpg">
<IMG SRC="$IMG_DIR/s_image3.jpg" BORDER=0 ALT="image3"></A>
</TD>
</TR>

</TABLE>
```

```
<HR>

<STRONG>Fill out the form below and click
"Preview Postcard"</STRONG>

<P>

<TABLE CELLPADDING=2 CELLSPACING=0>

<TR>
<TD VALIGN="TOP">
<FONT SIZE=2>Sender's first name:<BR>
<INPUT TYPE="TEXT" NAME="sender_name" SIZE=25>
<BR>
Sender's e-mail address:<BR>
<INPUT TYPE="TEXT" NAME="sender_email" SIZE=25>
<BR>
<P>
</TD>

<TD VALIGN="TOP">
Type your message below:
<BR>
<TEXTAREA NAME="message" ROWS=5 COLS=30 WRAP="SOFT"></TEXTAREA>
</FONT>
</TD>
</TR>

<TR>
<TD COLSPAN=2>
<P>
<STRONG>You may send this postcard to 1-5 recipients.</STRONG>
<P>
<TABLE WIDTH=600 CELLPADDING=2 CELLSPACING=0>

<TR NOBR>
<TD BGCOLOR="#EEEECC">
Recipient 1 name:<INPUT TYPE="TEXT" NAME="name1" SIZE=20>
e-mail:<INPUT TYPE="TEXT" NAME="email1" SIZE=20>
<BR>
</TD>
</TR>

<TR NOBR>
<TD BGCOLOR="#EEEECC">
Recipient 2 name:<INPUT TYPE="TEXT" NAME="name2" SIZE=20>
e-mail:<INPUT TYPE="TEXT" NAME="email2" SIZE=20>
<BR>
</TD>
</TR>
<TR NOBR>
<TD BGCOLOR="#EEEECC">
Recipient 3 name:<INPUT TYPE="TEXT" NAME="name3" SIZE=20>
```

```
e-mail:<INPUT TYPE="TEXT" NAME="email3" SIZE=20>
<BR>
</TD>
</TR>

<TR NOBR>
<TD BGCOLOR="#EEEECC">
Recipient 4 name:<INPUT TYPE="TEXT" NAME="name4" SIZE=20>
e-mail:<INPUT TYPE="TEXT" NAME="email4" SIZE=20>
<BR>
</TD>
</TR>

<TR NOBR>
<TD BGCOLOR="#EEEECC">
Recipient 5 name:<INPUT TYPE="TEXT" NAME="name5" SIZE=20>
e-mail:<INPUT TYPE="TEXT" NAME="email5" SIZE=20>
<BR>
</TD>
</TR>

</TABLE>

<P>

<CENTER>
<INPUT TYPE="SUBMIT" NAME="action" VALUE="Preview Postcard">
</CENTER>

</TD>
</TR>
</TABLE>

</FONT>
</FORM>
EOF

}
```

There are several variables in the configuration section. $TITLE sets the title of the HTML page. $IMG_DIR must be set to the path to where the postcard images are kept; this can be a relative or full path. $PCARD_DIR is the directory where the HTML files are kept; this can also be a relative or full path. The CGI script must be able to write to this directory. $PCARD_URL is the URL to the directory containing the HTML postcard files. $TEXT sets the text on the main postcard form.

We must create a "clean" environment because we are making a system call to sendmail later in the script.

```
# Setup Environment for taint
$ENV{PATH} = '';
```

We then print out the hidden variables that will go on each page. The names, email addresses, and message must be passed from the initial form to the preview page.

There are three main actions that the script can take: `preview_card()`, `send_card()`, or `print_form()`. The `print_form()` function is called the first time the script is run or when the user clicks the Redo button on the preview page. `print_form()` uses a here doc to print the HTML form because in this case, it is much easier than using the HTML shortcuts supplied by CGI.pm. The `preview_card()` function allows the user to preview the postcard before sending it. Figure 10.6 shows the preview page.

Figure 10.6
Postcard preview.

Like the guestbook script, we escape any HTML and convert line breaks in the message.

```
# Prevent HTML
$display_message = escapeHTML($display_message);
```

```
# Deal with line breaks
$display_message =~ s/(?:\015\012?|\012)/<BR>/g;
```

The `send_card()` function also escapes HTML and converts line breaks in the message. We then loop through the names and email addresses passed from the form. For each name and email combination that has been filled out, the script will create a postcard file and send out an email to the recipient. We use the epoch seconds generated by the Perl `time()` function as our postcard filename. We also add the loop number to create a unique postcard for each recipient. Once the file has been saved, an email is generated. We first check the email address and remove any spaces. Then we must do a taint check on the email address because it is used with a system call to `sendmail`:

```
# Remove any spaces
$to_email =~ s/\s+//g;
# Untaint data
$to_email =~ /^([a-zA-Z0-9_\.\@\+\-]+)$/ or die "Tainted data\n";
$to_email = $1;
```

We're checking only for valid characters, not valid email syntax. It's very difficult to check for a valid email address using a regex (see "How do I check a valid email address" in perlfaq9), and we're using the regex mainly to untaint the email address, so you might use a less restrictive regular expression such as:

```
$to_email =~ /(.*)/;
```

We then call the `mail_card()` function, which sends the email.

We keep track of how many cards were sent and the names and URLs of the cards. We use this information when printing the confirmation page to the user, as shown in Figure 10.7.

```
$pcount++;
$people .= "$to_name ($to_email)<BR>\n";
$filelist .= "<A HREF=\"$pcard_url\">" .
             "$pcard_url</A><BR>";
```

When recipients click the postcard links in their emails, they can view their postcards, as shown in Figure 10.8.

We should empty the postcard directory everyday so that it doesn't become full. Run a cron job once a day to delete files older than 14 days. You can do this by checking the file modification time with the Perl `stat()` function. You could also use the epoch seconds from the file

Figure 10.7
Confirmation page.

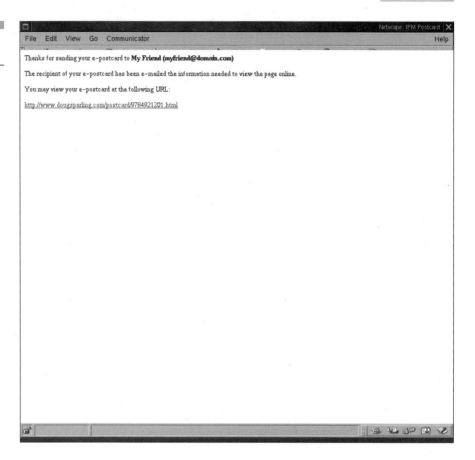

name (or you may want to put a human readable date in the file name).
The following two scripts use the stat() function.

The first script calculates the number of seconds in 14 days and uses
that number to determine whether the file should be deleted.

```perl
#!/usr/bin/perl -w
use strict;

# Directory containing HTML postcards
my $pcard_dir = '/usr/local/apache/htdocs/postcard/';

# How many days old should card be?
my $kill = 14 * 86400;

opendir(PCARD,"$pcard_dir") or die "Cannot open $pcard_dir: $!\n";
while(my $filename = readdir(PCARD)) {
    next if $filename =~ /^\.\.?/;
    my $full_path = $pcard_dir . $filename;
    # Get last modified time from file
```

Figure 10.8
Postcard.

```
my($mtime) = (stat($full_path))[9];
# Compute age of file
my $diff = time - $mtime;
# If file >+ kill time, delete file
if( $diff > $kill ) {
    unlink "$full_path";
}
}
close PCARD;
```

You could also use the `Date::Calc` module and find the difference in days between the files. However, this method is somewhat slower than that of the previous example.

```
#!/usr/bin/perl -w
use strict;
use Date::Calc qw/Delta_Days/;
```

```perl
# Directory containing HTML postcards
my $pcard_dir = '/usr/local/apache/htdocs/postcard/';

# Number of days to keep cards
my $card_days = 14;

# Get current date
my($cur_day, $cur_month, $cur_year) = (localtime)[3..5];
$cur_month += 1;
$cur_year += 1900;

opendir(PCARD,"$pcard_dir") or
  die "Cannot open $pcard_dir: $!\n";
while(my $filename = readdir(PCARD)) {
    next if $filename =~ /^\.\.?/;
    my $full_path = $pcard_dir . $filename;
    # Get last modified time from file
    my($mtime) = (stat($full_path))[9];
    my($file_day, $file_month,
        $file_year) = (localtime($mtime))[3..5];
    $file_month += 1;
    $file_year += 1900;

    # Compute difference of two dates (in days)
    my $diff = Delta_Days($cur_year, $cur_month, $cur_day,
                          $file_year, $file_month, $file_day);

    # If $diff > $card_days, delete file
    if( $diff > $card_days ) {
        unlink "$full_path";
    }
}
close PCARD;
```

Chat

You've probably used a chat client or instant messaging program before. This script will allow you to have a simple web-based chat application on your web site. Figure 10.9 shows the login screen. Figure 10.10 shows the chat client in action.

Here's the code:

```perl
#!/usr/bin/perl -Tw
use strict;
use CGI qw/:standard :netscape escapeHTML/;
use Fcntl qw/:flock/;
$|++;

# Config
my $TITLE = 'IPM CHAT';
```

Figure 10.9
Chat login.

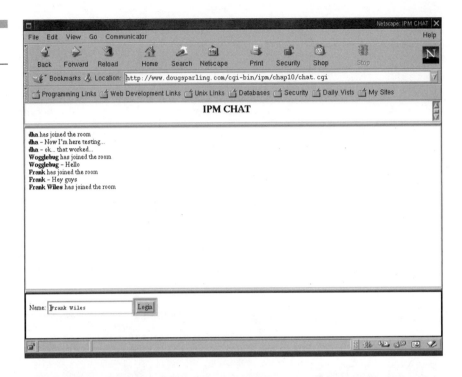

Figure 10.9
Chat login.

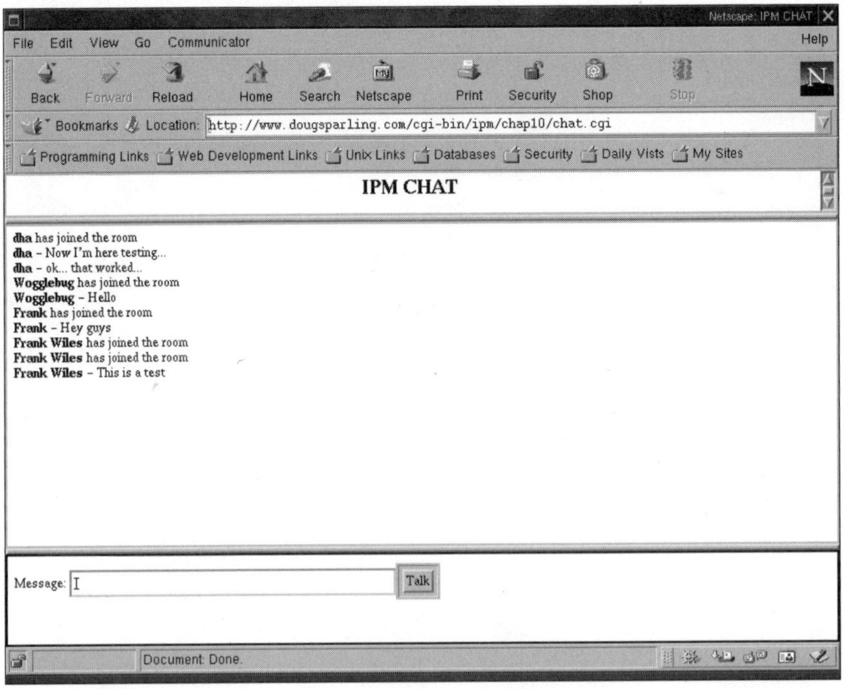

Figure 10.10
Web-based chat.

```perl
my $MSG_FILE = '/home/doug/chat/chat.txt';
my $REFRESH = 15;   # Refresh rate in seconds
my $MAX_NAME_LENGTH = 25; # Maximum length for name
my $MAX_MSG_LENGTH = 100; # Maximum length for message
my $MAX_MSGS = 10;  # Maximum number of messages to display
# End Config

my $frame_name = path_info();
$frame_name =~ s!^/!!;

if (!$frame_name) {
    print_frameset();
    exit 0;
}

print_top() if $frame_name eq 'top';
print_middle() if $frame_name eq 'middle';
print_bottom() if $frame_name eq 'bottom';

###########################################

sub print_frameset {
    print header;
    my $script = url();
    print title($TITLE),
          frameset({-rows=>'10%,70%,20%'},
            frame({-name=>'top',-src=>"$script/top"}),
            frame({-name=>'middle',-src=>"$script/middle"}),
            frame({-name=>'bottom',-src=>"$script/bottom"})
          );
    exit 0;

}

sub print_top {
    print header,
          start_html(-bgcolor=>'white'),
          center(h1($TITLE)),
          end_html;

}

sub print_middle {
    print header(-refresh=>$REFRESH),
          start_html(-bgcolor=>'white');

    # Read the data file and print
    open(FILE, "$MSG_FILE") or
      die "Cannot open $MSG_FILE: $!\n";
    flock(FILE, LOCK_SH); # Shared lock for reading

    my @data = (<FILE>);
```

```perl
        flock(FILE, LOCK_UN); # Unlock the file
        close FILE;

        # If more than MAX_MSGS messages, delete oldest
        if(@data > $MAX_MSGS) {
            open(FILE, ">$MSG_FILE") or
              die "Cannot open $MSG_FILE: $!\n";
            shift @data while @data > $MAX_MSGS;
            print FILE @data;
            close FILE;
        }

        # Print the messages
        for (@data) {
            print;
        }

        print end_html;

    }

sub print_bottom {
    print header,
          start_html(-bgcolor=>'white');
    my $script = url();

    if ( !param() ) {
        # Have user log in first time
        print start_form(-action=>"$script/bottom",
                        -target=>'bottom'),
            hidden(-name=>'first', -value=>'first'),
            'Name: ',
            textfield(-name=>'name', -size=>25),
            submit(-name=>'Login'),
            end_form;
    } else {
        # Once user logged in, allow them to post messages
        my $name = param('name');
        $name = substr($name, 0, $MAX_NAME_LENGTH);

        print start_form(-action=>"$script/bottom",
                        -target=>'bottom'),
            hidden(-name=>'name', value=>$name),
            'Message: ',
            textfield(-name=>'text', -size=>50,
                    -override=>1),
            submit(-name=>'Talk'),
            end_form;

        # If text sent, save to file
        # If user just logged in, save announcement to file
        if ( param('text') or param('first') ) {
```

```perl
open(FILE, ">>$MSG_FILE") or
    die "Cannot open $MSG_FILE: $!\n";
flock(FILE, LOCK_EX); # Exclusive lock for writing

if ( param('first') ) {
    print FILE "<STRONG>$name</STRONG> " .
                  "has joined the room<BR>\n";
} else {
    my $text = param('text');

    # Limit length of message
    $text = substr($text, 0, $MAX_MSG_LENGTH);

    # Escape HTML
    $text = escapeHTML($text);

    print FILE "<STRONG>$name</STRONG>" .
                  " - $text<BR>\n";
}

flock(FILE, LOCK_UN); # Unlock the file
close FILE;
    }
  }

  print end_html;

}
```

We import the `netscape` function set from `CGI.pm` because this script uses a frame set:

```perl
use CGI qw/:standard :netscape escapeHTML/;
```

Next we configure our script. `$TITLE` sets the title of our HTML page. `$MSG_FILE` is the location of our data file. `$REFRESH` is the refresh rate of our chat frame in seconds. `$MAX_NAME_LENGTH` sets maximum length of the name field. `$MAX_MSG_LENGTH` sets the maximum length of the message field. `$MAX_MSGS` sets the number of messages displayed. You may want to play around with the `$MAX_MSG_LENGTH` and `$MAX_MSGS` settings and find a combination that doesn't force the user to scroll too often, and leaves a reasonable amount of messages displayed to keep track of the conversation.

The chat CGI script uses a frame set consisting of three windows and three corresponding functions: `print_top()`, `print_middle()`, and `print_bottom()`. The top frame, generated by `print_top()`, displays the title of the chat room that is set in the `config` section of the script. The middle frame, generated by `print_middle`, displays the chat messages.

A meta-refresh automatically updates the frame with new messages at the rate set by the $REFRESH variable. If you're using an ISP, you might not want to set this rate too fast, because it can fill up the logs pretty quickly.

The number of messages is held to the amount set in the $MAX_MSGS variable:

```
# If more than MAX_MSGS messages, delete oldest
if(@data > $MAX_MSGS) {
    open(FILE, ">$MSG_FILE") or
      die "Cannot open $MSG_FILE: $!\n";
    shift @data while @data > $MAX_MSGS;
    print FILE @data;
    close FILE;
}
```

The bottom frame, generated by print_bottom(), has two main functions. The first time a user calls the script, a login box is displayed. The user must enter a username; once the user logs in, he or she will be identified by this name. Once the user logs in, a message box is displayed, allowing the user to chat. Like the previous scripts, the message is checked for length and HTML:

```
# Limit length of message
$text = substr($text, 0, $MAX_MSG_LENGTH);

# Escape HTML
$text = escapeHTML($text);
```

Once the user clicks the Talk button, the message will be saved to the data file and displayed on the next refresh to the middle screen.

Summary

This chapter has presented some of the classic CGI scripts that you may have seen on many web sites. These are simple scripts that should run right out of the box, but you probably will want to modify them to suit your own needs. This gives your scripts a personalized touch and gives you the opportunity to learn more about CGI programming with Perl.

CGI and
Databases

Introduction

▬ ▬ ▬ ▬ ▬ ▬ ▬ ▬ ▬ ▬ ▬ ▬ ▬ ▬ ▬ ▬ ▬ ▬ ▬

```
DBI: /CPAN/DBI-1.14.tar.gz
DBD::Pg: /CPAN/DBD-Pg-0.95.tar.gz
```

In Chapter 10, we built a few simple applications using CGI.pm. All those scripts saved data to flat-file databases that were simply ASCII text files that contained one record per line and a delimiter to separate the fields. Although a flat-file database may serve simple applications, more complex applications need a more robust system for storing and querying data. In this chapter, we will use the PostgreSQL relational database to store and query the data used in the applications.

Feedback Form

We will start with a simple form used to gather feedback from a user. This script will save the user's name, email address, comments, and the time the form was submitted into a table in the database.

First, we'll open a database session and build the table. We are assuming that you have already created a database called 'ipm'.

```
ipm=> CREATE TABLE feedback (
ipm->             id INTEGER,
ipm->             submit_date TIMESTAMP,
ipm->             name VARCHAR(50),
ipm->             email VARCHAR(50),
ipm->             comments TEXT
ipm-> );
CREATE
ipm=>
```

The following lines create a sequence that we'll use to auto-increment the ID field.

```
ipm=> CREATE SEQUENCE feedback_id_seq;
CREATE
ipm=>
```

Next, we need to change the table's permission so the web server can access the table.

```
ipm=> GRANT ALL ON feedback TO nobody;
CHANGE
ipm=> GRANT ALL ON feedback_id_seq TO nobody;
CHANGE
ipm=>
```

The first time the script is called, the input form is displayed as shown in Figure 11.1. After the user submits the form, a thank-you page is displayed, as shown in Figure 11.2.

Figure 11.1
Feedback form.

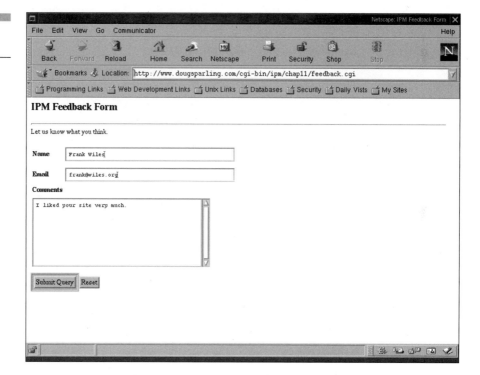

Here's the code for the feedback form:

```perl
#!/usr/bin/perl -w
use strict;
use CGI qw/:standard/;
use DBI;
$|++;

# Config - Limit length of comments
```

Figure 11.2
Thank-you page.

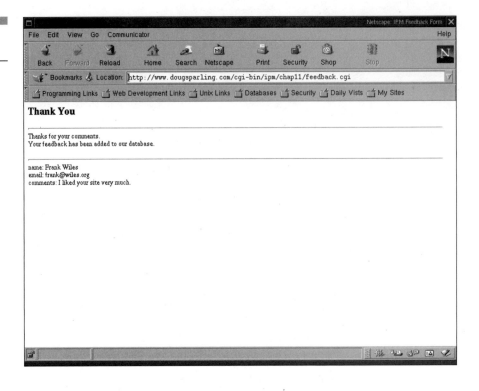

```
my $MAX_COMMENTS_LENGTH = 300;

print header,
      start_html(-title=>'IPM Feedback Form',
                  -bgcolor=>'white');

if( !param() ) {
    print_form();
} else {
    print_thanks();
}

print end_html;

#########################################

sub print_form {
    print h1('IPM Feedback Form'),
          hr,
          'Let us know what you think.';

    print start_form,
          table({-border=>0},
              Tr(td([b('Name'),textfield(-name=>'name',
                                          -size=>50)])),
```

```
                            Tr(td([b('Email'),textfield(-name=>'email',
                                                      -size=>50)])),
                            Tr(td([b('Comments')])),
                            Tr(td{-colspan=>2},
                                ([textarea(-name=>'comments',
                                           -rows=>10,
                                           -columns=>50,
                                           -wrap=>'physical')]))
                    ),
                    submit,
                    reset,
                    end_form;

}

sub print_thanks {
    # Connect to database
    my $dbh = DBI->connect('dbi:Pg:dbname=ipm', 'nobody', '')
      or die "Cannot connect to database: $!\n";

    # Get current date/time
    my $time = localtime();

    # Get form variables
    my $name = param('name');
    my $email = param('email');
    my $comments = param('comments');

    # Prepare comments for insertion
    $comments =~ s/\\/\\\\/g;
    $comments =~ s/'/''/g;

    # Limit length of comments field
    $comments = substr($comments, 0, $MAX_COMMENTS_LENGTH);

    $dbh->do("INSERT INTO feedback VALUES (
        NEXTVAL('feedback_id_seq'),
        '$time',
        '$name',
        '$email',
        '$comments')");

    $dbh->disconnect;

    # Print output to user
    print h1('Thank You'),
          hr,
          'Thanks for your comments.',
          br,
          'Your feedback has been added to our database.',
          p,
          hr;

    # Print all parameters
```

```
    foreach my $name ( param() ) {
        my $value = param($name);
        print "$name: $value<BR>\n";
    }

}
```

The beginning of this script should look familiar because it is very similar to the one in Chapter 10:

```
#!/usr/bin/perl -w
use strict;
use CGI qw/:standard/;
use DBI;
$|++;
```

We use the following line to load the DBI module to interface with the database:

```
use DBI;
```

When the script is first called (with no parameters), the form is displayed. Once the form is submitted, a thank-you page is displayed:

```
if( !param() ) {
    print_form();
} else {
    print_thanks();
}
```

We use CGI.pm's HTML shortcuts to build a simple table to align the form elements:

```
print start_form,
    table({-border=>0},
        Tr(td([b('Name'),textfield(-name=>'name',
                                    -size=>50)])),
        Tr(td([b('Email'),textfield(-name=>'email',
                                    -size=>50)])),
        Tr(td([b('Comments')])),
        Tr(td{-colspan=>2},
            ([textarea(-name=>'comments',
                        -rows=>10,
                        -columns=>50,
                        -wrap=>'physical')]))
    ),
    submit,
    reset,
    end_form;
```

We connect to the database in the `print_thank()` you **subroutine:**

```
# Connect to database
my $dbh = DBI->connect('dbi:Pg:dbname=ipm', 'nobody', '')  or
  die "Cannot connect to database: $!\n";
```

```
Next, we get the current time:
# Get current date/time
my $time = localtime();
```

```
We get the form parameters and place them in variables:
# Get form variables
my $name = param('name');
my $email = param('email');
my $comments = param('comments');
```

The user's comments might contain characters that can cause errors when the characters are inserted into the database, so we use the following code to prepare the comments before doing the INSERT:

```
# Prepare comments for insertion
$comments =~ s/\\/\\\\/g;
$comments =~ s/'/''/g;
```

To keep a user from manipulating the form and exceeding the limit for the comments text area, we use the following line:

```
# Limit length of comments field
$comments = substr($comments, 0, $MAX_COMMENTS_LENGTH);
```

This will prevent any errors when trying to put too much text into the comments field in the table.

Now we're ready to insert the user's data into the table:

```
$dbh->do("INSERT INTO feedback VALUES (
    NEXTVAL('feedback_id_seq'),
    '$time',
    '$name',
    '$email',
    '$comments')");
```

Finally, we print the user's input back on the thank-you page:

```
# Print all parameters
foreach my $name ( param() ) {
    my $value = param($name);
    print "$name: $value<BR>\n";
}
```

This script can be modified and used to create all types of web-based forms. In fact, we'll do just that and build another simple web-based form for submitting resumes.

Resume Submit Form

This script is a variation of the feedback form. As before, we'll take some input from a user and store it in a table. This time we'll store the user's name, phone number, email address, resume, and the time the form was submitted in a table.

First, we need to create our table:

```
ipm=> CREATE TABLE resume (
ipm->                id INTEGER,
ipm->                submit_date TIMESTAMP,
ipm->                name VARCHAR(50),
ipm->                phone VARCHAR(50),
ipm->                email VARCHAR(50),
ipm->                address VARCHAR(100),
ipm->                resume TEXT
ipm-> );
CREATE
ipm=>
```

Create a sequence so we can easily auto-increment the id:

```
ipm=> CREATE SEQUENCE resume_id_seq;
CREATE
ipm=>
```

and then change the table's permission so it can be accessed by the web user.

```
ipm=> GRANT ALL ON resume TO nobody;
CHANGE
ipm=> GRANT ALL ON resume_id_seq TO nobody;
CHANGE
ipm=>
```

Like the previous script, the form is displayed the first time the script is called, as shown in Figure 11.3. After the form is submitted, a thank-you page is displayed to the user, as shown in Figure 11.4.

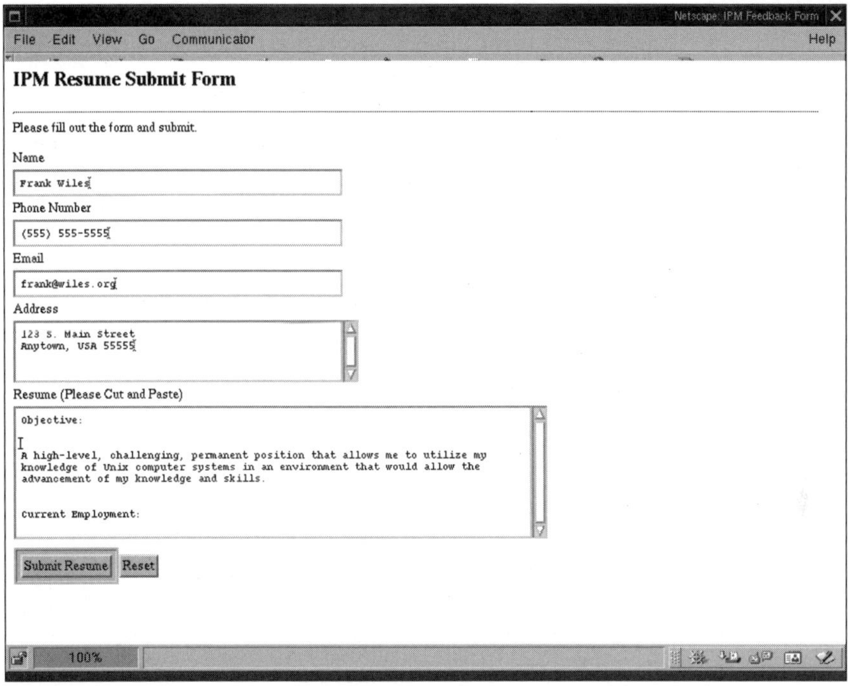

Figure 11.3
Resume submit form.

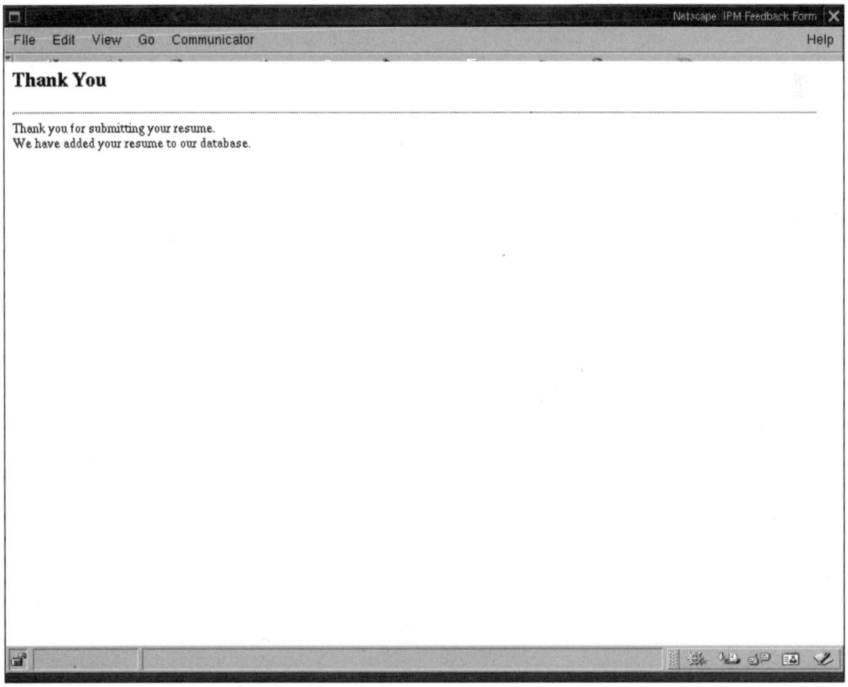

Figure 11.4
Thank-you page.

Here's the code for the resume submit script:

```perl
#!/usr/bin/perl -w
use strict;
use CGI qw/:standard/;
use DBI;
$|++;

# Config - Limit length of comments
my $MAX_RESUME_LENGTH = 500;

print header,
      start_html(-title=>'IPM Feedback Form',
                 -bgcolor=>'white');

if( !param() ) {
    print_form();
} else {
    print_thanks();
}

print end_html;

##########################################

sub print_form {
    print h1('IPM Resume Submit Form'),
          hr,
          'Please fill out the form and submit.';

    print start_form,
          'Name',
          br,
          textfield(-name=>'name',-size=>50),
          br,
          'Phone Number',
          br,
          textfield(-name=>'phone',-size=>50),
          br,
          'Email',
          br,
          textfield(-name=>'email',-size=>50),
          br,
          'Address',
          br,
          textarea(-name=>'address',
                   -rows=>4,
                   -columns=>50,
                   -wrap=>'physical'),
          br,
          'Resume (Please Cut and Paste)',
          br,
```

```perl
                textarea(-name=>'resume',
                        -rows=>10,
                        -columns=>80,
                        -wrap=>'physical'),
            br,
            submit(-name=>'Submit Resume'),
            reset,
            end_form;

    }

sub print_thanks {
    # Connect to database
    my $dbh = DBI->connect('dbi:Pg:dbname=ipm', 'nobody', '')
        or die "Cannot connect to database: $!\n";

    # Get current date/time
    my $time = localtime();

    # Get form variables
    my $name = param('name');
    my $phone = param('phone');
    my $email = param('email');
    my $address = param('address');
    my $resume = param('resume');

    # Prepare resume for insertion
    $resume =~ s/\\/\\\\/g;
    $resume =~ s/'/''/g;

    # Limit length of comments field
    $resume = substr($resume, 0, $MAX_RESUME_LENGTH);

    $dbh->do("INSERT INTO resume VALUES (
        NEXTVAL('resume_id_seq'),
        '$time',
        '$name',
        '$phone',
        '$email',
        '$address',
        '$resume')");

    $dbh->disconnect;

    # Print output to user
    print h1('Thank You'),
          hr,
          'Thank you for submitting your resume.',
          br,
          'We have added your resume to our database.';

    }
```

There's not much new in this script; we've simply modified the feed-back script from the previous section. The form itself is a bit different because we're getting different input from the user.

The `print_thanks()` function is called when the user submits the form. Like the feedback script, we make a connection to the database and get the current time and form variables. We then check the length of the resume field and check for quotes before inserting the user's infor-mation into the database. We insert the information like this:

```
$dbh->do("INSERT INTO resume VALUES (
    NEXTVAL('resume_id_seq'),
    '$time',
    '$name',
    '$phone',
    '$email',
    '$address',
    '$resume')");
```

Finally, we print a thank-you page letting the user know that we have accepted their information:

```
# Print output to user
print h1('Thank You'),
    hr,
    'Thank you for submitting your resume.',
    br,
    'We have added your resume to our database.';
```

Job Board

Now that we've built a resume submit form, it makes sense to build a job board. The job board script will allow a user to search for a job by location, category, and/or keywords. The initial search form is show in Figure 11.5. The results of the search are displayed in Figure 11.6. Each job displayed has a link that will take the user to a page that provides more details about the job. Figure 11.7 shows a job detail page. Each job detail page has a link that allows the user to submit a resume for that particular job. The resume page, as shown in Figure 11.8, is very similar to the resume submit page we built in the previous section.

Figure 11.5
Job search form.

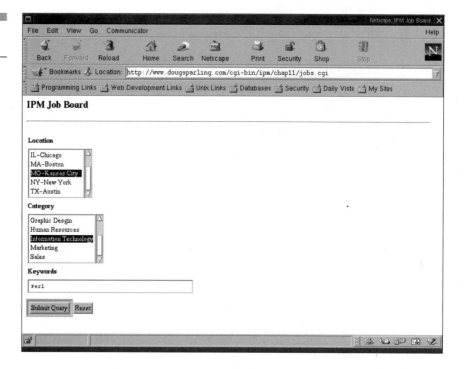

Figure 11.5
Job search form.

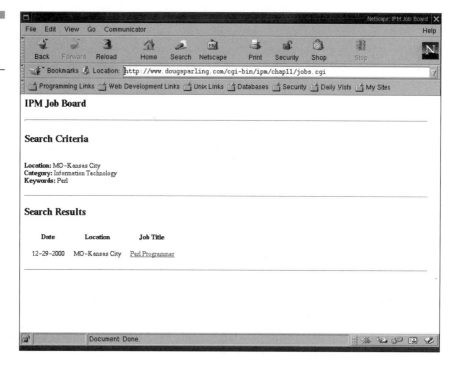

Figure 11.6
Job search results
page.

Figure 11.7
Job detail page.

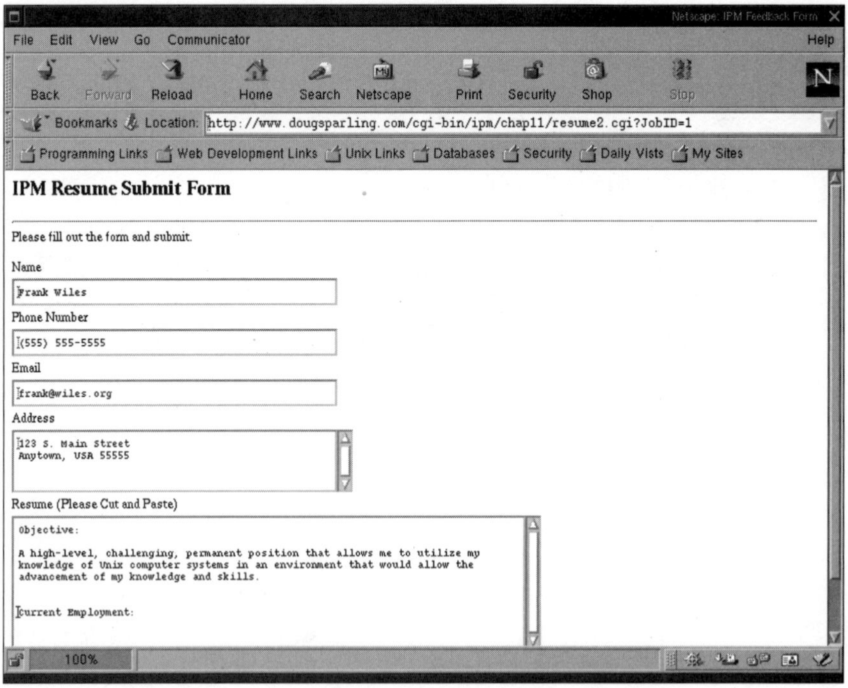

Figure 11.8
Resume submit form.

This job board script uses three tables: jobs, locations, and categories. The jobs table is where we store information about each job.

```
ipm=> CREATE TABLE jobs (
ipm->              id INTEGER,
ipm->              title VARCHAR(50),
ipm->              category INTEGER,
ipm->              date DATE,
ipm->              location INTEGER,
ipm->              description TEXT,
ipm->              salary VARCHAR(50),
ipm->              keywords VARCHAR(50)
ipm-> );
CREATE
ipm=>
```

This table contains two foreign keys, location and category, which join the jobs table with the locations and categories tables.

Each record in the locations table contains a numeric key and a corresponding location string.

```
ipm=> CREATE TABLE locations (
ipm->              id INTEGER,
ipm->              location VARCHAR(50)
ipm-> );
CREATE
ipm=>
```

The categories table contains a numeric key and a corresponding category string.

```
ipm=> CREATE TABLE categories (
ipm->              id INTEGER,
ipm->              category VARCHAR(50)
ipm-> );
CREATE
ipm=>
```

Before we put data into our tables, we must create the sequences and change the tables' permissions so that the web user can access them.

```
ipm=> CREATE SEQUENCE jobs_id_seq;
CREATE
ipm=> GRANT ALL ON jobs TO nobody;
CHANGE
ipm=> GRANT ALL ON jobs_id_seq TO nobody;
CHANGE
ipm=>
```

```
ipm=> CREATE SEQUENCE locations_id_seq;
CREATE
ipm=> GRANT ALL ON locations TO nobody;
CHANGE
ipm=> GRANT ALL ON locations_id_seq TO nobody;
CHANGE
ipm=>

ipm=> CREATE SEQUENCE categories_id_seq;
CREATE
ipm=> GRANT ALL ON categories TO nobody;
CHANGE
ipm=> GRANT ALL ON categories_id_seq TO nobody;
CHANGE
ipm=>
```

Now let's put some data in our tables. First, we'll enter a job in the jobs table:

```
ipm=> INSERT INTO jobs
ipm-> VALUES (
ipm->         NEXTVAL('jobs_id_seq'),
ipm->         'Perl Programmer'
ipm->         6,
ipm->         '12/9/2000',
ipm->         5,
ipm->         'Create web-based databases using Perl.',
ipm->         '50,000',
ipm->         'Perl,Unix'
ipm-> );
INSERT 19330 1
ipm=>
```

NOTE

The keywords are separated by commas.

Next, we enter the location information in the locations table:

```
ipm=> INSERT INTO locations
ipm-> VALUES (
ipm->         NEXTVAL('locations_id_seq'),
ipm->         '----- Any -----'
ipm-> );
INSERT 19331 1
ipm=> INSERT INTO locations
ipm-> VALUES (
ipm->         NEXTVAL('locations_id_seq'),
```

```
ipm->             'CA-San Francisco'
ipm-> );
INSERT 19332 1
ipm=> INSERT INTO locations
ipm-> VALUES (
ipm->             NEXTVAL('locations_id_seq'),
ipm->             'IL-Chicago'
ipm-> );
INSERT 19333 1
ipm=> INSERT INTO locations
ipm-> VALUES (
ipm->             NEXTVAL('locations_id_seq'),
ipm->             'MA-Boston'
ipm-> );
INSERT 19334 1
ipm=> INSERT INTO locations
ipm-> VALUES (
ipm->             NEXTVAL('locations_id_seq'),
ipm->             'MO-Kansas City'
ipm-> );
INSERT 19335 1
ipm=> INSERT INTO locations
ipm-> VALUES (
ipm->             NEXTVAL('locations_id_seq'),
ipm->             'NY-New York'
ipm-> );
INSERT 19336 1
ipm=> INSERT INTO locations
ipm-> VALUES (
ipm->             NEXTVAL('locations_id_seq'),
ipm->             'TX-Austin'
ipm-> );
INSERT 19337 1
```

Finally, we'll put some categories into the categories table:

```
ipm=> INSERT INTO categories
ipm-> VALUES (
ipm->             NEXTVAL('categories_id_seq'),
ipm->             '----- Any -----'
ipm-> );
INSERT 19338 1
ipm=> INSERT INTO categories
ipm-> VALUES (
ipm->             NEXTVAL('categories_id_seq'),
ipm->             'Accounting'
ipm-> );
INSERT 19339 1
ipm=> INSERT INTO categories
ipm-> VALUES (
ipm->             NEXTVAL('categories_id_seq'),
ipm->             'Administrative'
ipm-> );
```

```
INSERT 19340 1
ipm=> INSERT INTO categories
ipm-> VALUES (
ipm->          NEXTVAL('categories_id_seq'),
ipm->          'Graphic Design'
ipm-> );
INSERT 19341 1
ipm=> INSERT INTO categories
ipm-> VALUES (
ipm->          NEXTVAL('categories_id_seq'),
ipm->          'Human Resources'
ipm-> );
INSERT 19342 1
ipm=> INSERT INTO categories
ipm-> VALUES (
ipm->          NEXTVAL('categories_id_seq'),
ipm->          'Information Technology'
ipm-> );
INSERT 19343 1
ipm=> INSERT INTO categories
ipm-> VALUES (
ipm->          NEXTVAL('categories_id_seq'),
ipm->          'Marketing'
ipm-> );
INSERT 19344 1
ipm=> INSERT INTO categories
ipm-> VALUES (
ipm->          NEXTVAL('categories_id_seq'),
ipm->          'Sales'
ipm-> );
INSERT 19345 1
```

The resume script uses one table:

```
ipm=> CREATE TABLE resume2 (
ipm->              id INTEGER,
ipm->              submit_date TIMESTAMP,
ipm->              name VARCHAR(50),
ipm->              phone VARCHAR(50),
ipm->              email VARCHAR(50),
ipm->              address VARCHAR(100),
ipm->              resume TEXT,
ipm->              job_id INTEGER
ipm-> );
CREATE
ipm=>
```

This table is similar to the resume table we built earlier in the chapter with the addition of a job_id field.

We need to create the sequences and change the tables' permissions so that the web user can access them.

```
Ipm=> CREATE SEQUENCE resume2_id_seq;
CREATE
ipm=> GRANT ALL ON resume2 TO nobody;
CHANGE
ipm=> GRANT ALL ON resume2_id_seq TO nobody;
CHANGE
ipm=>
```

Here's the code for the jobs board:

```perl
#!/usr/bin/perl -w
use strict;
use CGI qw/:standard/;
use DBI;
$|++;

# Config
my $TITLE = 'IPM Job Search';
my $APPLY_URL = 'http://localhost/cgi-bin/ipm/'.
                'chap11/resume2.cgi';

print header,
      start_html(-title=>$TITLE, -bgcolor=>'white');

if( !param() ) {
    print_form();
} elsif ( param('JobID') ) {
    get_job( param('JobID') );
} else {
    print_results();
}

print end_html;

#########################################

sub print_form {
    # Connect to database
    my $dbh = DBI->connect('dbi:Pg:dbname=ipm', 'nobody', '')
      or die "Cannot connect to database: $!\n";

    # Get locations
    my $sql = "SELECT * FROM locations";
    my $sth = $dbh->prepare($sql);
    $sth->execute;

    my %location_labels;
    my @locations;
    while (my ($id, $location) = $sth->fetchrow) {
        $location_labels{$id}=$location;
        push(@locations, $id);
    }
```

```
        $sth->finish;

        # Get categories
        $sql = "SELECT * FROM categories";
        $sth = $dbh->prepare($sql);
        $sth->execute;

        my %category_labels;
        my @categories;
        while( my ($id, $category) = $sth->fetchrow) {
            $category_labels{$id}=$category;
            push(@categories, $id);
        }

        $sth->finish;
        $dbh->disconnect;

        print h1($TITLE),
              hr;

        print start_form,
              table({-border=>0},
                Tr(td([b('Location')])),
                Tr(td([scrolling_list(
                        -name=>'location',
                        -value=>\@locations,
                        -size=>5,
                        -multiple=>1,
                        -labels=>\%location_labels)])),
                Tr(td([b('Category')])),
                Tr(td([scrolling_list(
                        -name=>'category',
                        -value=>\@categories,
                        -size=>5,
                        -multiple=>1,
                        -labels=>\%category_labels)])),
                Tr(td([b('Keywords')])),
                Tr(td([textfield(-name=>'keywords',-size=>50)]))
              );

        print submit,
              reset;

    }

sub print_results {
    my $dbh;
    my $sql;
    my $sth;

    # Get form variables
    my @locations = param('location');
    my @categories = param('category');
    my $keywords = param('keywords');
```

```perl
# Clear arrays if 'Any' is selected
@locations = () if grep /\b1\b/, @locations;
@categories = () if grep /\b1\b/, @categories;

# Connect to database
$dbh = DBI->connect('dbi:Pg:dbname=ipm', 'nobody', '') or
  die "Cannot connect to database: $!\n";

# Get location name
my @location_names;
my $location_names;
if (@locations) {
    foreach my $location (@locations) {
        $sql = "SELECT location FROM locations " .
               "WHERE id=$location";
        $sth = $dbh->prepare($sql);
        $sth->execute;

        my $location_name = $sth->fetchrow;
        push (@location_names, $location_name);
    }
    $location_names = join(', ', @location_names);
    $sth->finish;
} else {
    $location_names = 'Any';
}

# Get category name
my @category_names;
my $category_names;
if (@categories) {
    foreach my $category (@categories) {
        $sql = "SELECT category FROM categories " .
               "WHERE id=$category";
        $sth = $dbh->prepare($sql);
        $sth->execute;

        my $category_name = $sth->fetchrow;
        push (@category_names, $category_name);
    }

    $category_names = join(', ', @category_names);
    $sth->finish;
} else {
    $category_names = 'Any';
}

# Print output to user
print h1($TITLE),
      hr,
      h2('Search Criteria'),
      br,
      b('Location: '),
```

```perl
        $location_names,
        br,
        b('Category: '),
        $category_names,
        br,
        b('Keywords: '),
        $keywords,
        p,
        hr,
        h2('Search Results');

# Find jobs that match criteria
$sql = "SELECT * FROM jobs ";

# Check if we need a WHERE
if (@locations || @categories || $keywords) {
    $sql .= "WHERE ";

    # Location
    if (@locations == 1) {
        $sql .= "location=$locations[0]";
    } elsif (@locations > 1) {
        $sql .= '(';
        for (my $i = 0; $i <= $#locations; $i++) {
            if ($i < $#locations) {
                $sql .= "location=$locations[$i] OR ";
            } else {
                $sql .= "location=$locations[$i])";
            }
        }
    }

    if (@categories == 1) {
        if (@locations) {
            $sql .= ' AND ';
        }
        $sql .= "category=$categories[0]";
    } elsif (@categories > 1) {
        if (@locations) {
            $sql .= ' AND ';
        }
        $sql .= '(';
      for (my $i = 0; $i <= $#categories; $i++) {
            if ($i < $#categories) {
                $sql .= "category=$categories[$i] OR ";
            } else {
                $sql .= "category=$categories[$i])";
            }
        }
    }

    if ($keywords) {
        my @keywords = split(/\s+/, $keywords);
        if (@locations or @categories) {
```

```
                            $sql .= ' AND ';
                        }
                        $sql .= '(' if @keywords > 1;
                        for (my $i = 0; $i <= $#keywords; $i++) {
                            if ($i < $#keywords) {
                                $sql .= "keywords LIKE " .
                                        "'%$keywords[$i]%' OR ";
                            } else {
                                $sql .= "keywords LIKE '%$keywords[$i]%'";
                                $sql .= ')' if @keywords > 1;
                            }
                        }
                    }
                }
            }

            $sth = $dbh->prepare($sql);
            $sth->execute;

            # Print results
            print "<TABLE BORDER=0 CELLSPACING=15>";
            print "<TH>Date</TH>";
            print "<TH>Location</TH>";
            print "<TH>Job Title</TH>";
            while( my($id, $title, $cat, $date, $loc_id, $desc,
                    $sal) = $sth->fetchrow ) {
                print "<TR>";
                $sql = "SELECT location FROM locations WHERE " .
                        "id=$loc_id";
                $sth = $dbh->prepare($sql);
                $sth->execute;
                my $loc = $sth->fetchrow;
                $sth->finish;
                print "<TD>$date</TD>";
                print "<TD>$loc</TD>";
                my $script = url();
                $script .= "?JobID=$id";
                print "<TD><A HREF=\"$script\">$title</A></TD>\n";
                print "</TR>";
            }
            print "</TABLE>";
            print hr;

            $sth->finish;
            $dbh->disconnect;

        }

        sub get_job {
            my $job_id = shift;

            my $dbh;
            my $sql;
            my $sth;
```

```
# Connect to database
$dbh = DBI->connect('dbi:Pg:dbname=ipm', 'nobody', '') or
   die "Cannot connect to database: $!\n";

# Get selected job info
$sql = "SELECT j.title, l.location, j.description, " .
       "j.salary FROM jobs j, locations l " .
       "WHERE j.id=$job_id AND j.location=l.id";

$sth = $dbh->prepare($sql);
$sth->execute;

my ($title,$location,$desc,$salary) = $sth->fetchrow;

$sth->finish;

if (!$title) {
    print "Invalid JobID<BR>\n";
    $dbh->disconnect;
    exit;
}

$dbh->disconnect;

# Print the job information
print h1($title),
      h2($location),
      hr,
      p($desc),
      hr,
      b('Salary: '),
      $salary,
      hr,
      a({-href=>"$APPLY_URL?JobID=$job_id"},
        "Apply Online");

}
```

We set the path to the resume CGI script in the config section of the script. You'll need to change this to match the path on your system:

```
my $APPLY_URL = 'http://localhost/cgi-bin/ipm/' .
                'chap11/resume2.cgi';
```

This script has three main functions: print_form(), get_job(), and print_results(). The print_form() function is called the first time the CGI is run. The print_form() function displays the search form. The print_results() function is called when the user submits the search form. This function will display any jobs that match the user's selected criteria. The get_job() function takes a JobID as a parameter and will display details of the selected job.

```
if( !param() ) {
    print_form();
} elsif ( param('JobID') ) {
    get_job( param('JobID') );
} else {
    print_results();
}
```

The locations and categories drop-down boxes are built dynamically with information contained in the locations and categories tables, respectively. First, we make a database connection:

```
# Connect to database
my $dbh = DBI->connect('dbi:Pg:dbname=ipm', 'nobody', '')
    or die "Cannot connect to database: $!\n";
```

We then query the locations table and save the location strings in a hash and the IDs in an array. This will be used later to build a drop-down box.

```
# Get locations
my $sql = "SELECT * FROM locations";
my $sth = $dbh->prepare($sql);
$sth->execute;

my %location_labels;
my @locations;
while (my ($id, $location) = $sth->fetchrow) {
    $location_labels{$id}=$location;
    push(@locations, $id);
}

$sth->finish;
```

Next we query the categories table and save the category strings in a hash and the IDs in an array:

```
# Get categories
$sql = "SELECT * FROM categories";
$sth = $dbh->prepare($sql);
$sth->execute;

my %category_labels;
my @categories;
while( my ($id, $category) = $sth->fetchrow) {
    $category_labels{$id}=$category;
    push(@categories, $id);
}

$sth->finish;
```

Now we can create the form with the location and category information that we pulled from the database. To create a scrolling list, we use a
reference to the array of keys for the –value parameter and a reference
to the hash of strings for the –labels parameter.

```
print start_form,
      table({-border=>0},
         Tr(td([b('Location')])),
         Tr(td([scrolling_list(
                 -name=>'location',
                 -value=>\@locations,
                 -size=>5,
                 -multiple=>1,
                 -labels=>\%location_labels)])),
         Tr(td([b('Category')])),
         Tr(td([scrolling_list(
                 -name=>'category',
                 -value=>\@categories,
                 -size=>5,
                 -multiple=>1,
                 -labels=>\%category_labels)])),
         Tr(td([b('Keywords')])),
         Tr(td([textfield(-name=>'keywords',-size=>50)])))
);

print submit,
      reset;
```

In the print_results() function, we get the form variables and use
them to build an SQL statement to query the jobs table. The location
and category parameters can take many values (from the scrolling lists),
so their values are stored in arrays. The keywords (from a textfield)
should be a string containing one or more keywords separated by whitespace. These are stored in a scalar:

```
# Get form variables
my @locations = param('location');
my @categories = param('category');
my $keywords = param('keywords');
```

If the user selects 'Any' (value=1) for locations or categories, we must
clear the corresponding array:

```
# Clear array if 'Any' is selected
@locations = () if grep /\b1\b/, @locations;
@categories = () if grep /\b1\b/, @categories;
```

The locations and categories arrays contain keys, so we need to find the corresponding names that will be displayed on the results page. We store the location names in the @location_names array that will be used to build an SQL statement. We also save each name to a scalar $location_names, which contains a comma-separated string to display the search criteria to the user. If @locations is empty, then $location_names is set to 'Any':

```
# Get location name
my @location_names;
my $location_names;
if (@locations) {
    foreach my $location (@locations) {
        $sql = "SELECT location FROM locations " .
               "WHERE id=$location";
        $sth = $dbh->prepare($sql);
        $sth->execute;

        my $location_name = $sth->fetchrow;
        push (@location_names, $location_name);
    }
    $location_names = join(', ', @location_names);
    $sth->finish;
} else {
    $location_names = 'Any';
}
```

We do the same thing for the category names:

```
# Get category name
my @category_names;
my $category_names;
if (@categories) {
    foreach my $category (@categories) {
        $sql = "SELECT category FROM categories " .
               "WHERE id=$category";
        $sth = $dbh->prepare($sql);
        $sth->execute;

        my $category_name = $sth->fetchrow;
        push (@category_names, $category_name);
    }

    $category_names = join(', ', @category_names);
    $sth->finish;
} else {
    $location_names = 'Any';
}
```

With the variables `$location_names`, `$category_names`, and `$keywords`, we display the search criteria for the user:

```
print h1($TITLE),
      hr,
      h2('Search Criteria'),
      br,
      b('Location: '),
      $location_names,
      br,
      b('Category: '),
      $category_names,
      br,
      b('Keywords: '),
      $keywords,
      p,
      hr,
      h2('Search Results');
```

With all the criteria that the user selected, we can now dynamically build an SQL statement.

First, we create the base statement:

```
# Find jobs that match criteria
$sql = "SELECT * FROM jobs ";
```

Next, we need to check whether the user has entered any criteria. If so, we need to add the WHERE clause to the SQL statement:

```
# Check if we need a WHERE
if (@locations || @categories || $keywords) {
    $sql .= "WHERE ";
```

Now we need to add the specific conditions for the WHERE clause. First, we check the `@locations` array. If only one selection has been selected, then we simply add `"location=$locations[0]"` to the WHERE clause. If there is more than one location, then we must add the OR statement between each location (but not at the end of the last location). If no locations are selected, then we query on all locations.

```
# Location
if (@locations == 1) {
    $sql .= "location=$locations[0]";
} elsif (@locations > 1) {
    $sql .= '(';
    for (my $i = 0; $i <= $#locations; $i++) {
        if ($i < $#locations) {
            $sql .= "location=$locations[$i] OR ";
```

```
        } else {
            $sql .= "location=$locations[$i])";
        }
    }
}
```

Next we check if any categories have been selected; if so, we build another string to add to the WHERE clause. However, we first check if there were any locations selected in the previous code and add an AND statement, if there were. For example, if we selected a location and a category, we would have a WHERE clause something like: WHERE location=1 AND category=3.

```
if (@categories == 1) {
    if (@locations) {
        $sql .= ' AND ';
    }
    $sql .= "category=$categories[0]";
} elsif (@categories > 1) {
    if (@locations) {
        $sql .= ' AND ';
    }
    $sql .= '(';
    for (my $i = 0; $i <= $#categories; $i++) {
        if ($i < $#categories) {
            $sql .= "category=$categories[$i] OR ";
        } else {
            $sql .= "category=$categories[$i])";
        }
    }
}
```

Finally, we check whether any keywords were entered and build another string to add to the WHERE clause. We split the $keywords variable on whitespace to get the individual keywords.

```
if ($keywords) {
    my @keywords = split(/\s+/, $keywords);
    if (@locations or @categories) {
        $sql .= ' AND ';
    }
    $sql .= '(' if @keywords > 1;
    for (my $i = 0; $i <= $#keywords; $i++) {
        if ($i < $#keywords) {
            $sql .= "keywords LIKE " .
                    "'%$keywords[$i]%' OR ";
        } else {
            $sql .= "keywords LIKE '%$keywords[$i]%'";
            $sql .= ')' if @keywords > 1;
        }
    }
}
```

```
      }
}
```

We use this SQL statement to query the jobs table. Each job found that matched the selected criteria is displayed for the user. The job title is set as a hyperlink that can be used to query the database so that information for that specific job can be displayed:

```
my $script = url();
$script .= "?JobID=$id";
print "<TD><A HREF=\"$script\">$title</A></TD>\n";
```

The get_job() function displays information for a specific job selected by the user from the results page. We need to get information from the jobs table (title, description, and salary) and the locations table (location string). We use an SQL statement that joins the two tables:

```
# Get selected job info
$sql = "SELECT j.title, l.location, j.description, " .
       "j.salary FROM jobs j, locations l " .
       "WHERE j.id=$job_id AND j.location=l.id";
```

We then query the database and fetch the information:

```
my ($title,$location,$desc,$salary) = $sth->fetchrow;
```

We need to check that the job ID is valid and alert the user if it's not:

```
if (!$title) {
    print "Invalid JobID<BR>\n";
    $dbh->disconnect;
    exit;
}
```

If we have a valid job ID, then we display the job information to the user, including a link to the resume script so that the user can apply for this job:

```
# Print the job information
print h1($title),
      h2($location),
      hr,
      p($desc),
      hr,
      b('Salary: '),
      $salary,
      hr,
      a({-href=>"$APPLY_URL?JobID=$job_id"},
        "Apply Online");
}
```

The resume script is similar to the script we built earlier in the chapter. We've added a `JobID` parameter so that the user can apply for a specific job:

```perl
my $job_id = param('JobID');
```

We use `$job_id` in a hidden form variable so that it can be inserted into the database:

```perl
hidden(-name=>'job_id',-value=>$job_id),
```

Here's the complete code for the modified resume script:

```perl
#!/usr/bin/perl -w
use strict;
use CGI qw/:standard/;
use DBI;
$|++;

# Config - Limit length of comments
my $MAX_RESUME_LENGTH = 500;

print header,
      start_html(-title=>'IPM Feedback Form',
                 -bgcolor=>'white');

if( !param() or param('JobID') ) {
    print_form();
} else {
    print_thanks();
}

print end_html;

#########################################

sub print_form {
    my $job_id = param('JobID');
    print h1('IPM Resume Submit Form'),
          hr,
          'Please fill out the form and submit.',
          start_form,
          hidden(-name=>'job_id',-value=>$job_id),
          'Name',
          br,
          textfield(-name=>'name',-size=>50),
          br,
          'Phone Number',
          br,
          textfield(-name=>'phone',-size=>50),
```

```perl
            br,
            'Email',
            br,
            textfield(-name=>'email',-size=>50),
            br,
            'Address',
            br,
            textarea(-name=>'address',
                     -rows=>4,
                     -columns=>50,
                     -wrap=>'physical'),
            br,
            'Resume (Please Cut and Paste)',
            br,
            textarea(-name=>'resume',
                     -rows=>10,
                     -columns=>80,
                     -wrap=>'physical'),
            br,
            submit(-name=>'Submit Resume'),
            reset;

    }

sub print_thanks {
    # Connect to database
    my $dbh = DBI->connect('dbi:Pg:dbname=ipm', 'nobody', '')
      or die "Cannot connect to database: $!\n";

    # Get current date/time
    my $time = localtime();

    # Get form variables
    my $name = param('name');
    my $phone = param('phone');
    my $email = param('email');
    my $address = param('address');
    my $resume = param('resume');
    my $job_id = param('job_id');

    # Prepare resume for insertion
    $resume =~ s/\\/\\\\/g;
    $resume =~ s/'/''/g;

    # Limit length of comments field
    $resume = substr($resume, 0, $MAX_RESUME_LENGTH);

    $dbh->do("INSERT INTO resume2 VALUES (
        NEXTVAL('resume2_id_seq'),
        '$time',
        '$name',
        '$phone',
```

```
                        '$email',
                        '$address',
                        '$resume',
                        $job_id)");

        $dbh->disconnect;

        # Print output to user
        print h1('Thank You'),
                hr,
                'Thank you for submitting your resume.',
                br,
                'We have added your resume to our database.';

}
```

CD Database

I've got hundreds of CDs lying around the house and I thought it would be a good idea to get organized and create a database containing information about all those CDs. The script that I created allows me to search the database by CD title or the artist's name. The search form is shown in Figure 11.9. If a search is successful, then a list of CDs is displayed, as shown in Figure 11.10. To make this script more useful, each CD title is a link that will query the database and display the tracks from that CD. Figure 11.11 shows the tracks from a selected CD.

This script uses two tables: one table to store the CD information (artist, title, label, and genre) and another table to store all the tracks from the CDs in the first table.

First, we create the CD table:

```
ipm=> CREATE TABLE cd (
ipm->                 id INTEGER,
ipm->                 artist VARCHAR(50),
ipm->                 title VARCHAR(50),
ipm->                 label VARCHAR(50),
ipm->                 type VARCHAR(50)
ipm-> );
CREATE
ipm=>
```

Next, we create the table that will contain all the song titles from the CDs. The cd_id field is a foreign key that ties this table with the CD table.

Figure 11.9
The CD search form.

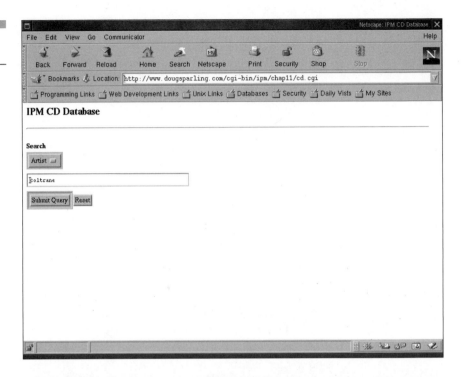

Figure 11.10
The search results
page.

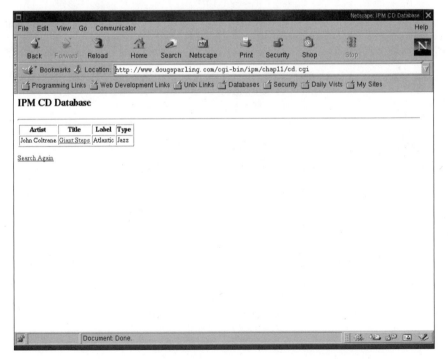

Figure 11.11
The tracks from a
selected CD.

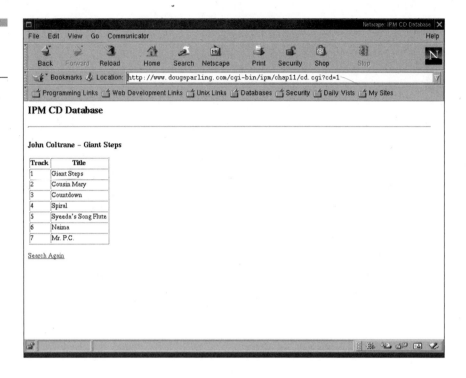

```
ipm=> CREATE TABLE cd_titles (
ipm->                id INTEGER,
ipm->                cd_id INTEGER,
ipm->                track INTEGER,
ipm->                name VARCHAR(50)
ipm-> );
CREATE
ipm=>
```

Now we create the sequences needed for the auto-increment ID fields.

```
ipm=> CREATE SEQUENCE cd_id_seq;
CREATE
ipm=> CREATE SEQUENCE cd_titles_id_seq;
CREATE
ipm=>
```

Finally, we change the table's permissions so that it can be accessed by the web user:

```
ipm=> GRANT ALL ON cd TO nobody;
CHANGE
ipm=> GRANT ALL ON cd_titles TO nobody;
```

```
CHANGE
ipm=> GRANT ALL ON cd_id_seq TO nobody;
CHANGE
ipm=> GRANT ALL ON cd_titles_id_seq TO nobody;
CHANGE
ipm=>
```

To get started, we'll manually enter a few CD titles into our database.

```
ipm=> INSERT INTO cd VALUES (
ipm->                              NEXTVAL('cd_id_seq'),
ipm->                              'John Coltrane',
ipm->                              'Giant Steps',
ipm->                              'Atlantic',
ipm->                              'Jazz'
ipm-> );
INSERT 19765 1
ipm=> INSERT INTO cd VALUES (
ipm->                              NEXTVAL('cd_id_seq'),
ipm->                              'Miles Davis',
ipm->                              'Kind of Blue',
ipm->                              'Columbia',
ipm->                              'Jazz'
ipm-> );
INSERT 19766 1
ipm=> INSERT INTO cd_titles
ipm-> VALUES (
ipm->         NEXTVAL('cd_titles_id_seq'),
ipm->         1,
ipm->         1,
ipm->         'Giant Steps'
ipm-> );
INSERT 19767 1
ipm=> INSERT INTO cd_titles
ipm-> VALUES (
ipm->         NEXTVAL('cd_titles_id_seq'),
ipm->         1,
ipm->         2,
ipm->         'Cousin Mary'
ipm-> );
INSERT 19768 1
ipm=> INSERT INTO cd_titles
ipm-> VALUES (
ipm->         NEXTVAL('cd_titles_id_seq'),
ipm->         1,
ipm->         3,
ipm->         'Countdown'
ipm-> );
INSERT 19769 1
ipm=> INSERT INTO cd_titles
ipm-> VALUES (
ipm->         NEXTVAL('cd_titles_id_seq'),
ipm->         1,
```

```
ipm->          4,
ipm->          'Spiral'
ipm-> );
INSERT 19770 1
ipm=> INSERT INTO cd_titles
ipm-> VALUES (
ipm->          NEXTVAL('cd_titles_id_seq'),
ipm->          1,
ipm->          5,
ipm->          'Syeeda\'s Song Flute'
ipm-> );
INSERT 19771 1
ipm=> INSERT INTO cd_titles
ipm-> VALUES (
ipm->          NEXTVAL('cd_titles_id_seq'),
ipm->          1,
ipm->          6,
ipm->          'Naima'
ipm-> );
INSERT 19772 1
ipm=> INSERT INTO cd_titles
ipm-> VALUES (
ipm->          NEXTVAL('cd_titles_id_seq'),
ipm->          1,
ipm->          7,
ipm->          'Mr. P.C.'
ipm-> );
INSERT 19773 1
ipm=> INSERT INTO cd_titles
ipm-> VALUES (
ipm->          NEXTVAL('cd_titles_id_seq'),
ipm->          2,
ipm->          1,
ipm->          'So What'
ipm-> );
INSERT 19774 1
ipm=> INSERT INTO cd_titles
ipm-> VALUES (
ipm->          NEXTVAL('cd_titles_id_seq'),
ipm->          2,
ipm->          2,
ipm->          'Freddie Freeloader'
ipm-> );
INSERT 19775 1
ipm=> INSERT INTO cd_titles
ipm-> VALUES (
ipm->          NEXTVAL('cd_titles_id_seq'),
ipm->          2,
ipm->          3,
ipm->          'Blue In Green'
ipm-> );
INSERT 19776 1
ipm=> INSERT INTO cd_titles
ipm-> VALUES (
```

```
ipm->           NEXTVAL('cd_titles_id_seq'),
ipm->           2,
ipm->           4,
ipm->           'All Blues'
ipm-> );
INSERT 19777 1
ipm=> INSERT INTO cd_titles
ipm-> VALUES (
ipm->           NEXTVAL('cd_titles_id_seq'),
ipm->           2,
ipm->           5,
ipm->           'Flamenco Sketches'
ipm-> );
INSERT 19778 1
ipm=>
```

Here's the code for the CD database script:

```perl
#!/usr/bin/perl -w
use strict;
use CGI qw/:standard/;
use DBI;
$|++;

# Config
my $TITLE = 'IPM CD Database';
my $MAX_QUERY_LENGTH = 50;

print header,
      start_html(-title=>$TITLE, -bgcolor=>'white');

if( !param() ) {
    print_form();
} elsif ( param('search_type') ) {
    search_cd();
} elsif ( param('cd') ) {
    print_titles();
} else {
    print_form();
}

print end_html;

##########################################

sub print_form {
    print h1($TITLE),
          hr;

    print start_form,
          b('Search'),
          br,
          scrolling_list(-name=>'search_type',
```

```
                              -value=>['Artist', 'Title'],
                              -size=>1),
                  br,
                  textfield(-name=>'query',-size=>50),
                  br,
                  submit,
                  reset,
                  end_form;

}

sub search_cd {
    my $dbh;
    my $sql;
    my $sth;

    # Connect to database
    $dbh = DBI->connect('dbi:Pg:dbname=ipm', 'nobody', '')
      or die "Cannot connect to database: $!\n";

    # Get form variables
    my $search_type = param('search_type');
    my $query = param('query');

    # Get script url
    my $script = url();

    # Limit length of artist and title fields
    $query = substr($query, 0, $MAX_QUERY_LENGTH);

    # Remove leading and trailing white space
    $query =~ s/^\s+//;
    $query =~ s/\s+$//;
    # Convert multiple white space to single white space
    $query =~ s/\s{2,}/ /g;

    $sql = "SELECT id, artist, title, label, type FROM cd ";
    if ($search_type eq 'Artist') {
        $sql .= "WHERE artist ~* '$query'";
    } elsif ($search_type eq 'Title') {
        $sql .= "WHERE title ~* '$query'";
    }
    $sth = $dbh->prepare($sql);
    $sth->execute;

    # Print output to user
    print h1($TITLE),
    hr;

    print "<TABLE BORDER=1>\n";
    print "<TH>Artist</TH>\n";
    print "<TH>Title</TH>\n";
    print "<TH>Label</TH>\n";
    print "<TH>Type</TH>\n";
```

```perl
        my $found = 0;
        while ( my($cd_id, $cd_artist, $cd_title,
                   $cd_label, $cd_type) = $sth->fetchrow ) {
            $found++;
            print "<TR>\n";
            print "<TD>$cd_artist</TD>\n";
            print "<TD><A HREF=\"$script?cd=$cd_id\">" .
                  "$cd_title</A></TD>\n";
            print "<TD>$cd_label</TD>\n";
            print "<TD>$cd_type</TD>\n";
            print "</TR>\n";
        }
        print "</TABLE>\n";

        $sth->finish;
        $dbh->disconnect;

        # Check if records found
        if (!$found) {
            print 'No records found';
        }

        # Print link back to search form
        print br;
        print "<A HREF=\"$script\">Search Again</A>\n";

}

sub print_titles {
    my $sql;
    my $sth;
    my $dbh;

    # Connect to the database
    $dbh = DBI->connect('dbi:Pg:dbname=ipm', 'nobody', '') or
      die "Cannot connect to database: $!\n";

    # Get form variable
    my $cd_id = param('cd');

    # Get artist and title
    $sql = "SELECT artist, title FROM cd WHERE id=$cd_id";
    $sth = $dbh->prepare($sql);
    $sth->execute;

    my($artist, $title) = $sth->fetchrow;

    $sth->finish;

    # Get track titles
    $sql = "SELECT track, name FROM cd_titles WHERE " .
           "cd_id=$cd_id";
    $sth = $dbh->prepare($sql);
```

```
$sth->execute;

# Print track titles
print h1($TITLE),
        hr;

print h3($artist, ' - ', $title);

print "<TABLE BORDER=1>\n";
print "<TH>Track</TH>\n";
print "<TH>Title</TH>\n";

while ( my($track, $name) = $sth->fetchrow ) {
    print "<TR>\n";
    print "<TD>$track</TD>\n";
    print "<TD>$name</TD>\n";
    print "</TR>\n";
}
print "</TABLE>\n";

$sth->finish;
$dbh->disconnect;

# Get script url
my $script = url();

# Print link back to search form
print br;
print "<A HREF=\"$script\">Search Again</A>\n";

}
```

This script has three main functions: print_form(), search_cd(), and print_titles().

```
if( !param() ) {
    print_form();
} elsif ( param('search_type') ) {
    search_cd();
} elsif ( param('cd') ) {
    print_titles();
} else {
    print_form();
}
```

The first time the script is called (or when the Search again link is clicked), the print_form() function is called. The following code contained in print_form() will display the simple search form:

```
print start_form,
        b('Search'),
```

```
        br,
        scrolling_list(-name=>'search_type',
                      -value=>['Artist', 'Title'],
                      -size=>1),
        br,
        textfield(-name=>'query',-size=>50),
        br,
        submit,
        reset,
        end_form;

}
```

The `search_cd()` function will search the database using the user's input as search criteria. The scrolling list indicates the type of search: CD title or artist's name. The user can enter the title or name in the textfield.

```
# Get form variables
my $search_type = param('search_type');
my $query = param('query');
```

Before querying the database, we'll tidy up the information entered in the textfield. We'll remove any leading or trailing whitespace and convert any multiple whitespaces to a single whitespace.

```
# Remove leading and trailing white space
$query =~ s/^\s+//;
$query =~ s/\s+$//;
# Convert multiple white space to single white space
$query =~ s/\s{2,}/ /g;
```

Next we build the SQL statement with the Postgres regular expression comparison. The ~ operator is the regular expression operator, and * means to make a case-insensitive comparison.

```
$sql = "SELECT id, artist, title, label, type FROM cd ";
if ($search_type eq 'Artist') {
    $sql .= "WHERE artist ~* '$query'";
} elsif ($search_type eq 'Title') {
    $sql .= "WHERE title ~* '$query'";
}
```

We print all the matches (if any) and increment $found, which determines whether we actually had any matches. The CD title is printed as a link, which will be used to query the database for the tracks on the CD.

```
while ( my($cd_id, $cd_artist, $cd_title,
            $cd_label, $cd_type) = $sth->fetchrow ) {
    $found++;
    print "<TR>\n";
    print "<TD>$cd_artist</TD>\n";
    print "<TD><A HREF=\"$script?cd=$cd_id\">" .
          "$cd_title</A></TD>\n";
    print "<TD>$cd_label</TD>\n";
    print "<TD>$cd_type</TD>\n";
    print "</TR>\n";
}
```

If no matches are found, we inform the user:

```
# Check if records found
if (!$found) {
    print 'No records found';
}
```

We then offer the user the option to search again:

```
# Print link back to search form
print br;
print "<A HREF=\"$script\">Search Again</A>\n";
```

The URL of the script is set earlier in the search_cd() subroutine:

```
# Get script url
my $script = url();
```

The print_titles() function will query the database for the selected CD. First, we must retrieve the CD id parameter:

```
# Get form variable
my $cd_id = param('cd');
```

Then we query the database to find the artist and CD title for this id:

```
# Get artist and title
$sql = "SELECT artist, title FROM cd WHERE id=$cd_id";
```

Now we can query the database to get the tracks for the selected CD:

```
# Get track titles
$sql = "SELECT track, name FROM cd_titles WHERE cd_id=$cd_id";
```

We loop through the record set and print the track numbers and titles:

```
while ( my($track, $name) = $sth->fetchrow ) {
    print "<TR>\n";
    print "<TD>$track</TD>\n";
    print "<TD>$name</TD>\n";
    print "</TR>\n";
}
```

Finally, we print a link so that the user can search again:

```
my $script = url();

# Print link back to search form
print br;
print "<A HREF=\"$script\">Search Again</A>\n";
```

Summary

This chapter has shown how easy and useful it is to use a database with your CGI scripts. Using a relational database will allow you to perform complex queries that might be difficult (or impossible) using simple flat files. Using a database is a good way to manage large amounts of data, and using Perl DBI should speed up access to that data.

CGI: Commerce and Community

Introduction

```
DBI: /CPAN/DBI-1.14.tar.gz
DBD::Pg: /CPAN/DBD-Pg-0.95.tar.gz
```

In this chapter we show two more practical applications of Perl CGI scripts. These scripts are a little more involved than our previous examples and focus heavily on the use of databases to store our information. These examples show you how to write larger web applications. Although they can be used as shown, you can customize and expand on them to fit your particular needs.

Our first example shows a simple online computer ordering application that allows web users to configure, price, and order a computer that they have designed. The second example is a fully threaded online discussion forum. This type of script is seen on many web sites and is commonly requested. The example provided shows a simple database solution to a common problem.

Online Computer Store

In this example, we implement an online computer store by using a simple set of small tables to store name and price information about different types of computer parts. Users can then, via pull-down menus, select which components they want in their computer and quickly calculate the price. We have also included a table to allow for the storing of billing information so that users can actually order the computer.

Here is the database table structure for our `'cmpstore'` database:

```
CREATE SEQUENCE orders_seq;
CREATE TABLE orders (
            id int4 PRIMARY KEY DEFAULT
            NEXTVAL('orders_seq'),
            order_ts datetime,
            customer_id int4,
            processor_id int4,
            video_id int4,
            memory_id int4,
            harddrive_id int4,
            monitor_id int4
```

```
);
GRANT ALL ON orders TO nobody;
GRANT ALL ON orders_seq TO nobody;
```

This table stores the information regarding the order. Each integer value such as `customer_id` and `processor_id`, store the ID we relate to the other tables defined below. `order_ts` is a time stamp that shows when the order came in and can be used by an administration application to only show new orders to the storeowner.

```
CREATE SEQUENCE customer_seq;
CREATE TABLE customer (
            id int4,
            first_name text,
            last_name text,
            address text,
            city  text,
            state text,
            zip text,
            phone text,
            email text
);
GRANT ALL ON customer TO nobody;
GRANT ALL ON customer_seq TO nobody;
```

The customer table shown above stores all the necessary billing information about the web user who wants to order the defined system.

```
CREATE SEQUENCE processor_seq;
CREATE TABLE processor (
            id int4 PRIMARY KEY DEFAULT
            NEXTVAL('processor_seq'),
            name text,
            price numeric
);
GRANT ALL ON processor TO nobody;
GRANT ALL ON processor_seq TO nobody;

CREATE SEQUENCE video_seq;
CREATE TABLE video (
            id int4 PRIMARY KEY DEFAULT
            NEXTVAL('video_seq'),
            name text,
            price numeric
);
GRANT ALL ON video TO nobody;
GRANT ALL ON video_seq TO nobody;

CREATE SEQUENCE memory_seq;
CREATE TABLE memory (
```

```
                     id int4 PRIMARY KEY DEFAULT
                     NEXTVAL('memory_seq'),
                     name text,
                     price numeric
);
GRANT ALL ON memory TO nobody;
GRANT ALL ON memory_seq TO nobody;

CREATE SEQUENCE harddrive_seq;
CREATE TABLE harddrive (
                     id int4 PRIMARY KEY DEFAULT
                     NEXTVAL('harddrive_seq'),
                     name text,
                     price numeric
);
GRANT ALL ON harddrive TO nobody;
GRANT ALL ON harddrive_seq TO nobody;

CREATE SEQUENCE monitor_seq;
CREATE TABLE monitor (
                     id int4 PRIMARY KEY DEFAULT
                     NEXTVAL('monitor_seq'),
                     name text,
                     price numeric
);
GRANT ALL ON monitor TO nobody;
GRANT ALL ON monitor_seq TO nobody;
```

These tables actually store our individual parts. We have defined five basic types of computer hardware and have created a separate table for each. We also could have created a generic 'parts' table and used another table to relate what type of part it was.

Here is a list of the source code of this CGI script:

```perl
#!/usr/bin/perl -w

use strict;
use CGI qw(:standard);
use DBI;

# Create our database connection
my $dbh = DBI->connect('dbi:Pg:dbname=cmpstore', '', '') or
  die "Cannot connect to database: $!\n";

# Start our HTML output
print header;
print start_html(-bgcolor=>'white'),
     h2('IPM Computer Store'),
     qq!<HR SIZE="1" NOSHADE>!;

# Get what our action is
```

```perl
my $param = param('action');

# Determine what our user would like us to do
main($param);

print end_html;

# Functions

sub main {
    my $a = shift; # Our action
    print "<!-- action $a -->\n";

    # Determine based on our action what we are
    # supposed to be doing
    SWITCH: {
        if( $a eq '' )        { display_menu(); last SWITCH; }
        if( $a =~ /update/i ) { display_menu(); last SWITCH; }
        if( $a =~ /save/i )   { do_save(); last SWITCH; }
        if( $a =~ /order/i )  { do_order(); last SWITCH; }
    }

}

# This function retrieves all of our possible
# items for this type of part
sub get_parts {
    my $table = shift;
    my %tmp;

    my $sth = $dbh->prepare(
                "SELECT * FROM $table ORDER BY name"
            );
    $sth->execute;

    while( my($id, $name, $price) = $sth->fetchrow ) {

        # Fix our $price to only have two decimal digits
        $price =~ s/^(.*?\.\d\d).*?$/$1/o;

        $tmp{$id} = "$name -- \$$price";
    }
    $sth->finish;

    # Setup a starting point for them
    $tmp{0} = '-- None Selected --';

    return(%tmp);

}

sub get_part_name {
    my ($id, $table) = @_;
```

```perl
    my $sth = $dbh->prepare(
                  "SELECT name FROM $table WHERE id=$id"
               );
    $sth->execute;

    my $tmp = $sth->fetchrow;

    $sth->finish;

    return($tmp);

}

sub get_price {
    my ($id, $table) = @_;

    if( $id == 0 ) {
        return(0);
    }

    my $sth = $dbh->prepare(
                  "SELECT price FROM $table WHERE id=$id"
               );
    $sth->execute;

    my $tmp = $sth->fetchrow;

    $sth->finish;

    $tmp =~ s/^(.*?\.\d\d).*?$/$1/o;

    return($tmp)

}

sub get_price_total {

    my $proc_price = get_price( param('processor'),
                                'processor');
    my $vid_price  = get_price( param('video'), 'video');
    my $mem_price  = get_price( param('memory'), 'memory');
    my $drive_price = get_price( param('harddrive'),
                                 'harddrive');
    my $monitor_price = get_price( param('monitor'),
                                   'monitor');

    my $total = $proc_price + $vid_price + $mem_price
                + $drive_price + $monitor_price;

    $total =~ s/^(.*?\.\d\d).*?$/$1/o;

    return($total);

}
```

```perl
sub display_menu {

    # Get all of our values from the database
    my %processor = get_parts('processor');
    my %video = get_parts('video');
    my %memory = get_parts('memory');
    my %harddrive = get_parts('harddrive');
    my %monitor = get_parts('monitor');

    # Setup a default value for our menus
    my $default_processor = param('processor') || 0;
    my $default_video = param('video') || 0;
    my $default_memory = param('memory') || 0;
    my $default_harddrive = param('harddrive') || 0;
    my $default_monitor = param('monitor')   || 0;

    # Determine our price
    my $price = get_price_total();

    print start_form,
        b("Current Price: \$$price"),
        br,
        qq!<TABLE BORDER=0><TR><TD>!,
        b('Processors:'),
        qq!</TD><TD>!,
        popup_menu('processor', [keys(%processor)],
                   $default_processor, \%processor),
        qq!</TD></TR><TR><TD>!,
        b('Video Card:'),
        qq!</TD><TD>!,
        popup_menu('video', [keys(%video)],
                   $default_video, \%video),
        qq!</TD></TR><TR><TD>!,
        b('Memory:'),
        qq!</TD><TD>!,
        popup_menu('memory', [keys(%memory)],
                   $default_memory, \%memory),
        qq!</TD></TR><TR><TD>!,
        b('Harddrive:'),
        qq!</TD><TD>!,
        popup_menu('harddrive', [keys(%harddrive)],
                   $default_harddrive, \%harddrive),
        qq!</TD></TR><TR><TD>!,
        b('Monitor:'),
        qq!</TD><TD>!,
        popup_menu('monitor', [keys(%monitor)],
                   $default_monitor, \%monitor),
        qq!</TD></TR></TABLE>!,
        submit('action', 'Update Price'),
        submit('action', 'Place Order'),
        end_form;

}
```

```perl
sub do_order {
    my @errors;

    # Check to make sure everything is filled out
    if( param('processor') == 0 ) {
        push(@errors, 'No processor selected!' );
    }

    if( param('video') == 0 ) {
        push(@errors, 'No video card selected!' );
    }

    if( param('memory') == 0 ) {
        push(@errors, 'No memory selected!' );
    }

    if( param('harddrive') == 0 ) {
        push(@errors, 'No hard drive selected!' );
    }

    if( param('monitor') == 0 ) {
        push(@errors, 'No monitor selected!' );
    }

    # An error has occurred if we find anything in
    # @errors, display the error(s) and re-show the menu
    if(@errors) {

        print qq!<B>Some errors have occurred:</B><BR>!,
        join('<BR>', @errors);

        display_menu();

        exit();

    }

    # The names and prices of our parts
    my $proc_name = get_part_name( param('processor'),
                                    'processor');
    my $vid_name = get_part_name( param('video'), 'video');
    my $mem_name = get_part_name( param('memory'), 'memory');
    my $drive_name = get_part_name( param('harddrive'),
                                    'harddrive');
    my $monitor_name = get_part_name( param('monitor'),
                                        'monitor');

    my $proc_price = get_price( param('processor'),
                                'processor');
    my $vid_price = get_price( param('video'), 'video');
    my $mem_price = get_price( param('memory'), 'memory');
    my $drive_price = get_price( param('harddrive'),
                                    'harddrive');
```

```perl
my $monitor_price = get_price( param('monitor'),
                               'monitor');

# Get our total price
my $total = get_price_total();

# Display the user's order and a form
# for them to give us billing information
print start_form,
      hidden('processor', param('processor')),
      hidden('video', param('video')),
      hidden('memory', param('memory')),
      hidden('harddrive', param('harddrive')),
      hidden('monitor', param('monitor'));

print qq!<CENTER>!,
      b('Your Order:'),
      br,
      qq!<TABLE BORDER="0">!,
      qq!<TR><TD><B>Processor:</B></TD>!,
      qq!<TD>$proc_name</TD>!,
      qq!<TD ALIGN="RIGHT">\$$proc_price</TD></TR>!,
      qq!<TR><TD><B>Video Card:</B></TD>!,
      qq!<TD>$vid_name</TD>!,
      qq!<TD ALIGN="RIGHT">\$$vid_price</TD></TR>!,
      qq!<TR><TD><B>Memory:</B></TD><TD>$mem_name</TD>!,
      qq!<TD ALIGN="RIGHT">\$$mem_price</TD></TR>!,
      qq!<TR><TD><B>Hard Drive:</B></TD>!,
      qq!<TD>$drive_name</TD>!,
      qq!<TD ALIGN="RIGHT">\$$drive_price</TD></TR>!,
      qq!<TR><TD><B>Monitor:</B></TD>!,
      qq!<TD>$monitor_name</TD>!,
      qq!<TD ALIGN="RIGHT">\$$monitor_price</TD></TR>!,
      qq!<TR><TD COLSPAN="2"><B>Total:</B>!,
      qq!<TD ALIGN="RIGHT">!,
      qq!\$$total</TD></TR></TABLE><P>!;

print qq!<B>Billing Information:</B>!,
      qq!<TABLE BORDER="0">!,
      qq!<TR><TD>First Name:</TD><TD>!,
      textfield('first_name'),
      qq!</TD></TR>!,
      qq!<TR><TD>Last Name:</TD><TD>!,
      textfield('last_name'),
      qq!</TD></TR>!,
      qq!<TR><TD>Address:</TD><TD>!,
      textfield('address'),
      qq!</TD></TR>!,
      qq!<TR><TD>City:</TD><TD>!,
      textfield('city'),
      qq!</TD></TR>!,
      qq!<TR><TD>State:</TD><TD>!,
      textfield('state'),
      qq!</TD></TR>!,
```

```
        qq!<TR><TD>Zip Code:</TD><TD>!,
        textfield('zip'),
        qq!</TD></TR>!,
        qq!<TR><TD>Phone:</TD><TD>!,
        textfield('phone'),
        qq!</TD></TR>!,
        qq!<TR><TD>E-mail:</TD><TD>!,
        textfield('email'),
        qq!</TD></TR></TABLE>!,
        submit('action', 'Save Order');

}

sub do_save {
    my @errors;

    # Check to make sure we have all the required values
    if( param('first_name') eq '' ) {
        push(@errors, 'First name is a required field');
    }

    if( param('last_name') eq '' ) {
        push(@errors, 'Last name is a required field');
    }

    if( param('address') eq '' ) {
        push(@errors, 'Address is a required field');
    }

    if( param('city') eq '' ) {
        push(@errors, 'City is a required field');
    }

    if( param('state') eq '' ) {
        push(@errors, 'State is a required field');
    }

    if( param('zip') eq '' ) {
        push(@errors, 'Zip Code is a required field');
    }

    if( param('phone') eq '' ) {
        push(@errors, 'Phone is a required field');
    }

    # If we find anything in @errors then display what
    # went wrong and the order menu again
    if(@errors) {
        print "<CENTER><B>Some errors have occurred:</B>";
        print join('<BR>', @errors);
        do_order();

        return();
    }
```

```
# Get our new customer id from the database sequence
my $sth = $dbh->prepare("SELECT NEXTVAL('customer_seq')");
$sth->execute;

my $customer_id = $sth->fetchrow;

$sth->finish;

# Insert our customer information
my $fname = param('first_name');
my $lname = param('last_name');
my $add = param('address');
my $city = param('city');
my $state = param('state');
my $zip = param('zip');
my $phone = param('phone');
my $email = param('email');

my $sql = "INSERT INTO customer VALUES ($customer_id, " .
          "'$fname', '$lname', '$add', '$city', " .
          "'$state', '$zip', '$phone', '$email')";

$dbh->do($sql) or die "Could not insert customer data: $!";


# Insert our order information
my $proc_id = param('processor');
my $vid_id = param('video');
my $mem_id = param('memory');
my $drive_id = param('harddrive');
my $monitor_id = param('monitor');

$sql = "INSERT INTO orders (order_ts, customer_id, " .
       "processor_id, video_id, memory_id, " .
       "harddrive_id, monitor_id) VALUES ( 'now', " .
       "$customer_id, $proc_id, $vid_id, $mem_id, " .
       "$drive_id, $monitor_id)";

$dbh->do($sql) or die "Could not insert order data: $!";

print "<CENTER><B>Thank you for your order</B></CENTER>";

}
```

As you can see this script is very similar to those from previous chapters. Probably the most notable difference is how we handled our program flow. Instead of using a large block of nested if/else statements, we used:

```
SWITCH: {
        if( $a eq '' ) { display_menu(); last SWITCH; }
        if( $a =~ /update/i ) { display_menu(); last SWITCH; }
```

```
        if( $a =~ /save/I ) { do_save(); last SWITCH; }
        if( $a =~ /order/i ) { do_order(); last SWITCH; }
}
```

In Perl you can name a block of code, and we use that to our advantage here. By naming this block of code 'SWITCH', we can exit the block by calling the built-in function last(). Because Perl does not have a case statement, common in other languages, we simulate it here with this code structure.

Our first function defined in this example is get_parts(). get_parts() takes one argument, which is the type of part we are trying to retrieve. Based on that input, we retrieve the ID, name, and price of all the rows in this table. We store these values in a hash that gets used as the labels for subsequent popup_menu() calls. Because we use the numeric data type in our tables for our price fields, we must remove all the trailing zeros with the following regular expression:

```
$price =~ s/^(.*?\.\d\d).*?$/$1/o;
```

If we did not use this regex, our prices would resemble $12.00000000000000000000 instead of the desired $12.00.

After defining get_parts(), we lay out two functions, get_part_name() and get_price(). These two functions take two arguments each, the first being the unique ID of the part, and the second being the table where this part is located.

get_price_total() is called when we want to update the total price based on input from the user. It calls get_price() for each of the five types of parts we have and then simply adds them together.

display_menu() displays for the user an HTML form with all of the types of parts that are available. Users will not have chosen anything at the first call; on subsequent calls to update the price, the menu will adjust automatically. This adjustment is handled in part by the ability of popup_menu() to display the last chosen item, and because we call get_price_total() on each display. Figure 12.1 shows the output of display_menu() when first entering the site. Figure 12.2 shows display_menu() after some parts have been selected.

Our do_order() function displays the last parts selected by users and an HTML form for them to input their billing information. This form posts to do_save(), which actually inserts the customer and order information into the database. It then displays a simple "Thank You" message. Figures 12.3 and 12.4 show the ordering and "Thank You" pages.

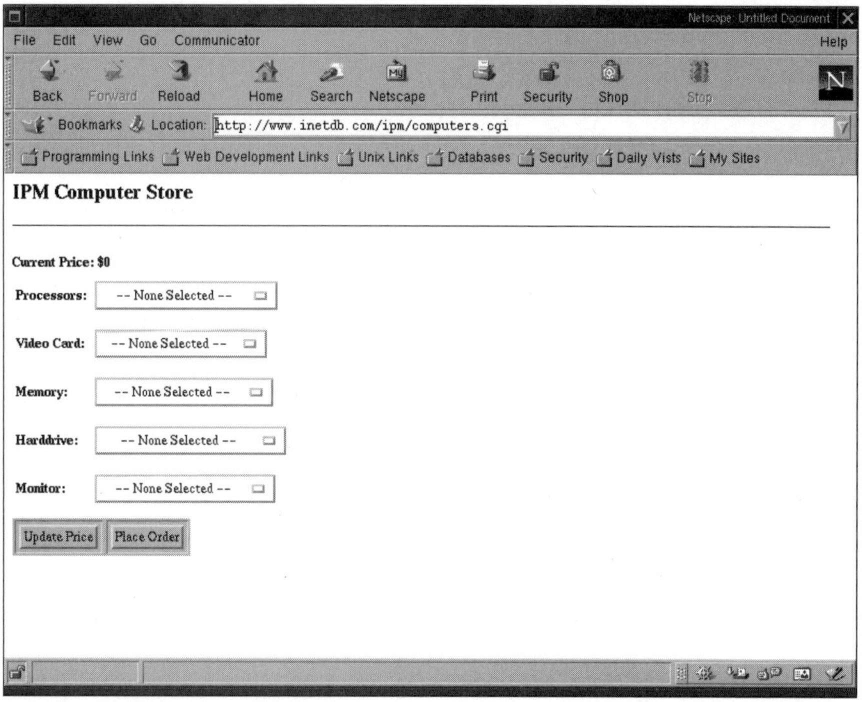

Figure 12.1
Output of
display_menu() when
first entering the site.

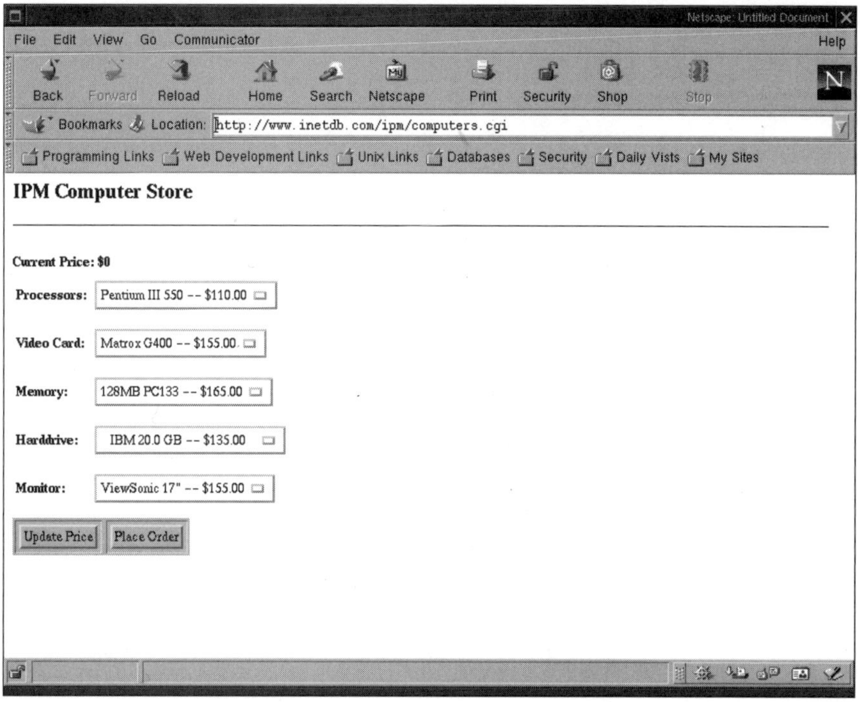

Figure 12.2
Output of
display_menu() after
some parts have
been selected.

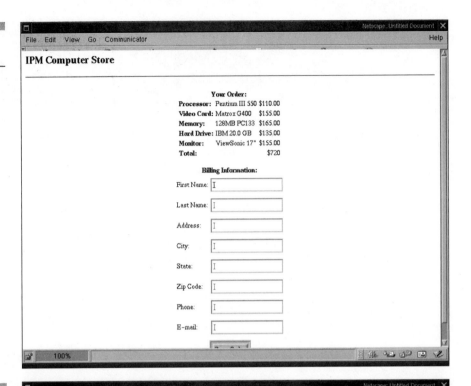

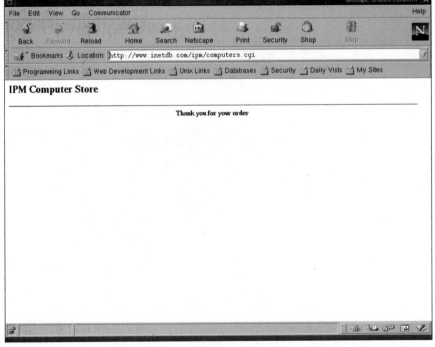

Online Forum

This script is an example of a threaded online discussion forum. We have taken a different stylistic approach in writing this CGI script in the spirit of Perl's motto: "There Is More Than One Way To Do It."

The two biggest differences are our use of subroutine references to handle program flow and the fact that we store all of our output in an array, sending it to the browser at the end of the script. We also wrap the content-generation section of this script in an `eval`. This lets us catch any possible fatal errors in the script and display a useful error message to the users, as opposed to simply sending them to the webserver's error log.

For this forum we use a PostgreSQL database to store the message and threading information.

Here is the table structure for our 'forum' database:

```
CREATE SEQUENCE msg_seq;
CREATE TABLE msg (
            id int4 PRIMARY KEY DEFAULT NEXTVAL('msg_seq'),
            parent_id int4,
            created datetime,
            title varchar(50),
            name varchar(50),
            email varchar(50),
            link varchar(255),
            message text
);
GRANT ALL ON msg TO nobody;
GRANT ALL ON msg_seq TO nobody;
CREATE INDEX msg_idx1 ON msg(parent_id, id);
CREATE INDEX msg_idx2 ON msg(created);
```

We create an SQL sequence to give each message a unique ID number, which will be the default value on all message inserts. The most interesting part of the 'msg' table is the `parent_id`, which will store the ID number of the message that was replied to or zero if this message is the start of a thread. This form of threading is very common; the idea of the parent/child relationship is evident in our choice of variable and function names.

After granting permission to the user the webserver runs as, we create two indexes: one on the `parent_id` and the message id, and another on the creation date and time of the message. These indexes will speed our database queries when looking for messages by their `parent_id` or by the time at which they were created.

```perl
#!/usr/bin/perl -w
use strict;
use CGI qw(:standard);
use DBI;

# URI location of this script
my $script = '/ipm/forum.cgi';

# Different actions of our page
my %Cmds = (
    'main'  => \&do_main,
    'post'  => \&do_post,
    'reply' => \&do_reply,
    'save'  => \&do_save,
    'view'  => \&do_view,
);

# Array of lines of HTML we gather and eventually
# display to the user just before exiting
my @lines;

# Our database connection
my $dbh;

# Make our database connection and execute the chosen
# action wrapping everything in an eval to catch any errors
eval {

    # Create our database connection
    $dbh = DBI->connect('dbi:Pg:dbname=forum', '', '') or
      die "Cannot create database connection: $!";

    # Start our HTML output
    print header;
    print start_html(-bgcolor=>'white');
    print h2('IPM Forum') . qq!<HR SIZE="1" NOSHADE>!;
    print qq!<A HREF="$script?action=post">!;
    print qq!Start a New Thread</A>!;
    print qq!   !;
    print qq!<A HREF="$script">Back to Threads</A><P>!;

    # Determine our action and default to the main view
    my $action = param('action') || 'main';

    # Try to find the action
    if( my $func = $Cmds{$action} ) {
        push(@lines, &$func() );
    } else {
        push(@lines, qq!The action "$action" is not valid!);
    }

};

# Let the user know of any fatal errors
```

```perl
if($@) {
    push(@lines, "An error has occurred: $@");
}

# Send our collected output to the user and end our HTML
print join("\n", @lines);
print end_html;

# Functions

# This function displays the threaded list of messages
sub do_main {

    # Get the ids of the threads
    my @thread_ids = get_thread_ids();

    # Start our output table
    push(@lines, qq!<TABLE BORDER=0>!);

    # Loop over each id displaying the threads
    foreach my $id ( @thread_ids ) {
        push(@lines,
            qq!<TR><TD>!,
            get_thread_messages($id, 0),
            qq!</TD></TR>!,
        );
    }

    # Close up our HTML table
    push(@lines, qq!</TABLE>!);

    return();

}

# Generate our new thread form
sub do_post {

    # Overwrite our current action so that we save this message
    param('action', 'save');

    # Push our HTML output onto our output array
    push(@lines,
        start_form,
        hidden('parent_id', 0),
        qq!<TABLE BORDER=0><TR><TD><B>Title:</B></TD><TD>!,
        textfield(-name=>'title', -maxlength=>50),
        qq!</TD></TR><TR><TD><B>Your Name:</B></TD><TD>!,
        textfield(-name=>'name', -maxlength=>50),
        qq!</TD></TR><TR><TD><B>Your E-mail:</B></TD><TD>!,
        textfield(-name=>'email', -maxlength=>50),
        qq!</TD></TR><TR><TR><TD>!,
        qq!<B>Optional Link:</B></TD><TD>!,
        textfield(-name=>'link', -maxlength=>255),
```

```
            qq!</TD></TR><TR><TD VALIGN="middle">!,
            qq!<B>Message:</B></TD>!,
            qq!<TD>!,
            textarea(-name=>'message',-rows=>8,-columns=>50),
            qq!</TD></TR></TABLE>!,
            hidden('action'),
            submit('Post Message'),
            reset,
            end_form,
        );

        return();

}

sub do_reply {

    # Fix our action
    param('action', 'save');

    # Get our parent message's title and message text
    my $parent_id = param('parent_id');
    my $sql = "SELECT title, message FROM msg " .
              "WHERE id=$parent_id";

    my $sth = $dbh->prepare($sql) or
      die "ERROR: Invalid SQL in do_reply(): $!";

    $sth->execute;

    my ($title, $message) = $sth->fetchrow;

    $sth->finish;

    # Change the title to show that this is a response
    $title = 'Re: ' . $title;

    # Change our message to look like a response
    $message =~ s/^/\>/mg;

    # Push our output onto our output array
    push(@lines,
        start_form,
        hidden('parent_id', $parent_id),
        qq!<TABLE BORDER=0><TR><TD><B>Title:</B></TD><TD>!,
        textfield(-name=>'title', -default=>"$title",
                  -maxlength=>50),
        qq!</TD></TR><TR><TD><B>Your Name:</B></TD><TD>!,
        textfield(-name=>'name', -maxlength=>50),
        qq!</TD></TR><TR><TD><B>Your E-mail:</B></TD><TD>!,
        textfield(-name=>'email', -maxlength=>50),
        qq!</TD></TR><TR><TR><TD>!,
        qq!<B>Optional Link:</B></TD><TD>!,
        textfield(-name=>'link', -maxlength=>255),
```

```
            qq!</TD></TR><TR>!,
            qq!<TD VALIGN="middle"><B>Message:</B></TD>!,
            qq!<TD>!,
            textarea(-name=>'message',-default=>"$message",
                    -rows=>8,-columns=>50),
            qq!</TD></TR></TABLE>!,
            hidden('action'),
            submit('Save Reply'),
            reset,
            end_form,
        );

        return();

    }

    sub do_save {
        my %vars;
        my @errors;

        # Store all of our inputs into a hash
        foreach my $key ( param() ) {
            $vars{$key} = param($key);
        }

        # Check to make sure all required fields are filled out
        if( $vars{title} eq '' ) {
            push(@errors, 'Title is a required field');
        }

        if( $vars{name} eq '' ) {
            push(@errors, 'Name is a required field');
        }

        if( $vars{message} eq '' ) {
            push(@errors, 'You did not input a message');
        }

        # If we have any errors show them to the user and
        # redisplay the correct form
        if(@errors) {
            push(@lines,
                qq!<B>Some errors occurred:</B>!,
                join('<BR>', @errors),
            );

            if( $vars{action} =~ /Post/ ) {
                push(@lines, do_post());
            } else {
                push(@lines, do_reply());
            }

            return();
```

```
        }

        # Prepare our data to be inserted into the database
        $vars{message} =~ s/'/''/g;
        $vars{message} =~ s/\\/\\\\/g;
        $vars{message} =~ s/\</\&lt;/g;
        $vars{message} =~ s/\>/\&gt;/g;

        $vars{name} =~ s/'/''/g;
        $vars{name} =~ s/\\/\\\\/g;

        $vars{title} =~ s/'/''/g;
        $vars{title} =~ s/\\/\\\\/g;

        # Prepare our insert statement
        my $sql = "INSERT INTO msg (parent_id, created, title, " .
                  " name, email, link, message) VALUES (" .
                  "$vars{parent_id}, 'now', '$vars{title}', " .
                  "'$vars{name}', '$vars{email}', " .
                  "'$vars{link}', '$vars{message}')";

        $dbh->do($sql) or
          die "ERROR in saving message: $!";

        push(@lines,
            qq!<CENTER><B>Thank you for your submission</B><BR>!,
            qq!<A HREF="$script">Back to Threads</A></CENTER>!,
        );

        return();

    }

# Actually view the message
sub do_view {
    my $id = param('id');

    # Retrieve the contents of this message
    my $sth = $dbh->prepare("SELECT * FROM msg WHERE id=$id")
      or die "ERROR: Invalid SQL in do_view(): $!";

    $sth->execute;

    my ($cid, $pid, $created, $title, $name, $email,
        $link, $message ) = $sth->fetchrow;

    # Output this message to the user
    push(@lines,
        qq!<TABLE BORDER="0">!,
        qq!<TR><TD><B>Title:</B></TD><TD>$title</TD></TR>!,
    );

    # Output the name with a link for their E-mail
```

```perl
        # if they gave us one
        if($email ne '' ) {
            push(@lines,
                qq!<TR><TD><B>Name:</B></TD><TD>!,
                qq!<A HREF="mailto:$email">$name</A></TD></TR>!,
            );
        } else {
            push(@lines,
                qq!<TR><TD><B>Name:</TD><TD>!,
                qq!$name</TD></TR>!
            );
        }

        # Show the user a link if one was given to us
        if($link ne '' ) {
            push(@lines,
                qq!<TR><TD><B>Link:</B></TD>!,
                qq!<TD><A HREF="$link">$link!,
                qq!</A></TD></TR>!,
            );
        }

        # Make our message look nice
        $message =~ s/\n/<BR>/g;

        push(@lines,
            qq!<TR><TD VALIGN="TOP"><B>Message:</B></TD>!,
            qq!<TD>$message</TD></TR></TABLE><P>!,
            qq!<A HREF="$script?action=reply\&parent_id=$id">!,
            qq!Reply to this message</A>!,
        );

        push(@lines,
            qq!<P><B>Replies:</B><HR SIZE="1">!,
            get_thread_messages($id, 0, 'replies'),
        );

        return();

    }

# Get the ids of the start of all threads
sub get_thread_ids {
    my @ids;

    # This works because all threads have a parent_id of zero
    my $sql = "SELECT id FROM msg WHERE parent_id=0 " .
            "ORDER BY created";

    my $sth = $dbh->prepare($sql) or
        die "ERROR: invalid SQL in get_thread_ids(): $!";

    $sth->execute;
```

```perl
    while( my ($id) = $sth->fetchrow ) {
        push(@ids, $id);
    }

    $sth->finish;

    return(@ids);

}

# Get a thread based on it's parent id
sub get_thread_messages {
    my ($parent_id, $depth, $replies) = @_;
    my $output;

    # Setup this messages link
    if( !$replies ) {
        $output .= generate_link($parent_id, $depth);
    }

    # Get the ids of any children
    my $sql = "SELECT id FROM msg " .
              "WHERE parent_id=$parent_id " .
              "ORDER BY created";

    # Get all the sub-threads of this parent
    my $sth = $dbh->prepare($sql) or
      die "ERROR: invalid SQL in get_thread_messages(): $!";

    $sth->execute;

    # Loop on each child found and if it has children recurse
    # on this function, if not generate the link
    while( my $id = $sth->fetchrow ) {

        # Test to see if this child message
        # in fact has children
        if( has_children($id) ) {
            $output .= get_thread_messages($id, $depth + 2);
        } else {
            $output .= generate_link($id, $depth+2);
        }
    }

    $sth->finish;

    return($output);

}

# See if this ID has any children
sub has_children {
    my $id = shift;
```

```perl
    my $sql = "SELECT count(*) FROM msg WHERE parent_id=$id";

    my $sth = $dbh->prepare($sql) or
        die "ERROR: Invalid SQL in has_children(): $!";

    $sth->execute;

    # Save how many children this message ID has
    my $count = $sth->fetchrow;

    $sth->finish;

    if( $count > 0 ) {
        return(1);
    } else {
        return(0);
    }

}

# Generate this message's HTML link
sub generate_link {
    my ($id, $depth) = @_;
    my $output;

    my $sql = "SELECT title, name FROM msg WHERE id=$id";

    # Get the title of this message
    my $sth = $dbh->prepare($sql) or
        die "ERROR: Invalid SQL in generate_link(): $!";

    $sth->execute;

    my ($title, $name, $created) = $sth->fetchrow;

    $output = '  ' x $depth .
            qq!<A HREF="$script?action=view\&id=$id">! .
            qq!$title</A>$name <BR>\n!;

    return($output);

}
```

In our `eval` at the beginning of the script, we connect to our database, find our action function, and execute it. If we could not connect or execute our function, users would get the error in their browsers instead of a blank page. This is useful for letting users know that they are indeed on the right page, that it cannot currently be displayed, and, most importantly that it is not their fault.

Without this sort of error message, users might assume that the address they have for the page is wrong, or that the page never existed.

By seeing this message instead of a blank page, they can attempt to revisit your site in the future when it is working.

```
# Determine our action and default to the main view
my $action = param('action') || 'main';

if( my $func = $Cmds{$action} ) {
    push(@lines, &$func() );
} else {
    push(@lines, qq!The action "$action" is not valid!);
}
```

The code above checks the `action` parameter to see if it is set to anything and, if not, assigns it the default of `'main'`, which is the front page of this script. We do this by keeping a hash with the keys representing actions that we have set up and the values being references to subroutines.

If `$func` were to contain `'reply'`, then `&$func()` would call `&reply()`. It is probably easiest to think of these references as holding the name of the subroutine; however, references in Perl are more complicated and beyond the scope of this book.

Our `do_main()` function and the functions it calls are definitely the most complicated pieces of this application. In `do_main()`, we first get a list of messages with a `parent_id` of zero using `get_thread_ids()`. This is our clue that this message is the start of a thread and not a reply. We then build a simple HTML table, where each row is the output of `get_thread_messages()`, with one of our IDs from `get_thread_ids()`. The second argument to `get_thread_messages()` is the depth of the message; this provides a simple way to indent our messages. Figure 12.5 shows the main menu.

We indent our messages using HTML's representation of a space, which is `' '`. This method is trivial and can easily be done by using more complicated tables or even cascading style sheets so that the generated HTML is smaller. Making the display page smaller is advantageous on larger sites and should be explored if you plan to use this code in such a manner.

Below is some code from `get_thread_messages()`, which is the real meat of our application. It uses the tried-and-true computer-science idea of *recursion*. Recursion is simply a function calling itself repeatedly with new information to get to the bottom of a problem. This function takes three arguments: the ID of the current message, the current depth, and whether or not we're using a message in our `do_reply()` function. If `$replies` is defined, we do not generate the HTML for the current mes-

Figure 12.5
Main menu.

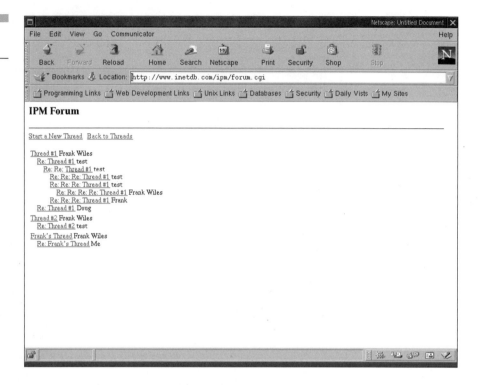

sage, only the replies. If we are not replying, we call `generate_link()` with the passed-in message ID and at the current depth:

```
if( !$replies ) {
    $output .= generate_link($parent_id, $depth);
}
```

After we have displayed the link for the current message, we query the database for all messages that have this message as their parent message, with the following code:

```
# Get the ids of any children
my $sql = "SELECT id FROM msg " .
          "WHERE parent_id=$parent_id " .
          "ORDER BY created";

# Get all the sub-threads of this parent
my $sth = $dbh->prepare($sql) or
  die "ERROR: invalid SQL in get_thread_messages(): $!";

$sth->execute;
```

From this database query, we check each message to see if it has any children of its own. If it does have children, we call `get_thread_messages()` again with its unique ID and increase the depth of indention. This is when the recursion is applied. If the message doesn't have any children, we simply call `generate_link()` to display it on the page.

```
while( my $id = $sth->fetchrow ) {

    # Test to see if this child message
    # in fact has children
    if( has_children($id) ) {
        $output .= get_thread_messages($id, $depth + 2);
    } else {
        $output .= generate_link($id, $depth+2);
    }
}
```

The functions `do_post()` and `do_reply()` provide essentially the same functionality, but there are several small differences in `do_reply()` that set it apart. `do_reply()` sets the `parent_id` input value to the message being replied to and modifies the title and contents of the message to more resemble an e-mail reply. Figure 12.6 shows the `do_post()` generated form, and Figure 12.7 shows the reply to such a message.

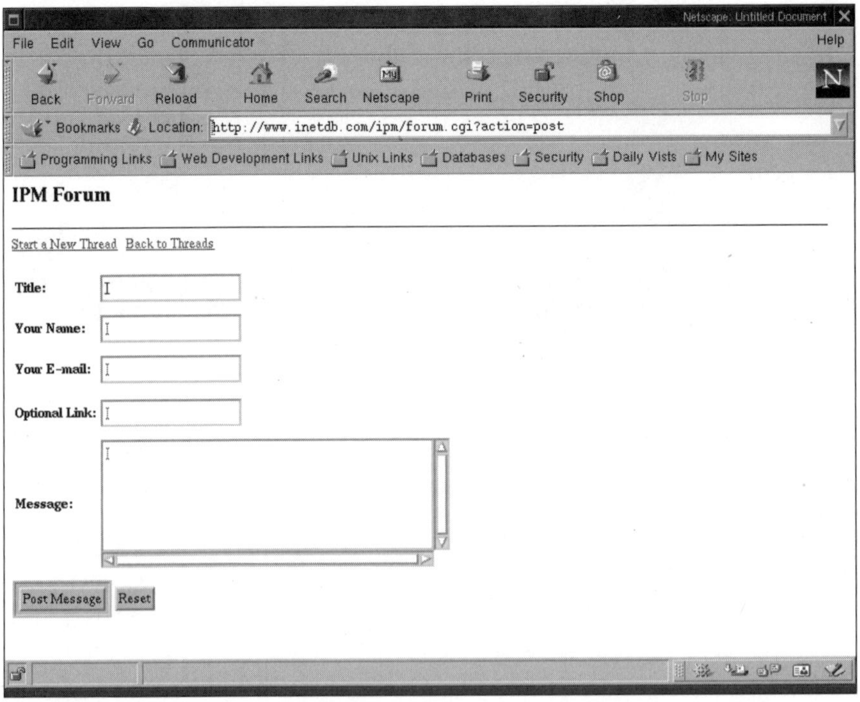

Figure 12.6
Form generated by
do_post().

Figure 12.7
Reply to a do_view()
message.

Figure 12.7
Reply to a do_view()
message.

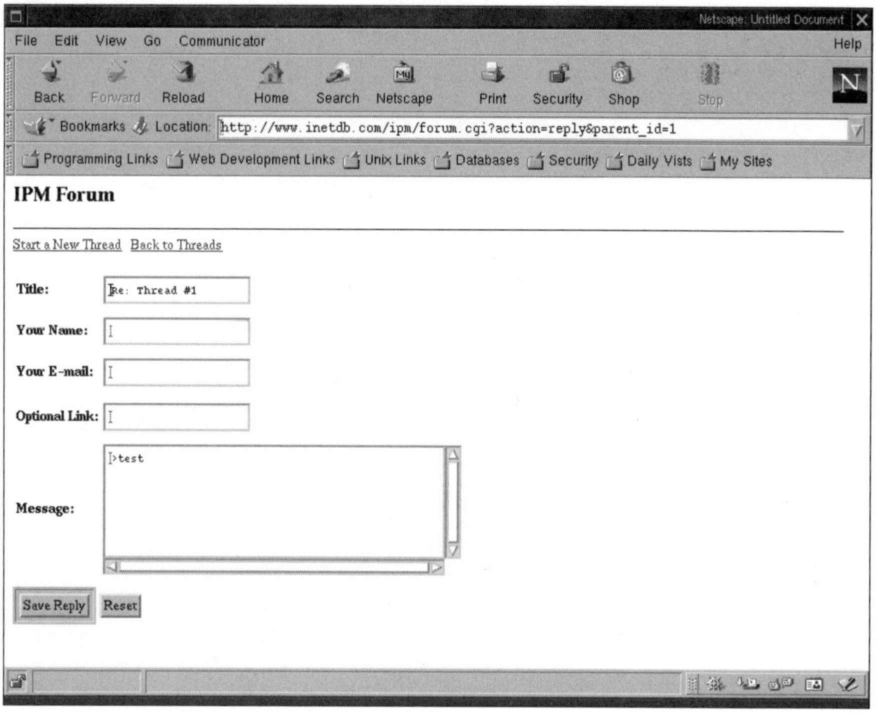

Our function `do_view()` displays all of the contents of the message in the database, including a mail-to and option link, if they are found. The usefulness of this function is also greatly increased by displaying all the children below this message. This allows the user to quickly read an entire thread. Figure 12.8 shows how a message looks when viewed.

Our `do_save` function first puts all of the available input parameters from CGI.pm into a hash:

```
foreach my $key ( param() ) {
    $vars{$key} = param($key);
}
```

Although this trick uses more memory, it increases programmer efficiency and the speed with which this function executes by removing any extra function calls to `param()`.

We use the following regular expressions on the user's name, title, and the message body. This is necessary to ensure these go easily into our PostgreSQL database.

```
s/'/''/g;
s/\\/\\\\/g;
```

Figure 12.8

Viewing a do_view()
message.

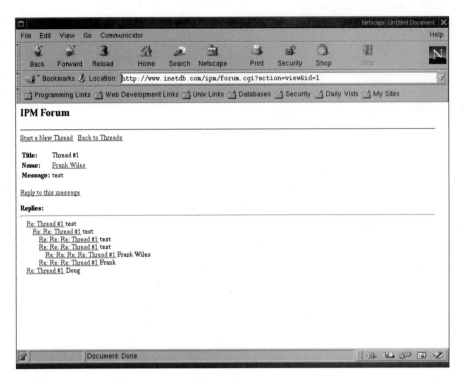

We also want to ensure that no HTML input is accepted in the message body as improperly formatted HTML, which would disrupt its display. To do this, we replace all angle brackets with

```
s/\</\&lt;/g;
s/\>/\&gt;/g;
```

has_children() uses the SQL function count() to return the number of rows found matching the given WHERE clause. If the message ID given to this function has any children, we return true; otherwise we return false.

Summary

We hope this chapter has shown you a couple of more full-featured practical applications using some of the skills learned so far in this book. By using a few simple coding tricks with regard to program flow and databases as a storage method, you can quickly and easily design and build useful applications.

Site
Administration

Introduction

The day-to-day operations of maintaining a web site can easily over-whelm one person in a surprisingly short time. In this chapter we show some simple Perl scripts that can reduce the time spent on trivial but common web site management tasks.

Our HTML Editor and htaccess examples help with remote server administration by providing a web interface for editing HTML files and modifying Apache access controls. And our server log parsing and port checking scripts help address common requests from management by providing server statistics and 24/7 monitoring of the site(s).

Online HTML Editor

This CGI script allows you to edit HTML files from a specific directory from any web browser. Careful consideration needs to be taken with regard to security. You must password-protect this script with whatever security mechanisms are available in your web server. Without this protection, any Internet user who knows the URL to this script can edit the files.

At your first visit to the CGI script, it displays a pull down list of files currently in the directory specified by the variable $DIR. It also allows you to create new files in this directory by leaving the default choice of Create New File in the select box and entering a filename in the text box below.

When a file is chosen for editing or a filename is submitted for creation, the script displays an HTML form containing the contents of the file in a text area. The contents of this text area can then be edited and saved by the user.

```perl
#!/usr/bin/perl -Tw
use strict;
use CGI qw/:standard/;

# Setup Environment for taint
$ENV{PATH} = '';

# Directory to store files
my $DIR = '/home/httpd/content/html';

# Determine if we are to save a file,
# open a file for edit, or simply display
# the form for a user to choose which file to edit
if( param('filename') ) {
```

```perl
        save_html_file( param('filename') );
    } elsif( param('display') ) {
        display_form( param('display') );
    } else {
        display_form();
    }

    #######################################

    sub display_form {
        my $file = shift;
        my @lines;

        # Used to determine if this file is new or not
        my $new = 0;

        # Start our HTML output and give a title
        print header;
        print start_html(-bgcolor=>'white'),
              h1('IPM HTML Editor'),
              $file,
              start_form;

        # Create our new file
        if( $file =~ /Create New File/ ) {
            $file = param('new');
            $new = 1;
        }

        # Remove taint
        $file =~ s/^\.+//;
        $file =~ s/\///g;
        $file =~ /^\s*(.*?)\s*$/;
        $file = $1;

        # If we have gotten a file argument from
        # the user, check to make sure the file exists
        # and that it is safe to open
        if( $file ) {

            # Don't open symlinks for security
            if( -l "$DIR/$file" ) {
                die "File is not a regular file";
            }

            # If our file is new, create it
            # otherwise read in the file for editing.
            if( $new ) {
                open(INPUT, ">$DIR/$file") or
                  die "Can't create $file: $!\n";
            } else {
                open(INPUT, "$DIR/$file") or
                  die "Cannot open $file: $!\n";
```

```perl
            @lines = <INPUT>;
        }

        close(INPUT);
        my $content = join('', @lines);

        # Free unused and possibly large variable
        undef(@lines);

        print hidden('filename', $file),
              textarea(-name=>'content',
                       -default=>$content,
                       -rows=>15,
                       -columns=>50,
                       -wrap=>'virtual'),
              submit(-name=>'Save');

    } else {
        my @files;

        # Give users ability to create a new file
        push(@files, 'Create New File');

        # Get a list of all the files in the directory
        # the user can edit
        opendir(LIST, $DIR) or
          die "Cannot open input directory: $!\n";

        while( my $f = readdir(LIST) ) {

            # Skip files that start with a period
            if( $f =~ /^\./ ) { next; }
            push(@files, $f);
        }

        close(LIST);

        # Print a pull down box of file names that
        # currently exist and a box for them
        # to create new files
        print b('Choose a file to edit:'),
              popup_menu(-name=>'display',
                         -values=>\@files, ),
              br,
              b('Create New:'),
              textfield(-name=>'new', -size=>25),
              submit(-name=>'Edit');
    }

    print end_form,
          end_html;
}
```

```
sub save_html_file {
    my $file = shift;

    # Remove taint by making sure
    # the user does not attempt to fool our
    # script into editing a file it shouldn't
    $file =~ s/^\.+//;
    $file =~ s/\///g;
    $file =~ /^\s*(.*?)\s*$/;
    $file = $1;

    # Don't save files that aren't plain text
    # files or those that are symbolic links
    if( !-e "$DIR/$file" || -l "$DIR/$file" ) {
        die "Cannot save file: $!\n";
    }

    open(OUT, ">$DIR/$file")
      or die "Can't save $file: $!\n";

    print OUT param('content');

    close(OUT);

    print header,
          start_html(-bgcolor=>'white'),
          h1("$file was saved successfully"),
          end_html;
}
```

In the main section of this program we use the HTML form elements from this script to determine the next action. If no inputs exist, we know this is the user's first time to the page and we simply display our file list (Figure 13.1). If we have an input from param() named "display," we display the second page of this script, which allows the user to edit or create the contents of this file (Figure 13.2). When the input named "filename" is present, we save any changes the user has made to file.

There are two subroutines in the script: display_form() and save_html(). display_form() generates the introduction and editing pages with the chosen file's contents. save_html() writes the contents of the text area to the file after the user clicks the Save button on the editing page.

Note that this example does not handle the race condition, where one user opens a file for editing and another opens it at nearly the same time. Whichever user saves last will overwrite any changes made by the other. The htaccess example later in this chapter and Appendix C address this matter further.

Figure 13.1
Form displaying file
names.

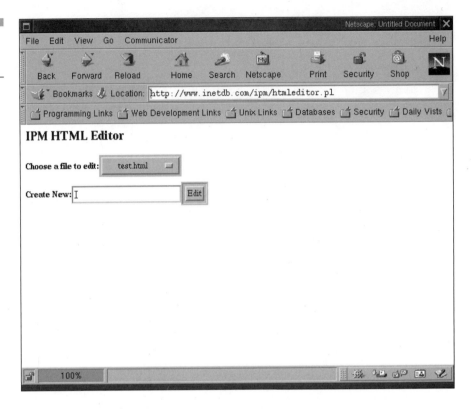

Most of the code in this example should be familiar from Chapters 9 through 12; however, the regular expressions that check to make sure we did not edit files outside of the area designated by $DIR should be explained.

```
$file =~ s/^\.+//;
$file =~ s/\///g;
$file =~ /^\s*(.*?)\s*$/;
$file = $1;
```

The first and second regular expressions remove any forward slashes and any periods at the beginning of the filename. The third expression removes any spaces before or after the file name, extracting out the base filename into $1, which is reassigned to our $file variable.

These checks remove the taint attached to this variable and provide a reasonable amount of assurance that the user cannot trick the script into doing something it shouldn't.

Figure 13.2
HTML edit form.

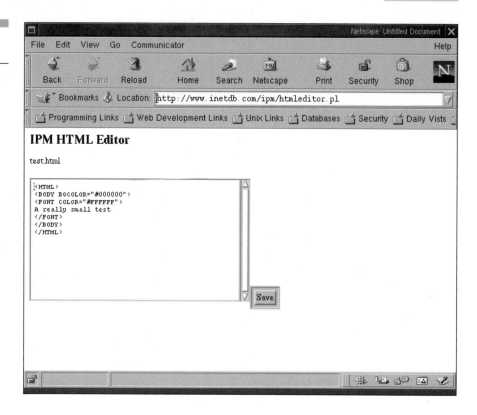

```
if( !-e "$DIR/$file" || -l "$DIR/$file" ) {
    die "Cannot save file";
}
```

This `if` statement checks that our file exists and that it is not a symbolic link to another file. `display_form()` creates new files as directed by the user; by the time a user has come to this point, the file should exist or something is wrong. We don't allow writing to symbolic links to avoid the possibility of someone adding a link to another file on the system that we don't want to overwrite.

Parsing Log Files

All web servers have the ability to log the requests they have received and tried to process. These logs are useful to see which parts of a site are popular or which parts are broken. They are also very useful in gathering statistics about who has come to see the site. We provide some simple examples of parsing what is known as the Common Log Format, which is the default logging format of the most popular web server, known as Apache. Below is an example of a common line from a log file. This would be one long line in the actual file but has been broken due to space constraints.

```
206.52.158.167 - - [28/Nov/2000:15:14:56 -0600]
"GET / HTTP/1.0" 200 1364
```

This log entry contains the IP address of the person making the request, the date and time of the request, and the requested page. The last two numbers in the entry are the HTTP status code of the request (in this case, success) and the amount of data transferred in bytes.

One common request of management is determining how many "people" have visited a site. It is nearly impossible to gauge exactly how many individuals have visited a web site, but you can give management an exact number of unique IP addresses, which is a fair approximation. Confusion can arise because any user coming from behind firewalls and proxy servers will appear as a unique user. Cookies can increase the accuracy of this information, but some people do browse the web with cookies turned off. Therefore, there is no easy way of obtaining a number that is 100% accurate.

```perl
# Location of our log file
my $logfile = '/var/log/httpd/access_log';

# Hash to stores users in
my %users;

open(INPUT, $logfile) or die "Can't open $logfile: $!\n";

while( my $line = <INPUT> ) {
    chomp($line);
    $line =~ /^(\d+\.\d+\.\d+\.\d+)/o;

    # Increment our users hash
    $users{$1}++;
}

close(INPUT);

print "Total Unique Users: " . scalar(keys(%users)) . "\n\n";
```

With this script, we simply traverse the file and grab the IP addresses that appear at the beginning of the line in the standard format of 'xxx.xxx.xxx.xxx'.

This script is easily changed to show how many times each user has accessed the web site by adding the following code to the end of the script:

```perl
foreach my $ip ( keys(%users) ) {
    print "$ip: $users{$ip}\n";
}
```

Another task typically asked of programmers to show how many web hits each page has received. This is achieved in much the same manner only with more use of regular expressions:

```perl
# Location of our log file
my $logfile = '/var/log/httpd/access_log';

# Hashes to store pages
my %get_pages;
my %post_pages;

open(INPUT, $logfile) or die "Can't open $logfile: $!\n";

while( my $line = <INPUT> ) {
    chomp($line);
    my $request;

    # Retrieve the actual request
    $line =~ /\"(.*?)\"/o;
    $request = $1;

    # Determine if this is a GET request or not
    if( $request =~ /^GET/o ) {
        $request =~ /^GET\s(.*?)\s.*?$/;
        $request = $1;
        $get_pages{$request}++;
    } else {
        $request =~ /^POST\s(.*?)\s.*?$/;
        $request = $1;
        $post_pages{$request}++;
    }

}

close(INPUT);

# Print out a header
print "Page\tViews\tPosts\n";
```

```
print '-' x 60 . "\n";

# Print out our GET requested pages and
# their relative POSTs if any
foreach my $key ( keys(%get_pages) ) {
    print "$key\t$get_pages{$key}\t$post_pages{$key}\n";
    delete($post_pages{$key});
}

# Print out pages that were only POSTed to
foreach my $key ( keys(%post_pages) ) {
    print "$key\t\t$post_pages{$key}\n";
}
```

Here is some sample output from this script when I ran it against one of my web server log files:

```
Page     Views   Posts
-------------------------------------------------------------
/usage/usage_0699.html   1
/usage/ctry_usage_0499.gif   6
/ipm/htmleditor.pl   17   31
/robots.txt 97
/icons/image2.gif    2
/archived_html/docs/postgres      1
```

htaccess

htaccess is the standard method by which an administrator password for an Apache web server protects an entire website or individual directories within a site. This is useful for restricting content to certain users who can supply a valid userid and password. Apache stores these userids and passwords in a plain text file in the format of:

```
userid:encrypted password
```

Here is a small example of how this file looks:

```
doug:DsJs7vPfKaFPY
frank:2cTzL31QhFdZQ
admin:LfraIUw.lvI.c
```

This example is a Perl CGI script that adds, edits, and removes users from this file. This is useful because many people can be given access to this script and update the file remotely without knowing how the web server actually accomplishes the task. Figure 13.3 shows the CGI script's HTML interface.

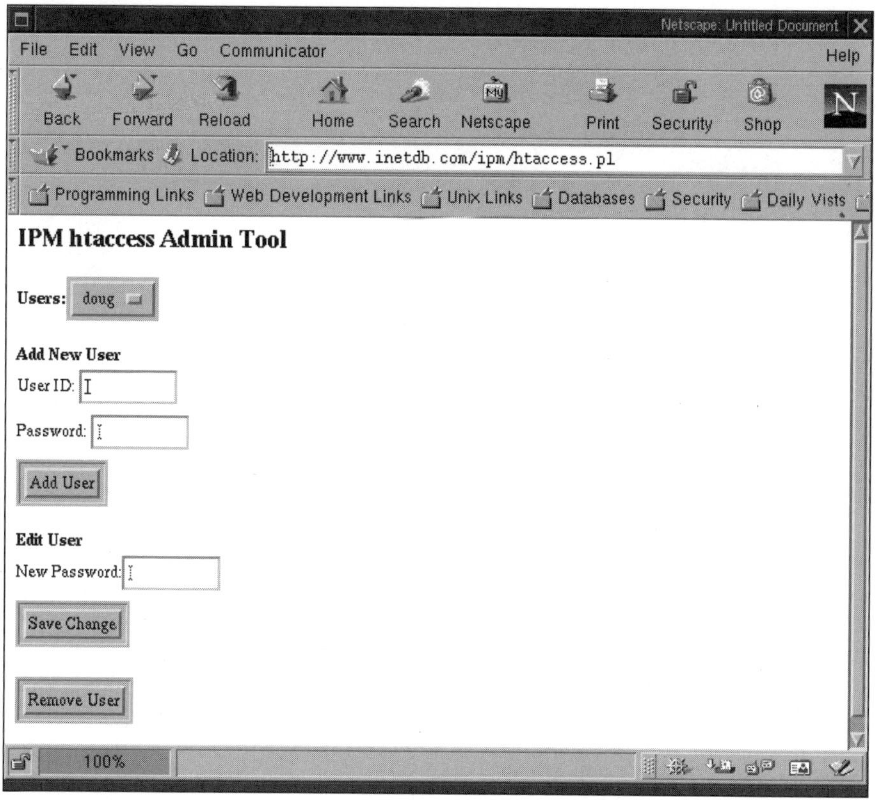

Figure 13.3
htaccess Admin Tool.

```perl
#!/usr/bin/perl -w
use strict;
use CGI qw(:standard);
use Fcntl qw(:flock);
use POSIX;

# Variables
my $userfile = '/home/httpd/secure/passwd';

# Determine if the user wants to add, edit, or remove
# a user from this htaccess file
if( param('submit_add')   ) {
    save_user();
} elsif( param('submit_edit') ) {
    save_user();
} elsif( param('submit_remove')  ) {
```

```perl
        remove_user();
    } else {
        display_menu();
    }

    # subroutine to handle actually encrypting the password
    sub encrypt_password {
        my $password = shift;

        # Build a salt for this password
        my $salt = join("", ('.','/',0..9,'A'..'Z','a'..'z')
            [rand 64 , rand 64] );

        # Encrypt the supplied password with our salt
        my $encrypted = crypt($password, $salt);

        return($encrypted);
    }

    sub display_menu {

        print header;
        print start_html(-bgcolor=>'white'),
                h1('IPM htaccess Admin Tool'),
                start_form;

        my @users = get_users();

        print b('Users:'),
                popup_menu(-name=>'user',
                            -values=>\@users),
                br,
                br,
                b('Add New User'),
                br,
                'User ID: ',
                textfield(-name=>'new_userid', -size=>10),
                br,
                'Password: ',
                textfield(-name=>'new_password', -size=>10),
                br,
                submit(-name=>'submit_add', -value=>'Add User' ),
                br,
                br,
                b('Edit User'),
                br,
                'New Password:',
                textfield(-name=>'edit_password', -size=>10),
                br,
                submit( -name=>'submit_edit', -value=>'Save Change' ),
                br,
                br,
                submit(-name=>'submit_remove',
                        -value=>'Remove User');
```

```perl
    print end_form,
        end_html;
}

sub save_user {
    my $user;
    my $pass;
    my $add = 1;

    if( param('submit_add' ) ) {
        $user = param('new_userid');
        $pass = param('new_password');
    } else {
        $user = param('user');
        $pass = param('edit_password');
        $add = 0;
    }

    if( $user eq '' ) {
        die "No user selected";
    }

    if( $pass eq '' ) {
        die "No password";
    }

    my $encrypted = encrypt_password($pass);

    if( $add ) {
        if( grep(/$user/, get_users()) ) {
            die "User already exists";
        }

        open(INPUT, ">> $userfile") or
          die "Can't open userfile: $!\n";

        flock(INPUT, LOCK_EX);
        print INPUT "$user:$encrypted\n";
        flock(INPUT, LOCK_UN);
        close(INPUT);

    } else {

        # Edit our file in place without a temporary file
        # this is not advisable if your access file is large
        open(USERFILE, "+< $userfile") or
          die "Can't edit userfile: $!\n";

        flock(USERFILE, LOCK_EX);
        my @lines;

        while( my $line = <USERFILE> ) {
            chomp($line);
```

```perl
            if( $line =~ /^$user:/o ) {
                $line = "$user:$encrypted";
            }

            push(@lines, $line);
        }

        seek(USERFILE, 0, 0);
        print USERFILE join("\n",@lines);
        truncate(USERFILE, tell(USERFILE));

        flock(USERFILE, LOCK_UN);
        close(USERFILE);
    }

    print header;

    print start_html(-bgcolor=>'white'),
          h1('User Saved'),
          end_html;
}

sub remove_user {
    my $user = param('user');

    open(USERFILE, "+< $userfile") or
      die "Can't edit userfile: $!\n";

    flock(USERFILE, LOCK_EX);

    my @lines;

    while( my $line = <USERFILE> ') {

        if( $line =~ /^$user:/o ) {
            next;
        } else {
            push(@lines, $line);
        }
    }

    seek(USERFILE, 0, 0);
    print USERFILE join('', @lines);
    truncate(USERFILE, tell(USERFILE));

    flock(USERFILE, LOCK_UN);
    close(USERFILE);

    print header;

    print start_html(-bgcolor=>'white'),
```

```
                h1('User Removed'),
                end_html;
        }

    sub get_users {
        my @users;

        if( !-e $userfile ) {
            open(INPUT, ">$userfile") or
                die "Cannot create userfile: $!\n";
            close(INPUT);
        }

        # Open our file and put each user into the array
        open(INPUT, $userfile) or die "Cannot open userfile: $!\n";

        while( my $line = <INPUT> ) {
            chomp($line);

            $line =~ /^(.*?):/;
            my $current_user = $1;

            push(@users, $current_user);

        }

        close(INPUT);

        # Populate the array with a message if no users found
        if( @users == 0 ) {
            push(@users, "No Users In System");
        }

        return(@users);
    }
```

Like our HTML Editor, most of the source code to this CGI script should be very familiar. In the main section of this script, we decide which action to take by looking for which named submit button the user clicked. Afterward we use the subroutines encrypt_password(), display_menu(), save_user(), remove_user(), and get_users() to handle all of the rest of the logic.

encrypt_password() uses the standard Perl crypt() function and a random two-character "salt" to obscure the password so it cannot be determined by reading the passwd file.

display_menu() displays our HTML form with which the user will interact. It uses get_users() to populate the pulldown select box with the users currently in the file and to give the user the option of creating a new user.

save_user() determines whether this is a new user or an edit of the password of an existing user. If we are adding a new user, we open the password file in append mode and acquire a file lock so that no one else can read or write to the password file while we are editing it.

If we are editing a user's password, we lock the password file with the line:

```
flock(USERFILE, LOCK_EX);
```

After we have read in the contents of the file into the @lines array with our modified data, we use the line:

```
seek(USERFILE, 0, 0);
```

to bring our filehandle back to the start of the file. We then write the contents of @lines back onto the file, thereby overwriting all previous data.

```
truncate(USERFILE, tell(USERFILE));
```

This line directs Perl to set the length of the file to where we are currently in case the length of the file was shortened by our modification.

After completing these steps, we give up our exclusive lock and close the file with these lines:

```
flock(USERFILE, LOCK_UN);
close(USERFILE);
```

The operations performed by remove_user() are almost the same as the editing portion of save_user(). We use the same locking mechanisms, but rather than pushing modified data onto our @lines array when we find the user, we move on with the next command. Afterward we rewrite the contents of the file as we did in save_user().

Checking Server Ports

```
libwww-perl: /CPAN/libwww-perl-5.48.tar.gz
Net::FTP: /CPAN/libnet-1.0703.tar.gz
Net::SMTP: /CPAN/libnet-1.0703.tar.gz
Net::DNS: /CPAN/Net-DNS-0.12.tar.gz
```

If you are a system administrator in charge of systems that need to be up all day every day, this script is for you. The first time a crucial system goes down in the middle of the night and no one notices until morning, management will ask for this script the very next day.

This script should be run periodically throughout the day to verify that all the system's services are functioning properly. It has the ability to check web, FTP, mail, POP3, IMAP, and DNS servers. It will also ping a server to verify that it is awake and listening.

It uses a simple config file that specifies e-mail addresses to which error messages should be sent. The script verifies that its own network is functioning properly by pinging a set of IP addresses. This prevents the script from sending out error messages for every test if the computer running with this script has network problems.

Here is a sample configuration file:

```
email admin@mydomain.com
email root@mydomain.com
email mypager@mypager.com

# Sample IP addresses
test 10.0.0.1
test 10.0.1.0

server mail.mydomain.com mail
server mail.mydomain.com pop
server www.mydomain.com www
server ftp.mydomain.com ftp

server otherserver.mydomain.com ping
```

This simple configuration would mail the three e-mails provided when the script detected an error with any of the services specified. The test directives are the IP addresses that the script should attempt to ping before testing the servers. Each server line is the fully qualified domain name of the server to be tested and the service that should be tested on it.

If the script is unable to pull a web page from www.mydomain.com, an e-mail similar to the following will be generated:

```
From: monitor@mydomain.com
To: admin@mydomain.com
Subject: Network Monitoring Event

Could not pull www page from http://www.mydomain.com
Date: Thu Nov 30 21:31:52 CST 2000
```

Here is the source code for the monitoring script:

```perl
#!/usr/bin/perl -w
use strict;
use Net::Ping;
use LWP::UserAgent;
use Net::FTP;
use Net::SMTP;
use Net::DNS;
use IO::Socket;
use HTTP::Status;

# Location of config file
my $config = '/home/admin/monitor.config';

# Array of E-mail addresses to send to
my @emails;

# Array of servers and what we are to test
my @servers;

# List of IP addresses to test pings to before starting tests
my @ips;

# Location of the sendmail binary
my $sendmail = '/usr/sbin/sendmail';

sub parse_config {
    my $file = shift;

    open(IN, $file) or die "Can't open $file: $!\n";

    while( my $line = <IN> ) {
        chomp($line);

        if( $line =~ /^\s+|\#/ ) { next; }
        if( $line eq '' ) { next; }

        if( $line =~ /^email\s(.*?)$/i ) {
            push(@emails, $1);
        } elsif( $line =~ /^test\s(.*?)$/i ) {
            push(@ips, $1);
        } elsif( $line =~ /^server\s(.*?)\s(.*?)$/i ) {
            push(@servers, "$1:$2");
        } else {
            warn "Config file error: $line\n";
        }
    }

    close(IN);

}

sub test_network {
```

```perl
    # Make sure we have some IPs to test
    if( @ips == 0 ) {
        return();
    }

    # Get a ping object and setup a watch variable
    # to see if we found any of the ips up
    my $found = 0;

    foreach my $ip ( @ips ) {

        $ip =~ s/\s//g;

        my $p = Net::Ping->new("icmp") or
          die "Can't create a Net::Ping object: $!\n";

        if( !$p->ping($ip) ) {
          warn "Can't ping $ip: $!\n";
        } else {
            $found = 1;
        }

        $p->close();
        undef($p);

    }

    if(!$found) {
        die "Can't ping any test IPs";
    }

}

sub check_servers {

    foreach my $serv_line ( @servers ) {

        $serv_line =~ s/\s//g;
        my($host, $type) = split(/:/, $serv_line);

        if( $host eq '' || $type eq '' ) {
          die "Error in server line 'server $host $type'\n";
        }

        if( $type eq 'www' ) {
            check_www($host);
        } elsif ( $type eq 'ftp' ) {
            check_ftp($host);
        } elsif ( $type eq 'mail' ) {
            check_mail($host);
        } elsif ( $type eq 'dns' ) {
            check_dns($host);
        } elsif ( $type eq 'ping' ) {
            check_ping($host);
```

```perl
        } elsif ( $type eq 'pop' ) {
            check_pop($host);
        } elsif ( $type eq 'imap' ) {
            check_imap($host);
        } else {
            warn "ERROR: unknown check '$type' encountered\n";
        }

    }

}
sub check_www {
    my $host = shift;

    my $ua = new LWP::UserAgent;

    $ua->agent("IPM Network Monitor/0.1" . $ua->agent);

    my $req = new HTTP::Request( GET => "http://$host" );

    my $res = $ua->request($req);

    if( $res->is_error ) {
        send_mail("Could not pull www page from ".
            "http://$host: ".$res->as_string);
    }

}

sub check_ftp {
    my $host = shift;

    my $ftp = Net::FTP->new($host) or
      send_mail("Could not access FTP on $host");

}

sub check_mail {
    my $host = shift;

    my $smtp = Net::SMTP->new($host) or
      send_mail("Could not access SMTP on $host");

}

sub check_dns {
    my $host = shift;

    my $dns = new Net::DNS::Resolver;
    $dns->nameservers("$host");
    my $query = $dns->query("mydomain.com", "NS");

    if(!$query) {
        send_mail("Could not get DNS request for $host");
```

```perl
        }

    }

    sub check_ping {
        my $host = shift;

        my $p = Net::Ping->new("icmp");

        if( !$p->ping($host) ) {
            send_mail("Could not ping $host");
        }

        $p->close();

    }

    sub check_pop {
        my $host = shift;

        my $sock = IO::Socket::INET->new(PeerAddr => $host,
                                         PeerPort => 110,
                                         Proto => 'tcp');

        if( !$sock ) {
            send_mail("Could not connect to POP3 server on $host");
        }

    }

    sub check_imap {
        my $host = shift;

        my $sock = IO::Socket::INET->new(PeerAddr => $host,
                                         PeerPort => 143,
                                         Proto => 'tcp');

        if( !$sock ) {
            send_mail("Could not connect to IMAP server on $host");
        }

    }

    sub send_mail {
        my $msg = shift;

        foreach my $addr ( @emails ) {

            open(OUT, "|$sendmail $addr") or
              die "Can't find $sendmail: $!\n";

            print OUT "From: monitor\@sunflower.com\n";
            print OUT "To: $addr\n";
            print OUT "Subject: Network Monitoring Event\n\n";
```

```
        print OUT "$msg\nDate: " . localtime() . "\n";

        close(OUT);

    }

}

# Make sure our config file exists
if( !-e $config ) {
    die "ERROR: $config does not exist!: $!\n";
}

# Get our configurations
parse_config($config);

# Make sure our network connectivity is up
test_network();

# Check out servers out
check_servers();
```

In this script we use the `parse_config()` subroutine to get the desired configuration from our config file. We then ping the IP addresses provided with the test directives in the `test_network()` routine.

The real work of this script is done within the `check_servers()` subroutine that tests each server configuration directive in turn. It determines the type of service to be tested and then calls the appropriate subroutine to actually test it. If that subroutine cannot accomplish its test, it calls `send_mail()` with an error message to be sent to all of the users in the `@emails` array.

All of the network modules used in the testing subroutines should be familiar to you from Chapter 8 on Internet Protocols.

Summary

We hope these scripts have shown you how easy it is to perform system administration tasks using Perl. Whether you need to edit HTML, change passwords, or verify that your server is functioning, Perl is a good choice.

Perl is probably the second-most used programming language for UNIX system administration tasks, rivaled only by Bourne Shell. Windows admins are also starting to use Perl in their system administration tasks, and we hope we have shown you why.

Site Utilities

Introduction

This chapter focuses on utilities that are common on many websites or could be of use to a Webmaster on his personal site. Searching the contents of a local site, querying a search engine, and banner ad rotation can be found on many popular websites. The examples that follow should show you how to add these features to your website and customize them as you wish.

Our Perl syntax checker and notes database are examples of utilities that might be useful to a Webmaster on a password-protected site or on a company's Intranet.

All of these utilities, with the help of some modules from CPAN and Perl's standard library, are relatively simple to build and understand.

Site Search

By using a combination of two standard Perl modules you can create a fairly accurate website search utility. We use Perl's `File::Find` module, which simplifies the searching of nested directories full of files by traversing the file system. Of course, we use the CGI module for our HTML form and output.

Here is the script:

```perl
#!/usr/bin/perl -w
use strict;
use CGI qw(:standard);
use File::Find;

# Root directory of our website
my $webroot = '/ipm/';

print header;
print start_html(-bgcolor=>'white');

if( param('criteria') ) {
    find(\&search_file, $webroot);
} else {
    display_menu();
}

print end_html;

# Subroutines
```

```perl
sub search_file {

    my $criteria = param('criteria');

    # Only search text and HTML files
    if( $_ !~ /html|txt$/o ) {
        return;
    }

    open(IN, "$_") or warn "Can't open $_: $!\n";

    while ( my $line = <IN> ) {
        chomp($line);

        # Remove HTML from the line
        $line =~ s/\<.*?\>//g;

        # Cleanup our filename and turn it into a valid
        # relative URL so that it can be used as a link
        my $uri = $File::Find::name;
        $uri =~ s/^$webroot//;
        $uri = "$uri";

        if( $line =~ /$criteria/o ) {
            print "<A HREF=$uri>$_</A><BR>";
        }

    }
    close(IN);

}

sub display_menu {

    print start_form,
        b('Search this site for:'),
        br,
        textfield(-name=>'criteria'),
        br,
        submit(-name=>'Search'),
        end_form;

}
```

The find() function from File::Find takes two arguments: the first is a reference to a subroutine that will process each file and the second is a directory from where the search begins. If we have received input from the user in the criteria parameter we perform the search by calling this function.

The search_files() subroutine handles opening and searching through each file. File::Find sets some variables that will assist us (Table 14.1).

$_	Current Filename Being Processed
$File::Find::dir	Current directory
$File::Find::name	Full path to the file (`$File::Find::dir/$_`)

`File::Find`, `chdir()` moves you into the directory. This allows you to:

```
open(IN, "$_");
```

rather than:

```
open(IN, "$File::Find::name");
```

When first entering `search_file()`, check to make sure the name of the file ends in `.html` or `.txt`, which are probably the only files we will want to search. There is not much point in searching the website's images for instance. If the current file is an html or text document, we strip out HTML by removing anything within angle brackets (< and >). We then test whether our file has the search criteria given to us by the user. If it does, we output a link to the file by removing parts of the path in `$File::Find::name` and putting a slash before it to make it a relative URL. Figures 14.1 and 14.2 show the search form and results, respectively.

If we did not receive input from the user, we display an HTML form that will allow users to define their search criteria. This search script should work for most small- to medium-sized websites. If your site is very large or contains hundreds of files, it would probably be best to store the text contents of your site in a database and search it because it is very expensive to `open()` a file.

Searching the Web

CPAN contains a useful module named `WWW:Search` that will allow you to use popular search engines. The base module supports search engines such as AltaVista, Excite News, Infoseek, MetaCrawler, and WebCrawler. You can also expand your ability to search by adding more modules that are site specific. Some examples are Deja News, Lycos, and Yahoo! News.

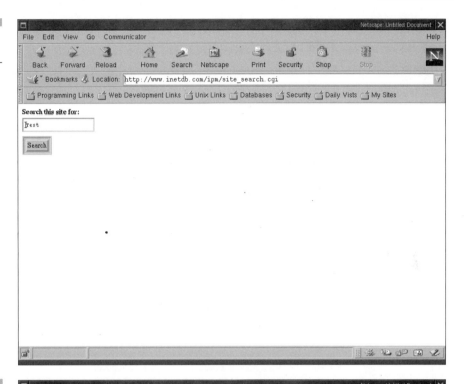

Figure 14.1
Search form.

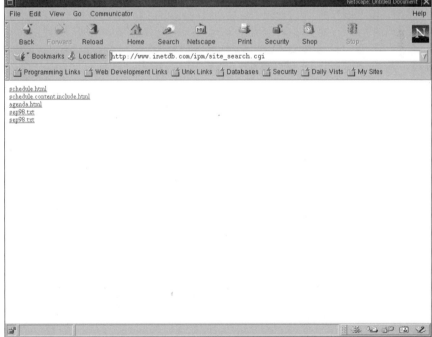

Figure 14.2
Search results.

The interface is in a straightforward object-oriented style. Here is a small example:

```perl
#!/usr/bin/perl -w
use strict;
use WWW::Search;

# Create our search object
my $search = new WWW::Search('AltaVista');

# What we want to search for
my $query = 'Instant+Perl+Modules';

# Actually perform the search
$search->native_query(WWW::Search::escape_query($query));

# Display our results
while( my $result = $search->next_result() ) {
    print $result->url . "\n";
}
```

Here are some sample results:

```
http://www.pbg.mcgraw-hill.com/betabooks/
http://www.dougsparling.com/
http://extras.ids.net/tech.html
http://www.books.mcgraw-hill.com/betabooks/
http://www.softpanorama.org/Bookshelf/perl.shtml
```

There are several options you can set using WWW::Search, such as the maximum number of results to retrieve, a timeout value, and the ability to seek to a particular result. Below is another example that sets our maximum to retrieve to 5 and gives a timeout of 5 seconds to ensure this query returns quickly or not at all.

```perl
#!/usr/bin/perl -w
use strict;
use WWW::Search;

# Create our search object
my $search = new WWW::Search('AltaVista');

# A vanity search
my $query = 'Frank+Wiles';

# Set our max retrieve and timeout options
$search->maximum_to_retrieve(5);
$search->timeout(5);

$search->native_query(WWW::Search::escape_query($query));

# Display our results
while( my $result = $search->next_result() ) {
```

```
    print $result->url . "\n";
}
```

Here are the results from this script:

```
http://staff.daemonnews.org/credits.shtml
http://bugs.gnome.org/db/si/pendinggrave.html
http://frank.wiles.org/
http://www.mindsec.com/
http://www.wiles.org/resume/
```

It is useful to set maximum_to_retrieve() because the module defaults to 500, which is a lot of URLs to wade through. These searches output to STDOUT, but usually you would want this sent to a browser. Below is a CGI script that will take a simple search engine query and return the first 20 results from AltaVista:

```perl
#!/usr/bin/perl -w
use strict;
use CGI qw(:standard);
use WWW::Search;

# Start our HTML output
print header;
print start_html(-bgcolor=>'white');

# Determine what our user would like us to do
if( param('criteria') ) {
    do_search();
} else {
    display_menu();
}

print end_html;

# Subroutines

sub do_search {

    # Create our search object
    my $search = new WWW::Search('AltaVista');

    # Set some options
    $search->maximum_to_retrieve(20);
    $search->timeout(10);

    # Setup our query
    my $query = param('criteria');
    $query =~ s/\s/+/g;

    # Actually perform our search
```

```
$search->native_query(WWW::Search::escape_query($query));

while( my $result = $search->next_result() ) {
    my $url = $result->url;

    print qq!<A HREF="$url">$url</A><BR>!;
}
}

sub display_menu {

    print start_form,
        b('Search AltaVista for:'),
        br,
        textfield(-name=>'criteria'),
        br,
        submit(-name=>'Search'),
        end_form;

}
```

After we have started our HTML output, we check to see if this is the
first or second time through the script by checking for input in our text
field. If the user has given us some search criteria, we process the
search by calling do_search(); otherwise, we simply display our HTML
form.

In the search we set our maximum number to retrieve to 20 and our
timeout to 10 seconds. Before we send the query, we use a regular
expression to replace all whitespace with plus symbols so that the
search engine will process it correctly. We print our output with the
same while loop as in the previous examples, modified to print HTML
links for each URL we received from the search engine. Figures 14.3 and
14.4 show the search form and results respectively.

Recommend a Site

One frequent feature of websites is the ability for the web user to quickly and easily send the URL of the page being viewed to a friend who
might find the site interesting. This can be accomplished across an
entire site with only one script by using the HTTP_REFERER environment
variable that is set based on the last page the user visited. We also use
the Net::SMTP module discussed in detail in Chapter 7.

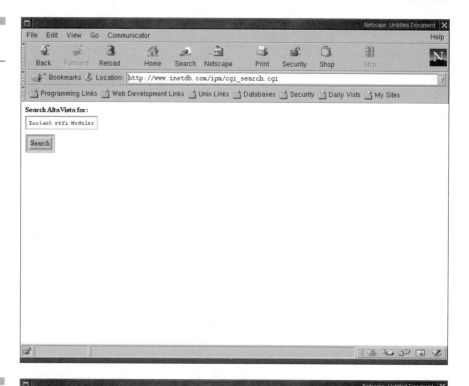

Figure 14.3
Search form.

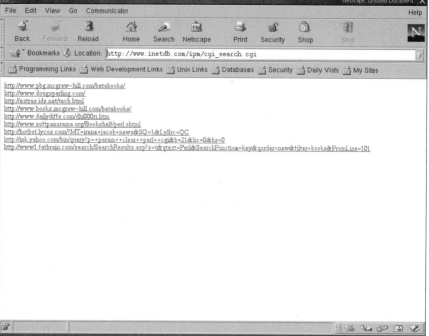

Figure 14.4
Search results.

```perl
#!/usr/bin/perl -w
use strict;
use CGI qw(:standard);
use Net::SMTP;

# Address to say this E-mail is from
my $address = 'mysite@mydomain.com';

# An E-mail server we can use
my $server = 'mail.mydomain.com';

# If we have an address that means we need to send
# the E-mail, otherwise we need to prompt the
# user for an E-mail address to send this note
# to as well as some other information
if( param('address') ) {
    send_email();
} else {
    display_menu();
}

# Function to send our E-mail address
sub send_email {
    # Address we are sending to
    my $to_address = param('address');

    # Address of the web user, or our default address
    my $from_address = param('from_address') || $address;

    # Name of the web user
    my $from_name = param('name');

    # Subject for this E-mail
    my $subject = param('subject');

    # Comments from our web user
    my $comment = param('comment');

    # Page that the user last visited
    my $page = param('url');

    # Create our E-mail object
    my $smtp = Net::SMTP->new($server) or
      die "Error making connection to $server: $!\n";

    # Address this E-mail is from
    $smtp->mail($from_address);

    # Address this E-mail it to
    $smtp->to($to_address);

    # Start sending this message
    $smtp->data();
```

```perl
        # Send some in message headers including our subject
        $smtp->datasend("From: $from_address\n");
        $smtp->datasend("To: $to_address\n");
        $smtp->datasend("Subject: $subject\n");
        $smtp->datasend("\n");

        # Actually send the text of our message
        $smtp->datasend(" $from_name has suggested that you".
                        " visit:\n\n");
        $smtp->datasend(" $page\n\n");

        $smtp->datasend(" Here is what they had to say about".
                        " this");
        $smtp->datasend(" page:\n\n $comment\n\n");

        $smtp->dataend();
        $smtp->quit;

        # Give the web user a message letting them know
        # that their request was processed successfully
        print    header;

        print start_html(-bgcolor=>'white'),
              h1("Your recommendation has been sent ".
                 "to $to_address"),
              end_html;

}

# Display our HTML form for the web user to give us some
# information to send in our E-mail message such as
# the address they wish to send this recommendation to,
# a message subject, some comments, etc.
sub display_menu {

    print header;

    print start_html(-bgcolor=>'white'),
          h1('Recommend this page to a friend'),
          start_form,
          hidden('url', $ENV{HTTP_REFERER}),
          h3("Recipient's Information"),
          b('E-mail Address:'),
          br,
          textfield(-name=>'address'),
          br,
          h3('Your information'),
          b('Name:'),
          br,
          textfield(-name=>'name'),
          br,
          b('E-mail address:'),
          br,
          textfield(-name=>'from_address'),
          br,
```

```
           b('Subject:'),
           br,
           textfield(-name=>'subject'),
           br,
           b('Comments to include in this E-mail:'),
           br,
           textarea(-name=>'comment',
                   -rows=>8,
                   -columns=>40,
                   -wrap=>'virtual'),
           br,
           br,
           submit(-name=>'Send Recommendation');

    print end_form,
          end_html;


}
```

Most of the code in the example above should seem very familiar by now from previous chapters. However, this script is commonly requested and some people make it much harder than it really is. Because of the HTTP_REFERER environment variable, you can use a simple HTML form and Net::SMTP to send this email message. Figure 14.5 shows how the input form looks.

Figure 14.5
Recommend a site input form.

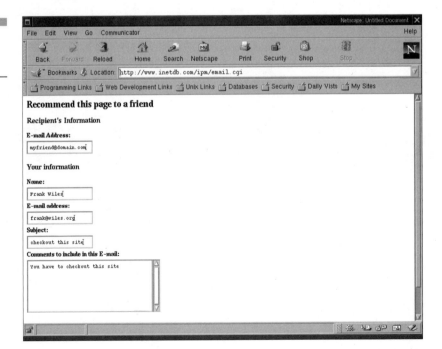

Banner Ad Rotation

Most commercial websites have banner advertisements. It is useful to have these banners rotate so that visitors to the site see different advertisements at each visit. In this section we will build a simple banner ad system that can be incorporated into a website. This system has two pieces: an administration program that tracks banner images and the URL these banners should link to, and a script that generates the HTML needed to show a random banner. We also try to guarantee that a user does not see the same banner twice in a row by keeping track of the last banner viewed by the user.

First, we will build our administration interface. This CGI script handles the addition and removal of banner images and the URL that they link to by a simple HTML form. We store this information in a DBM file database. The information is stored with a unique integer as its key. The image's filename and the URL to which it should point are stored in tab delimited format as the value for this key.

Here is the Perl for the admin tool:

```perl
#!/usr/bin/perl -w
use strict;
use CGI qw(:standard);
use Fcntl;
use SDBM_File;

# Name of this script
my $script = 'banneradmin.pl';

# The path to our lockfile
my $lock = 'banners.lock';

# Path and name for our banner database
my $banner_filename = 'banners.dat';

# Hash to tie our banner DBM file to
my %banners;

# Location of the web document root
my $webroot = '/ipm/images';

# Wait until we any currently existing locks are gone
while( -e $lock ) {
    sleep(1);
}

# Set a lock file
open(LOCK, ">$lock") or die "Can't open $lock: $!";
```

```perl
# Tie our DBM file to our hash so that we can begin using it
tie(%banners, 'SDBM_File', $banner_filename,
    O_RDWR|O_CREAT, 0666) or
  die "Can't create or open $banner_filename: $!";

# Start our HTML output
print header;
print start_html(-bgcolor=>'white');

# Figure out based on the presence of inputs what
# the web user would like us to do
if( param('remove') ) {
    remove_banner( param('remove') );
    display_form();
} elsif( param('filename') ) {
    add_banner();
    display_form();
} else {
    display_form();
}

untie(%banners);

# Close and remove our lock file
close(LOCK);
unlink($lock) or die "Cannot remove $lock: $!";

# Subroutines

# Routine to remove this chosen banner and
# display a success message
sub remove_banner {
    my $id = shift;

    # Remove this banner from the DBM file
    delete( $banners{$id} );

    # Make sure our banner was deleted
    my $line = $banners{$id};

    if( $line ) {
        die "Could not remove banner $id: $!\n";
    }

    # Print out a message letting the user
    # know everything went ok
    print h1("Banner $id removed successfully"),
          br,
          br;
}

# Routine to add a banner to the system and verify the data
sub add_banner {
```

```perl
    my $file = param('filename');
    my $url  = param('url');

    # Make sure our filename and our url don't contain
    # any tab characters
    if( $file =~ /\t/ || $url  =~ /\t/ ) {
        die "ERROR: The filename or url provided cannot".
            "contain a tab";
    }

    # Make sure this file exists on the system already
    if( !-e "$webroot/$file" ) {
        die "ERROR: $webroot/$file does not exist: $!";
    }

    # Try to make sure the URL is valid
    if( $url !~ /^http:\/\/.*?\..*?$/ ) {
        die "ERROR: $url is not a valid URL";
    }

    # If everything has gone alright up to now, actually
    # store the banner information

    # First we get our highest banner id to get a unique id
    my $count = 0;
    foreach my $key ( sort(keys(%banners)) ) {
        if( $key > $count ) {
            $count = $key;
        }
    }

    # Increment our banner id to ensure uniqueness
    $count++;

    # Actually store the information
    $banners{$count} = "$file\t$url";

    # Tell the user everything went alright
    print h1("Banner $count added successfully"),
          br,
          br;

}

# Routine to display the HTML form for our web user
sub display_form {

    # Start our output table
    print '<TABLE BORDER=0>';

    # Loop through each banner displaying its information
    # and a link to remove it
    foreach my $key ( sort(keys(%banners)) ) {
```

```
        # Get our banner information
        my( $file, $url ) = split(/\t/, $banners{$key}, 2);

        # Display our info and link
        print qq!<TR><TD>$file</TD><TD>$url</TD><TD>!;
        print qq!<A HREF="$script?remove=$key">!.
              qq!Remove</A></TD></TR>!;

    }

    # Close our HTML table
    print '</TABLE>';

    # Print out our HTML form for adding a new banner
    print start_form,
          br,
          br,
          br,
          h1('Insert a New Banner'),
          b('Filename:'),
          br,
          textfield(-name=>'filename'),
          br,
          b('URL to redirect to:'),
          br,
          textfield(-name=>'url'),
          br,
          submit(-name=>'Save This Banner'),
          end_form,
          end_html;

}
```

We then define some variables, such as the name of our banner ad database, the name of our lock file, and the location where these images should reside. We wait until there is no lock file from another process. When it is our turn, we create a lock file ourselves. The ensures that no two processes are reading or writing to the DBM file at the same time. There is a small race condition between when a process recognizes that there is no lock file and when a new lock file is created. We would have used flock() to better guarantee our file locking, but flock() does not work with SDBM database files.

After we have our lock, we determine what our user would like us to do by checking for certain input values. Based on which inputs exist, we add a new banner, remove an existing banner, or display the menu with a list of the banners currently in the system.

If the remove input is set, we know the user would like us to remove the banner with the associated ID number in our DBM file. We remove it by using the delete() function on the hash we tied to our DBM file.

Unfortunately, `SDBM_File` does not provide functionality for the useful `exists()` function. To test that we have actually removed the banner, we try to get its information again and should get an error. If we are successful, we give the user a short message saying that we have removed the banner and then redisplay the menu.

To add a banner, we use the `add_banner()` subroutine that does some simple checks on the information provided to us by the user. We first make sure that neither the filename nor the URL contains any tab characters that would conflict with our storage method. We then test to make sure the image file the user has given us really does exist in the correct directory. We also verify that the URL given is in the correct format. If all of these tests succeed we tell the user and display the menu again.

When adding a banner, we must give it a unique identifying number. We determine this number by finding the highest number currently in the database and incrementing it by one. If no user input exists, we display our menu, which generates a table of the banner ads currently in the system with links next to each one that allow for the removal of that banner. The menu also defines the HTML form for adding new banners to the system. Figure 14.6 shows the administration interface with a few sample banners.

Figure 14.6
Administration
interface.

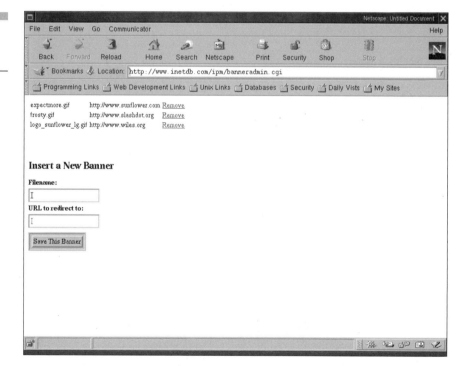

The other part of this system is the script that will find and display a random banner from our database. This is the code for that script:

```perl
#!/usr/bin/perl -w
use strict;
use CGI qw(:standard);
use Fcntl;
use SDBM_File;

# Our lockfile name
my $lock = 'banners.lock';

# Path and name for our banner database
my $banner_filename = 'banners.dat';

# Last viewed file
my $lastview_filename = 'lastview.dat';

# Hash to tie our banner DBM file to
my %banners;

# Hash to tie to our last viewed DBM file
my %last_viewed;

# The number of banner ads we have
my $banner_count = 0;

# Wait until our lock file is gone by testing
# for its existence
while( -e $lock ) {
    sleep(1);
}

# There is a possible race condition here between
# when we find that the lock is gone and before
# we create our new lock file
open(LOCK, ">$lock") or die "Can't open $lock: $!";

# Actually tie our DBM files to our hashes
# or create them if it they don't exist.
tie(%banners, 'SDBM_File', $banner_filename,
    O_RDWR|O_CREAT, 0666) or die
  "Can't create or open $banner_filename: $!";

tie(%last_viewed, 'SDBM_File', $lastview_filename,
    O_RDWR|O_CREAT, 0666) or
  die "Can't create or open $lastview_filename: $!";

# Get our banner count
$banner_count = get_banner_count();

# Get a banner id
my $id = get_random_banner();
```

```perl
# Get this banners info
my ($img, $url) = get_banner_info($id);

# Save this banner id associated with this user's IP
# address so that they do not see the same banner
# multiple times in a row
log_lastviewed($id);

# Actually output the desired banner and link information
print header;
print qq!<A HREF="$url"><IMG SRC="images/$img"!.
    qq!BORDER="0"></A>!;

# Cleanup old last viewed banner info
cleanup_lastviewed();

# Close and remove our lock file so that other processes
# can get their banner ads

untie(%banners);
untie(%last_viewed);

close(LOCK);
unlink($lock);

# Subroutines

# Determine the number of banner ads
# that we currently have in our system
sub get_banner_count {
    my $tmp_count = 0;

    foreach my $current_num ( sort(keys(%banners)) ) {

        if( $current_num > $tmp_count ) {
            $tmp_count = $current_num;
        }

    }

    return($tmp_count);

}

# Get a random banner id
sub get_random_banner {
    # Variable to test if we have a good banner or not
    my $bad_banner = 1;

    # Increment our banner count so that we can
    # show the newest banner
    $banner_count++;
```

```perl
    # Get a random banner, it's information,
    # and this web user's last_viewed information
    my $banner_id = int( rand($banner_count) );
    my $banner_info = $banners{$banner_id};
    my $last_viewed_banner = $last_viewed{$ENV{REMOTE_ADDR}};

    # Test to see if the banner is good and
    # not the same as the last one they saw.
    if( $banner_info && $last_viewed_banner !~
        /^$banner_id\t/ ) {
        $bad_banner = 0;
    }

    # If the banner is zero it is a bad banner
    if( $banner_id == 0 ) {
        $bad_banner = 1;
    }

    # Loop until we find a good banner
    while( $bad_banner ) {

        $banner_id = int( rand($banner_count) );

        $banner_info = $banners{$banner_id};
        $last_viewed_banner = $last_viewed{$ENV{REMOTE_ADDR}};

        if( $banner_info && $last_viewed_banner !~
            /^$banner_id\t/ ) {
            $bad_banner = 0;
        }

        if( $banner_id == 0 ) {
            $bad_banner = 1;
        }
    }

    return($banner_id);

}

# Get a banner's information
sub get_banner_info {
    my $banner_id = shift;
    my $image_file;
    my $redirect_url;

    # Make sure this banner really does exist
    my $banner_info = $banners{$banner_id};
    if( !$banner_info ) {
        die "Banner $banner_id does not exist";
    }

    my $line = $banners{$banner_id};
```

```
    # Retrieve our information using a regular expression
    $line =~ /^(.*?)\t(.*?)$/;

    $image_file = $1;
    $redirect_url = $2;

    # Return the information we found to the caller
    return( $image_file, $redirect_url );

}

# Get rid of old last viewed information
sub cleanup_lastviewed {

    # Current time in seconds from the Epoch
    my $current_time = time();

    foreach my $key ( keys(%last_viewed) ) {
        my $time;

        $last_viewed{$key} =~ /^\d+\t(\d+)$/o;
        $time = $1;

        # If the time associated with this user
        # is greater than 15 minutes remove it
        if( $current_time < ( $time + 900 ) ) {
            delete($last_viewed{$key});
        }

    }
}

# store our last viewed information
sub log_lastviewed {
    my $banner_id = shift;

    my $current_time = time();

    $last_viewed{$ENV{REMOTE_ADDR}} =
        "$banner_id\t$current_time";
}
```

We use the same DBM file, image location, and lock file names as our admin script. However, in this script, we add a 'last_viewed' DBM file that uses a web user's IP address as its key and stores the time and ID number of the last banner viewed by the user. When a random banner is generated, it is checked against this database so that the same banner is not seen twice in a row by the user.

Each time this script is run, we find a random banner ID in the banner database and we retrieve and parse out its information. After that, we log the banner ID and time of the banner we are about to show with the user's IP address into our 'last_viewed' database. We then output the HTML link and image tag necessary to display the banner. Next we spin through each key in our last_viewed database and remove any information that is more than 15 minutes old so that we don't waste disk space. We remove our lockfile and exit so that other processes can use the banner database. get_random_banner() is probably the most difficult part of the script to understand. Because we don't have the ability to test whether a key exists in a hash with exists() when using SDBM databases, we have to retrieve the information associated with a key. If we successfully retrieve information, then the key must exist. If the key exists, we test whether this banner was the last one viewed by this IP address by checking in the last_viewed database. We also make sure the banner ID is not 0 because that banner does not exist in our database. If all of these conditions are met, we return the banner ID and display the banner for the user. If one of these conditions fails, we continue to loop until we find a suitable banner.

To use this system on a website, you must use server-side includes (SSIs). Here is an example of a small HTML page that contains two banner ads on a page. The actual location of the display script will change based on where you put it on your website.

```
<HTML>
<BODY>
<!--#include virtual="/ipm/bannerads.pl" -->
<BR>
<!--#include virtual="/ipm/bannerads.pl" -->
</BODY>
</HTML>
```

Online Perl Syntax Checker

In some college programming courses, assignments are accepted from an HTML form and cataloged for the instructor. The CGI script below accepts Perl source code in an HTML textarea and by using Perl checks that the syntax of the code is valid.

Here is the code:

```
#!/usr/bin/perl -w
use strict;
use CGI qw(:standard);
use POSIX;
```

```perl
use IPC::Open3;

if( param('code') ) {
    my $filename = param('filename');

    # Check to make sure our file is safe
    if( $filename =~ /\.\./ ) {
        die "Temporary file $filename contains dots";
    }

    # Make sure our temporary file is in the right place
    if( $filename !~ /^\/tmp\// ) {
        die "Temporary file $filename not in /tmp: $!";
    }

    open(CODE, ">$filename") or
      die "Can't create $filename: $!";

    print CODE param('code');

    close(CODE);

    open3(\*WRITE, \*READ, \*ERROR, "perl -c -w $filename") or
      die "Can't execute perl -c -w $filename: $!";

    print header;
    print start_html(-bgcolor=>'white'),
          h1('Perl had this to say about your source code:'),
          br,
          br;

    print map("$_<BR>", <ERROR>);

    close(WRITE);
    close(READ);
    close(ERROR);

    print end_html;

    # Remove our file when we are done
    unlink($filename);

} else {

    # Get a good filename
    my $filename = POSIX::tmpnam();

    print header;
    print start_html(-bgcolor=>'white'),
          start_form,
          hidden(-name=>'filename', -value=>$filename),
          h1('Enter your Perl code below:'),
          textarea(-name=>'code',
                   -rows=>25,
```

```
            -columns=>50,
            -wrap=>'virtual'),
    br,
    submit(-name=>'Check Syntax'),
    end_form,
    end_html;
}
```

We begin this script by checking whether we have input and, if not, display a small HTML form. This form uses the POSIX module's `tmp-name()` function to generate a safe, temporary filename that is passed as a hidden parameter back to this script. This file is where we will store the Perl source code given to us to check. Figure 14.7 shows the input the web user will see. After the form has been displayed and the user has entered some source and clicked the submit button, we check the code syntax. We perform the following regular expressions on the temporary filename to ensure that it wasn't tampered with by a malicious user.

Figure 14.7
Input form.

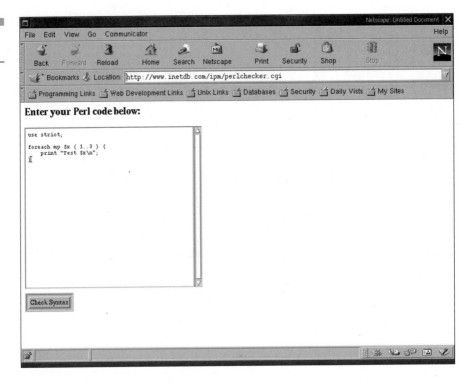

```
# Check to make sure our file is safe
if( $filename =~ /\.\./ ) {
    die "Temporary file $filename contains dots";
}
```

```
# Make sure our temporary file is in the right place
if( $filename !~ /^\/tmp\// ) {
    die "Temporary file $filename not in /tmp: $!";
}
```

We then make sure our filename does not contain a '..', which would allow the user to overwrite an arbitrary file on the system. We also test that this filename is located in the /tmp directory.

After we have written the code to be tested to our temporary file, we use IPC::Open3 to open another process and control its standard input, standard output, and standard error.

```
open3(\*WRITE, \*READ, \*ERROR, "perl -c -w $filename") or
    die "Can't execute perl -c -w $filename: $!";
```

The call to open3() takes three typeglobs, which will be STDIN, STDOUT, and STDERR for this process. We use this because all output of perl -c is sent to STDERR. If it was sent to STDOUT, we could use back ticks to execute and gather the output.

After the open3() call, we start our HTML output and send each line of output on STDERR to the user's browser. Once this has been completed, we clean up by removing the temporary file that stored the source code. Figure 14.8 shows the output of a code sample. The ideas in this script can be used to store Perl source on a remote computer and guarantee that the code is syntactically correct or expanded into a script to grade students' submissions in a class.

Online Notes

```
DBI: /CPAN/DBI-1.14.tar.gz
DBD::Pg: /CPAN/DBD-Pg-0.95.tar.gz
```

This script uses a database to store small notes via a web browser, which might be useful for many reasons. Maybe you want to store a phone number of one of your contacts and access it from home as well as in the office. Maybe you want to have a page where many people can store information regarding a project. This script was designed to be generic, to show you the basic ideas involved with CGI scripts that

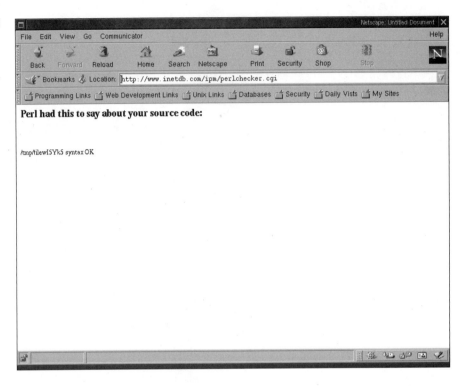

access a database. The following code can easily be modified to fit your
particular needs.

We store our notes in a PostgreSQL database, which is accessible
through DBI provided you have the DBD::Pg module installed. To do
this, we must create a couple of data structures inside the database:

```
CREATE SEQUENCE notes_seq;
```

We create a SQL sequence named 'notes_seq', which is a counter
variable. This variable will be incremented each time it is used to store
a new note.

```
CREATE TABLE notes (
    id int4 PRIMARY KEY DEFAULT( NEXTVAL('notes_seq') ),
    title text,
    content text,
    date datetime,
    link text
);
```

We then create our notes table, which will store all of our note information such as title, content, date and time of creation, and an HTML

link. The ID field might look a little strange, but it means that the ID will be numeric, that it will be the primary key, and that an index will be created to speed our lookups. The DEFAULT keyword also instructs the database to fill this field with the result of NEXTVAL('notes_seq'). NEXTVAL('notes_seq') will increment and return the next value of our 'notes_seq' counter variable inside the database.

```
GRANT ALL ON notes_seq TO nobody;
GRANT ALL ON notes TO nobody;
```

We must grant permission for user 'nobody' to read and write the sequence and the table. User 'nobody' is typically the user your web server runs as. If yours is different, modify those lines to match.

Now that our database is ready, here is the code:

```
#!/usr/bin/perl -w
use strict;
use CGI qw(:standard);
use DBI;

# The location of this script
my $script = '/ipm/notes.pl';

# Our connection to the database
my $dbh = DBI->connect('dbi:Pg:dbname=notes', '', '') or
  die "Cannot connect to database: $!\n";

# Start our HTML output
print header;
print start_html(-bgcolor=>'white');

# Determine what our user would like to do
if( param('remove') ) {
    remove_note( param('remove') );
    display_menu();
} elsif( param('view') ) {
    view_note( param('view') );
} elsif( param('add') ) {
    add_note();
    display_menu();
} else {
    display_menu()
}

# Close our database connection
$dbh->disconnect();

# Subroutines

sub remove_note {
```

```
    my $id = shift;

    # Make sure the id we received is numeric
    if( $id =~ /\D/ ) {
        print "ERROR: Note ID must be numeric";
        return();
    }

    # Actually remove this note
    $dbh->do("DELETE FROM notes WHERE id=$id") or
      die "Can't remove note: $!";

        print b("Note $id removed"), br;

}

sub view_note {
    my $id = shift;

    # Make sure our id is numeric
    if( $id =~ /\D/ ) {
        print "ERROR: Note ID must be numeric";
        return();
    }

    # Retrieve everything for this note
    my $sth = $dbh->prepare("SELECT * FROM notes".
                            "WHERE id=$id");
    $sth->execute or die "Could not execute query: $!";

    my ($tid, $title, $content, $date, $link) = $sth->fetchrow;

    # Display this note in a HTML table
    print "<TABLE BORDER=0>\n";
    print "<TR><TH>Title:</TH><TD>$title</TD></TR>\n";
    print "<TR><TH>Created:</TH><TD>$date</TD></TR>\n";
    print "<TR><TH VALIGN=TOP>Content:</TH>".
          "<TD>$content</TD></TR>\n";
    print "<TR><TH>Link:</TH><TD><A HREF=$link>$link</A>".
          "</TD></TR>\n";
    print "</TABLE>\n";

}

sub add_note {

    # Save our inputs to temporary values
    my $title = param('title');
    my $link = param('link');
    my $content = param('content');

    # Make sure they have given us a title
    if( !$title ) {
        print "ERROR: You must include a title for this note";
```

```perl
        return();
    }

    # Make sure our data is safe to insert into the database
    $title =~ s/'/''/g;
    $title =~ s/\\/\\\\/g;
    $link =~ s/'/''/g;
    $link =~ s/\\/\\\\/g;
    $content =~ s/'/''/g;
    $content =~ s/\\/\\\\/g;

    # Change newlines to <BR> HTML tags
    $content =~ s/\n/<BR>/g;

    # Build our SQL query
    my $sql = "INSERT INTO notes (title, content, date, link) ".
              "VALUES( '$title', '$content', 'now', '$link')";

    # Actually add this note
    $dbh->do($sql) or die "Can't save note: $!";

    print b('Note saved'), br;
}

sub display_menu {

    # Get all of our current notes from the database
    my $sth = $dbh->prepare("SELECT id, title, date".
                            "FROM notes");
    $sth->execute or die "Could not execute query: $!";

    # Start an HTML table for output
    print "<TABLE BORDER=0>\n";

    # Loop over our results displaying them
    while( my ($id, $title, $date) = $sth->fetchrow ) {

        print "<TR><TD><A HREF=\"$script?view=$id\">".
              "$title</A></TD>";
        print "<TD><A HREF=\"$script?remove=$id\">".
              "Remove</A></TD>";
        print "<TD>$date</TD></TR>\n";

    }

    # Free resources taken up by this query
    $sth->finish;

    # Close our HTML table
    print "</TABLE>\n<HR SIZE=1 NOSHADE>\n";

    # Display our HTML form
    print start_form,
          hidden(-name=>'add', -value=>'1'),
```

```
             h2('New Note'),
             b('Title:'),
             br,
             textfield(-name=>'title'),
             br,
             b('Link:'),
             br,
             textfield(-name=>'link'),
             br,
             textarea(-name=>'content',
                      -columns=> 50,
                      -rows=> 7,
                      -wrap=>'virtual'),
             br,
             submit(-name=>'Save Note'),
             end_form;

}
```

The CGI code in this example should look familiar from previous examples. Based on user input in the form of `param()` values, we determine whether the user wants us to add, remove, or view a note. If no input is given, we display a menu with an HTML form that will allow a user to add a new note or display a list of the notes currently in the system. This list of notes has a link to view its contents and a link to remove the note.

The DBI code should look familiar from the DBI section in Chapter 4. In `display_menu()`, we execute a search using DBI to display any notes currently in the system. After this search has completed, we display our HTML form that allows for the addition of new notes. Figure 14.9 shows this menu with a few sample notes. `remove_note()` verifies that the data passed to it is numeric and removes the note with the ID passed to it from the database with the following code:

```
$dbh->do("DELETE FROM notes WHERE id=$id") or
  die "Can't remove note: $!";
```

`add_note()` is the most complicated subroutine in this example because it has the job of saving the note in the database and verifying that the data will go into it cleanly. In SQL, single quotations wrap around character string values; we must escape these strings by doubling them with regular expressions such as:

```
$title =~ s/'/''/g;
```

SQL also uses backslashes to escape characters; we fix this by doubling them too:

Figure 14.9
Add notes form.

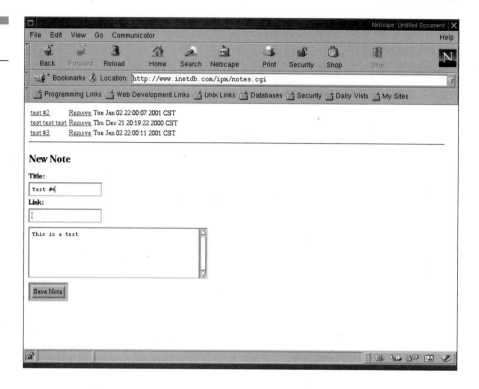

```
$title =~ s/\\/\\\\/g;
```

After making these changes, we convert new line characters from our text area into HTML `<BR>` tags, which display the data as the user intended. Once we have checked that our data will go cleanly into our database, we build our SQL query with:

```
my $sql = "INSERT INTO notes (title, content, date, link)".
          "VALUES( '$title', '$content', 'now', '$link')";
```

This insert statement is fairly simple, but the `'now'` might confuse you. `'now'` is a reserved word in PostgreSQL that is for fields that have a type of `'datetime'`. It simply replaces `'now'` with the current date and time so that you don't have to look it up yourself. If the note was inserted properly, we display a short message telling the user.

`view_note()` takes a note's ID as its input and uses that uniquely identifying number to retrieve that note's contents. After it has retrieved the values into temporary variables, it displays them in a small HTML table, making sure to wrap the link in a `<A HREF>` tag.

Figure 14.10 shows the detailed view of a note. Minus the use of NEXTVAL() and 'now' in our SQL, this script can be modified easily for use with MySQL, Oracle, or any other database that DBI can access.

Figure 14.10
Detailed view of a note.

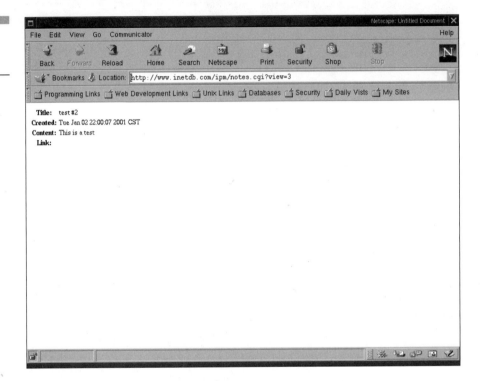

Summary

We hope this chapter has shown you how easy some of these tasks truly are with the help of the modules that handle most of the dirty work for you. Although these examples will work as shown with few modifications, it is probably in your best interest to tailor them to your site's particular needs.

Web
Programming

Web Automation with LWP

 libwww-perl: /CPAN/libwww-perl-5.48.tar.gz

You've probably needed to download a Web page to process locally at one time or another. Or maybe you've wanted to check all the links on a Web site to make sure that they're still valid. You could use your browser to manually perform these types of tasks, but this may entail a lot of unnecessary work. What if you needed to retrieve several documents, or the documents update frequently? Instead of manually using your browser, you could automate these processes using Perl.

The LWP (library for WWW access in Perl), written by Gisle Aas and Martijn Koster (with help from countless others), is a set of Perl modules that is used for working with the World Wide Web. LWP is normally used to create Web clients, which can be used to fetch Web pages from remote servers, mirror documents from remote servers, and post data to Web servers. LWP can be downloaded as a single file, libwww-perl, from CPAN and includes a "cookbook," lwpcook, which provides several examples of using LWP.

Now let's take a look at two useful modules that are part of the LWP package, LWP::Simple and LWP::UserAgent.

Getting Web Documents with LWP::Simple

LWP::Simple is a function-oriented module that is used to create simple, easy-to-use Web clients. LWP::Simple exports five functions used for retrieving a document from a specified URL: get(), head(), getprint(), getstore(), and mirror(). LWP::Simple also exports the constants and functions from the HTTP::Status module (included with libwww-perl), which can be used to check the response code returned from the getprint(), getstore(), and mirror() methods.

get($url)

The get() function retrieves the document found at the specified URL ($url can be either a string or a reference to a URI object). If the function fails, it returns undef.

```
use LWP::Simple;

my $url = 'http://www.perl.com';
my $html = get($url);

if (defined $html) {
    print $html . "\n";
} else {
    print "Error getting $url\n";
}
```

head($url)

The head() function gets the headers from the document found at the specified URL. If successful, the function returns a list containing the following five values: ($content_type, $document_length, $modified_time, $expires, $server). If the request fails, it returns an empty list.

```
use LWP::Simple;

my $url = 'http://www.perl.com';

my @headers = head($url);

if (@headers) {
    print "content type: $headers[0]\n" if $headers[0];
    print "document length: $headers[1]\n" if $headers[1];
    print "modified time: $headers[2]\n" if $headers[2];
    print "expires: $headers[3]\n" if $headers[3];
    print "server: $headers[4]\n" if $headers[4];
} else {
    print "Request failed\n";
}
```

The head() function can also be used to check for the existence of a document. When used in a scalar context, the head() function returns true, if successful, and false, if it fails.

```
use LWP::Simple;

my $url = 'http://www.perl.com/';

if (head($url)) {
    print "Document exists\n";
} else {
    print "Document not found\n";
}
```

getprint($url)

The getprint() function will get the document from the specified URL and print it to STDOUT. The status code and message are printed to STDERR if the request fails. The return value is the HTTP response code, which can be used by the HTTP::Status is_error() method (described later in this section) to handle errors.

```
use LWP::Simple;

my $url = 'http://www.perl.com/';

my $rc = getprint($url);

if (is_error($rc)) {
    print "Error getting document\n";
}
```

It is also possible to use getprint() as a one-liner:

```
% perl -MLWP::Simple -e 'getprint("http://www.perl.com")'
```

getstore($url,$file)

The getstore() function will get the document from the specified URL and store it in the specified file. The return value is the HTTP response code. In this example, we use the HTTP::Status is_success() method (described later in this section) to report on whether our request was successful.

```
use LWP::Simple;

my $url = 'http://www.perl.com/';
my $file = 'perl_index.html';

my $rc = getstore($url, $file);

if (is_success($rc)) {
    print "File saved\n";
} else {
    print "Error getting document\n";
}
```

Here's a one-liner:

```
% perl -MLWP::Simple -e 'getstore("http://www.perl.com/",
"perl_index.html")'
```

Note that this one-liner fails silently on error.

mirror($url,$file)

The `mirror()` function is similar to the `getstore()` function, except that it will only save the document found at the URL if it is newer than the file that is saved locally. This function is used to create a mirrored document. Note that we use a few of the `HTTP::Status` constants, described in the next section, for error handling.

```
use LWP::Simple;

my $url - 'http://www.cpan.org/';
my $file = 'cpan_index.html';

my $rc = mirror($url, $file);

if ($rc == RC_NOT_MODIFIED) {
    print "Document is current - no copy\n";
} elsif ($rc == RC_OK) {
    print "Document updated\n";
} else {
    print "Error getting document\n";
}
```

The one-liner:

```
% perl -MLWP::Simple -e 'mirror("http://www.cpan.com/",
"cpan_index.html")'
```

Note that this one-liner fails silently on error.

As mentioned previously, the `LWP::Simple` module exports the `HTTP::Status` constants and methods. The following list shows the constants.

RC_CONTINUE	(100)
RC_SWITCHING_PROTOCOLS	(101)
RC_OK	(200)
RC_CREATED	(201)
RC_ACCEPTED	(202)
RC_NON_AUTHORITATIVE_INFORMATION	(203)
RC_NO_CONTENT	(204)
RC_RESET_CONENT	(205)
RC_PARTIAL_CONTENT	(206)
RC_MULTIPLE_CHOICES	(300)
RC_MOVED_PERMANENTLY	(301)

RC_FOUND	(302)
RC_SEE_OTHER	(303)
RC_NOT_MODIFIED	(304)
RC_USE_PROXY	(305)
RC_TEMPORARY_REDIRECT	(307)
RC_BAD_REQUEST	(400)
RC_UNAUTHORIZED	(401)
RC_PAYMENT_REQUIRED	(402)
RC_FORBIDDEN	(403)
RC_NOT_FOUND	(404)
RC_METHOD_NOT_ALLOWED	(405)
RC_NOT_ACCEPTABLE	(406)
RC_PROXY_AUTHENTICATION_REQUIRED	(407)
RC_REQUEST_TIMEOUT	(408)
RC_CONFLICT	(409)
RC_GONE	(410)
RC_LENGTH_REQUIRED	(411)
RC_PRECONDITION_FAILED	(412)
RC_REQUEST_ENTITY_TOO_LARGE	(413)
RC_REQUEST_URI_TOO_LARGE	(414)
RC_UNSUPPORTED_MEDIA_TYPE	(415)
RC_REQUEST_RANGE_NOT_SATISFIABLE	(416)
RC_EXPECTATION_FAILED	(417)
RC_INTERNAL_SERVER_ERROR	(500)
RC_NOT_IMPLEMENTED	(501)
RC_BAD_GATEWAY	(502)
RC_SERVICE_UNAVAILABLE	(503)
RC_GATEWAY_TIMEOUT	(504)
RC_HTTP_VERSION_NOT_SUPPORTED	(505)

The HTTP::Status includes the following methods.

is_success($rc)

is_success() returns true if the response code showed that the request was successful (response codes 200 through 299).

is_error($rc)

is_error() returns true if the response code showed that the request failed (response codes 400 through 599).

is_redirect($rc)

`is_redirect()` returns `true` if the response received is a redirect (response codes 300 through 399).

status_message($rc)

`status_message()` returns the constant that corresponds to the return code.

We can take our `getstore()` example and add a more detailed error handling by checking the return code to see why the request failed (if it failed).

```
use LWP::Simple;

my $url = 'http://www.perl.com/';
my $file = 'perl_index.html';

my $rc = getstore($url, $file);

if (is_success($rc)) {
    print "File saved\n";
} else {
    if ($rc == RC_NOT_FOUND) {
        print "Document not found\n";
    } elsif ($rc == RC_INTERNAL_SERVER_ERROR) {
        print "Internal server error\n";
    } else {
        print "Other error getting document\n";
    }
}
```

Getting Web Documents with LWP::UserAgent

`LWP::UserAgent` is an object-oriented module that is used to create flexible, full-featured Web clients. Normally, when you build a Web client application, you will first create and configure a `UserAgent` object. After the `UserAgent` object is created, you then need to create and configure an `HTTP::Request` object and pass it to the `UserAgent request()` method. After the request is made, a response is returned from the server in the form of an `HTTP::Response` object. Let's take a look at this process in more detail.

You can create a `UserAgent` object by using the `LWP::UserAgent` constructor method.

```
use LWP::UserAgent;
my $ua = new LWP::UserAgent;
```

or

```
use LWP::UserAgent;
my $ua = LWP::UserAgent->new();
```

LWP::UserAgent provides several methods, which can be used to configure attributes of the UserAgent object that alter the behavior of the UserAgent request() method. Some of the more common methods follow.

agent([$product_id])

The agent() method specifies the name that is used to identify your application to the Web server. This name will be saved in the Web server's log files. You can think of your UserAgent as a mini Web browser. You can give your UserAgent a name and an optional software version. For example:

```
$ua->agent('SecretBrowser');
```

or

```
$ua->agent('SecretBrowser/007');
```

The default value is libwww-perl/#.##, where #.## is replaced with the version number of the current LWP library.

timeout([$secs])

The timeout() method sets the number of seconds that the request will wait for a response from the server. The default period is 180 seconds (3 minutes).

Once we have configured the UserAgent object, we need to create an HTTP::Request object that we will pass to the UserAgent request() method. Note that the HTTP::Request object can be used for all Internet protocols, not just HTTP, as the name would imply.

You can use the following line to create an HTTP::Request object:

```
$request = HTTP::Request->new($method, $url,
          [$header,[$content]]);
```

The four attributes of an HTTP::Request object are:

- **Method**—String specifying the request method, normally GET, POST or HEAD.
- **URL**—String or URI object specifying the protocol, server, and document.
- **Header**—Optional argument. Reference to HTTP::Headers object.
- **Content**—Optional argument. POST data (POST method only).

Here are two examples of creating an HTTP::Request object:

```
my $url = 'http://www.perl.com/';
my $request = HTTP::Request->new('GET', $url);
```

or

```
my $url = 'http://www.perl.com/';
my $request = HTTP::Request->new(GET => $url);
```

Now let's pass the HTTP::Request object to the UserAgent request() method:

```
my $response = $ua->request($request);
```

There are actually three ways to call the UserAgent request() method:

1. `$ua->request($request);`
   $request—Reference to an HTTP::Request object.
2. `$ua->request($request, $filename);`
   $filename—Local file name that will store the contents of the response.
3. `$ua->request($request, \&callback, [$chunksize]);`
   \&callback—Reference to a subroutine that is called to process response data.
   $chunksize—Optional argument. Chunk size (in bytes) of content that is required before the referenced subroutine will be called.

After the request is made, the server will return a response in the form of an HTTP::Reponse object. The HTTP::Response object has the following attributes:

- **Code**—Numeric response code.
- **Message**—String that corresponds to the response code.

- **Header**—Any returned headers.
- **Content**—Content returned (possibly empty).

The values of these attributes can be retrieved with the following corresponding methods:

```
$response->code();
$response->message();
$response->headers_as_string();
$response->content();
```

NOTE

HTTP::Response *is a subclass of* HTTP::Message *and inherits its methods, including the methods* headers_as_string() *and* content().

Other useful HTTP::Response methods include status_line(), base(), is_success(), and is_error().

status_line()

The response code and message can be retrieved as the string <code><message> by using the status_line() method:

```
$reponse->status_line();
```

base()

The base() method will return the base URL for the response. The base URL is obtained from a BASE HREF tag embedded in the document, a Content-Base or Content-Location header in the response, or the URL of the response (which may differ from the URL passed to the request method due to a redirect).

is_success()

Returns true if the response was successful.

is_error()

Returns true if the response an error.

Let's build a simple Web client using the LWP::UserAgent module:

```perl
use LWP::UserAgent;

my $url = 'http://www.perl.com/';

# Create new UserAgent object (browser)
my $ua = LWP::UserAgent->new();

# Give the browser a name
$ua->agent('SecretBrowser/007');

# Set the timeout value - only wait 60 seconds.
$ua->timeout(60);

# Create HTTP GET request
my $request = HTTP::Request->new(GET => $url);
# Execute HTTP request
my $response = $ua->request($request);

# Check success
if ($response->is_success) {
    # Request was successful - print the contents of the response
    print $response->content;
} else {
    # Request failed - print response code and message
    print "Error getting document: ",
          $response->status_line, "\n";
}
```

It is also possible to mirror a Web document with LWP::UserAgent by using the mirror() method. The mirror() function will save the document found at the URL only if it is newer than the file that is saved locally.

```perl
use LWP::UserAgent;
use HTTP::Status;

my $url = 'http://www.cpan.org/';
my $file = 'cpan_index.html';

my $ua = LWP::UserAgent->new();

my $res = $ua->mirror($url, $file);
my $rc = $res->code();

if (($rc == RC_NOT_MODIFIED)) {
    print "Document is current - no copy\n";
} elsif ($rc == RC_OK) {
    print "Document updated\n";}
else {
    print "Error getting document\n";
}
```

Getting Protected Documents with LWP::UserAgent

If a document is protected using basic authorization, you can still retrieve the document provided that you are authorized and have the password.

```perl
use LWP::UserAgent;

my $ua = new LWP::UserAgent;

my $request = new HTTP::Request GET =>
              'http://www.hostname.com/';
$request->authorization_basic('name', 'password');

my $response = $ua->request($request);

# Check success
if ($response->is_success) {
    # Request was successful - print the contents of the response
    print $response->content;
} else {
    # Request failed - print response code and message
    print "Error getting document: ",
          $response->status_line, "\n";
}
```

Automating Form Submission

LWP can be used to post data to a Web server. We'll take a look at a couple of examples of posting form data.

The first example uses the GET method to submit form data to a server. After viewing the HTML source of the CPAN search page, I found that two arguments are being passed to the server: query and mode. The query argument is a string entered by the user into a text box on the form. The mode argument is a selection from a menu that categorizes what the user is looking for: module, distribution, author, or documentation. For example, if we wanted to look for the LWP module, the form would generate the following URL:

```
http://search.cpan.org/search?mode=module&query=LWP
```

This script could be used to automate the form submission by using the query_form() method of the URI::URL module:

```
use LWP::Simple;
use URI::URL;

my $url = URI::URL->new('http://search.cpan.org/search');

# Select box, name = mode
# Values: module (Module), dist (Distribution),
#          author (Author), doc (Documentation)
$url->query_form(mode  => 'module',
                 query => 'LWP'
);

my $content = get($url);

print $content, "\n";
```

Of course, you don't really need to use the URI::URL module, as long as you encode the query string yourself:

```
use LWP::Simple;

my $html =
    get('http://search.cpan.org/search?mode=module&query=LWP');

print $html, "\n";
```

We can also use LWP to submit a form using the POST method. I viewed the HTML source of the Perl search page and found that this form passes a search string and one or more search options. The search string is text entered by a user in a text box named s. There are also a few checkboxes that give the user a choice of the number of hits to be shown and where the search will take place: perl, perlref, cpan, and meercat. The following script will automate the form submission for a search for LWP, showing up 50 hits at www.perl.com and the www.perl.com reference database.

━━ ━━ ━━ ━━ ━━ ━━ ━━ ━━ ━━ ━━ ━━ ━━ ━━ ━━ ━━ ━━ ━━ ━━

If the form on the Web server is ever changed, your script may need to be modified to reflect those changes.

NOTE

```
use LWP::UserAgent;

my $url = 'http://www.perl.com/search/';

# Create new UserAgent object (browser)
my $ua = LWP::UserAgent->new();
```

```
# Give the browser a name
$ua->agent("SecretBrowser/007");

# Create HTTP POST request
my $request = HTTP::Request->new(POST => $url);
$request->content_type('application/x-www-form-urlencoded');
# Text box:
# name = s
# Checkbox:
# name = perl value = 50, www.perl.com The Source for Perl
# name = perlref value = 50, www.perl.com Reference- A database
# of Perl Resources
# name = cpan value = 10, The Comprehensive Perl Archive Network
# name = meerkat value = 10, Syndicated Perl-related news stories
$request->content('s=LWP&perl=50&perlref=50');

# Execute HTTP request
my $response = $ua->request($request);

# Check success
if ($response->is_success) {
    print $response->content;
} else {
    print "Error getting document: ",
          $response->status_line, "\n";
}
```

Specifying and Converting URLs with URI::URL

URI::URL: /CPAN/URI-1.07.tar.gz

The URI::URL module can be used to create URI objects that allow you to specify elements of a URL and convert between absolute and relative URLs.

Specifying URLs

The following example uses some of the common functions that can be used to specify elements of a URL:

```
use URI::URL;

my $url = URI::URL->new(
          'http://search.cpan.org/search?mode=module&query=LWP');
```

```
# Use various methods to print elements of the URL
print "\$url->as_string(): ", $url->as_string(), "\n";
print "\$url->scheme(): ", $url->scheme(), "\n";
print "\$url->host(): ", $url->host(), "\n";
print "\$url->default_port(): ", $url->default_port(), "\n";
print "\$url->port(): ", $url->port(), "\n";
print "\$url->path(): ", $url->path(), "\n";
print "\$url->full_path: ", $url->full_path(), "\n";
print "\$url->query(): ", $url->query(), "\n";

# Print the parameter key/value pairs
my %form_data = $url->query_form();
print "\$url->query_form():\n";
foreach my $item (keys %form_data) {
    print "  $item => $form_data{$item}\n";
}
```

```
% perl uri1.pl
$url->as_string():
http://search.cpan.org/search?mode=module&query=LWP
$url->scheme(): http
$url->host(): search.cpan.org
$url->default_port(): 80
$url->port(): 80
$url->path(): /search
$url->full_path: /search?mode=module&query=LWP
$url->query(): mode=module&query=LWP
$url->query_form():
  mode => module
  query => LWP
```

Converting Relative URLs to Absolute URLs

The next script creates a new URI object that contains a relative URL.
The abs() method is used to convert the relative URL to an absolute
URL.

```
use URI::URL;

my $base_url = URI::URL->new('http://www.perl.com/');
my $rel_url = URI::URL->new('images/perl.gif');
my $abs_url = $rel_url->abs($base_url);

print "Rel URL: ", $rel_url->as_string(), "\n";
print "Abs URL: ", $abs_url->as_string, "\n";
```

```
% perl uri2.pl
Rel URL: images/perl.gif
Abs URL: http://www.perl.com/images/perl.gif
```

We can also pass the base URL as an optional parameter to the URI::URL *new* constructor:

```
$url = new URI::URL($url_string, $base_url);
```

For example, if we provide the relative URL /images and the base URL http://www.perl.com/images/perl.gif, we can then find the absolute URL.

```
use URI::URL;

my $url = URI::URL->new('/images',
        'http://www.perl.com/images/perl.gif');

print "Rel URL: ", $url->as_string(), "\n";
print "Abs URL: ", $url->abs(), "\n";
```

```
% perl uri3.pl
Rel URL: /images
Abs URL: http://www.perl.com/images
```

Converting Absolute URLs to Relative URLs

The following example will convert an absolute URL to a relative URL by using the rel() method.

```
use URI::URL;

my $base_url = URI::URL->new('http://www.perl.com');
my $abs_url = URI::URL->new(
            'http://www.perl.com/images/perl.gif');

my $rel_url = $abs_url->rel($base_url);

print "Abs URL: ", $abs_url->as_string(), "\n";
print "Rel URL: ", $rel_url->as_string(), "\n";
```

```
% perl uri4.pl
Abs URL: http://www.perl.com/images/perl.gif
Rel URL: images/perl.gif
```

We can also pass the optional base URL to the URI::URL new constructor.

```
use URI::URL;

my $url = URI::URL->new('http://www.perl.com/images/perl.gif',
                        'http://www.perl.com/');

print "Rel: ", $url->rel(), "\n";
print "Abs: ", $url->as_string(), "\n";
```

```
% perl uri5.pl
Rel URL: images/perl.gif
Abs URL: http://www.perl.com/images/perl.gif
```

Parsing and Processing HTML

HTML-Parser: /CPAN/HTML-Parser-3.08.tar.gz

In the first part of this chapter we learned how to retrieve an HTML document from a remote server. Now let's take a look at how we can process an HTML document. To do this, we'll use a few of the modules included in the HTML-Parser package: HTML::Parser, HTML::LinkExtor, and HTML::Entities.

Parsing HTML with HTML::Parser

Once you've downloaded a document, you may want to parse the HTML to display the plain text. Although it is possible to parse the HTML using complex regular expressions, it is much easier (and usually more correct and safer) to use the HTML::Parser module, written by Gisle Aas and Michael A. Chase. There are two versions of HTML::Parser available. We'll take a look at version 2 and version 3.

HTML::Parser can be used to parse HTML from either a string or a file by using the parse($string) and parse_file($file) methods, respectively. HTML::Parser takes HTML input and divides it up into pieces: start tags, end tags, text, comments, and declarations. Each separate piece is sent to a corresponding subroutine: start(), end(), text(), comment(), and declaration().

To use HTML::Parser, *you must either create a subclass and override the parsing functions or specify event handlers when the* HTML::Parser *constructor is called (version 3 only).*

This example demonstrates how HTML::Parser divides the HTML input into separate pieces and calls the corresponding function.

```perl
package MyHTMLparser;
use HTML::Parser;
@ISA = qw /HTML::Parser/;

sub start {
    my($self, $tag, $attr, $attrseq, $origtext) = @_;
    print "START: $origtext\n";
}

sub end {
    my($self, $tag, $origtext) = @_;
    print "END: $origtext\n";
}

sub text {
    my($self, $text) = @_;
    print "TEXT: $text\n";
}

sub comment {
    my($self, $comment) = @_;
    print "COMMENT: $comment\n";
}

sub declaration {
    my($self, $decl) = @_;
    print "DECL: $decl\n";
}

package main;

my $p = MyHTMLparser->new;
$p->parse('<!DOCTYPE HTML PUBLIC "-//W3C//DTD HTML 4.0'
        'Transitional//EN">');
$p->parse('<!--HTML Comment-->');
$p->parse('<H1>Perl Links</H1>');
$p->parse('<A HREF="http://www.perl.com/">Perl</A>');
```

This script will produce the following output:

```
% perl html_parser1.pl
DECL: DOCTYPE HTML PUBLIC "-//W3C//DTD HTML 4.0 Transitional//EN"
```

```
COMMENT: HTML Comment
START: <H1>
TEXT: Perl Links
END: </H1>
START: <A HREF="http:/www.perl.com">
TEXT: Perl
END: </A>
```

In the following example, we simply parse the text from the HTML string.

```perl
package MyHTMLparser;
use HTML::Parser;
@ISA = qw /HTML::Parser/;

sub text {
    my($self, $text) = @_;
    print "$text\n";
}


package main;

my $p = MyHTMLparser->new;
$p->parse('<!DOCTYPE HTML PUBLIC "-//W3C//DTD HTML 4.0'
        'Transitional//EN">');
$p->parse('<!--HTML Comment-->');
$p->parse('<H1>Perl Links</H1>');
$p->parse('<A HREF="http://www.perl.com/">Perl</A>');
```

Running this script will output the text parsed from the HTML in the string.

```
% perl html_parser2.pl
Perl Links
Perl
```

This example shows how to strip all tags from an HTML file and save the plain text to another file.

```perl
package MyHTMLparser;
use HTML::Parser;
@ISA = qw /HTML::Parser/;

sub text {
    my ($self, $text) = @_;
    $self->{myText} .= $text;
}

package main;
```

```
# Select an HTML file to be parsed
my $in_file = 'in_file.html';

# Parse the file
my $p = MyHTMLparser->new;
$p->parse_file($in_file);

# Save parsed file to output file
$out_file = 'out_file.txt';
open(FILE, ">$out_file") or
     die "Cannot open $out_file for writing: $!\n";
print FILE $p->{myText};
close FILE;
```

Version 3 of HTML::Parser allows you to use handlers instead of having to subclass the module (although you can still subclass if you wish). Version 3 also includes the ability to deal with XML constructs.

The following example shows how to parse out the various HTML components from a string using HTML::Parser, version 3:

```
use HTML::Parser;

my $p = HTML::Parser->new(
        api_version => 3,
        start_h => [\&start, "self, tagname, attr, attrseq, text"],
        end_h => [\&end, "self, tagname, text"],
        text_h => [\&text, "self, text"],
        comment_h => [\&comment, "self, text"],
        declaration_h => [\&decl, "self, text"]
);

sub start {
    my($self, $tagname, $attr, $attrseq, $origtext) = @_;
    print "START: $origtext\n";
}

sub end {
    my($self, $tagname, $origtext) = @_;
    print "END: $origtext\n";
}

sub text {
    my($self, $text) = @_;
    print "TEXT: $text\n";
}

sub comment {
    my($self, $comment) = @_;
    print "COMMENT: $comment\n";
}
```

```
sub decl {
    my($self, $decl) = @_;
    print "DECL: $decl\n";
}

$p->parse('<!DOCTYPE HTML PUBLIC "-//W3C//DTD HTML 4.0
Transitional//EN">');
$p >parse('<!--HTML Comment-->');
$p->parse('<H1>Perl Links</H1>');
$p->parse('<A HREF="http://www.perl.com/">Perl</A>');
```

```
% perl html_parser_ver3.pl
DECL: <!DOCTYPE HTML PUBLIC "-//W3C//DTD HTML 4.0
Transitional//EN">
COMMENT: <!--HTML Comment(
START: <H1>
TEXT: Perl Links
END: </H1>
START: <A HREF="http:/www.perl.com">
TEXT: Perl
END: </A>
```

Extracting Links with HTML::LinkExtor

When parsing an HTML document, you may want to extract any links that it contains. The HTML::LinkExtor module, which is a subclass of HTML::Parser, makes the process very simple.

Finding Links on a Web Page

The following example uses LWP::UserAgent to fetch an HTML document from the Web and then uses HTML::LinkExtor to extract all the links from that document. We use the abs() method from URI::URL to create absolute URLs from any relative URLs found in the document.

```
use LWP::UserAgent;
use HTML::LinkExtor;
use URI::URL;

my $url = URI::URL->new('http://www.perl.com/');
my $base_url;

# Create new UserAgent object (browser)
my $ua = LWP::UserAgent->new();

# Give our agent a name
$ua->agent("Mozilla/4.7");
```

```perl
# Create HTTP GET request
my $request = HTTP::Request->new(GET => $url);

# Execute HTTP request
my $response = $ua->request($request);

# Check success
if ($response->is_success &&
    $response->content_type eq 'text/html') {
    # Request was successful and is html
    $base_url = $response->base();
    print "Base URL: $base_url\n";
    my $link_extor = HTML::LinkExtor->new(\&extract_links);
    $link_extor->parse($response->content);
} else {
    # Request failed - print response code and message
    print "Error getting document: ",
          $response->status_line, "\n";
}

sub extract_links {
    my ($tag, %attr) = @_;

    if ($tag eq 'a' or $tag eq 'img') {
        foreach my $key (keys %attr) {
            if ($key eq 'href' or $key eq 'src') {
                my $link_url = URI->new($attr{$key});
                my $full_url = $link_url->abs($base_url);
                print "LINK: $full_url\n";
            }
        }
    }
}
```

Checking for Dead Links

Keeping track of dead links can be a time-consuming chore. We can automate this task by using a few Perl modules. The following example will check all the hyperlinks and image links found on a Web page.

```perl
use LWP::UserAgent;
use HTML::LinkExtor;
use URI::URL;

# Create new URI object
my $url = URI::URL->new('http://www.perl.com/');
my $base_url;

# Create new UserAgent object (browser)
my $ua = LWP::UserAgent->new();

# Give our agent a name
```

```perl
$ua->agent("Mozilla/4.7");

# Create HTTP GET request
my $request = HTTP::Request->new(GET => $url);

# Execute HTTP request
my $response = $ua->request($request);

# Check success
if ($response->is_success &&
    $response->content_type eq 'text/html') {
    # Request was successful and is html document
    $base_url = $response->base();
    print "Base URL: $base_url\n";
    # Extract links
    my $link_extor = HTML::LinkExtor->new(\&extract_links);
    $link_extor->parse($response->content);
} else {
    # Request failed - print response code and message
    print "Error getting document: ",
          $response->status_line, "\n";
}

sub extract_links {
    my ($tag, %attr) = @_;

    # Look for anchor and image tags
    if ($tag eq 'a' or $tag eq 'img') {
        foreach my $key (keys %attr) {
            if ($key eq 'href' or $key eq 'src') {
                my $link_url = URI->new($attr{$key});
                my $full_url = $link_url->abs($base_url);
                next unless ($full_url->scheme =~
                    /\b(?:https?|ftp|file)\b/);

                # Create HTTP HEAD request
                my $request = HTTP::Request->new(
                            HEAD => $full_url);

                # Execute HTTP request
                my $response = $ua->request($request);

                # Check response
                if($response->status_line eq '200 OK') {
                    print "$full_url OK\n";
                } else {
                    print "$full_url BAD - ",
                          $response->status_line, "\n";
                }
            }
        }
    }
}
```

Let's take a closer look at this example and see what's going on.

This example has three major steps that are used to find the status of our links.

1. Get the HTML document that contains the links that we want to check.
2. Extract the anchor and image links (if the request was successful).
3. Create a HEAD request for each link and check the response.

To add a little more detail, we begin by creating a URI object.

```
my $url = URI::URL->new('http://www.perl.com/');
```

This URI object will be used later in the example to convert relative URLs to absolute URLs.

Next, we use LWP::UserAgent to retrieve the URL specified by the URI object. We covered the creation and use of a LWP::UserAgent object in detail earlier in this chapter.

We then check the response to see whether our request was successful. Because we will be parsing HTML, we want to make sure that the document returned is actually an HTML document.

```
if ($response->is_success &&
    $response->content_type eq 'text/html') {
```

After we've successfully retrieved the document, we set the base URL by using the HTTP::Response base() method. This URL may differ from the original URL if the response was a redirect.

```
$base_url = $response->base();
```

We now want to extract the links contained in the HTML document.

```
my $link_extor = HTML::LinkExtor->new(\&extract_links);
$link_extor->parse($response->content);
```

We can extract the links in one of two ways: by specifying a call-back routine in the HTML::LinkExtor constructor or by using the links() method, which stores all the links contained in the document. The call-back routine is called as each link is found, whereas the links() method contains all the links after the document has been processed. In this example, we use the call-back routine. To actually extract the links, the document must be passed to the `parse()` method. It is also possible to parse an HTML document that has been saved to a file by using the `parse_file()` method.

We check our links in the call-back routine. Each time a link is found in the HTML document, the call-back routine is called. The tag and any link attributes are passed to the routine. The attributes are passed as key/value pairs. Note that the tag and attribute names are all lower-case.

```
my ($tag, %attr) = @_;
```

Because we are only looking for anchor and image links, we first check to see whether the tag is an a or an img.

```
if ($tag eq 'a' or $tag eq 'img') {
```

Once we have an anchor or image tag, we need to extract the link. The link will be the value of the key/value pair corresponding to the key *href* for an anchor tag or *src* for an image tag. We then create a new URI object and use the `abs()` method to convert any relative URLs to absolute URLs. We use the `scheme()` method of the URI::URL module to limit the links we check to the following: *http, https, ftp,* and *file.*

```
if ($key eq 'href' or $key eq 'src') {
    my $link_url = URI->new($attr{$key});
    my $full_url = $link_url->abs($base_url);
    next unless ($full_url->scheme =~ /\b(?:https?|ftp|file)\b/);
```

Next we create a new HTTP::Request HEAD request. Because we only need a return code, using a HEAD request will be faster than downloading the entire page with GET.

```
my $request = HTTP::Request->new(HEAD => $full_url);
my $response = $ua->request($request);
```

Finally, we check the response code to see whether the link is good or bad.

```
if($response->status_line eq '200 OK') {
    print "$full_url OK\n";
} else {
    print "$full_url BAD - ", $response->status_line, "\n";
}
```

Note that we don't catch redirects. This can be left as an exercise for the reader. This is a fairly basic script and could be used in many ways. For example, this script could be easily modified to check several URLs and then have a list of any bad links found e-mailed to the user. This could be automated by running the script as a cron job.

HTML::Entities

The HTML::Entities module is used to decode and encode strings that contain HTML character entities (e.g., characters '< > & " '). This module can come in handy when you want to use a browser to display a string containing an HTML character entity without it being parsed as HTML. For example, let's say that you store an HTML template in a database and you want to view and modify the template using a Web-based admin tool (using a browser). The browser will parse any HTML tags that are in the template, so to view the actual HTML you need to encode all the character entities. This is easily done using the decode_entities() and encode_entities() methods exported by HTML::Entities.

The following example will print the character entities contained in $string, encode them, and then decode them back to their original values:

```
use HTML::Entities;

my $string = '< > & "';
print "HTML Entities: $string\n";

encode_entities($string);
print "Encoded: $string\n";

decode_entities($string);
print "Decoded: $string\n";
```

If you save this example as html_entities.pl and run it, you should see the following output:

```
% perl html_entities.pl
HTML Entities: < > & "
Encoded: &lt; &gt; &amp; &quot;
Decoded: < > & "
```

Summary

In this chapter we have shown how it is possible to automate many Web-based tasks using the LWP modules. We have also shown how to work with URLs, parse HTML, extract links from HTML, and encode and decode HTML character entities. The modules covered in this chapter are extremely useful, and we've only scratched the surface on how they can be used. Be sure to read the documentation and take some time to work with these powerful Perl modules.

# CHAPTER 16

Win32

The Win32 Library

This chapter covers the Win32 library that comes with the ActiveState (http://www.activestate.com/activeperl/) distribution of Perl. If you are using the standard distribution, you can download the libwin32 library from CPAN. This chapter assumes that you have installed the ActiveState port of Perl.

The Win32 library is a group of modules that allow you to do Windows-specific tasks such as retrieve and format Win32 error messages, create and manage processes, use OLE automation, and connect to a Microsoft Access database using ODBC.

The Win32 Module

The Win32 module provides several functions that interface with the Win32 APIs. We'll take a look at a few of them here. The complete list of functions can be found in the perlwin32 perldoc.

Error Handling

Win32 has two functions for reporting errors, `Win32::GetLastError()` and `Win32::FormatMessage()`. These are useful functions because errors generated by Win32 modules and extensions do not normally use the `$!` variable that Perl uses.

The `Win32::GetLastError()` function returns the error code of the last error generated by a Win32 API function call.

```
use Win32;
my $error = Win32::GetLastError();
```

The error code can be converted to a human-friendly string by using the `Win32::FormatMessage()` function.

You can create a useful error-reporting routine by using `Win32::GetLastError()` with `Win32::FormatMessage()` as follows:

```
sub win32_error {
    return Win32::FormatMessage(Win32::GetLastError());
}
```

One reason to use a routine like this is that some Win32 modules may set $! when generating an error. The problem in such cases is that $! has been set with a Win32 error number, not a Perl error number, so the error message may not be correct.

OS and Build Information

It is possible to gather information about the operating system using the Win32::GetOSVersion() function. This function will return a list containing information about the operating system: ($service_pack, $major, $minor, $build, $platform_id).

- $service_pack—A string containing the service pack version number
- $major—The major version number of the operating system
- $minor—The minor version number of the operating system
- $build—The Win32 build number
- $platform_id—A digit that represents the operating system name: the possible values are 0 for generic Win32, 1 for Win95/Win98, and 2 for WinNT

```
use Win32;
my($service_pack, $major, $minor, $build,
    $platform_id) = Win32::GetOSVersion();
my @os = qw(Win32s Win95/98 WinNT);
print "OS: $os[$platform_id] $major\.$minor $service_pack\n";
print "Build: $build\n";
```

When I run this on my NT machine, I get the following output:

```
D:\ipm\chap16>perl os.pl
OS: WinNT 4.0 Service Pack 6
Build: 1381
```

On my Win98 machine, I get a slightly different output:

```
D:\ipm\chap16>perl os.pl
OS: Win95/98 4.10  A
Build: 67766446
```

Win32::BuildNumber() will return the Perl Win32 build number.

```
use Win32;
my $build = Win32::BuildNumber();
print "Build: $build\n";
```

On both my NT and Win98 boxes, I get the following output:

```
D:\ipm\chap16>perl build.pl
Build: 616
```

You can check which Windows operating system is running by using
`Win32::IsWinNT()` and `Win32::IsWin95()`. Both functions return a
Boolean value, which can be useful if your program has operating system–specific code. Note that `Win32::IsWin95()` will return true for Windows 95 and Windows 98.

```
use Win32;
print "WinNT\n" if Win32::IsWinNT();
print "Win9x\n" if Win32::IsWin95();
```

Running this function on my NT machine produces:

```
D:\ipm\chap16>perl is_win.pl
WinNT
```

On my Win98 machine, this function produces:

```
D:\ipm\chap16>perl is_win.pl
Win9x
```

User, Machine, and Domain Names

The Win32 module provides three functions that can be used to determine the user, machine, and domain names.

- `Win32::LoginName()` returns the login name of the user who owns the
  current Perl process.
- `Win32::NodeName()` returns the Microsoft Network node name of the
  machine on which the script is running.
- `Win32::DomainName()` returns the Microsoft Network domain name
  that the owner of the current Perl process is logged into.

```
use Win32;

my $user = Win32::LoginName();
my $node = Win32::NodeName();
my $domain = Win32::DomainName();

print "Current User: $user\n";
```

```
print "Node: $node\n";
print "Domain: $domain\n";
```

Running this on my NT box produces the following output:

```
D:\ipm\chap16>perl user.pl
Current User: doug
Node: SETUP123
Domain: UCLICK
```

Finding and Changing the Current Working Directory

`Win32::GetCwd()` can be used to find the current working directory.

```
use Win32;

my $cwd = Win32::GetCwd();
print "Cwd: $cwd\n";
```

Running this script generates the following output:

```
D:\ipm\chap16>perl getcwd.pl
Cwd: D:\ipm\chap16
```

It is also possible to change the current working directory by using `Win32::SetCwd()`. The parameter to `Win32::SetCwd()` must be a relative or full path, not a UNC. If successful, `Win32::SetCwd()` will return a True value (1) and change the working directory. If the function fails, it returns an `undef`.

```
use Win32;

my $cwd = Win32::GetCwd();
print "Cwd: $cwd\n";

# move up a directory
my $new_cwd = '..';

if( Win32::SetCwd($new_cwd) ) {
    $cwd = Win32::GetCwd();
    print "Directory changed\n";
    print "Cwd: $cwd\n";
} else {
    print "Directory not changed\n";
```

```
    print "Cwd: $cwd\n";
}
```

Running this script should give you an output similar to:

```
D:\ipm\chap16>perl setcwd.pl
Cwd: D:\ipm\chap16
Directory changed
Cwd: D:\ipm
```

File System

You can find the file system of a drive by using the Win32::FsType()
function. Win32::FsType() will return a string representing the file system of the current drive:

```
use Win32;

my $file_system = Win32::FsType();
print "File System: $file_system\n";
```

Running this on NT, I get the following output:

```
D:\ipm\chap16>perl fstype.pl
File System: NTFS
```

On Win98, I get this output:

```
D:\ipm\chap16>perl fstype.pl
File System: FAT32
```

As of Perl 5.005, Win32::FsType() can also return a list containing
the following elements: ($file_system, $flags, $max_chars).
$file_system is a string representing the file system type (FAT, FAT32
or NTFS). $flags is a numeric value that represents the various flags
set by the drive. $max_chars is a numeric value that represents the
maximum permissible length of file or directory names.

```
use Win32;

my ($file_system, $flags, $max_chars) = Win32::FsType();

print "File System: $file_system\n";
print "Flags: $flags\n";
print "Max Chars: $max_chars\n";
```

Running this on NT, I get the following:

```
D:\ipm\chap16>perl fstype2.pl
File System: NTFS
Flags: 31
Max Chars: 255
```

On Win98, the script produces:

```
D:\ipm\chap16>perl fstype2.pl
File System: FAT32
Flags: 16390
Max Chars: 255
```

It is also possible to find the file system used on a drive other than the current one by changing the current working directory.

```perl
use Win32;

my $drive = 'C:';
if (Win32::SetCwd($drive)) {
    print_drive();
}

$drive = 'D:';
if (Win32::SetCwd($drive)) {
    print_drive();
}

sub print_drive {
    my ($file_system, $flags, $max_chars) = Win32::FsType();
    print "Drive: $drive\n";
    print "File System: $file_system\n";
    print "Flags: $flags\n";
    print "Max Chars: $max_chars\n\n";
}
```

Running this on NT, I get the following output:

```
D:\ipm\chap16>perl fstype3.pl
Drive: C:
File System: FAT
Flags: 6
Max Chars: 255

Drive: D:
File System: NTFS
Flags: 31
Max Chars: 255
```

On Win98, I get get:

```
D:\ipm\chap16>perl fstype3.pl
Drive: C:
File System: FAT
Flags: 16390
Max Chars: 255

Drive: D:
File System: FAT32
Flags: 16390
Max Chars: 255
```

Next Available Drive

The `Win32::GetNextAvailDrive()` function will return the next available drive letter.

```
use Win32;

my $next_drive = Win32::GetNextAvailDrive();
print "Next Available Drive: $next_drive\n";
```

Running this script, you should see something similar to the following output, depending on the layout of your system:

```
D:\ipm\chap16>perl nextdrive.pl
Next Available Drive: F:
```

Tick Count

The `Win32::GetTickCount()` function returns the number of milliseconds that have elapsed since the system started.

```
use Win32;

my $tick = Win32::GetTickCount();
print "Tick Count: $tick milliseconds\n";
```

You should see something similar to the following output, with the number of milliseconds determined by when you run the script:

```
D:\ipm\chap16>perl tick.pl
Tick Count: 4588909 milliseconds
```

Message Box

The `Win32::MsgBox()` function allows you to display a message box from your script. The `Win32::MsgBox()` function takes three arguments: a message string, a flag that specifies the type of message box, and an optional title string (the default is "Perl").

The possible values for the flag are:

```
MB_ICONHAND
MB_ICONQUESTION
MB_ICONEXCLAMATION
MB_ICONASTERISK
MB_ICONWARNING
MB_ICONERROR
MB_ICONINFORMATION
MB_ICONSTOP
```

The following script will create a dialog box with an "OK" button, an information icon (the letter "i" in a bubble), a title, and a message.

```
use Win32;

my $message = 'Your message here';
my $flag = MB_ICONINFORMATION;
my $title = 'Your Perl App';

Win32::MsgBox($message, $flag, $title);
```

The second argument can also be a number that represents the buttons and icon used. To determine the number for the second argument, choose one number from "button codes" and one number for "icon codes" and add them together (Table 16.1).

TABLE 16.1

Determining the Number for the Second Argument

Button Codes		Icon Codes	
Code	Result	Code	Result
0	OK	16	Hand
1	OK and Cancel	32	Question (?)
2	Abort, Retry, Ignore	48	Exclamation point (!)
3	Yes, No, and Cancel	64	Asterisk (*)
4	Yes and No		
5	Retry and Cancel		

You can also find a return value to determine which button the user clicked. Table 16.2 lists the possible return codes.

TABLE 16.2

Button (Return) Codes

Code	Button Clicked
1	OK
2	Cancel
3	Abort
4	Retry
5	Ignore
6	Yes
7	No

The following script will create a message box with a question icon, three buttons (Yes, No, and Cancel), a title, and a message. The flag variable is set to 35, which is the result of adding 3 (button code for Yes, No, and Cancel) and 32 (code for question icon).

```
use Win32;

my $message = 'Save changes to file?';
my $flag = 35;
my $title = 'Perl App';

my $return = Win32::MsgBox($message, $flag, $title);
print "Return: $return\n";
```

Processes

There are several ways to run external programs using Perl: backticks, system(), exec(), open(), and fork(). As an alternative, you can use the Win32::Spawn() function (part of the Win32 module) or the Win32::Process module to create and manage processes.

Win32::Spawn

An easy way to run an external program is to use the Win32::Spawn() function. On the downside, once a process is created, you have no control over it, although it is possible to stop it with the `kill()` function. Also, the Perl script will continue execution after the external program has started.

The following script will open a file in Notepad. If no file is found, you will be asked if you want to create a new file. One minor annoyance when using `Win32::Spawn()` is that Notepad is opened minimized.

```perl
use Win32;

my $command = 'c:\windows\notepad.exe';
my $args = 'notepad.exe c:\my documents\test.txt';
my $pid = 0;

Win32::Spawn($command, $args, $pid) or die win32_error();
print "Spawned PID $pid\n";

sub win32_error {
    return Win32::FormatMessage(Win32::GetLastError());
}
```

The `$command` variable is set to the full path of the application that we want to run. The `$args` variable contains the name of our application (which is ignored) and the full path to the file we want to open.

Win32::Process

The `Win32::Process` module is more flexible and gives us more control by allowing us to start, kill, suspend, resume, and set the priority of a process. Note that `Win32::Spawn()` has been deprecated in favor of `Win32::Process`.

The `Win32::Process::Create()` function is used to create a new process and takes the following form (Table 16.3):

```perl
Win32::Process::Create($process, $program, $commandline,
                       $handles, $options, $dir);
```

TABLE 16.3		
Win32::Process Functions	$process	Reference to new process object (if successfully created)
	$program	Full path to executable program
	$commandline	How program would be called at command line
	$handles	Whether new process should inherit file handles from the parent process
	$options	List of options governing the creation and speed of the process
	$dir	Working directory for the new process

The $handles argument takes a value of 1 to specify that the process should inherit file handles from the parent process. A value of 0 signifies that the process should not inherit the file handles of its parent process.

The $options argument consists of a list of logically OR'd option flags used to create a new process (Table 16.4). The list may also contain one priority class that controls the priority level of the process (Table 16.5). For our example, we chose NORMAL_PRIORITY_CLASS, which is the standard process level.

TABLE 16.4

Option Flags

CREATE_DEFAULT_ERROR_MODE	Process object will use default error mode
CREATE_NEW_CONSOLE	Process object will have new console created for it; cannot be used with DETACHED_PROCESS option
CREATE_NEW_PROCESS_GROUP	New process set as root of new process group
CREATE_SEPARATE_WOW_VDM	New process will run in its own 16-bit Virtual DOS Machine (VDM)
CREATE_SUSPENDED	New process created in suspended state
CREATE_UNICODE_ENVIRONMENT	New process uses Unicode characters
DEBUG_PROCESS	New process and any child processes are debugged by calling process
DEBUG_ONLY_THIS_PROCESS	Only new process is debugged by calling process
DETACHED_PROCESS	New process has no access to the console of the calling process; cannot be used with CREATE_NEW_CONSOLE option

TABLE 16.5

Priority Classes

IDLE_PRIORITY_CLASS	Process only runs when system is idle
NORMAL_PRIORITY_CLASS	Process runs as normal process
HIGH_PRIORITY_CLASS	Process runs at above-normal priority; receives more CPU time than IDLE and NORMAL priority processes
REALTIME_PRIORITY_CLASS	Process receives as much CPU time as the OS will allow

The following script will open a file in Notepad. This time, the Notepad application is opened maximized.

```
use Win32;
use Win32::Process;
```

```
my $process;
my $command = 'c:\windows\notepad.exe';
my $commandline = 'notepad.exe c:\my documents\test.txt';
my $handles = 0;
my $options = NORMAL_PRIORITY_CLASS;
my $dir = '.';

Win32::Process::Create($process, $command, $commandline,
                       $handles, $options, $dir) or
    die win32_error();

sub win32_error {
    return Win32::FormatMessage(Win32::GetLastError());
}
```

Once again, the script will continue executing after the new process has been created. To prevent this, we can use the `Win32::Process` `Wait()` method. The `Wait()` method takes one argument, the amount of time to wait before continuing. You can use the constant `INFINITE` or the value in milliseconds; for example:

```
# Wait indefinitely
$process->Wait(INFINITE);
# Wait 500 milliseconds
$process->Wait(500);
```

To see this pause, we'll add the `Wait()` function and a print statement to the previous code. After the new process has been created, the `Wait()` function causes the script to wait 5 seconds to print out the message "Hello" to the command line.

```
use Win32;
use Win32::Process;

my $process;
my $command = 'c:\windows\notepad.exe';
my $commandline = 'notepad.exe c:\my documents\test.txt';
my $handles = 0;
my $options = NORMAL_PRIOIRTY_CLASS;
my $dir = '.';

Win32::Process::Create($process, $command, $commandline,
                       $handles, $options, $dir) or
    die Win32_error();

# Wait 5 seconds
$process->Wait(5000);
print "Hello\n";
```

```
sub Win32_error {
    return Win32::FormatMessage(Win32::GetLastError());
}
```

We can kill the current process by calling the `Kill()` method. The `Kill()` method takes a single argument, which is the exit code to be returned; for example:

```
$process->Kill($exit_code);
```

We can suspend and restart a process by using the `Suspend()` and `Resume()` methods; for example:

```
$process->Suspend();
$process->Resume();
```

We can get and set the priority of a process by using the `GetPriorityClass()` and `SetPriorityClass()` methods; for example, to get the priority of the current process:

```
$priority = $process->GetPriorityClass();
```

To change the priority of a process, you would pass a priority class constant (see Table 16.5) to the `SetPriorityClass()` method; for example:

```
$process->SetPriorityClass(HIGH_PRIORITY_CLASS);
```

We can get the process ID by using the `GetProcessID()` method:

```
$id = $process->GetProcessID();
```

To get the exit code returned by the process, use the `GetExitCode()` method:

```
$process->GetExitCode($ExitCode);
```

OLE Automation

Perl provides an interface to OLE automation with the `Win32::OLE` module. OLE was originally used to embed one application into another (for example, embedding an Excel spreadsheet into a Word document).

Win32::OLE also allows us to manipulate Windows applications that support OLE.

Using Win32::OLE, we can create an object that represents a Windows application. Once we create a Win32::OLE object, we can communicate with an application that supports OLE (like Excel) and send it various commands.

The ActiveState documentation includes a FAQ, "Using OLE with Perl," that provides the basis for the next few examples.

Creating and Writing to an Excel Spreadsheet

The following script will create an Excel spreadsheet, write data to selected cells, and then save the data to a file. This fictitious example writes the number of page views for three different Web sites to the spreadsheet.

```perl
use Win32::OLE;

# Create a new Win32::OLE object
my $excel = Win32::OLE->new('Excel.Application', 'Quit') or
    die ("Can't create object: ", Win32::OLE->LastError());

# Create new workbook
$excel->Workbooks->Add;

# Set cell values
$excel->Cells(1,1)->{Value} = "Site";
$excel->Cells(1,2)->{Value} = "Page Views";

$excel->Cells(2,1)->{Value} = "Perl";
$excel->Cells(2,2)->{Value} = "67845";

$excel->Cells(3,1)->{Value} = "Java";
$excel->Cells(3,2)->{Value} = "21345";

$excel->Cells(4,1)->{Value} = "Python";
$excel->Cells(4,2)->{Value} = "12462";

# Save file
$excel->Workbooks(1)->SaveAs('D:\ipm\code\chap16\ole\stats.xls');
```

In this example, we first create a Win32::OLE object:

```perl
my $excel = Win32::OLE->new('Excel.Application', 'Quit') or
    die ("Can't create object: ", Win32::OLE->LastError());
```

In the call to the constructor method, we provide two arguments, `'Excel.Application'` and `'Quit'`. `'Excel.Application'` is the ProgID, which in this case is an Excel application. `'Quit'` is a method of Excel.Application that closes the Excel application.

Extracting Data from an Excel Spreadsheet

This script will extract the data loaded into an Excel spreadsheet by the previous example.

```
use Win32::OLE;

# Create a new Win32::OLE object
my $excel = Win32::OLE->new('Excel.Application', 'Quit') or
    die ("Can't create object: ", Win32::OLE->LastError());

# Open workbook
my $file = 'D:\ipm\code\chap16\ole\stats.xls';
my $workbook = $excel->Workbooks->Open(@file) or
    die ("Can't open Workbook: ", Win32::OLE->LastError());

# Get worksheet and values in cell range
my $worksheet = $workbook->Worksheets(1);
my $range = $worksheet->Range("A1:B4")->{'Value'};

# Close workbook
$workbook->close;

# Print out cells
foreach my $row (@$range) {
    foreach my $cell (@$row) {
        print "$cell\t";
    }
    print "\n";
}
```

Running this script will provide the following output provided that you ran the previous script that created the spreadsheet:

```
D:\ipm\code\chap16\ole>perl ole2.pl
Site    Page Views
Perl    67845
Java    21345
Python  12462
```

Creating a Chart with Excel

The following script will create a pie chart from the data loaded into the spreadsheet:

```perl
use Win32::OLE;
use Win32::OLE::Const 'Microsoft Excel';

# Create a new Win32::OLE object
my $excel = Win32::OLE->new('Excel.Application') or
  die ("Can't create object: ", Win32::OLE->LastError());

# Set to visible
$excel->{Visible} = 1;

# Open workbook
my $file = 'D:\ipm\code\chap16\ole\stats.xls';
my $workbook = $excel->Workbooks->Open(@file) or
  die ("Can't open Workbook: ", Win32::OLE->LastError());

# Get worksheet and values in cell range
my $worksheet = $workbook->Worksheets(1);
my $range = $worksheet->Range("A1:B4");

# Add chart
my $chart = $excel->Charts->Add();

# Set chart type to Pie
$chart->{ChartType} = xlPie;
# Set source data and plot instructions
$chart->SetSourceData({Source=>$range, PlotBy=>xlColumns});
# Set chart title
$chart->{HasTitle} = 1;
$chart->ChartTitle->{Text} = "Site Page Views";
```

In this example, we need the application to be visible so we can see the pie chart. We do this by setting the `Visible` property:

```perl
$excel->{Visible} = 1;
```

You can interact with automation objects by setting or getting properties, as we did with the `Visible` property, or by calling a method. We called the following method to open a workbook:

```perl
my $workbook = $excel->Workbooks->Open($file) or
  die ("Can't open Workbook: ", Win32::OLE->LastError());
```

Database Access with ODBC

The `Win32::ODBC` module provides an object-oriented interface to ODBC-compliant databases. We'll take a look at the steps required to use `Win32::ODBC` and then build a small database application.

Using Win32::ODBC

For the following examples, I used Microsoft Access 97 and created a DSN for my database. To run the following example, you will need to use an ODBC-compliant database and create a DSN.

Load Win32::ODBC

First you must load the `Win32::ODBC` extension. Normally, you will want to place the following line at the beginning of the script:

```
use Win32::ODBC;
```

Open Connection to Database

Then you open a database connection by creating a new `Win32::ODBC` object:

```
my $db = new Win32::ODBC("MyDSN" [, (Option1,Value1),
                                    (Option2,Value2)…]);
```

MyDSN can be a previously configured DSN or an actual DSN connect string. The DSN connect string can contain user ID and password information:

```
# Previously configured DSN
my $db = new Win32::ODBC("FilmDB");
```

or

```
# DSN connect string
my $db = new Win32::ODBC("DSN=FilmDB;UID=Doug;PWD=ipm");
```

If the connection fails, the database object will be undefined, so you may want to check the return value. For example:

```
# Create new Win32::ODBC object
my $db = new Win32::ODBC("FilmDB") or
   die "Can't open FilmDB: ", Win32::ODBC::Error();
```

Once a connection has been established, you can execute queries and extract data from the database.

Execute Query

To execute a query, you will use a line similar to the following:

```
$db->Sql("SELECT * FROM film");
```

In this case, if the command is successful, it will return a record set that contains all fields from all the rows in the "film" table. An error number is returned if the command is not successful.

You can use any valid SQL statement as a parameter to the Sql() method.

Process Record Set

If the execution of an SQL statement returns a record set, you may process the record set row by row to extract the data. The FetchRow() method is used to traverse through the record set, a row at a time. Once you have created a record set, no row is being pointed to, so you must call FetchRow() to move to the first row of the record set. Each subsequent call to FetchRow() will move to the next available row. Fetchrow() will return true if a row is returned and false if nothing is returned (when you reach the end of the record set). With this in mind, it is possible to process a record set as follows:

```
while( $db->FetchRow() ) {
    # extract and process data
}
```

Extract Data

There are two methods for extracting data from a row: Data() and DataHash().

To use the Data() method, you pass the names of the columns you want to extract as parameters. The values returned are in the same order as the parameters. If no column names are passed, all the column values are returned in the order they are found in the row.

```
while ($db->FetchRow()) {
    my @data = $db->Data('title', 'year', 'director', 'cast');
    print "Title: ", $data[0], "\n";
    print "Year: ", $data[1], "\n";
    print "Director: ", $data[2], "\n";
    print "Cast: ", $data[3], "\n\n";
}
```

It is also possible to extract the fields by name:

```
while ($db->FetchRow()) {
    print "Title: ", $db->Data('title'), "\n";
    print "Year: ", $db->Data('year'), "\n";
    print "Director: ", $db->Data('director'), "\n";
    print "Cast: ", $db->Data('cast'), "\n\n";
}
```

The `DataHash()` method is useful because it returns a hash with column names as the keys (or `undef` if it fails). You may pass parameters corresponding to the columns you wish to retrieve; if no parameters are passed, all columns are returned.

```
while ($db->FetchRow()) {
    # Clear the hash to prevent retention of previous values
    my %data = undef;
    %data = $db->DataHash();
    print "Title: ", $data{'title'}, "\n";
    print "Year: ", $data{'year'}, "\n";
    print "Director: ", $data{'director'}, "\n";
    print "Cast: ", $data{'cast'}, "\n\n";
}
```

Close Connection to Database

Once you have extracted all your data, you need to close the database connection. You can do this by using the `Close()` method.

```
$db->Close()
```

Film Database Application

I have created a simple database, `film.mdb`, to use with this application. It consists of one table, film, which contains four fields: title, year, director, and cast. I have separated the example into two scripts, one for inserting and deleting records from the database and the other to make queries.

Inserting and Deleting Records

The following code allows you to insert new records and delete existing ones from the database:

```perl
use Getopt::Std;
use Win32::ODBC;

my %opts;
# a=add, d=delete
getopt('a:d:', \%opts);

my $DSN = 'FilmDB';

# Create new Win32::ODBC object
my $db = new Win32::ODBC($DSN) or
  die "Can't open $DSN: ", Win32::ODBC::Error();

add_record() if $opts{a};
delete_record() if $opts{d};

sub add_record {
    # expected input string in
    # "title":year:"director":"cast" format.
    my($title, $year, $director, $cast) = split(':', $opts{a});

    my $sql = "INSERT INTO film ".
              "(title, year, director, cast) ".
              "VALUES ".
              "('$title', $year, '$director', '$cast')";

    unless ($db->Sql($sql)) {
        print "Record added";
        $db->Close();
    } else {
        print "Database Error: ", $db->Error();
    }
}

sub delete_record {

    my $dql = "DELETE FROM film WHERE title='$opts{d}'";
    unless ($db->Sql($sql)) {
        print "Record Deleted\n";
        $db->Close();
    } else {
        print "Database Error: ", $db->Error();
    }
}
```

To add a film to the database, you use the option flag –a followed by a colon-separated list containing the movie title, year of release, director, and cast. For example:

```
D:\ipm\chap16\ODBC>perl filmdb1.pl -a "An Autumn Tale":1999:"Eric
Rohmer":"Marie Rivier,Beatrice Romand"
```

I chose to use the film title as the key to delete on. Use a –d option flag followed by the film's title:

```
D:\ipm\chap16\ODBC>perl filmdb1.pl -d "An Autumn Tale"
```

Querying the Database

To retrieve data from the database, you can choose the film title, year of release, director, or actor. This simple example doesn't include the functionality to perform Boolean searches, but that would be a useful feature to add.

```
use Getopt::Std;
use Win32::ODBC;

my %opts;
# t=title, y=year, d=director, a=actor/actress
getopt('t:y:d:a:', \%opts);

my $DSN='FilmDB';

# Create new Win32::ODBC object
my $db = new Win32::ODBC($DSN) or
  die "Cannot open $DSN: ", Win32::ODBC::Error();

my $sql;

# Create SQL statement
if ($opts{t}) {
    $opts{t} =~ s/'/''/g; # Escape single quotes
    $sql = "SELECT * FROM film WHERE title LIKE '%$opts{t}%'";
} elsif ($opts{y}) {
    $sql = "SELECT * FROM film WHERE year=$opts{y}";
} elsif ($opts{d}) {
    $opts{d} =~ s/'/''/g;
    $sql = "SELECT * FROM film WHERE director LIKE '%$opts{d}%'";
} elsif ($opts{a}) {
    $opts{a} =~ s/'/''/g;
    $sql = "SELECT * FROM film WHERE cast LIKE '%$opts{a}%'";
} else {
    $sql = "SELECT * FROM film";
}
```

```
unless ($db->Sql($sql)) {
    my $count = 0;
    while ($db->FetchRow()) {
        print "Title: ", $db->Data('title'), "\n";
        print "Year: ", $db->Data('year'), "\n";
        print "Director: ", $db->Data('director'), "\n";
        print "Cast: ", $db->Data('cast'), "\n\n";
        $count++;
    }
    print "No records found\n" if !$count;
    $db->Close();
} else {
    print "Database Error: ", $db->Error();
}
```

In the following example, we search for all films in the database that were directed by Claude Berri:

```
D:\ipm\chap16\ODBC>perl filmdb2.pl -d "Berri"
Title: Jean de Florette
Year: 1986
Director: Claude Berri
Cast: Yves Montand,Gerard Depardieu,Daniel Auteuil

Title: Manon of the Spring
Year: 1986
Director: Claude Berri
Cast: Yves Montand,Daniel Auteuil,Emmanuelle Beart
```

The next example shows the results after querying the database for films with actress Irene Jacob:

```
D:\ipm\chap16\ODBC>perl filmdb2.pl -a "Irene Jacob"
Title: Red
Year: 1994
Director: Krzysztof Kieslowski
Cast: Irene Jacob,Jean-Louis Trintignant

Title: The Double Life of Veronique
Year: 1991
Director: Krzysztof Kieslowski
Cast: Irene Jacob,Wladyslaw Kowalski

Title: Au Revoir Les Enfants
Year: 1987
Director: Louis Malle
Cast: Gaspard Manesse,Raphael Fejto,Irene Jacob
```

We query the database for all films released in 1960. In this case, no records were found.

```
D:\ipm\chap16\ODBC>perl filmdb2.pl -y 1960
No records found
```

Summary

In this chapter we have shown how to use Win32 modules to obtain information about the Windows environment, create and manage processes, use OLE automation, and interact with an ODBC-compliant database such as Microsoft Access. There are many other Windows-based tasks that can be performed with Win32 modules such as network administration, file management, and manipulation of the registry, to name just a few. If you are interested in more information about programming with Perl on the Windows platform, read *Active Perl Developer's Guide* by Martin Brown and *Win32 Perl Programming: The Standard Extensions* by Dave Roth.

XML

Introduction

Extensible Markup Language (XML), a subset of the more complex Standard Generalized Markup Language (SGML), is a metalanguage that is used to define new markup languages for structured documents. Unlike HTML, which is used for document presentation (tags represent how the document should be displayed), XML is used to represent the document structure (tags represent the organization of the document). XML can be used for many tasks, including exchanging, storing, and representing data, message exchange, and RDF Site Summary (RSS) news feeds.

In this chapter, we will show how to parse an XML document using the XML::Parser module. We will also use the XML::RSS module to create an RDF channel and convert an RSS news feed into HTML.

This chapter is not meant to be a tutorial on XML. More information on XML can be found at **http://www.xml.com** and **http://www.w3.org/ XML/**. Additional information on Perl and XML can be found at **http://www.perlxml.com**.

Parsing XML with XML::Parser

```
XML::Parser: /CPAN/XML-Parser.2.30.tar.gz
expat: /misc/expat-1.95.1.tar.gz
```

Overview of XML::Parser

XML::Parser was originally developed by Larry Wall and is now maintained by Clark Cooper. XML::Parser is an interface to James Clark's XML parser, Expat, a nonvalidating parser written in C. If you are using the ActiveState version of Perl, XML::Parser is already installed on your system. Otherwise, you must install the module yourself.

As of version 2.30 of XML::Parser, *Expat is no longer included with the package. If Expat is not already installed on your system, you can download it (release 1.95.0 or later) from* **http://www.sourceforge.net/projects/ expat** *or install it from the CD-ROM.*

NOTE

XML::Parser is an event-based parser, which means we must register event handlers (callbacks) with the parser to process an XML document. As the document is parsed, the event handlers are called when the corresponding events are detected.

There are several handlers, but most applications will only need the Start, End, and Char handlers. See the module documentation for a list of all the handlers.

Parsing a Simple XML Document

In this example we'll create a simple XML document and use XML::Parser to parse the Start, End, and Char parts of the document.

First we'll create a simple XML document, cat.xml:

```
<?xml version="1.0"?>
<cat>
  <name>Harry</name>
  <breed>Tabby</breed>
  <color>Red</color>
  <sex>Male</sex>
  <weight unit="pound">12</weight>
</cat>
```

Next, we'll create a simple script, xmlparser1.pl, that uses XML::Parser:

```
#!/usr/bin/perl -w
use XML::Parser;
use strict;

die "Usage: xmlparser1.pl <file>" unless @ARGV == 1;

my $file = shift;

die qq!Can't find file "$file"! unless -f $file;

my $parser = new XML::Parser(
                Handlers => {Start => \&start_handler,
                             End   => \&end_handler,
                             Char  => \&char_handler});

$parser->parsefile($file);

############
# Handlers
############
```

```perl
sub start_handler {
    my $expat = shift;
    my $element = shift;

    print "START: $element\n";

    # Handle the attributes
    while (@_) {
        my $attr = shift;
        my $val = shift;
        print qq!ATTR: $attr="$val"\n!;
    }

}

sub end_handler {
    my($expat, $element) = @_;
    print "END: $element\n";

}

sub char_handler {
    my($expat, $data) = @_;
    return if $data =~ /^\s+$/;
    print "CHAR: $data\n";

}
```

Running the script,

```
% perl xmlparser1.pl cat.xml
```

will produce the following output:

```
START: cat
START: name
CHAR: Harry
END: name
START: breed
CHAR: Tabby
END: breed
START: color
CHAR: Red
END: color
START: sex
CHAR: Male
END: sex
START: weight
ATTR: unit="pound"
CHAR: 12
END: weight
END: cat
```

Although not particularly useful, this example should clarify how the event handlers operate. The `Start` handler is called each time the parser encounters an XML start tag. `$element` will contain the name of the XML element. We also print the name and value of each attribute (if any) in the start tag.

The `End` handler is called each time the parser encounters an XML end tag. `$element` will contain the name of the XML element. The `Char` handler is called when nonmarkup text is encountered between the start and end tags.

Converting XML to Text

Now let's look at a slightly more pragmatic example. We're going to store some contact information in an XML file and use a Perl script to print it as text.

Here's the XML file, `contacts.xml`:

```
<?xml version="1.0"?>
<contacts>
  <contact>
    <name>
      <first>Doug</first>
      <last>Sparling</last>
    </name>
    <address>
      <street>123 Maple</street>
      <city>Some City</city>
      <state>Some State</state>
      <zip>12345</zip>
    </address>
    <tel type="home">555.555.5555</tel>
    <tel type="work">555.123.4567</tel>
    <email>doug@dougsparling.com</email>
  </contact>
  <contact>
    <name>
      <first>Frank</first>
      <last>Wiles</last>
    </name>
    <address>
      <street>456 Oak</street>
      <city>Some City</city>
      <state>Some State</state>
      <zip>12345</zip>
    </address>
    <tel type="home">555.444.4444</tel>
    <tel type="work">555.123.4568</tel>
```

```
    <email>frank@wiles.org</email>
  </contact>
</contacts>
```

Here's the code for the Perl script, xmlparser2.pl:

```perl
#!/usr/bin/perl -w
use XML::Parser;
use strict;

die "Usage: xmlparser2.pl <file>" unless @ARGV == 1;

my $file = shift;

die qq!Can't find file "$file"! unless -f $file;

my $parser = new XML::Parser(ErrorContext => 2);
$parser->setHandlers(Start => \&start_handler,
                     End   => \&end_handler,
                     Char  => \&char_handler);

$parser->parsefile($file);

############
# Handlers
############

sub start_handler {
    my $expat = shift;
    my $element = shift;
    my %attribs = @_;

    if ( $element =~ /\bfirst\b/i ) {
        print "First Name: ";
    } elsif ( $element =~ /\blast\b/i ) {
        print "Last Name: ";
    } elsif ( $element =~ /\bstreet\b/i ) {
        print "Street: ";
    } elsif ( $element =~ /\bcity\b/i ) {
        print "City: ";
    } elsif ( $element =~ /\bstate\b/i ) {
        print "State: ";
    } elsif ( $element =~ /\bzip\b/i ) {
        print "Zip: ";
    } elsif ( $element =~ /\btel\b/i ) {
        print "Phone ($attribs{'type'}): ";
    } elsif ( $element =~ /\bemail\b/i ) {
        print "Email: ";
    }

}

sub end_handler {
```

```
    my($expat, $element) = @_;

    if ( $element =~ /\bcontact\b/i ) {
        print "\n";
    }

}

sub char_handler {
    my($expat, $data) = @_;
    return if $data =~ /^\s+$/;
    print "$data\n";

}
```

Running the script

```
% perl xmlparser2.pl contacts.xml
```

will produce the following output:

```
First Name: Doug
Last Name: Sparling
Street: 123 Maple
City: Some City
State: Some State
Zip: 12345
Phone (home): 555.555.5555
Phone (work): 555.123.4567
Email: doug@dougsparling.com

First Name: Frank
Last Name: Wiles
Street: 456 Oak
City: Some City
State: Some State
Zip: 12345
Phone (home): 555.444.4444
Phone (work): 555.123.4568
Email: frank@wiles.org
```

To create a text file, simply redirect the output:

```
% perl xmlparser2.pl contacts.xml > contacts.txt
```

In this script, we used the XML::Parser ErrorContext() method, which is an Expat option:

```
my $parser = new XML::Parser(ErrorContext => 2);
$parser->setHandlers(Start => \&start_handler,
```

```
          End   => \&end_handler,
          Char  => \&char_handler);
```

Setting the `ErrorContext` option to 2 provides two lines of context, one line for each side of an error. For example, if there were a typo in our XML document like this:

```
<firs>Doug</first>
```

we would see an error message similar to this:

```
mismatched tag at line 5, column 18, byte 78:
  <contact>
    <name>
      <firs>Doug</first>
================^
      <last>Sparling</last>
    </name>
  at /usr/lib/perl5/site_perl/5.005/i386-linux/XML/Parser.pm
    line 185
```

Converting XML to HTML

In this example, we'll convert an XML file to an HTML document. This type of script can be useful if you are using XML to store data and would like to display it on a web page.

First we'll create an XML document, `books.xml`:

```
<?xml version="1.0"?>
<books>
  <book>
    <title>Instant Perl Modules</title>
    <author>Doug Sparling, Frank Wiles</author>
    <publisher>McGraw-Hill</publisher>
    <year>2001</year>
    <isbn>0-07-212962-X</isbn>
  </book>
  <book>
    <title>Perl Programmer's Reference</title>
    <author>Martin C. Brown</author>
    <publisher>McGraw-Hill</publisher>
    <year>1999</year>
    <isbn>0-07-212142-4</isbn>
  </book>
</books>
```

Here's the code for `xmlparser3.pl`, the script responsible for creating the web page:

```perl
#!/usr/bin/perl -w
use XML::Parser;
use strict;

die "Usage: xmlparser3.pl <file>" unless @ARGV == 1;

my $file = shift;

die qq!Can't find file "$file"! unless -f $file;

my $parser = new XML::Parser(ErrorContext => 2);
$parser->setHandlers(Init  => \&init_handler,
                     Final => \&final_handler,
                     Start => \&start_handler,
                     End   => \&end_handler,
                     Char  => \&char_handler);

$parser->parsefile($file);

############
# Handlers
############

sub init_handler {
    print "<HTML><BODY BGCOLOR=\"#FFFFFF\">";
}

sub final_handler {
    print "</BODY></HTML>";
}

sub start_handler {
    my($expat, $element) = @_;

    if ( $element =~ /\bbook\b/i ) {
        print "<CENTER>";
    } elsif ( $element =~ /\btitle\b/i ) {
        print "<H1>";
    } elsif ( $element =~ /\bauthor\b/i ) {
        print "Author: <B>";
    } elsif ( $element =~ /\bpublisher\b/i ) {
        print "Publisher: <B>";
    } elsif ( $element =~ /\byear\b/i ) {
        print "Year: <B>";
    } elsif ( $element =~ /\bisbn\b/i ) {
        print "ISBN: <B>";
    }

}
```

```perl
sub end_handler {
    my($expat, $element) = @_;

    if ( $element =~ /\bbook\b/i ) {
        print "</CENTER><HR>";
    } elsif ( $element =~ /\btitle\b/i ) {
        print "</H1>";
    } elsif ( $element =~ /\bauthor\b/i ) {
        print "</B><BR>";
    } elsif ( $element =~ /\bpublisher\b/i ) {
        print "</B><BR>";
    } elsif ( $element =~ /\byear\b/i ) {
        print "</B><BR>";
    } elsif ( $element =~ /\bisbn\b/i ) {
        print "</B>";
    }

}

sub char_handler {
    my($expat, $data) = @_;
    print $data;

}
```

Running the script

```
% perl xmlparser3.pl books.xml > books.html
```

will create a file containing the following HTML:

```html
<HTML><BODY BGCOLOR="#FFFFFF">
  <CENTER>
    <H1>Instant Perl Modules</H1>
    Author: <B>Doug Sparling, Frank Wiles</B><BR>
    Publisher: <B>McGraw-Hill</B><BR>
    Year: <B>2001</B><BR>
    ISBN: <B>0-07-212962-X</B>
  </CENTER><HR>
  <CENTER>
    <H1>Perl Programmer's Reference</H1>
    Author: <B>Martin C. Brown</B><BR>
    Publisher: <B>McGraw-Hill</B><BR>
    Year: <B>1999</B><BR>
    ISBN: <B>0-07-212142-4</B>
  </CENTER><HR>
</BODY></HTML>
```

In this script we used the Init and Final handlers. The Init handler is called when the start of the XML document is encountered, and the Final handler is called when the end of the XML document is encountered.

XML::RSS

XML::Parser: /CPAN/XML-RSS-0.95.tar.gz

Overview

XML::RSS is a module by Jonathan Eisenzopf that can be used to create and update RSS files. XML::RSS also can be used to convert RSS to HTML (which is an easy way to add news feeds to your web site). RSS is an XML grammar that was developed by Netscape to create channels on Netscape Netcenter (**http://www.my.netscape.com**). RSS is now used by many content providers as a simple syndication format, commonly used to distribute daily news headlines. Sites that use RSS include Slashdot, Freshmeat, CNN, CNET, and Salon.

There are many types of channels available. The following websites publish RSS URLs:

- http://www.xmltree.com (search for RSS)
- http://my.netscape.com
- http://my.userland.com

RSS Syntax

An RSS file describes a channel's content. The top-level element of an RSS file is the rss element and it must specify an RSS version number (0.9, 0.91, or 1.0), the default being 1.0. The rss element also can specify the encoding attribute, with UTF-8 being the default:

```
<?xml version="1.0" encoding="ISO-8859-1"?>
```

The rss element cannot contain more than one channel element. The channel element must contain a few required elements (Table 17.1) and various optional elements (Table 17.2).

TABLE 17.1	title	Channel name
Required Channel Elements	description	Short description of channel
	link	HTML link to the web site of the channel
	language	Language encoding of channel
	item	Content being distributed, 1–15 items

TABLE 17.2	rating	PICS rating for channel web site
Optional Channel Elements	copyright	Content copyright
	pubDate	Publish date of channel
	lastBuildDate	Date RSS file was last updated
	docs	Additional channel information
	managingEditor	Managing editor of channel
	webMaster	Webmaster of channel
	image	Channel image
	textinput	Text box for a form
	skipHours	Hours the aggregator should not collect the RSS file
	skipDays	Days the aggregator should not collect the RSS file

Two of the optional channel elements can contain other elements: image and textinput. The image element is used to display a channel image or logo. The textinput element allows a user to enter text in an HTML text field and submit a query to a server-side program. The image element has the properties shown in Table 17.3. The title and url properties are required. The textinput element has the properties shown in Table 17.4. We'll look at an RSS file in the next section.

TABLE 17.3	title	Title of image; used as image ALT tag
Image Element's Properties	url	URL of image
	link	Link associated with image
	height	Height of image
	width	Width of image
	description	Description of image

TABLE 17.4	title	Submit button label
Textinput Element's Properties	description	Text input description
	name	Name of text input
	link	Action URL of form

Create an RSS Channel

Although you can create an RSS file by hand, the XML::RSS module makes this task painless. We use the channel(), image(), textinput(), and add_item() methods to build our RSS file.

Here's the code to build a simple RSS file.

```perl
#!/usr/bin/perl -w
use strict;
use XML::RSS;

# Create an RSS 1.0 file
my $rss = new XML::RSS (output => '1.0');

# Channel
$rss->channel(
    title       => 'IPM',
    link        => 'http://www.dougsparling.com/ipm/',
    description => 'Instant Perl Modules'
);

# Image
$rss->image(
    title => 'dougsparling.com',
    url   => 'http://dougsparling.com/images/dss.jpg'
);

# Textinput
$rss->textinput(
    title       => 'Search',
    descripiton => 'Search dougsparling.com',
    name        => 'text',
    link    => 'http://www.dougsparling.com/cgi-bin/search.cgi'
);

# Items
$rss->add_item(
    title => 'IPM News',
    link  => 'http://www.dougsparling.com/ipm/index.html'
);

# Save the file
```

```
$rss->save('channel.rss');
```

Running this script

```
% perl rss_channel.pl
```

will produce a file that looks like this:

```
<?xml version="1.0" encoding="UTF-8"?>

<rdf:RDF
 xmlns:rdf=http://www.w3.org/1999/02/22-rdf-syntax-ns#
 xmlns=http://purl.org/rss/1.0/
 xmlns:dc=http://purl.org/dc/elements/1.1/
 xmlns:syn=http://purl.org/rss/1.0/modules/syndication/
>

<channel rdf:about="http://www.dougsparling.com/ipm/">
<title>IPM</title>
<link>http://www.dougsparling.com/ipm/</link>
<description>Instant Perl Modules</description>
<items>
 <rdf:Seq>
  <rdf:li
rdf:resource="http://www.dougsparling.com/ipm/index.html" />
 </rdf:Seq>
</items>
<image rdf:resource="http://dougsparling.com/images/dss.jpg" />
<textinput rdf:resource="http://www.dougsparling.com/cgi-
bin/search.cgi" />
</channel>

<image rdf:about="http://dougsparling.com/images/dss.jpg">
<title>dougsparling.com</title>
<url>http://dougsparling.com/images/dss.jpg</url>
</image>

<item rdf:about="http://www.dougsparling.com/ipm/index.html">
<title>IPM News</title>
<link>http://www.dougsparling.com/ipm/index.html</link>
</item>

<textinput rdf:about="http://www.dougsparling.com/cgi-bin/search.cgi">
<title>Search</title>
<description></description>
<name>text</name>
<link>http://www.dougsparling.com/cgi-bin/search.cgi</link>
</textinput>

</rdf:RDF>
```

Converting RSS to HTML

Jonathan Eisenzopf, the author of XML::RSS, wrote a script that converts RSS to HTML. This script, rss2html.pl, is included with the XML::RSS module. Instead of reinventing the wheel, I'll just include his script here (altered slightly to fit the format of this book):

```perl
#!/usr/bin/perl -w
# rss2html - converts an RSS file to HTML
# It take one argument, either a file on the local system,
# or an HTTP URL like http://slashdot.org/slashdot.rdf
# by Jonathan Eisenzopf. v1.0 19990901
# See http://www.webreference.com/perl for more information

# INCLUDES
use strict;
use XML::RSS;
use LWP::Simple;

# Declare variables
my $content;
my $file;

# MAIN
# check for command-line argument
die "Usage: rss2html.pl (<RSS file> | <URL>)\n"
  unless @ARGV == 1;

# get the command-line argument
my $arg = shift;

# create new instance of XML::RSS
my $rss = new XML::RSS;

# argument is a URL
if ($arg=~ /http:/i) {
    $content = get($arg);
    die "Could not retrieve $arg" unless $content;
    # parse the RSS content
    $rss->parse($content);

# argument is a file
} else {
    $file = $arg;
    die "File \"$file\" does't exist.\n" unless -e $file;
    # parse the RSS file
    $rss->parsefile($file);
}

# print the HTML channel
&print_html($rss);
```

```perl
# SUBROUTINES
sub print_html {
    my $rss = shift;
    print <<HTML;
<table bgcolor="#000000" border="0" width="200"><tr><td>
<TABLE CELLSPACING="1" CELLPADDING="4" BGCOLOR="#FFFFFF"
 BORDER=0 width="100%">
  <tr>
  <td valign="middle" align="center" bgcolor="#EEEEEE">
  <font color="#000000" face="Arial,Helvetica"><B>
  <a href="$rss->{'channel'}->{'link'}">
  $rss->{'channel'}->{'title'}</a></B></font></td></tr>
  <tr><td>
HTML

    # print channel image
    if ($rss->{'image'}->{'link'}) {
      print <<HTML;
<center>
<p><a href="$rss->{'image'}->{'link'}">
<img src="$rss->{'image'}->{'url'}"
alt="$rss->{'image'}->{'title'}" border="0"
HTML
        print " width=\"$rss->{'image'}->{'width'}\""
          if $rss->{'image'}->{'width'};
        print " height=\"$rss->{'image'}->{'height'}\""
          if $rss->{'image'}->{'height'};
        print "></a></center><p>\n";
    }

    # print the channel items
    foreach my $item (@{$rss->{'items'}}) {
      next unless defined($item->{'title'}) &&
        defined($item->{'link'});
      print "<li><a href=\"$item->{'link'}\">
            $item->{'title'}</a><BR>\n";
    }

    # if there's a textinput element
    if ($rss->{'textinput'}->{'title'}) {
      print <<HTML;
<form method="get" action="$rss->{'textinput'}->{'link'}">
$rss->{'textinput'}->{'description'}<BR>
<input type="text" name="$rss->{'textinput'}->{'name'}"><BR>
<input type="submit" value="$rss->{'textinput'}->{'title'}">
</form>
HTML
    }

    # if there's a copyright element
    if ($rss->{'channel'}->{'copyright'}) {
      print <<HTML;
```

```
<p><sub>$rss->{'channel'}->{'copyright'}</sub></p>
HTML
    }

    print <<HTML;
</td>
</TR>
</TABLE>
</td></tr></table>
HTML
}
```

To get the latest RSS file from **www.news.perl.org** and convert it to HTML, run the script like this:

```
% perl rss2html.pl http://www.news.perl.org/perl-news-short.rdf
  > perl_news.html
```

This script will use the LWP::Simple module to fetch the RSS file, and then XML::RSS will convert it to HTML. By redirecting the output to a file, the HTML is saved in a file that we may use as an include file.

To give you an idea what an RSS file looks like, I've included the RSS file that was used to create the HTML. This is the source the script used to create its output and it won't be saved on your machine:

```
<?xml version="1.0" encoding="ISO-8859-1"?>

<!DOCTYPE rss PUBLIC "-//Netscape Communications//DTD RSS
0.91//EN" "http://my.netscape.com/publish/formats/rss-0.91.dtd">

<rss version="0.91">

<channel>
<title>Perl News</title>
<link>http://www.news.perl.org/</link>
<description>News for the Perl Community</description>
<language>en</language>
<copyright>Copyright 2000, Chris Nandor</copyright>
<pubDate>Mon, 18 Dec 2000 08:53:56 EST</pubDate>
<lastBuildDate>Mon, 18 Dec 2000 08:53:56 EST</lastBuildDate>
<managingEditor>news@perl.org</managingEditor>
<webMaster>news@perl.org</webMaster>

<image>
<title>Perl News</title>
<url>http://www.news.perl.org/perl-news-small.gif</url>
<link>http://www.news.perl.org/</link>
<width>119</width>
<height>30</height>
</image>
```

```
<item>
<title>Perl News Downtime</title>
<link>http://www.news.perl.org/perl-
news.cgi?item=977147331%7C11450</link>
</item>

<item>
<title>Perl Conference 5 Call For Participation</title>
<link>http://www.news.perl.org/perl-
news.cgi?item=977147339%7C11451</link>
</item>

<item>
<title>perl 5.6.1 TRIAL1 Released</title>
<link>http://www.news.perl.org/perl-
news.cgi?item=977147342%7C11452</link>
</item>

<item>
<title>perljvm Under Active Development Again</title>
<link>http://www.news.perl.org/perl-
news.cgi?item=977147349%7C11453</link>
</item>

<item>
<title>New www.perl.com Articles</title>
<link>http://www.news.perl.org/perl-
news.cgi?item=977147357%7C11455</link>
</item>

<item>
<title>mod_perl for ActivePerl</title>
<link>http://www.news.perl.org/perl-
news.cgi?item=977147365%7C11456</link>
</item>

<item>
<title>Jabber Programming with Perl</title>
<link>http://www.news.perl.org/perl-
news.cgi?item=977147370%7C11457</link>
</item>

<item>
<title>New Modules  1-17 December 2000</title>
<link>http://www.news.perl.org/perl-
news.cgi?item=977147390%7C11459</link>
</item>

<textinput>
<title>Search Perl News</title>
<description>Search the Perl News database</description>
<name>text</name>
<link>http://www.news.perl.org/perl-news.cgi</link>
```

```
</textinput>

</channel>
</rss>
```

The HTML file produced looks likes this:

```html
<table bgcolor-"#000000" border="0" width="200"><tr><td>
<TABLE CELLSPACING="1" CELLPADDING="4" BGCOLOR="#FFFFFF"
  BORDER=0 width="100%">
  <tr>
  <td valign="middle" align="center" bgcolor="#EEEEEE">
  <font color="#000000" face="Arial,Helvetica"><B>
  <a href="http://www.news.perl.org/">
  Perl News</a></B></font></td></tr>
  <tr><td>
<center>
<p><a href="http://www.news.perl.org/">
<img src="http://www.news.perl.org/perl-news-small.gif"
alt="Perl News" border="0"
 width="119" height="30"></a></center><p>
<li><a href="http://www.news.perl.org/perl-
news.cgi?item=977147331%7C11450">
          Perl News Downtime</a><BR>
<li><a href="http://www.news.perl.org/perl-
news.cgi?item=977147339%7C11451">
          Perl Conference 5 Call For Participation</a><BR>
<li><a href="http://www.news.perl.org/perl-
news.cgi?item=977147342%7C11452">
          perl 5.6.1 TRIAL1 Released</a><BR>
<li><a href="http://www.news.perl.org/perl-
news.cgi?item=977147349%7C11453">
          perljvm Under Active Development Again</a><BR>
<li><a href="http://www.news.perl.org/perl-
news.cgi?item=977147357%7C11455">
          New www.perl.com Articles</a><BR>
<li><a href="http://www.news.perl.org/perl-
news.cgi?item=977147365%7C11456">
          mod_perl for ActivePerl</a><BR>
<li><a href="http://www.news.perl.org/perl-
news.cgi?item=977147370%7C11457">
          Jabber Programming with Perl</a><BR>
<li><a href="http://www.news.perl.org/perl-
news.cgi?item=977147390%7C11459">
          New Modules  1-17 December 2000</a><BR>
<form method="get" action="http://www.news.perl.org/perl-
news.cgi">
Search the Perl News database<BR>
<input type="text" name="text"><BR>
<input type="submit" value="Search Perl News">
</form>
<p><sub>Copyright 2000, Chris Nandor</sub></p>
</td>
```

```
</TR>
</TABLE>
</td></tr></table>
```

Now that we've seen how to fetch an RSS file and convert it to HTML, let's build a script that we can cron and use to update a web page. We'll fetch an RSS file, convert it to HTML, and then save it to a file that can be included by a web page using SSI. This script will use the `mirror()` function of `LWP::Simple` to check if we need to download and process the RSS file. This will keep us from rebuilding our include file needlessly if the RSS file hasn't updated since the last time we fetched it. This script uses the same table layout as Jonathan Eisenzopf's `rss2html.pl` script. I got the idea for this script after reading Randal Schwartz's column in the January 2000 *Web Techniques* magazine (**http://www.stonehenge. com/merlyn/WebTechniques/col45.html**).

Here's the script:

```
#!/usr/bin/perl -w
use strict;
use LWP::Simple;
use XML::RSS;

# Config
my $DESC = 0; # Non-zero to show channel description
my $RSS_DIR = '/home/doug/rss';
my $INCLUDE_DIR = '/usr/local/apache/htdocs/includes';
my @CHANNELS = ('http://www.news.perl.org/perl-news-short.rdf'
                => 'perl_news',
                'http://www.slashdot.org/slashdot.rdf'
                => 'slashdot');

while (@CHANNELS >= 2) {
    my $url = shift @CHANNELS;
    my $filename = shift @CHANNELS;
    my $rss_filename = "$RSS_DIR/$filename.rss";

    # Next if the file is up-to-date
    next unless is_success(mirror($url, $rss_filename));

    my $rss = XML::RSS->new or
      die "Can't create new XML::RSS object: $!\n";
    $rss->parsefile($rss_filename) or
      warn "Can't parse $rss_filename: $!\n";

    # Create html and save inc file
    print_html($rss, $filename);

}
```

```perl
sub print_html {
    my $rss = shift;
    my $filename = shift;

    # Build the HTML that we'll save
    my $html = qq!<TABLE BGCOLOR="#000000" BORDER=0 ! .
               qq!WIDTH=200>\n!;
    $html .= "<TR>\n";
    $html .= "<TD>\n";
    $html .= qq!<TABLE BGCOLOR="#FFFFFF" BORDER=0 ! .
             qq!CELLSPACING=1 WIDTH="100%">\n!;
    $html .= "<TR>\n";
    $html .= qq!<TD BGCOLOR="#EEEEEE" ALIGN="center">\n!;

    # Channel title and link
    $html .= qq!<B><A HREF="$rss->{'channel'}->{'link'}">! .
             qq!$rss->{'channel'}->{'title'}</A></B>\n!;
    $html .= "</TD></TR>\n";

    $html .= "<TR>\n";
    $html .= "<TD>\n";

    # Channel image
    if ($rss->{'image'}->{'link'}) {
        $html .= "<CENTER>\n";
        $html .= qq!<P><A HREF="$rss->{'image'}->{'link'}">!;
        $html .= qq!<IMG SRC="$rss->{'image'}->{'url'}"!;
        $html .= qq! ALT="$rss->{'image'}->{'title'}" ! .
                 qq!BORDER=0!;

        # Height and Width tags
        $html .= qq! WIDTH="$rss->{'image'}->{'width'}"!
          if $rss->{'image'}->{'width'};
        $html .= qq! HEIGHT="$rss->{'image'}->{'height'}"!
          if $rss->{'image'}->{'height'};

        # Close IMG SRC tag
        $html .= qq!></A>\n!;
        $html .= qq!</CENTER><P>\n!;
    }

    # Channel items
    foreach my $item (@{$rss->{'items'}}) {
        next unless defined($item->{'title'})
          && defined($item->{'link'});
        $html .= qq!<LI><A HREF="$item->{'link'}">! .
                 qq!$item->{'title'}</A><BR>\n!;
        $html .= qq!$item->{'description'}\n!
          if $item->{'description'} and $DESC;
    }

    # Text input
    if ($rss->{'textinput'}->{'title'}) {
```

```
        $html .= qq!<FORM METHOD="get" ! .
                qq!ACTION="$rss->{'textinput'}->{'link'}">\n!;
        $html .= qq!$rss->{'textinput'}->{'description'}! .
                qq!<BR>\n!;
        $html .= qq!<INPUT TYPE="text" ! .
                qq!NAME="$rss->{'textinput'}->{'name'}">! .
                qq!<BR>\n!;
        $html .= qq!<INPUT TYPE="submit" ! .
                qq!VALUE="$rss->{'textinput'}->{'title'}">\n!;
        $html .= "</FORM>\n";
    }

    # Copyright
    if ($rss->{'channel'}->{'copyright'}) {
        $html .= "<P><SUB>$rss->{'channel'}->{'copyright'}" .
                "</SUB>\n";
    }

    $html .= "</TD></TR>\n";
    $html .= "</TABLE>\n";
    $html .= "</TD>\n";
    $html .= "</TR>\n";
    $html .= "</TABLE>\n";

    # Save the html file
    my $inc_file = "$INCLUDE_DIR/$filename.inc";
    open(FILE, ">$inc_file") or
      die "Cannot open $inc_file: $!\n";
    print FILE $html;
    close FILE;

}
```

An easy way to add these headlines to a web page is to use server-side includes. Here is an example of a small HTML page (Figure 17.1) that contains our headlines. The actual location of the include files will differ based on where you put it on your website.

```
<HTML>
<BODY>
<!--#include virtual="/includes/perl_news.inc" -->
<BR>
<!--#include virtual="/includes/slashdot.inc" -->
</BODY>
</HTML>
```

If your system doesn't allow server-side includes or you don't wish to use them, you can still build a single HTML page containing your news headlines. You'll need to modify this script so that, instead of creating an HTML include file for each RSS news feed, you place the HTML for each news feed in a table in a single HTML file.

Figure 17.1
Web page with news
headlines.

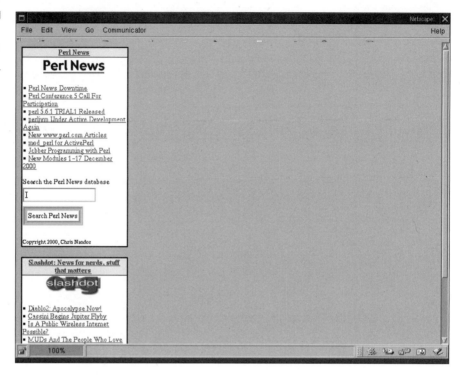

Summary

In this chapter we have shown you how to parse an XML document, how to create an RSS file, and how to convert RSS to HTML. Although XML::Parser and XML:RSS are two very useful modules, there are several other XML modules available at CPAN that are worth investigating. We hope this chapter inspires you to do so.

APPENDIX A

PRAGMAS

Introduction

Pragmas, also known as pragmatic modules, are a special type of module that comes with the standard Perl distribution. Pragmas affect the compilation and, in some cases, the execution of your script. A pragma can be thought of as a hint or suggestion given to the compiler. By convention, pragma names are in lowercase, whereas the other Perl modules have names that begin with an uppercase letter.

Pragmas are invoked using the `use` and `no` directives. Most pragmas are lexically scoped, meaning that they affect the block in which they are invoked. It is possible to turn off or countermand a pragma by using the `no` directive. Most pragmas can be turned off until they are turned back on by using a new `use` directive:

```
use strict;
# Code run under strict

no strict;
# Code not run under strict

use strict;
# Code run under strict
```

They also can be temporarily turned off in an inner block:

```
use strict;
# Code run under strict

{
```

```
    no strict;
    # Code not run under strict
}

# Code run under strict
```

A few pragmas aren't lexically scoped but instead affect the current package. These pragmas cannot be countermanded. For example, use vars and use subs can be used to predeclare variables and subroutines in a file, but no cannot be used to turn off either of these pragmas.

There are only a handful of pragmas that come with the standard Perl distribution. To find the programs that are installed on your system, type:

```
% man perlmodlib
```

or

```
% perldoc perlmodlib
```

which will display the Perl module library man page. Included in the output is the following list of pragmatic modules:

attributes	Get/set subroutine or variable attributes
attrs	Set/get attributes of a subroutine (deprecated)
autouse	Postpone load of modules until a function is used
base	Establish IS-A relationship with base class at compile time
blib	Use MakeMaker's uninstalled version of a package
caller	Inherit pragmatic attributes from caller's context
charnames	Define character names for \N{named} string literal escape
constant	Declare constants
diagnostics	Force verbose warning diagnostics
fields	Declare a class's attribute fields at compile-time
filetest	Control the filetest operators like '-r', '-w' for AFS, etc.
integer	Compute arithmetic in integer instead of double
less	Request less of something from the compiler (unimplemented)
lib	Manipulate @INC at compile time
locale	Use or avoid POSIX locales for built-in operations
ops	Restrict unsafe operations when compiling
overload	Overload Perl operations
re	Alter regular expression behavior
sigtrap	Enable simple signal handling
strict	Restrict unsafe constructs
subs	Predeclare subroutine names
utf8	Turn on UTF-8 and Unicode support

vars	Predeclare global variable names (obsoleted by our())
warnings	Control optional warnings

Each pragma comes with its own documentation, and most can be viewed using the respective man pages or `perldoc` command. Let's take a closer look at a few of these pragmatic modules.

constant

The `constant` pragma allows you to declare constants at compile-time. The values are evaluated in list context by default, but you may override this with `scalar`; for example:

```
use constant PI => 3.14159;
use constant USERINFO => getpwuid($<);
use constant USERNAME => scalar getpwuid($<);
```

List constants are returned as lists, not as arrays, so if we declare the following constant:

```
use constant MONTHS => qw (Jan Feb Mar Apr May Jun
                           Jul Aug Sep Oct Nov Dec);
```

then the following statement is incorrect:

```
$month = MONTHS[3];
```

You must use the following form:

```
$month = (MONTHS)[3];
```

It is also possible to use an expression when declaring a constant:

```
use constant PI => 22/7;
```

Constants cannot be interpolated directly in double quotation marks, but they may be interpolated indirectly:

```
use constant PI => 3.14159;
print "PI = @{[PI]}\n";
```

diagnostics

The `diagnostics` pragma is used to expand the standard warning and error messages by including the more descriptive messages from the `perldiag` man page. Duplicate messages are suppressed. The `diagnostics` pragma can be used at compile-time and runtime.

To invoke `diagnostics` in your script, add the following line near the top of your program to automatically enable Perl's `-w` flag:

```
use diagnostics;
```

The `-verbose` flag will cause the introduction from the `perldiag` man page to be printed before any other diagnostic messages.

```
use diagnostics -verbose;
```

The `$diagnostics::PRETTY` variable can be used to create nicer output for pagers (`less` or `more`). This variable must be set before the `diagnostics` module is loaded:

```
BEGIN { $diagnostics::PRETTY = 1 }
use diagnostics;
```

You can turn diagnostics on and off at runtime (assuming that you invoke `diagnostics` with `use` first) by using the following commands:

```
use diagnostics;
# code run under diagnostics

disable diagnostics;
# code run without diagnostics

enable diagnostics;
# code run under diagnostics
```

NOTE

The diagnostics *pragma uses* enable *and* disable *instead of* use *and* not, *which are used by most other pragmas.*

integer

The `integer` pragma tells Perl to use integer arithmetic instead of the default double precision floating-point arithmetic. This is useful for the rare machine without floating point hardware or with scripts that use only integers. The `integer` pragma is lexically scoped, so it will affect the remainder of the enclosing block in which it is invoked. The `integer` pragma may be turned off by using the `no` directive. Note that the `integer` pragma will affect arithmetic operations, not the actual numbers.

```
use integer;
print '22/7 = ', 22/7, "\n";

no integer;
print '22/7 = ', 22/7, "\n";
```

Running this script will give you the following output:

```
% perl integer.pl
22/7 = 3
22/7 = 3.14285714285714
```

lib

The `lib` pragma allows you to manipulate the `@INC` array at compile-time. This is commonly done to add private directories to Perl's search path so that modules not located in directories in the standard search path can be found (see Chapter 1).

```
use lib '/home/doug/perlmodules', '/home/doug/mymodules';
```

Each directory listed is added to the front of `@INC`. This will ensure that your private modules will be found before the standard ones. For each directory (`$dir`) listed, the `lib` module will check for a platform-specific directory, `$dir/$archname/auto`, and place it in front of `$dir`, if it exists. `$archname` is the name of the current platform.

Although rarely necessary, and not recommended, it is possible to remove directories from `@INC`:

```
no lib '/home/doug/perlmodules', '/home/doug/mymodules';
```

This will delete the first instance of each directory listed. For each directory listed, the `lib` module will also check for the directory `$dir/$archname/auto`. If this directory is found, `lib` will remove it as well.

To remove all instances of a directory, use :ALL as the first parameter to no lib:

```
no lib qw(:ALL /home/doug/perlmodules /home/doug/mymodules);
```

To restore @INC to its original value, use:

```
@INC = @lib::ORIG_INC;
```

strict

The strict pragma disallows unsafe constructs like symbolic references, global variables, and barewords. The strict pragma is lexically scoped and may be countermanded using the no directive. It is possible to enforce the restrictions separately, or all restrictions may be assumed if no import list is supplied.

```
use strict 'refs';    # disallow symbolic references
use strict 'vars';    # disallow global variables
use strict 'subs';    # disallow barewords
use strict;           # disallow symbolic references,
                      # global variables and barewords
```

strict 'refs'

Using strict 'refs' will disallow the use of symbolic references and will generate a runtime error if a symbolic reference is found:

```
use strict 'refs';
$symref = 'Dylan';
print $$symref;
```

```
% perl strict_refs1.pl
Can't use string ("Dylan") as a SCALAR ref while "strict refs" in
use at strict_ref1.pl line 3.
```

Hard links are permitted:

```
use strict 'refs';
$name = 'Dylan';
$symref = \$name;
print $$symref;
```

```
% perl strict_refs2.pl
Dylan
```

strict 'vars'

Using `strict 'vars'` will disallow accessing a variable that wasn't declared with `our` (global), `my` (lexical), or `use vars`, imported from another package, fully qualified, or predefined by Perl. In any of those cases, a compile-time error will be generated. Using the `local` operator with `strict 'vars'` will cause an error; for example:

```
use strict 'vars';
$director = 'Kieslowski';
```

```
% perl strict_vars1.pl
Global symbol "$director" requires explicit package name at
strict_vars1.pl line 2.
Execution of strict_vars1.pl aborted due to compilation errors.
```

This error can be fixed by using `my` with `our` variable:

```
use strict 'vars';
my $director = 'Kieslowski';
```

strict 'subs'

Using `strict 'subs'` will disallow the use of barewords (unquoted strings) and will generate a compile-time error if a bareword is found; for example:

```
use strict 'subs';
$color = red;
```

```
% perl strict_subs1.pl
Bareword "red" not allowed while "strict subs" in use at
strict_subs1.pl line 2.
Execution of strict_subs1.pl aborted due to compilation errors.
```

This is easily fixed by quoting the bareword:

```
use strict 'subs';
$color = 'red';
```

NOTE

Barewords inside curly braces or on the left-hand side of the `=>` *operator are considered to be quoted and hence allowed by* `use strict`.

```
use strict 'subs';
%capitals = (England => 'London', France => 'Paris',
             Italy => 'Rome');
$france_capital = $capitals{France};
```

Predeclared subroutines are also considered to be quoted:

```
use strict 'subs';
sub hello { return 'hello'};
$greeting = hello;
```

vars

The `vars` pragma allows you to predeclare global variables; that is, use variables that aren't fully qualified when running under the `strict` pragma. This also will disable any warnings generated by typographic errors.

```
use vars qw($actor @films %dates);
```

The `vars` pragma has been deprecated with Perl 5.6.0 and has been replaced with the `our` modifier. So the previous code can be written as:

```
our($director, @films, %dates);
```

or with initializations:

```
our $director = 'Eric Rohmer';
our @films = ('Le genou de Claire', 'Le rayon vert',
             'Conte de printemps');
our %dates = (1970 => 'Le genou de Claire',
              1986 => 'Le rayon vert',
              1990 => 'Conte de printemps');
```

Summary

With the use of pragmatic modules, it is possible to affect scripts at compile-time and add useful features such as creating constants, checking for unsafe constructs, or adding directories to `@INC` so that you can use modules in a private directory.

APPENDIX B

CREATING PERL MODULES

Over time, you will find yourself writing the same or very similar routines over and over again. Once you realize you're writing a routine yet again, but for a different project, a mental red flag should go up: put it in a module! Building Perl modules is easy and should be used often for many reasons. They should be built for reusability and clarity of your source code as well as for your own efficiency.

Libraries consisting of modules are a programmer's best friend and bag of magic tricks. Creating a good library takes time and effort, but the end result is definitely worth it. However, some people try to put everything into a module, which can decrease a program's readability and maintainability. Only common, seldom changing routines should be added to your bag of tricks. Modules should be used for things like database access, common error checking, and personal error logging routines.

In addition, even though your personal library should be filled with routines common for many applications, it is often useful to build a few modules that are specific to the application at hand. Perhaps the code in your personal library for connecting to your database needs to be modified just a bit for the application you are currently working on. In that case, build a special database library for that application.

There are two programming models for building modules, functional and object oriented. We will discuss both in terms of the pros and cons and where and how they should be used.

Building Modules the Smart Way

Perl comes with a handy utility called h2xs (typically located at /usr/bin/h2xs). This program, given a few options, creates a skeleton of a module from which you can create your own personal modules and have them install exactly like a CPAN module.

h2xs is typically used by programmers to extend Perl by incorporating the functionality of C libraries. However, it is also perfect for creating 100 percent Perl libraries.

To create module MyMod.pm in directory MyLib for use in your programs, for example:

```
use MyLib::MyMod
```

run h2xs with the following arguments and it will be created for you:

```
% h2xs -X -A -n MyLib::MyMod
```

NOTE

See perldoc h2xs *for information on the command-line switches.*

h2xs will create a directory MyLib under the directory you are currently in and a MyMod directory within that. Inside of the MyMod directory will reside five files that should look familiar (Table B.1).

TABLE B.1

Files created by h2xs in Directory MyMod

Changes	File to record significant changes to the module
MANIFEST	List of files in this package
Makefile.PL	The Perl script that will generate your Makefile for actually building and installing the module
MyMod.pm	A basically empty module file with some example POD documentation for you to fill in with your code; this includes all the necessary variables, requires, etc., for you to build a Perl module
test.pl	A sample test script that will be executed during a make test

By using this method before creating your personal library, you will be able to propagate changes across many servers or share your libraries with fellow programmers and maybe even get them put into CPAN. The base POD documentation and Changes file also remind you that documenting your work is nearly as important as writing it. Once your module is ready, you can install it into the default library directories for Perl in the standard way: perl Makefile.pl, make, make install. Otherwise, you would have to modify @INC to include the directory that contains your modules.

When writing a module from scratch, it should look very similar to the stub `.pm` file created by `h2xs`. Aside from the POD documentation, nearly everything is required when writing a module.

Module Internals—Functional

In this section we'll break down a simple example module line by line to show what each part does:

```
package MyLib::MyMod;

use strict;
use vars qw(@EXPORT @ISA $VERSION);
require Exporter;

@ISA = qw(Exporter);
$VERSION = '1.0';
@EXPORT = qw(
    add
    multiply
);

sub add {
    my ($x, $y) = @_;
    return( $x + $y );
}

sub multiply {
    my ($x, $y) = @_;
    return( $x * $y );
}

1;
```

We start off all modules with the `package` line, which Perl reads to determine whether this is the package it is looking for. It must have the same name as the `"use"` line from our programs. Next comes the `"use"` lines for the module, where we include any packages that this module will depend on such as `DBI`, `Date::Manip`, and `CGI.pm`.

The `"use strict"` line is optional, but it helps in making sure you write good clean Perl code. In my honest opinion, if you aren't using `strict` in your modules, then you are asking for all the debugging problems and weird quirks you will receive. After this we `"use vars"`, which will accomplish the same as:

```
my @EXPORT:
my @ISA;
my $VERSION;
```

We require `Exporter`, a module included in the standard Perl distribution. This module allows us to "export" symbols we place into our `@EXPORT` array to be used within our other programs. As you can see in the following script, we set up our two subroutines `add` and `multiply` to be exported into the using program's namespace:

```
@EXPORT = qw(
    add
    multiply
);
```

By doing this we can write a simple Perl script that can use these subroutines:

```
use MyLib::MyMod;

print "2 + 2 = " . add(2,2) . "\n";
print "2 x 2 = " . multiply(2,2) . "\n";
```

Without exporting `add` and `multiply`, the code above would look like:

```
use MyLib::MyMod;

print "2 + 2 = " . MyLib::MyMod::add(2,2) . "\n";
print "2 x 2 = " . MyLib::MyMod::multiple(2,2) . "\n";
```

Although we gain programmer efficiency by exporting our subroutines, we lose some program clarity because it is not immediately obvious that `add` and `multiply` are from our `MyLib::MyMod` module.

Now that we've built and explained a simple module, let's build a slightly more complex one, first in the functional style and then in object-oriented style. This module is modeled after one of my personal libraries for dealing with a PostgreSQL database. This module is essentially a wrapper around `DBI`, written for programmer efficiency.

```
package IPM::DB;

use strict;
use DBI;
use Carp;
use vars qw(@EXPORT @ISA);
require Exporter;

@EXPORT = qw(
    db_connect
    db_disconnect
```

```perl
            db_query
            db_run
            db_next
            db_nextvals
            db_finish
    );

    sub db_connect ($$$$) {
        my( $usr, $pwd, $db, $server ) = @_;

        my $dsn = "dbi:Pg:dbname=$db;host=$server";
        my $dbh = DBI->connect( $dsn, $user, $pwd ) or
            croak "Can't make connection to database: $!\n:;

        return($dbh);
    }

    sub db_disconnect ($) {
        my $dbh = shift;

        $dbh->disconnect;

    }

    sub db_query ($$@) {
        my ($dbh, $errmsg, @sql) = @_;

        my $sth = $dbh->prepare( join("\n", @sql) ) or
            croak "Prepare failed doing $errmsg: $!\n";

        $sth->execute or croak "Execute failed doing $errmsg: $!\n";

        return($sth);
    }

    sub db_run ($$@) {
        my ($dbh, $errmsg, @sql) = @_;

        $dbh->do( join("\n", @sql) ) or
            croak "SQL Query failed doing $errmsg: $!\n";

    }

    sub db_next ($) {
        my $sth = shift;

        return( $sth->fetchrow );
    }

    sub db_nextvals ($) {
        my $sth = shift;
```

```
        return( $sth->fetchrow_hashref );
}

sub db_finish ($) {
    my $sth = shift;

    $sth->finish;

    return;
}

1;
```

As an example, this module would be used in a program the following way:

```
use IPM::DB;

# Connect to our database
my $dbh = db_connect('ipm', 'secret', 'ipm_db', 'ipm.wiles.org');

# Insert some values
db_run($dbh, 'inserting some data',
        "INSERT INTO mytable (last_name, first_name) ",
        "VALUES ('Wiles', 'Frank')");

db_run($dbh, 'inserting some data',
        "INSERT INTO mytable (last_name, first_name) ",
        "VALUES ('Sparling', 'Doug')");

# Retrieve those values we just entered
my $res = db_query($dbh, 'retrieving some data',
                    "SELECT * FROM mytable");

while( my ($last_name, $first_name) = db_next($res) ) {
    print "$last_name, $first_name\n";
}

db_finish($res);
db_disconnect($dbh);
```

In the IPM::DB module, we load DBI and Carp for use. DBI is discussed at length in Chapter 4. Carp is a module useful in libraries and provides the croak() function call. It is similar to die, except in the way that it reports errors. If we had used die in this module, our error would resemble the following line:

```
Can't make connection to database: Error line 15 of DB.pm
```

This doesn't help us to determine from where our db_connection function was called. With croak, we get the line number of the calling program, not the library itself. As you've probably guessed, this greatly reduces debugging time.

Module Internals—Object Oriented

Now let's modify the previous example to be object oriented:

```perl
package IPM::DBOO;

use strict;
use DBI;
use Carp;

sub new {
    my $class = shift;
    my $self = {};
    bless($self, $class);
    return($self);
}

sub connect {
    my ($self, $user, $passwd, $db, $serv) = @_;

    # Save our instance data
    $self->{userid} = $user;
    $self->{passwd} = $passwd;
    $self->{db}     = $db;
    $self->{serv} = $serv;

    $self->{dbh} = DBI->connect("dbi:Pg:dbname=$db;host=$serv",
                                "$user",
                                "$passwd") or
                croak "Cannot make database connection: $!\n";
}

sub disconnect {
    my $self = shift;

    $self->{dbh}->disconnect;

    return;
}

sub query  {
    my ($self, $errmsg, @sql) = @_;
```

```perl
    $self->{sth} = $self->{dbh}->prepare( join("\n", @sql) ) or
      croak "Prepare failed doing $errmsg: $!\n";

    $self->{sth}->execute or
      croak "Execute failed doing $errmsg: $!\n";

    return;
}

sub run {
    my ($self, $errmsg, @sql) = @_;

    $self->{dbh}->do( join("\n", @sql) ) or
      croak "Cannot execute SQL while doing $errmsg: $!\n";

    return;
}

sub next {
    my $self = shift;

    return( $self->{sth}->fetchrow );
}

sub nextvals {
    my $self = shift;

    return( $self->{sth}->fetchrow_hashref );
}

sub finish {
    my $self = shift;

    $self->{sth}->finish;

    return;
}

1;
```

By writing this module in an object-oriented fashion we can get rid of the slightly annoying db_ prefixes on our module names and the Exporter module. Because of the way Perl handles object orientation, we do not need to "export" any of our symbols into the program's namespace. The methods are called simply by using the arrow operator (->) on the object itself.

The $self variable might seem odd at first; it is simply a hash that is "blessed" by Perl. "Blessing" turns a variable into an object in Perl's eyes. We use this hash to store all of the state information about this instance of the object. In the example above, we used this hash to store our userid, password, database handle, and current query, among other items.

Summary

With these two different styles of programming, it should be fairly apparent where the functional style makes more sense than the object-oriented style. Our example database module should probably be implemented in the object-oriented fashion. Modules in which the goal is to check or modify some data and return it are usually good candidates for functional-style modules. For instance, our first example using add() and multiply() should remain in the functional style. It would not be useful to create an $add object and then call $add->add(2,2).

I hope this appendix has shown you how using modules increases the efficiency, readability, and maintainability of your applications.

APPENDIX C

PERL SECURITY

Writing secure Perl programs should be on every Perl programmer's mind. Customers, users, your boss, and fellow programmers rely on the probability that the code you provide is secure. Unlike programming in stricter languages such as C and C++, programming in a secure manner with Perl is easy. There is simply one basic rule to follow: Do not assume anything! Don't make assumptions about your users' input, input from other programs, and definitely not input from network connections. Don't assume just because you designed your system around a set of standards that those standards will be followed.

Temp File Security

Opening a temporary file doesn't strike most programmers as a concern about security, but it should. On a UNIX system if an attacker can guess the name of your soon-to-be created temp file, he can place a symbolic link in its place.

Consider the code:

```
my $filename = '/tmp/example-temp-file' . time();
open(OUTPUT, ">$filename");
```

This is an example of an exploitable temporary file. If this script were run at a certain time (via cron, for instance) with administrator or root privilege, it would be easy for an attacker to create a symbolic link with the same name as the temporary file to /etc/passwd and have this script "accidentally" overwrite the system password file!

This common security problem is caused by the programmer assuming that this somewhat random temporary file does not already exist.

Here is a better way to create temporary files:

```
use IO::File;
my $file_handle = IO::File->new_tmpfile();
```

This piece of code uses the POSIX standard method for creating temporary files. You won't know its filename, but it will be destroyed when it is closed.

Using Taint

Using taint mode is probably the easiest way to provide a fair amount of security to your Perl scripts. Adding -T to the #!/usr/bin/perl line turns on taint mode. The Perl interpreter keeps track of which variables have been "tainted" by outside input and won't let that tainted data affect external programs. The easiest way to untaint a variable is to use regular expressions; for example:

```
#!/usr/bin/perl -T

# Make sure our environment variables are safe
$ENV{PATH} = '/bin:/usr/bin';
$ENV{ENV} = '';

my $input = $ARGV[0];   # Tainted user input

# Make sure we have all numeric input
$input =~ /^(\d+)$/ or die;
$input = $1;

system("echo $input");
```

If we run this script entirely with numeric input, it executes as expected, however, if we use a few alpha characters, $input is not set because of taint checking:

```
% perl taint1.pl 1234
1234

%

% perl taint1.pl 1234ad

%
```

Better Coding Practices

One unwritten rule in software development is that cleaner code runs better, is more easily maintained, and is more secure. Writing dirty code leads to confusion and mistakes, leading to less secure scripts.

By using some simple coding practices, you can increase your productivity, ability to maintain code, and provide better security. Here are some simple guidelines for writing Perl:

- *Use strict.* By using strict you force yourself to declare each variable and thus avoid accidentally creating global variables. This leads to cleaner, more readable code.
- *Use taint mode.* Using taint mode ensures against using malformed data when dealing with an external program, assuming that you have written your regular expression patterns correctly.
- *Pick a coding style and stick to it.* Nothing is worse than having to edit a script that uses one style of indentation for half and another style for the other half. If you are modifying someone else's code, use that style so that the script maintains readability.
- *Comment your code.* Ever see a section of Perl that confused you the day after you wrote it? This is exactly what comments are for. Use them; they are your friends. Some people say that you can comment too much, but too much is better than too little. Also, make use of Perl's POD to document the modules you create.
- *Use variable and subroutine names that reflect what they are or do.* This should be self-explanatory. Code such as `&foo_stuff($my_stuff);` doesn't mean anything to the person reading it. `&open_file($filename);` explains so much more.
- *Modularize or object-orient your code.* This automatically makes your code easier to read. If your code uses a modular or an object-oriented style, you will be able to spot security concerns more easily.

Summary

I hope I've demonstrated that writing more secure Perl is simple provided you follow a few basic rules when designing and developing applications. For more information, be sure to read the `perlsec` man page that comes with Perl and Lincoln Stein's World Wide Web Security FAQ available on **http://www.w3.org/Security/Faq/www-security-faq.html**.

APPENDIX D

PERL RESOURCES

There are a vast number of online resources to help you learn Perl, obtain answers to questions about Perl, and find code already written to do what you want. However, there are also a number of resources included with the standard Perl distribution. By fully using all these resources, you can save time and frustration by fully understanding the language and its constructs.

Online Resources

CPAN—http://www.cpan.org

CPAN is the Comprehensive Perl Archive Network. Nearly every module discussed in this book has been a module from CPAN. This is a great place to look for existing libraries and even some scripts. Before you begin coding a project always peruse its archives. You can look for modules to develop routines and save you the time of coding your own. You can search the entire CPAN web site in many ways, including by a module's name or author.

The Official Perl Site—http://www.perl.com

Perl.com has a wealth of information and news concerning the Perl community. This site not only has all the Perl manuals in HTML format but also FAQs, information on training, and featured articles about noteworthy Perl programmers.

use Perl—http://use.perl.org

use Perl can be described as the Slashdot.org of the Perl community. It contains news and interesting tidbits from around the globe for Perl programmers.

Perl Mongers—http://www.perl.org

This is the official homepage of the Perl Mongers User Groups. Information can be found on users groups in your area as well as links to many Perl-related sites.

Perldoc.com—http://www.perldoc.com

This site has more Perl documentation than you can shake a stick at, including lots of POD documentation, manual pages, and installation guides.

Perl Monks—http://www.perlmonks.com

Perl Monks is a fun and useful site. This website features question-and-answer forums where knowledgeable Perl programmers will help you solve any problems you might be having. It also features snippets of new and interesting uses for Perl, Perl poetry, and obfuscated Perl.

Randal Schwartz's Magazine Articles— http://www.stonehenge.com/merlyn/

Mr. Schwartz has kindly provided an online repository of all his magazine articles. He has written on a variety of Perl topics for several publications including *Web Techniques*, *Linux Magazine*, *SysAdmin*, and *UNIX Review*.

EFNet IRC Channel #perl

IRC (Internet Relay Chat) is a real-time textual chat network. There are many different "networks," each of which has many "servers." You must connect to a server that is a part of the IRC network you wish to chat with. Each network has thousands of channels that are basically chat rooms where some particular subject is typically discussed.

Channel #perl on the EFNet is a great source to talk with fellow Perl programmers about a problem you can't find any documentation for or just to sit around and chat. Listening in on this discussion can be just as helpful as actually participating because you get to see how many different programmers attack the same problem.

A list of EFNet servers can be found at: **http://www.efnet.org/ servers.html**.

Offline Resources

POD: Plain Old Documentation

Nearly every module from CPAN and those from the standard distribution of Perl come with built-in POD documentation. This documentation can be viewed using the perldoc utility. For example, the following command would display the POD documentation for Net::SMTP:

```
% perldoc Net::SMTP
```

Manual Pages—man

A great deal of POD documentation can be converted to UNIX man pages. Some systems come with the modules' POD translated for you; others you have to do yourself. These can be viewed with the man command:

```
% man Net::SMTP
```

The *Perl Journal*

This is a quarterly journal devoted to the Perl programming language. Columnists include Sean M. Burke, Damian Conway, Simon Cozens, Steve Lidie, Chris Nandor, Editor Jon Orwant, and Lincoln Stein. The magazine's web site can be found at **http://www.tpj.com**.

Perl Books

The following list is certainly not exhaustive but does contain some essential books for your Perl library.

- *Learning Perl*, Randal L. Schwartz & Tom Christiansen, O'Reilly & Associates
- *Programming Perl*, Larry Wall, Tom Christiansen & Jon Orwant, O'Reilly & Associates
- *Perl Cookbook*, Tom Christiansen & Nathan Torkington, O'Reilly & Associates
- *Programming the Perl DBI*, Alligator Descartes & Tim Bunce, O'Reilly & Associates
- *Official Guide to Programming with CGI.pm*, Lincoln Stein, Wiley
- *Effective Perl Programming*, Joseph N. Hall with Randal L. Schwartz, Addison-Wesley
- *Elements of Programming with Perl*, Andrew L. Johnson, Manning

Summary

There is a wealth of knowledge and help regarding Perl on the Internet and in the standard Perl distribution. If you have a problem and want to know the easiest, most speed efficient, or most memory efficient way of solving it, you now have a vast array of resources to call on.

APPENDIX E

INSTALLING THE POSTGRESQL DATABASE

Introduction

In many of the chapters in this book we show examples that utilize SQL databases. We have used the open source PostgreSQL database in all of our examples. This appendix is an instruction guide on installing and setting up a PostgreSQL database server.

PostgreSQL should run on all modern UNIX-compatible platforms; some examples include Linux, Solaris, FreeBSD, HP/UX, and IRIX. While PostgreSQL will compile and run under Windows NT, we have no experience doing this, so it will not be covered in this appendix. Please consult the PostgreSQL website or documentation for information on this particular installation.

If you are running a system that can use RPM packages such as Red Hat, Mandrake, or SuSE Linux, you can install PostgreSQL very easily. If you are running another type of UNIX-compatible system, then you will need to compile PostgreSQL from source. Both methods are covered in this appendix.

Installation from RPM

Installing PostgreSQL with an RPM package is by far the easiest method. You simply download the appropriate packages from PostgreSQL's FTP or website, and as the root user, type the command:

```
% rpm -Uvh postgresql-*.rpm
```

For a Red Hat Linux 6.2 computer we downloaded the following files from ftp://ftp.postgresql.org/pub/binary/v7.0.3/RPMS/RedHat-6.x/i386/:

postgresql-7.0.3-2.i386.rpm	the base distribution
postgresql-devel-7.0.3-2.i386.rpm	the development libraries
postgresql-server-7.0.3-2.i386.rpm	the server portion
postgresql-test-7.0.3-2.i386.rpm	the test suite

The RPM command shown above will verify that the current packages are not already installed, and if a previous version of PostgreSQL happens to be installed it will upgrade to this version.

Installation from Source

Installing PostgreSQL from source is very similar to installing many open source packages. It follows the typical process of:

```
% ./configure
% make
% make install
```

On most systems the commands above will configure, compile, and install a standard PostgreSQL system.

NOTE

The make install *step needs to be performed by the administrative root user.*

While the above commands will give you a default PostgreSQL installation, there are many options that you can choose from when configuring your installation.

Whether you choose to use any extra options or not, you will need to create a PostgreSQL *superuser account*. User 'postgres' is typically used. Please consult your system documentation on how to add users to your system. This superuser account will control access to all the PostgreSQL administrative functions.

After you have setup a PostgreSQL superuser you need to download the PostgreSQL source code. Since at the time of this writing the latest version of PostgreSQL was v7.0.3, we downloaded: ftp://ftp.postgresql.org/pub/v7.0.3/postgresql-7.0.3.tar.gz.

Once your download has completed you will need to uncompress and untar the source code. This is accomplished by issuing one of the following commands, depending on your system:

```
% tar -xvzf postgresql-7.0.3.tar.gz
```

or

```
% gzip -dc postgresql-7.0.3.tar.gz | tar -xvf -
```

After these steps have been completed, a directory named postgresql-7.0.3 will be created with all of the source code and documentation of this application. You will probably want to read the README and INSTALL files located in this newly created directory.

For the rest of this example we'll need to be in the postgresql-7.0.3/src directory. This is where we will begin configuring PostgreSQL.

Using the previously mentioned options occurs during the configuration stage. Some of the more commonly used options and what they do are shown in Table E1.

TABLE E1

Commonly Used Options

Option	Usage
--prefix=DIR	The directory you wish PostgreSQL to be installed in; the default is /usr/local/pgsql
--bindir=DIR	Directory to contain the PostgreSQL executable binary files
--sbindir=DIR	Directory to contain the administrative executables
--datadir=DIR	Directory where PostgreSQL will actually store its databases
--libdir=DIR	Directory where you would like PostgreSQL to store its object code libraries
--includedir=DIR	Directory to store C header files
--with-pgport=PORT	Default port number for the PostgreSQL server to use
--with-maxbackends=X	Sets the default maximum number of backend server processes you wish to have
--enable-multibyte	Allows the use of multibyte characters, which is needed for languages such as Japanese, Chinese, or Korean
--with-odbc	Builds the ODBC driver package

For more options you can run:

```
% ./configure —help
```

If you wish your PostgreSQL to be installed into /usr/local/postgresql instead of the default /usr/local/pgsql, and you also want PostgreSQL's server to run on the nondefault port of 1000, your configuration line would be:

```
% ./configure —prefix=/usr/local/postgresql —with-pgport=1000
```

When you run this command you will see lots of checking messages, as the configuration tries to determine various things about your system. Here are a few lines from a typical configuration:

```
creating cache ./config.cache
checking host system type... i686-pc-linux-gnu
checking echo setting...
checking setting template to... linux_i386
checking whether to support locale... disabled
checking whether to support cyrillic recode... disabled
checking whether to support multibyte... disabled
checking setting DEF_PGPORT... 5432
checking setting DEF_MAXBACKENDS... 32
checking setting USE_TCL... disabled
checking for gcc... gcc
checking whether the C compiler (gcc -O2 ) works... yes
checking whether we are using GNU C... yes
```

After the configuration has finished, it is time to compile PostgreSQL. This is accomplished by issuing the command:

```
% make
```

After running this command you should see output similar to the following:

```
make -C utils all
gcc -I../include -I../backend   -O2 -Wall -Wmissing-prototypes
   -Wmissing-declarations   -c -o version.o version.c
make -C backend all
gcc -I../../../include -I../../../backend   -O2 -Wall
   -Wmissing-prototypes -Wmissing-declarations -I../..
   -c -o heaptuple.o heaptuple.c
```

When the compilation has successfully finished, you should see the following message:

```
All of PostgreSQL is successfully made. Ready to install.
```

If you do not see this message, something has gone wrong with your compilation. Please consult the PostgreSQL documentation for more information on how to correct your problem.

After the compilation has finished, you need to execute the following command as the root user in order to install PostgreSQL:

```
# make install
```

This command will put all the necessary executables and libraries in the correct directories and create the proper directories for database storage.

Initial Database Setup

Once PostgreSQL is installed on your system you need to start the server process. On RPM-installed systems this is accomplished with the following command, executed as root:

```
# /etc/rc.d/init.d/postgresql start
```

For non-RPM installed systems you need to run:

```
# /usr/local/pgsql/bin/postmaster -D /usr/local/pgsql/data -S
```

If you chose to install PostgreSQL in a location other than the default, this command will need to be modified to reflect the directories in which it is actually installed.

Once the server is started you need to log in as the PostgreSQL superuser account you created before installing the software. When you are this user, you need to initialize PostgreSQL's databases with the following command:

```
% initdb —pgdata /usr/local/pgsql/data
```

Also, from this account you can add and remove individual databases to the system with the following command, where 'name' is what you would like to call this database:

```
% createdb name
```

If you created an 'ipm' database you can then access it using PostgreSQL's interactive SQL shell by issuing:

```
% psql ipm
```

From here you can execute SQL queries directly to the database for creating tables, setting up indexes, or retrieving actual data.

Summary

Hopefully this has shown you everything you need in order to successfully install a PostgreSQL database server. However if you have problems with any of these steps please consult the documentation that comes with the PostgreSQL source code or the project's website at **http://www.postgresql.org** for more information.

APPENDIX F

INSTALLING APACHE

Introduction

According to Netcraft (**http://www.netcraft.com/survey**) the Apache webserver is the most popular webserver on the Internet. Like most open source products, there are many different installation methods. In this appendix we'll show you two of the most common methods.

If you are running a RPM-based Linux distribution such as Red Hat, Mandrake, or SuSE, Apache is probably already installed for you. You can check by executing the following command:

```
% rpm -qa | grep apache
```

On our Red Hat Linux 6.2 box this is the output we received:

```
apache-1.3.12-2
apache-devel-1.3.12-2
apache-manual-1.3.12-2
%
```

If Apache is already be installed, then you simply need to configure it. Please consult the Apache documentation or the Apache web site at **http://www.apache.org**.

If Apache is not already installed on your computer there are two options for installation: binary and source. Binary is probably the easiest solution if you are not familiar with compiling software or your platform lacks a compiler (systems such as Windows).

To do a binary install, simply go to the following URL and choose the correct version to download, based on the system you are running: **http://httpd.apache.org/dist/binaries/**.

As binary installation differs among platforms, there is an accompanying README file that helps explain this process.

If your system does have a compiler, or you need to compile Apache with specific options to accomplish your task, then you need a copy of the Apache source code. The latest stable version of Apache at the time of this writing, is version 1.3.14, so this is the version we will be explaining.

First download the source code from: **http://httpd.apache.org/dist/**.

For version 1.3.14 we used the URL: **http://httpd.apache.org/dist/apache_1.3.14.tar.gz**.

After downloading the source code, you need to decompress and unpack it. Depending on the version of the utility `tar` on your system, you will need to execute one of the following commands:

```
% tar -xvzf apache_1.3.14.tar.gz
```

or

```
% gzip -dc apache_1.3.14.tar.gz | tar -xvf -
```

Once this is done, a directory named '`apache_1.3.14`' will have been created as a subdirectory from where the above commands were executed. Now we need to move into this directory by issuing the command:

```
% cd apache_1.3.14
```

For most people a default install of Apache is more than sufficient. The only option most people change is where Apache installs its files. It should be noted that for all of the examples in this book, a default installation of Apache will suffice.

For a default configuration of Apache, run the following command:

```
% ./configure
```

By default Apache installs into /usr/local/apache. If you would like to change this location replace `DIR` with the directory you would like Apache installed into:

```
% ./configure —prefix=DIR
```

To see how Apache is going to be installed you can run the command:

```
% ./configure --show-layout
```

Here is a sample configure command:

```
% ./configure --prefix=/usr/local --htdocsdir=/home/web \
> --sysconfdir=/etc/httpd --logfiledir=/var/log
```

The options above would put most of Apache in /usr/local/apache. However, the configuration files would reside in /etc/httpd/conf, the logs in /var/log, and the location for HTML pages would be /home/web.

As you can see, there are many different ways you can lay out your Apache config. For more configuration options simply execute:

```
% ./configure --help
```

After we have Apache configured the way we want it, we compile it by issuing the make command:

```
% make
```

While the make command is executing you will see output similar to:

```
sh ./mkh  -p regcomp.c >regcomp.ih
gcc -I.  -I../os/unix -I../include    -DLINUX=2 -DUSE_HSREGEX
       -DUSE_EXPAT -I../lib/expat-lite -DNO_DL_NEEDED `../apaci`
       -DPOSIX_MISTAKE -c -o regcomp.o regcom.c
gcc -I.  -I../os/unix -I../include    -DLINUX=2 -DUSE_HSREGEX
       -DUSE_EXPAT -I../lib/expat-lite -DNO_DL_NEEDED `../apaci`
       -DPOSIX_MISTAKE   -c -o regerror.o regerror.c
```

When Apache is done compiling you will be returned to your command prompt. For this next command, which actually installs Apache in the directories you specified above (or the defaults if you did not choose any), you will need to be the root user of the system. To install Apache, execute the following command as root:

```
# make install
```

Now that Apache is installed on your system, you can begin trying out some of the CGI script examples from the book. It should be noted that these scripts will need to reside in the cgi-bin directory within

Apache's installation. They will also need to be named with a cgi extension for Apache to execute them.

These and many other options can be configured from the httpd.conf file that defines the behavior of your Apache server. Please consult the Apache documentation on how to modify your server's configuration.

INDEX

Note: Boldface numbers indicate illustrations; italic t indicates a table.

INTERNATIONAL CONTACT INFORMATION

AUSTRALIA
McGraw-Hill Book Company Australia Pty. Ltd.
TEL +61-2-9417-9899
FAX +61-2-9417-5687
http://www.mcgraw-hill.com.au
books-it_sydney@mcgraw-hill.com

CANADA
McGraw-Hill Ryerson Ltd.
TEL +905-430-5000
FAX +905-430-5020
http://www.mcgrawhill.ca

GREECE, MIDDLE EAST,
NORTHERN AFRICA
McGraw-Hill Hellas
TEL +30-1-656-0990-3-4
FAX +30-1-654-5525

MEXICO (Also serving Latin America)
McGraw-Hill Interamericana Editores S.A. de C.V.
TEL +525-117-1583
FAX +525-117-1589
http://www.mcgraw-hill.com.mx
fernando_castellanos@mcgraw-hill.com

SINGAPORE (Serving Asia)
McGraw-Hill Book Company
TEL +65-863-1580
FAX +65-862-3354
http://www.mcgraw-hill.com.sg
mghasia@mcgraw-hill.com

SOUTH AFRICA
McGraw-Hill South Africa
TEL +27-11-622-7512
FAX +27-11-622-9045
robyn_swanepoel@mcgraw-hill.com

UNITED KINGDOM & EUROPE
(Excluding Southern Europe)
McGraw-Hill Publishing Company
TEL +44-1-628-502500
FAX +44-1-628-770224
http://www.mcgraw-hill.co.uk
computing_neurope@mcgraw-hill.com

ALL OTHER INQUIRIES Contact:
Osborne/McGraw-Hill
TEL +1-510-549-6600
FAX +1-510-883-7600
http://www.osborne.com
omg_international@mcgraw-hill.com

ABOUT THE AUTHORS

DOUG SPARLING is a Web developer with UClick, a company that acquires, develops, packages, sells and distributes compelling Web content and whose clients include CNN, Salon magazine, AOL, Lycos, and *The New York Times*, among others. Doug has developed applications for these sites using Perl, JavaScript, XML, Java, and C/C++. His Perl application, "Suitable for Framing" was noted in the August/99 issue of *Internet World* magazine; his other Perl exploits include custom log apps for Netscape and AOL, custom admin tools for Doonesbury, and extensive work with Perl modules.

FRANK WILES is a web developer and system administrator for The World Company who own 12 newspapers and a cable modem ISP. Previously, Frank worked as developer at UClick.com, focusing on Perl programming along with Web database work on Linux and Solaris machines.

ABOUT THE CD

The accompanying CD-ROM contains all the modules used in this book as well as the code for all the examples and applications presented in the chapters. We have also included the latest version of Perl, PostgreSQL and Apache. The CD-ROM contents are arranged as follows:

- /CPAN—Perl modules used in this book.
- /misc—PerlMagick and ImageMagick modules.
- /chapters—Directories containing example code for each chapter.
- /perl—Perl source and RPMs for Red Hat Linux 6.2.
- /postgresql—PostgreSQL source and RPMs for Red Hat Linux 6.2.
- /apache—Apache source and RPMs for Red Hat Linux 6.2.